measurement and evaluation in
PHYSICAL EDUCATION

BROWN

PHYSICAL EDUCATION SERIES

Edited by AILEENE LOCKHART,
University of Southern California, Los Angeles, Calif

measurement and evaluation in
PHYSICAL EDUCATION

M. GLADYS SCOTT
Professor of Physical Education and
Chairman, Department of Physical Education for Women
State University of Iowa

and

ESTHER FRENCH
Professor of Physical Education and
Chairman, Division of Physical Education for Women
The University of Michigan

WM. C. BROWN COMPANY PUBLISHERS, Dubuque, Iowa

660674

Manufactured by Wm. C. Brown Company, Inc.—Dubuque, Iowa
(Printed in U. S. A.)

It seems likely that we in America will, as Secretary Folsom has declared, "stick fiercely to the central objective of our society -- the fullest development of each individual as a free human spirit, not as a servant of the state." The modern physical education program centers on the meeting of student needs. These needs, and the extent to which they are being met, can be ascertained best through measurement and evaluation. It is inconceivable that instruction can be individualized without the use of evaluative procedures. The student's progress must be appraised in all of the basic objectives of the physical education program.

We have the knowledge and some of the tools but means must be found to close the gap between what we know about physical education and what we do about it. Many teachers spend too much time in mere repetition of what the student already knows and in having him practice skills which he has mastered. The program as conducted may not call upon the student to put forth enough muscular activity to meet his physiological needs, enough mental activity for good growth and development, and enough social activity to prepare him adequately for effective living. It is known that man does not live by brains alone but by and through the aggregate of all of his powers. If the physical education program is to be effective in improving the status of an individual, it must challenge him to put forth an ever increasing amount of effort. It must also produce attitudes that will be conducive to continued voluntary participation.

Better teaching can be accomplished by the intelligent use of measurements and evaluation. Testing of all types must be considered and used in relation to aims and objectives, and the values derived are dependent upon the benefit each student gains.

The purpose of this book is to give a nontechnical discussion of the uses of measurement and evaluation in physical education and to provide the student and teacher with a clear perspective on testing as a part of teaching and learning. The book provides a background for test construction, selection, and use, a background which is practically identical for those conducting boys' and girls' physical education programs.

All of the tests presented here have been studied and have undergone experimentation. The extent to which each meets the criteria of an effective test varies. The tests selected for inclusion have proved value but no claim is made that they are the final answer. Better tests are needed in all areas. Much work has been done recently in developing tests for elementary school children and a number of these tests appear in this book. All of the tests are described in sufficient detail to make it possible for them to be used without further sources.

The statistical methods are mainly those that are essential to enable the teacher or student to select tests and to analyze the scores obtained through their use. Progress in closing the gap between what is known and what is practiced is dependent upon the ability of physical education teachers to apply the results to the program. This simplified presentation should be helpful to the test user who has not specialized in research procedures. The methods used in constructing skill tests, in analyzing them, and in combining such tests into batteries are described in a separate chapter for those persons interested in improving or constructing tests.

Acknowledgments are made to many students and coworkers who have served as subjects and have developed many of the measures described in this book. It is impossible to list all of their names, except where references are made to their studies. Acknowledgments are also made to the many authors and publishers who have so generously permitted use of their materials which are given recognition in the text.

Iowa City, Iowa   M. Gladys Scott

Ann Arbor, Michigan   Esther French

TABLE OF CONTENTS

LIST OF TABLES

Chapter I

PURPOSES OF EVALUATION AND MEASUREMENT

The purposes of evaluation and measurement are not
always clearly understood. Evaluation is a process that
can serve many purposes. Sometimes there are misconcep-
tions as, for example, thinking of evaluation only as a
final act of judgment rather than as a means to further
progress. Another misconception results from thinking of
evaluation as being synonymous with measurement, which is
but one technique used in the process of evaluation.

Measurement makes use of many tools, such as tests, to
determine the status of students and the extent to which
the objectives of the program are being met. The tools and
the uses made of them have changed decidedly as physical
education, along with other branches of education, has developed. At one time many anthropometric measures were taken but these have decreased in popularity as interest
shifted from the size and build to what one could do with
one's body.

Larson and Yocum[4] have differentiated between measurement and evaluation by stating that measurement concerns
the product or outcome of educational activity while evaluation concerns the process of educational activity. Evaluation as they conceive of it concerns such things as the
nature of leadership, program materials, facilities, equipment, grading, program time, participation, and administration. It is the determination of how the objectives are
achieved while measurement is the determination of the
traits, abilities, and characteristics of the individual or
the group. Perhaps a clear-cut distinction between measurement and evaluation is not so important as is conceiving
of the scope of the program, and understanding that many
purposes are served.

Comments such as the following indicate a lack of understanding of the purposes of evaluation and measurement:

1

We don't give grades in my school so I don't need
to give tests.

Physical education should be fun and since everyone hates tests, why test?

What good does it do for a student to know he can
punt the football forty yards -- that isn't
going to teach him to punt it fifty yards.

I don't need to test -- I can tell whether a
player is good just by watching him.

Anyone who flunks a physical education test is so
dumb he shouldn't be in school.

My classes are too large to use tests -- I'd like
to see anyone administer tests to forty or
more students in one gymnasium.

I don't have time to test -- I'm too busy teaching.

We didn't have tests when I was in school.

How can you give a knowledge test in dance --
what in the world would you ask them? Let
them dance!

The tests aren't any good anyway, so why use
them?

How can they say that tests save time -- all I
can see is that they waste time!

Testing is for those Ph.D's who like to play with
figures -- me, I am interested in the boys and
girls.

How is a teacher to know that he is "teaching the
right things in the right way to the right people at the
right time"? If our practices are to be scientifically
based, evaluative techniques must be employed to help determine the answer to such questions. To say that a thing
is right or being done satisfactorily because that is the
way it was done when we were in school is to deny progress.
It also fails to take into account that the environment has
changed and that different abilities are needed today.
Some say that a way of doing something is right because it
works and they pride themselves on being practical. Without some measurement of their results, they have little
other than their own intuition or feelings of satisfaction

to guide them. Teachers and students with inquiring minds
seek improvement, and in so doing, advance their profession. Professional persons, regardless of the area in
which they specialize, have a moral obligation to keep informed of the research findings in their field and to adjust their methods of working in accordance with these
findings.

UNDERSTANDING THE STUDENTS

The modern physical education program has the same
goals as general education and is centered around meeting
student needs. These needs, and the extent to which they
are being met, are best ascertained through evaluative procedures. As class sizes increase, the individual's needs
are more likely than not to be overlooked.

The selection of the proper program for each student
requires information as to the individual's physical fitness, his recreational fitness, and his social fitness.
The problem is to recognize needs through various evaluative procedures such as individual conferences, case his-
tories, and measurement. In some cases, the cause for what
might be termed a deficiency must be determined before a
program can be selected. Our programs at one time were
concerned largely with amelioration of conditions revealed
by medical examiners, with little attention being given to
other types of fitness. In the thirties and forties, a
concern developed for recreational fitness with much emphasis being placed on carry-over activities. It is recognized that a student must have developed some skill in a
wide variety of activities if he is to be able to make best
use of leisure time in adulthood. It is most desirable to
have developed better than average skill in at least two or
three activities or voluntary participation is not likely to
occur, either while in school or afterwards. Concern has
extended to what has been called social fitness for want of
a better term -- the ability to get along well with others,
to be both a good leader and a good "team" member. Included in this broad category are elements which can be
measured, some more easily than others, such as attitudes,
appreciations, and emotional stability. The coeducational
physical education program provides some of the experiences needed by many students.

Insight into the needs of students, their aspirations
and abilities can be gained through the use of various

3

measures, many of which are within the scope of this book
and will be covered in later chapters. Understanding the
students is one of the more important purposes of evaluation and measurement.

LEARNING AND TEACHING

While one of the best known purposes of evaluation is
checking on progress toward the various educational objectives, less well-known is that the process itself is a very
potent means of producing progress. When evaluation and
measurement are well used, the student is stimulated. In
many instances, the amount of learning that takes place is
in direct proportion to the motivation to learn.

Any teaching device which motivates students to put
forth their best efforts and which gives them interest and
understanding merits inclusion in the instructional program. Probably the greatest source of satisfaction in any
learning situation is the feeling of accomplishment. Both
the teacher and the student share in this sense of achievement and are motivated to greater efforts by evidences of
improvement. Swimming or stunts gain almost immediate enthusiasm partly because the results are readily perceived.
Results in any activity can be made apparent during instructional and practice periods by frequent use of tests.
For example, does a player use a shot from specified points
around the basket with increasing accuracy? Can the softball be thrown farther today than two weeks ago? Is a
player's tennis stroke improved so that the number of continuous returns or length of the rally is increasing? Such
methods for obtaining more or less objective evidence may
be part of the regular practice and serve as a real source
of motivation.

The occasional student who lacks interest in self-
testing may be motivated by the knowledge that tests will
be given and that others will judge him by the skill he
demonstrates. Likes and dislikes are very closely connected with success and failure or the feeling of defeat.
For this reason, care must be taken to select tests within
the ability levels of all students if the tests are to motivate or challenge each student.

Some tests are diagnostic and enable the teacher to
single out the skills or areas of knowledge in which additional instruction is needed, or to single out the

4

individuals needing special instruction. If a choice is to be made in content to be taught or in amount of time to be devoted to various portions of an instructional unit, test results furnish evidence that will be helpful in making the decision.

Every test should serve the student in some way just as every activity and experience included in the program should be planned with the student's welfare uppermost in mind. For the student to receive greatest benefit and really understand the test, his score should be made known to him. This should be done as soon after the testing as possible, before he loses interest and in time for him to plan for improvement on the basis of the test results. Information concerning results is not complete without enough interpretation of the results to enable the student to really appreciate his own status, plan intelligently, and recognize accomplishment when it does occur.

Effort is greater when the test is accepted as a personal aid rather than something for the teacher's benefit. Then testing becomes important for the individual; he sees a means of learning faster, and therefore, the whole physical education program appears more significant to him. The discouraged student needs evidence that he is improving. The best answer for him is a test sufficiently easy to register performance and discriminating enough to indicate small increments of improvement. Students with low motor ability show increased interest in physical education and derive considerable satisfaction from modest amounts of improvement when testing procedures are used as an integral part of instruction.[2,5] Students with high motor ability need to be challenged to improve but rarely secure adequate attention and motivation in the regular physical education class. This condition can be alleviated somewhat if standardized tests are given; the superior student then is able to compare his scores with the performance of students in other classes and in other schools.

Students learn while preparing for knowledge tests. Class time used in going over the answers with the students is well spent, both for the students and the teacher, particularly if the group participates in a discussion of the reason for the correctness and incorrectness of answers. McClusky* has shown that groups which discuss test papers

---

*McClusky, H.Y.: An Experimental Comparison of Two Methods of Correcting The Outcome of an Examination, School and Society, 40: p. 566, 1934.

score much higher on a retest of the same content than groups which merely looked at their answer sheets and the test forms.

Tests which put an emphasis on individual improvement almost always appeal to the older children in the elementary school and to junior high school pupils. For that age, tests serve as a form of competition and an opportunity for individual recognition. The tests should be inclusive enough that the same students will not always be in the upper brackets. In order to utilize this competitive urge to the fullest extent, announcements should be made or posted of the individuals making the highest scores, of those making the greatest improvement, or the squads with the best scores.

The teacher must consider the proportion of time which can be devoted to measurement, including testing. He should do this in the same manner that he considers the proportion of time to be devoted to other phases of instruction, between drill and actual participation in the activity, the proportion given to discussion, verbal description, demonstration, and educational films. All are important but the objectives of physical education and the needs of the students must be kept in mind in determining relative proportions. Testing, for example, can provide some real values but should not be overdone. There may be situations in which the total time allotted to physical education is so brief that testing must be reduced to a minimum. The rule to follow is that every test should serve the student. If no time remains after the testing is done, no follow-up can be made and the test will be limited as to purpose served. If too little testing is done, inadequate information is available for best teaching.

Testing is a device for teaching and learning. The successful teacher knows the best devices and aids to learning and uses them skillfully. Under the direction of such a teacher tests fit in so smoothly and naturally that they are accepted and considered challenging by the students, are used by both the student and the teacher, are understood by other teachers in the schools, are appreciated by the parents, and actually are inseparable from the teaching--learning process.

CURRICULUM PLANNING AND REVISION

Those charged with the responsibility for making curriculum decisions need to be fully cognizant of student needs, of program strengths and weaknesses, and of the extent to which the overall objectives of physical education are being met. Many curricula have developed "like Topsy," with only patch work revisions, some of which appear to have been based on whims rather than factual evidence. It seems to be almost universally true that it is easier to get a subject or a course added to the curriculum than it is to get one dropped. This is particularly noticeable in the curricula of some professional schools where the number of required courses has increased to the point where no room remains for electives and students complain of the lack of flexibility.

A look at the physical education curricula of several colleges and universities reveals at least three types. Some of the departments are keeping pace with changes in general education, some have curricula which have been perpetuated in an unchanging form for years, while still others are fluctuating back and forth. For want of better terms, these might be called the modern, the traditional, and the "we can't quite make up our minds" curricula. Similar problems exist in curriculum planning and revision in the elementary and secondary schools, particularly where there is a rapid turnover in teachers. In the extremely small schools, with but one or two physical education teachers, curricula frequently are based on the interests of the teacher or teachers rather than on student needs.

Upon what bases are decisions regarding curricula being made? Subjective judgment always plays a part but it should not be relied upon to too great an extent. Some of us by nature are reactionaries, quick to condemn present practices and to jump on the band wagon for a new activity or a new method. Others of us are inclined to be easy going, perhaps to be too comfortable and smug and desire to retain the status quo. In between, there should be and are many who realize that there are always better methods or improvements possible and who prefer to weigh various factors, collect and examine objective evidence, yet not delay unnecessarily long.

Fortunately, a number of instruments or tools are available for use in evaluating outcomes and assessing student needs. Some forms for use in program evaluation appear in Chapter XIII. Instruments for measuring student attitudes toward physical education have also been developed and reference is made to them in Chapter XII. Tools such as these can be used to supplement the more objective, quantitative type of data yielded by measurements, which provide information concerning student abilities. Evaluation and measurement are essential as the basis for good curriculum planning and revision.

EVIDENCE OF RESULTS

Educators, including physical educators, are being pressured to produce results and to present tangible evidence to justify the ever increasing expenditures of public funds. The physical education teacher who has made good use of evaluation and measurement is in an advantageous position not only to defend his program but to secure additional support for it. He should be able to supply the evidence that will answer such questions as, "What is physical education doing for the students? What gains are being made"?

SUMMARY

Evaluation and measurement have been discussed in relation to their use in understanding the students, in increasing learning and improving teaching, in curriculum planning and revision, and in providing tangible evidence of the results being attained. Many purposes are served; these purposes vary so much that it is obvious that no one type of test or evaluative instrument will serve all purposes. Some choice is available among the various types; teachers should select the ones that are most effective for the purposes in their local situations. The application of measurements and evaluation to the program of physical education provides a scientific foundation for our practices.

SELECTED REFERENCES

1. Cowell, Charles C. and Schwehn, Hilda M.: Modern Principles and Methods in High School Physical Education. Boston, Allyn and Bacon, Inc., 1958, Chapter 9.

2. *Frey, Bernice G.: A Study of Teaching Procedures in Selected Physical Education Activities for College Women of Low Motor Ability, Unpublished Ph.D. Dissertation, State University of Iowa, 1947.

3. Halsey, Elizabeth and Porter, Lorena: Physical Education for Children, A Developmental Program. New York, The Dryden Press, 1958, Chapter 8.

4. Larson, Leonard A. and Yocum, Rachael: Measurement and Evaluation in Physical, Health and Recreation Education. St. Louis, The C. V. Mosby Company, 1951, p. 20.

5. Salit, Elizabeth Powell: The Development of Fundamental Sport Skills in Freshman College Women of Low Motor Ability, Research Quarterly, 15: 330, 1944.

---

*Also available in microcards from Harrison Clarke, University of Oregon, Eugene.

Chapter II

CHARACTERISTICS OF EFFECTIVE MEASURING TOOLS

CRITERIA FOR SKILL TESTS

If tests really serve the purposes which we expect of them, they must possess certain qualities. Fortunately there are enough measures available in some areas that a choice between tests is possible. The question is then, "What qualities are essential?" "If a test doesn't possess all of them, is it inadequate?" "What constitutes the best test available for a given purpose?" Actually the purpose of the test and the degree of refinement of tests relative to that activity or ability determine the answer to the question of "best test." The criteria for evaluating tests of motor skills will be described first in this chapter; suggestions for the evaluation of knowledge tests and subjective ratings will follow.

Criteria to be used in evaluating tests have been presented by many authors of books on tests and measurements. These authors are rather well agreed that the criteria to be applied included statistical measures supplemented by practical considerations and subjective opinion. Usually evidence on reliability and validity is presented. Objectivity, standardized directions, the type of scoring, ease of administration, economy of time, and availability of norms are some of the practical considerations. These and other criteria pertinent to the evaluation and selection of tests of motor skills will be discussed.

TESTS SHOULD MEASURE IMPORTANT ABILITIES

Tests of sport skills are usually given to determine general ability in a particular sport or specific ability in one technique essential to successful performance. The significance of a specific ability as a measure of success

in playing the game is dependent upon its relative importance to all of the techniques required in the game. The
total of all techniques is frequently large and it is not
always easy to determine their relative importance. Nor is
it easy to determine which are important enough to be included, in other words, to set a minimum standard of importance. If the purpose is evaluation of general playing
ability, it is a mistake to test unimportant skills. If
the purpose is diagnosis of abilities for teaching purposes or for selection of team members, then the standard
of importance is considerably lower.

Statistical evidence of the reliability and validity
of a test is not enough. For example, a test known as the
Distance Throw has been mistakenly given to measure basketball playing ability, largely because statistical evidence
has been presented to indicate that it correlates highly
with ratings made of basketball playing ability. One
should expect the Distance Throw scores to correlate rather
highly with general ability in basketball or with general
ability in almost any sport because throwing is a basic
skill and tests of throwing ability are included in almost
all batteries of general motor ability. In the game of
basketball, however, long passes have a limited use. Compared to such abilities as shooting, rebounding, dribbling,
and pivoting, the ability to make a long pass is relatively
unimportant. Since players with high general ability make
better basketball players than those with low ability, high
correlations can be obtained. An example of a relatively
unimportant skill in field hockey is the roll-in, used by
only a few players on each team when the ball has gone out
of bounds over the side line. Some hockey test batteries
include a test of the roll-in. Regardless of the validity
and reliability coefficients reported for a test of the
roll-in, it seems undesirable to use a roll-in test to
measure field hockey playing ability. Logical as well as
statistical considerations should govern the selection of
skill tests.

When selecting skill tests for sports the teacher
should make a list of the important skills involved in the
game and select tests which use one or more of those
skills. For example, field hockey playing requires primarily ability to play the ball and ability of the player to
move quickly and with good body control. Ability to play
the ball can be subdivided into passing, dribbling, goal
shooting, fielding, dodging, and tackling. In every case

this involves using the stick. Ability to move quickly and with good body control can be subdivided into running with the ball (dribbling), change of direction, and footwork for passing, shooting, dodging, and tackling. Control of body weight is inseparable from skillful manipulation of the ball with the stick and with maneuvering the body into position to receive a pass, to tackle an opponent, or to intercept a pass. Further study of the game reveals that the majority of passes are rather short, that passing is usually done while the player is moving, and that in goal shooting the play almost invariably involves a moving ball at some distance from the goal, frequently with interference between the player and the goal. With this type of analysis, the teacher would have little reason to select as tests of field hockey playing ability the roll-in or goal shooting from a stationary position.

TESTS SHOULD BE LIKE THE GAME SITUATIONS

The tests should be as nearly like game situations as possible. For example, a tennis player may drop the ball and drive it to the far end of the court. Tests may be set up for successive trials at a given target, and scores obtained on accuracy of hitting the target or court area. However, the strokes or returns in the game are made on an approaching ball which usually requires footwork timed with the flight of the ball. Seldom can play during a rally be slow or deliberate; these returns are continuous. To measure the same ability as that required in the game, the test should be continuous too.

A combination of skills does not necessarily make a test gamelike; it may even result in infringement of the game rules or in encouragement of poor playing form. A test so constructed makes a poor teaching device. Examples can be found in test batteries in basketball. "Pivot and Shoot" and "Bounce and Shoot" are scored by the number of successful goals. The tests add the game element of receiving the ball and maneuvering to a better or closer position for shooting. On first consideration it might seem that they have gamelike qualities. However, the lack of pressure for speedy action characteristic of the game partly nullifies the possible value. Nothing prevents the player from pausing before attempting the shot, which defeats the purpose of having the player do a pivot or bounce before shooting. Secondly, the violation of traveling may occur in the performance of both tests. If violations are considered in the scoring, an extra helper or judge is needed to administer the test and the decision of that person is subjective.

The time element is more important than is usually realized. In the development of an accuracy test in softball, it was noted that successive throws at a stationary target permitted the player to take more time to aim than is available in the game situation. The test was revised so that the player caught a ball sent by a catapult and threw immediately at a stationary target. That introduced another difficulty, the impracticability of a catapult in group testing. The player was still able to hesitate following the catch so that the situation was almost the same as in the stationary throw. The next step in the development of this test was to change the sequence and add a time control. The player then threw the ball at a wall, fielded the ball on the rebound, turned and ran to a specified spot on the floor which represented a base, and threw to a wall target which represented another baseman. The stop watch was started on the signal for the first throw and stopped when the ball hit the wall on the second throw. The accuracy of the second throw was recorded. The actual time accumulated for the ten trials proved relatively unimportant but it served to eliminate the long hesitation or pause before the throw to the target. Performance on this test corresponded more closely to actual performance in the game than did performance on either of the other two tests. The difference between the tests is comparable to the difference between pegging the ball around the bases for practice and actually trying to beat the runner to base for an out in a game situation.

TESTS SHOULD ENCOURAGE GOOD FORM

Measurement of form in most sports presents a real problem. For example, a tennis player may be able to make a high score on an accuracy test by tapping rather than stroking a ball into a specified area on the court. The flight of the ball may be slow, arched, and followed by a high bounce. Another player may stroke the ball in the same area so that it travels with speed, in a flat path, and results in a low bounce. To return this stroke is more difficult than to return the first player's ball.

Some tests fail to discriminate between these two players and yet, obviously, the latter player has made a far better tennis performance.

Various attempts have been made to encourage performance in good form. Subjective ratings of form have been used to supplement the test score; these can be effective in encouraging good form if the ratings are made during the test. The use of a time limit has been tried. When the total time is short, a high premium is set on the accuracy of the stop watch and the consistency of the timer's reaction time. The introduction of a time element is probably of greater value in promoting a gamelike performance than it is in encouraging good form. The problem of objective measurement of form has not been solved for any of the sports or for dance activities. In selecting tests, care should be taken to avoid tests in which players using poor form can score higher than players using good form.

TESTS SHOULD INVOLVE ONE PERFORMER ONLY

Previous discussion may have suggested the use of two or more players in a test situation since the player in the game must always consider the person from whom he receives the ball, the one to whom he sends it, and the action of his opponents. The use of several players would satisfy the standard of game similarity. However, the cooperation or competition for all players must be identical in a testing situation. The persons tested must have good balls, a target of the same size, and all other equipment must be the same for each person taking the test. One player should not be tested with a partner who fumbles or throws wildly while another person has a partner who is an excellent player. It is becoming apparent that no single standard can be considered in isolation from the rest.

The test should involve only the person being tested. Recognition of this need has resulted in many tests using rebounds or repeated plays at a wall. An objection to this type of test is the artificiality of the situation. A rebound test represents a compromise between the two criteria of game similarity and a single performer. Such a test does aid in producing game similarity in that the player both receives and sends the ball and the play is continuous. The pressure for speedy action is not dissimilar from that in the game. Moreover, the player alone is responsible for the results.

TESTS SHOULD BE INTERESTING AND MEANINGINGFUL

The tests should appeal to the students if best efforts are to be obtained. Tests frequently have certain inherent qualities which attract or repel student interest; one of the qualities which attracts interest is game similarity. Various means of motivation can be used: providing individuals with score cards for recording continuous records; posting as well as announcing the scores and names of the best performers, or of those persons making the greatest improvement; comparison of scores with previous classes, other groups, or with accepted standards.

The scoring system should be meaningful to the students. For example, some tests may be scored either on the basis of the number of hits made in a given time interval or in terms of the time required to make a specified number of hits. A student readily understands a successful hit on the target and his total score relative to the total number of throws he had. However, the student's concept of his performance is less clear when results are expressed in time intervals, the number of seconds. It is true that even though he does not fully comprehend the meaning of his score he can make comparisons with scores of others, but the standard of an optimum or ideal performance is lacking. Likewise, a score should not be reported to the student in terms of standard deviation or some other value which he has no basis for understanding.

Students will retain interest in tests only if use is made of the test scores. Test scores should be made known to the student as soon as possible; probably one reason for the popularity of basket shooting tests is that the results are known at once. Interest lessens quickly when tests are so time-consuming that there is no opportunity to engage in the activity itself or when the tests produce undesirable after-effects such as muscle soreness. Most sports tests produce no undesirable after-effects although some tests of endurance may. Proper conditioning before the tests are given will prevent muscle soreness and stiffness.

The testing time should fit into the time ordinarily devoted in the lesson to practice of techniques. The student then looks at the tests as a more objective form of practice and learns to make all practice a self-testing experience.

In selecting tests, consideration should be given to those that the students will understand and enjoy. This is not to imply that there is need to entertain students. However, maximum effort is needed from the student on each test and understanding and enjoyment are essential to wholehearted effort.

TESTS SHOULD BE OF SUITABLE DIFFICULTY

The difficulty level of the test should correspond to the ability of the group being tested. The scores should show a reasonable distribution with no massing of scores at any one point. Should the test be too easy, most of the scores will be high and the test will not discriminate between players of slightly different abilities. An easy test does not serve to motivate continued effort. Should the test be too difficult, most of the scores will be near zero. A difficult test discourages students and serves no function in discriminating between players possessing varying degrees of the ability being measured.

The test may be altered or postponed until the class has developed more ability, or a different form of the test may be selected. If revisions are made, the test should not be used for diagnosis or marking unless a statistical study of the modified form of the test has revealed satisfactory evidence of its worth. Revised tests must also have new norms or achievement scales established since the previous ones are no longer applicable.

TESTS SHOULD DIFFERENTIATE BETWEEN LEVELS OF ABILITY

Most of our practices in education are based on a recognition of individual differences of students. Certainly the whole basis of measurement and evaluation procedures is the recognition of these differences, and recognition of the changing status of each student as time, experience and practice modify his behavior. It follows then that test scores should reflect these differences or increments. If a group is highly variable in ability, the test scores should indicate that. If the group is homogeneous in

16

ability, there are still differences between individuals which we need to determine.

The extremes of the ability range are not hard to identify by the teacher during practice, during the game, or with most tests. However, it is much more difficult to differentiate during the regular class performance between the majority of students who fall within the middle range of ability. The tests should make this discrimination throughout this middle range as well as at the extremes. The purpose of the test is to obtain a ranking of members of the class according to their respective abilities so that interpretations can be made in fairness to each student.

The tests will achieve this high level of discrimination only if the difficulty of the task to be performed is suited to the ability level of the group. However, such a criterion of difficulty does not guarantee discrimination and other characteristics must also be considered.

TESTS SHOULD PROVIDE ACCURATE SCORING

The objectivity of a test depends to a large extent upon the accuracy of the scoring. Some tests can be scored with a fairly high degree of accuracy by means of a measuring tape or stop watch. Stunt tests which are scored as success or failure involve subjective opinion and some are difficult to score accurately. A basket with a net leaves little doubt as to whether the ball went through the rim or dropped outside. An arrow shot into a target can be scored accurately; a ball thrown at a target is more difficult to score.

Accuracy in scoring throws at a target composed of concentric circles can be facilitated by constructing the center circle and alternate circles of tin attached to a wooden background; the sound supplements vision. Targets can be painted in different colors to facilitate scoring; the archery target is a well-known example. When timing of races is judged by the zone in which the runner finished, errors in judgment sometimes occur. When such an event is administered indoors on a course adjacent to a wall, the accuracy of scoring can be increased if the zone numbers are painted on the wall rather than on the floor.

Tests which cannot be scored accurately are usually low in reliability as well as objectivity and they cause dissatisfaction among the performers.

TESTS SHOULD PROVIDE A SUFFICIENT NUMBER OF TRIALS

The number of trials should be sufficient to eliminate chance deviations. Most tests of maximum effort can be measured in one to three trials; examples are throws for distance, strength events, and speed events where control is not a major factor. When a high degree of accuracy is necessary for good performance, the number of trials must be greater. Speed on short runs will not vary much from day to day; ability to make free throws does vary considerably.

Only by experimentation can the number of trials necessary to provide a truly representative score be determined. The number of trials should increase as the element of chance increases. The type of scoring affects the number of trials. If each attempt on an accuracy test is scored on a success or failure basis, as in basket shooting, the number needs to be greater than if each attempt is scored for relative accuracy, as in a test using a concentric circle target. The number of trials required is related to the ability of the players; the number necessary for a group of advanced players will frequently be fewer than for less experienced players on the same test.

Whenever the test is being used for a practice device or for motivation, the trials may be reduced to a smaller number than that recommended for classification or for use as a partial basis in determining marks. The amount of time required for administration is usually a factor in selecting tests; fifteen or twenty trials may take more time than is available. Testing time cannot be estimated by the number of trials alone. Tests which must be administered individually, such as strength tests involving the use of a dynamometer, may be more time-consuming than tests which can be given to large numbers at the same time even with more trials required.

To measure abilities accurately, the number of trials must be sufficient to eliminate effects of chance fluctuations in ability. Rather than reducing the number of trials to save testing time, thus sacrificing accuracy, it

18

is preferable to limit the selection of tests to the most important abilities and to plan the administration of tests carefully to avoid wasting time. Additional preparation and care in the collection of data will amply repay the teacher for the time expended.

TESTS SHOULD BE JUDGED PARTLY BY STATISTICAL EVIDENCE

The usual textbook list of criteria for evaluating tests includes reliability, validity, objectivity, economy, and availability of norms. Are these criteria related to the ones discussed previously in this chapter? Does satisfying statistical criteria insure satisfactory attainment of the other characteristics? It is more apt to work in the opposite direction. In any case, that which produces an effective test is a product of many factors.

Reliability, or consistency of measurement of the same degree of ability, is possible only if the performer is interested enough to put forth maximum effort, if his own skill only is measured, if equipment and test conditions are uniform, if the trials are sufficient in number to eliminate chance variations, and if scoring of performance is objective.

Validity is defined as the degree to which a test measures what it purports to measure. Logic as well as statistics should be applied in studying validity. The term face validity is sometimes used. This is a rational analysis of the task involved in the test situation, or a determination of that which the test purports to measure. It would be foolhardy to try to establish worth to a test unless one is satisfied that it is good logic to assume that the test measures a given ability. It is the basis on which one builds either items for a knowledge test or performance measures in a skill test. However, it is desirable to check or confirm this reasoning and so a validity estimate is made in terms of one or more groups of students.

Economy results primarily from the careful selection of a few highly valid tests which are administered efficiently. Validity computations of batteries, or combinations of tests, help in this selection. Recognition of the fact that every skill in the activity can not and need not be measured will help to make the measurement sessions feasible. Administrative aids to economy will be discussed in Chapter XIV.

Norms or standards of achievement undoubtedly add to the usefulness of a test but their unavailability does not render a test worthless. Scales may be constructed from data collected by a teacher having several classes or sections of similar age and experience or from data from several schools. The T-scale has proved satisfactory and may be constructed on data from fifty or more cases (see page 63). Teacher-constructed scales may be preferable to the use of published scales if the latter do not fit the local group; frequently the published scales have been constructed on a small number of subjects from a particular locality. The value of national norms is questionable, but if they are to be usable, they need to provide standards for players of both sexes and with varying amounts of experience. One set of norms for a test in basketball, for example, will not be adequate. Size, age, and maturity of players need to be considered in setting up norms, especially for some tests and for certain age levels.

If one is to make use of the work done by others in the development of tests, certain statistical concepts are essential. Range of ability or distribution of scores is basic to most of these concepts. Within any large group unselected for the ability in question there will be considerable variation in the level of that ability. With an effective measuring device, the range of ability will be shown in the test scores. There will not be an equal number of individuals at all points along the range; toward the center of the range there will be many scores and there will be fewer scores toward each extreme. One can expect that in any large group many persons will make scores that are about average, a few persons will make excellent scores, and a few will make poor scores.

When portrayed in graphic form the scores of a large group make a symmetrical, bell-shaped curve. This can be visualized by imagining each individual as being represented by a child's playing block upon which the test score has been written. If two persons make the same score, one block would be placed on top of the other; if ten or more persons make the same score the blocks stack up in tower fashion. The concentration or piling up of blocks will be in the middle. Individuals tend to be alike in ability but there are always variations; some will be superior, and the blocks representing those individuals would be placed at the right-hand side of the blocks representing persons with average ability. The individuals with below average ability would be represented by blocks placed on the left-hand side of the middle at varying distances corresponding to their scores. An efficient measuring device must discriminate between all levels of ability. Discrimination is most likely to be inadequate in the middle of the range, or in the area of greatest similarity of abilities.

An achievement scale shows the distribution of ability of a given group on a particular test. Distributions vary for different groups. Since this is true, one justifiably expects every report of test construction to describe the population upon which the report is based. The report should state the age or grade level, the sex, the number of cases, the amount of experience of the players, and any special characteristics which affect the results.

The reliability and validity of a test are expressed as correlation coefficients. Such coefficients are numerical expressions of a degree of relationship. The reliability coefficient expresses the relationship between two consecutive administrations of the test and indicates the consistency with which the test measures whatever it measures. It is frequently impractical to give two duplicate administrations when studying tests. As a substitute on tests where several trials are given, the laternate trials may be correlated. For example, if the test consists of six trials, the scores made on trials 1, 3, and 5 (the odd-numbered trials) are totaled and correlated against the total of scores made on trials 2, 4, and 6 (the even-numbered trials). This would be done for all the individuals taking the test; the correlation coefficient which results indicates the consistency within the series of trials. Such a coefficient will usually be lower than if the entire test had been given twice, because the correlation is actually made on one-half of the series of trials. Correction for that difference is possible and is sometimes made. The method of correction most commonly used is by the Spearman-Brown Prophecy Formula which will be discussed in Chapter IV. The reader should note in every case whether such correction has been made in order to know how to interpret the reliability coefficient.

The validity coefficient expresses the degree of relationship between a criterion and the test. The higher the relationship, the more truly does the test appear to be measuring the ability in question, that is, the more nearly it confirms the basic assumption of face validity. The criterion against which the test scores are correlated may be another test of proved worth, or it may be some score determined subjectively such as that provided by ratings. Since the criterion is the yardstick against which the test is being measured, it is important that the criterion be appropriate and good. If the criterion is not good, one might be misled and discard a test which had more worth than the criterion; since the criterion is poor, the test appears poor.

The user of the test has the right to expect a statement of the criterion used in order that he may be able to interpret the validity coefficient. If ratings have been used as the criterion, the procedure which was employed should be acceptable (see page 38). Lower validity coefficients appear to result when the criterion is a subjectively derived set of scores than when the criterion is another test. Knowing this, the user of the test is better able to interpret the validity coefficient.

Since reliability and validity are expressed as correlation coefficients, some explanation of these quantitative values is needed so that they can be interpreted by persons unfamiliar with correlation techniques. One must understand the difference between .90 and .09, between .90 and .80, between +.90 and -.90, and why coefficients are always decimal values and never whole numbers.

The correlation coefficient is a mathematical expression of relationship between two factors or abilities as measured on a given group of persons. The correlation is essentially a process of plotting the two factors under consideration into a single graph, called a scattergram. The computation of a validity coefficient involves two factors, the criterion and the experimental measure or test being checked (see Figure 1). The vertical scale OC represents the distribution of cases on the criterion. If fifty cases had been placed in rank order on that scale, then number 1 is at the top or high end of the scale and number 50 at the low or zero end of the scale, with all other cases in successive order between these two. Each case would be placed on the XO scale according to the rank order of the scores made on the experimental measure or test.

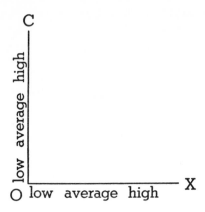

Figure 1. Diagram of correlation graph or scattergram.

The effects of similarity and discrepancy in these two rank orders are demonstrated in Figure 2. In Figure 2 a, two orders in perfect agreement are illustrated. The same person would be in top position in each scale and is represented by number 1 on the scattergram. All other cases would be similarly ranked and their placement on the graph would result in a straight line from O diagonally upward. The coefficient in this case would be 1.00. Such an instance would probably never occur because of chance variations, differences in effort, errors in measurement, and other shortcomings of all measuring techniques. Occasionally only slight variations in rank may occur and the plotting on the scattergram would appear as in Figure 2 b. This scattergram shows the same general direction in the design of the tallies across the graph but they do not hold to a narrow, straight line. A scattergram like b would give a coefficient of approximately .90 or some number indicating a relationship less perfect than a (1.00).

When there is no similarity between the scores on the experimental measure and the scores on the criterion, a scattergram such as c would occur. An individual who is low on one axis may be anywhere from high to low on the other. Such a heterogeneity of tallies would produce a coefficient at or near zero.

There might conceivably be instances where the rank order of one scale is completely reversed in the other. A scattergram representing complete reversal is shown in Figure 2 e. The tallies all fall in a straight line as

23

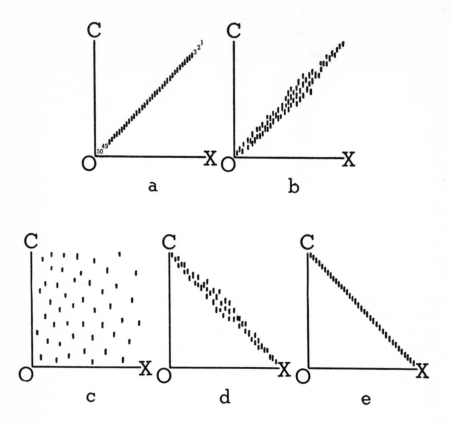

Figure 2. Scattergrams yielding different coefficients.

a = + 1.00 coefficient.
b = + .90 coefficient.
c = zero coefficient.
d = - .90 coefficient.
e = - 1.00 coefficient.

they do in a except that they run from C to X. The scattergram e would also give a coefficient of 1.00 but it would
be distinguished from the 1.00 coefficient in a by a negative sign. Part a shows a direct and exact correspondence
of the two scales; its coefficient is called positive (written +1.00) and it expresses relationship which is direct.
Part e shows a perfect reversal of the two rank orders; its
coefficient is called negative (written -1.00) and it expresses an inverse relationship between the two measures.

24

Perfect inverse relationships are no more likely to occur than perfect positive ones. Figure 2 d represents the more usual form of a high inverse relationship.

Questions are frequently asked regarding the size of correlation coefficients. No arbitrary size can be set as a minimum but generalizations can be made. Reliability coefficients can be expected to be higher than validity coefficients. Lower coefficients can be expected in tests of physical abilities than in tests of mental capacities, perhaps due to more fluctuation in the former. Tests given to girls usually yield lower reliabilities than when given to boys, probably due to the greater difficulty of motivating girls to put forth their best efforts. The performance of inexperienced players is usually less reliable than that of highly skilled ones. When a test is reported as having a reliability coefficient of .78, for example, this does not mean that any group using the same test would find exactly the same reliability coefficient when computed on its data. The reliability is specific to the group tested in the study; similar reliability coefficients may be expected only for similar groups under similar testing conditions.

The Repeated Volleys Test (see page 231) yielded a reliability coefficient of .78 for forty-seven senior high school girls, using as a score for the test the sum of the five best trials out of ten. The same test yielded a reliability coefficient of .92 for seventy-five college women using as a score for the test the sum of ten trials. (The latter reliability coefficient could have been corrected for length by the application of the Spearman-Brown Prophecy Formula but is reported here in its original size to facilitate comparison.) The difference is not believed to be entirely due to administration since the tests were given by the same person and under quite similar testing conditions. The number of trials used as the final score for the test may have caused the difference; it is known that up to a certain number the reliability of a measure increases with the number of trials. Quite a large share of the difference between the two coefficients can probably be accounted for by the difference in the experience of the players. The number of cases may also have affected the reliability somewhat; more reliance can be placed on the reliability coefficient computed on the larger number of cases.

With all of the above points in mind, a generalization can be made on the qualitative interpretations of numerical

25

coefficients. Anything above .85 is considered excellent; validity coefficients seldom go above .85; reliability coefficients frequently do. From .75 to .85 is considered adequate for many purposes. As reliability coefficients drop below .75 they indicate an inconsistent and poor measuring instrument. A validity coefficient below .60 to .65 indicates poor predictive value but the test may be used to serve other purposes, as will be discussed later.

Low coefficients indicate less relationship than do high ones and they should be interpreted accordingly. A low reliability coefficient indicates inconsistency in measurement and may suggest the need for additional trials or improvements in the details and conditions under which the test is conducted. A low validity coefficient would indicate that the test is worthless for predicting the ability it was assumed to measure, but if it appears subjectively to have some merit and is shown to be highly reliable, it might make a very good practice test and serve the purpose of securing interest and effort from the students.

Sometimes several tests are studied for their relationship to general ability in a sport. Each of them may show fairly high validity coefficients when correlated one test at a time against the criterion. It is possible that some of the tests may be measuring the same abilities as others; the tests are correlated against each other to determine the extent to which this is true. If the correlation coefficient between two tests is high, one test will probably be discarded in favor of the one with higher validity. A correlation between two tests is known as an intercorrelation. In combining tests to form a battery, those with low intercorrelations are selected because they measure different aspects of the general ability.

The validity of the total battery is computed by a multiple correlation (see page 92). To secure a high validity from a combination of tests, it is essential that each test be reliable and reasonably valid. Sometimes some tests are retained for future use because of their contribution to a battery although they do not have acceptable validity in and by themselves. The intercorrelations must necessarily be low. The following example illustrates these statements.

Imagine possessing a box that cannot be opened; its contents are unknown. One means of describing it to someone else would be subjectively by its shape or objectively by its external measurements. Its size can be measured by using a good cloth tape to determine its length, breadth, and thickness. It would add nothing to the description of the box to use a flexible steel tape and measure it again. The result would be two measures of the same thing, that is, two measures with high intercorrelations. It would be much more helpful to determine its weight as a second measure. While size and weight tend to be related, there doubtless would be a lower intercorrelation between weight and size than between size as measured by the cloth tape and size as measured by the steel tape. Knowing weight and size gives more of a clue to the contents than was known before. Additional qualities may be measured if means exist for measurement; additional measurement will be helpful only when it does not duplicate something already known.

Multiple correlation coefficients are expressed in the same form as those of the simple correlation but they are always positive. Somewhat higher values of multiple correlations are expected than in the case of a single test since more measurements are being considered.

The multiple correlation tells which tests to combine in a battery but it does not tell how to combine them. The multiple correlation (R) is actually a validity coefficient of the series or battery. In working with long experimental lists of tests, several combinations may be tried, and the R's indicate the relative validity of each combination, in terms of the original criterion. One may then choose a battery solely in terms of the highest R, or select the few most valid tests, considering also the administrative feasibility and cost, special equipment, relationship of the tests in terms of what students have been taught or what is expected from them, and other similar considerations. It must be remembered that numerical differences in the R are not always significant, and these other considerations are of real importance in the administration and use of the tests.

Frequently the units of scoring in one test are so different from those of another that the results of one test would completely dominate the final score if the raw scores were simply added together. For example, it might be desirable to combine scores from a softball throw for distance where the average score was 60 feet and the scores from an accuracy target throw where the average score was 15. The score on the distance throw is always so large

27

that variations in ability on the second test would fail to affect the final score proportionately. The two skills may not be of equal importance in measuring softball playing ability and the scores must be adjusted because of this difference in size of scores. Or the target throw might be more important in measuring playing ability and would need adjusting in relation to the distance throw. This adjustment, when combining tests into a battery, is called weighting. It is achieved by the regression equation (see page 93) which specifies the proportion of the raw scores to be used.

An alternative to the use of the regression equation when combining tests is to take the student's T-scores for each test and add them together. (See page 61 for explanation of T-scores.) Both procedures take into consideration the range of all scores and the ability of the student in relation to the rest of the group. The sum of the T-scores can be computed more quickly and is a satisfactory substitute when tests are approximately equal in value.

TESTS SHOULD PROVIDE A MEANS FOR INTERPRETING PERFORMANCE

A test score by itself is quite meaningless. Only when it is known how the test score relates to scores made by others can the performance represented by the score be interpreted. One way of interpreting the score is to relate it to the average (or mean), but this gives an inadequate description. Another measure of central tendency is the median; the median score is the middle point on the scale and is excelled by 50 per cent of the cases. Neither the mean nor the median is particularly useful to the teacher concerned with evaluating individual performance. Scores of 60 and 80 may both be above the mean and median, but is the score of 80 decidedly better than the score of 60? The measures of distribution (difference from the mean or from the median) are much more valuable. These measures are the quartile, percentile, and the standard deviation. The quartiles locate the scores between which 25 per cent of the cases fall. In other words, each half created by the establishment of the median is again halved. (See Figure 3.) The scores range from $\underline{A}$ (low) to $\underline{Z}$ (high); 25 per cent of the scores will fall in each quartile. Quartile point 2 coincides with the median. From $\underline{3}$ to $\underline{Z}$ is the fourth or upper quartile. The range of scores from $\underline{A}$ to the first

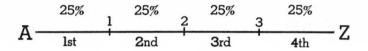

Figure 3. Quartiles.
A-Z = range of scores.
A-1 = lowest or first quartile.
1-2 = second quartile.
2-3 = third quartile.
3-Z = upper or fourth quartile.

quartile point will probably differ from the range between the first quartile point and the median, since the scores tend to concentrate around the middle portion of the distribution; the range will be greater toward the extremes. However, each score is located with respect to the rest of the group and a student understands very readily when told in which fourth of the class his score falls.

Percentiles follow the same plan with subdivisions into smaller units than 25 per cent. A score that falls at the sixty-fifth percentile point is readily understood by the student when he is told that his score is better than 65 per cent of the group but is surpassed by 35 per cent.

The standard deviation is a measure of distribution commonly applied to any symmetrical bell-shaped distribution of scores approximating the normal curve. The curve is bell-shaped because the frequencies decrease as the amount of deviation from the center increases in each direction. Since the standard deviation is a measurement yardstick, the units on it are the same length throughout the length of the scale. Each standard deviation is named according to its deviation from the mean. (See Figure 4.) Because of its specific location, each standard deviation has a specified percentage of frequencies in it equaled only by its partner at the opposite end of the distribution. The length of each standard deviation is uniform within each distribution but its length varies for each new group of cases or for each test, since the range varies and the distribution of cases through the range varies. The size of the standard deviation increases when the total range increases, or when the scores fall with greater frequency near the extremes.

The T-scale is an easy and practical interpretation of the standard deviation of a distribution and is the form

used for many achievement scales. The mean is always 50.
Each standard deviation equals 10 points on the T-scale.
Therefore, the limits of the scale are approximately 20 and
80. Two-thirds of the class will have scores between 40
and 60 or within one standard deviation above and below the
mean (see Figure 4). Of the scores, 68.2 per cent fall

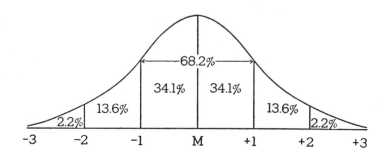

Figure 4. Standard deviations.

M = mean of the distribution.
+ = above the mean.
- = below the mean.
1 = first standard deviation from the mean.
2 = second standard deviation from the mean.
3 = third standard deviation from the mean.

between the limits of one standard deviation above the
mean and one standard deviation below the mean (approximately two-thirds of the cases). A simple explanation
which may be given to students follows: 50 is average on
the test; above 50 is better than average (the higher the
score, the better); below 50 is less than average (the
lower the score, the poorer it is).

One of the chief advantages of T-scores is that a direct comparison of performance on different tests is possible. It is not possible to say whether a 5--foot throw is
better than 10 points on a target test unless each is interpreted as good or poor. The T-scale makes this interpretation on the basis of standing with respect to the rest
of the group. Such a comparison is invaluable in diagnostic testing and in motivating student effort.

Other types of scales are available. Some achievement
scales range from 0 to 100 or 0 to 1000. These are

constructed on a plan similar to the T-scale except that
they are based on a 3 standard deviation range, which is
the practical rather than the theoretical range of population scores. The scale scores in each standard deviation
range are 16 2/3 instead of 10 as found in the T-scale. It
is, therefore, slightly more awkward for the teacher to interpret variability of the group than when using the T-
scale. It does have the advantage of spreading the middle
group a little more on the scale. The T-scales have an advantage not only in interpretation, but in greater motivation to the cases near the two ends of the distribution.

Closely related to the above are somewhat simpler
scales showing proportions of the total group in relation to
designated raw scores. Two of these in common use are
quartile divisions of the distribution and percentile values
for the respective raw scores.

The quartile division is made in similar fashion to
determination of the median. The median divides the cases
by locating the point above which 50% of the cases fall,
and below which the other 50% fall. In turn, the quartiles
divide each half so designated into halves again. Thus
three points are located along the distribution with one-
fourth of the total cases in each of the four groups so constructed.

The percentile indicates the percentage of the total
cases which are excelled by a particular score. For every
raw score made a percentile value is computed. Thus the
point dividing the lower and second quartile groups is the
25th percentile, the median or division between the second
and third quartiles is the 50th percentile, and the point
separating third and upper quartile is the 75th percentile.
The percentile values may vary more from group to group
than some of the other scales which have coarser categories
for interpretation.

Another method of scale construction utilizes what is
known as the principle of increased increments. This allows greater awards on the achievement scale in the upper
levels of skill where improvements are more difficult and
slow to achieve. McCloy[7] has prepared over fifty scoring
tables for a wide variety of strength, weight throwing,
running, walking, jumping and vaulting events. Such scales
would appear to be best adapted to groups above the beginners' level and where there is a wide range of ability represented.

Preference should be given to scales that provide a means of interpreting scores to the student and to those that can be readily computed. The T-scale or the 100-point scale is usually chosen for interpretation of scores derived on a class or a series of classes. There seems to be one advantage to the T-scale, particularly when used for stimulating student effort. The poor students may have tried hard and actually received some score on the test. If the 100-point scale is used, the reward is less than 10 and is very discouraging. If the T-scale is used, the reward is in the 20's. Such a score serves to give encouragement. At the other extreme of ability a student who makes in the 90's is likely to feel satisfied and not make much further effort. On the other hand, if the T-scale is used, the same student scores in the 70's; this seems to point up the fact that there is still opportunity for improvement. The choice of scale should be made on the basis of which one gives the student the best understanding of his performance and serves as the greatest aid to learning.

PRACTICAL CONSIDERATIONS IN APPLYING CRITERIA

Certain points should be kept in mind in applying the above criteria.

1. All criteria can not be met fully in any one test. The function to be served will help determine which criteria have priority. In general, perhaps the following are most essential; validity, reliability, accuracy, one performer involved, encouragement of good form.

2. A test or battery can only sample the many skills involved in an activity, or the many aspects of the broadly defined capacities. A small sample frequently can be adequate here just as in many other situations. The attempt to be comprehensive often defeats the purpose and discourages both students and instructor.

3. Effective test results are dependent upon maximum effort of each student. This is not always obtained and therefore, validation efforts fall down and instructional follow-ups are weakened. Motivation, administrative technique are the primary keys to student effort. Student attitudes usually reflect teacher attitudes.

4. Tests are tools for estimating individual abilities, and individual differences in abilities. The test administrator is the craftsman employing those tools. Like any craftsman or professional technician, a teacher may be clumsy or an artist in the use of the skills. A teacher should not feel above learning the art of test administration and constantly trying to improve.

5. A test is not the game itself, except perhaps in the case of a Columbia Round, a bowling line, or a few other such exceptions. The fact that there is some discrepancy between test and game is not necessarily serious. If the task in the test calls forth abilities in the same relative amounts as the game abilities, then the test will have served one purpose, that of determining relative abilities of class members. The test, however, should not be so artificial that it is disinteresting to students.

6. Groups differ, so the norms and achievement scales must differ. This will be discussed in the next section of this chapter.

CRITERIA FOR ACHIEVEMENT SCALES

ACHIEVEMENT SCALES MUST BE UNDERSTANDABLE TO THE STUDENT

The purpose of an achievement scale is to help the student interpret his performance. Therefore, he should understand the actual scale and the point values and understand his own changes in status as they occur. A standard deviation value is not apt to be meaningful to a student, but a scale based on a standard deviation may be easily comprehended. Scales based on a continuous range, with high numerical values for the better scores appear reasonable. The T-scale is one which does this. In contrast z-scores are not very meaningful or happily used by students. In such a scale the scores are all deviations from the mean and all cases below the mean receive negative scores.

ACHIEVEMENT SCALES MUST ACKNOWLEDGE DIFFERENCES IN ABILITY

The purpose of the test is differentiation between abilities. This should not be lost by translating into an achievement scale. Any single figure, whether a mean, a top score, or any other given value, is not satisfactory as a norm or point of reference for the student.

Quartiles give better differentiation than a single point and may be adequate for some uses. However, usually a continuous scale with numerous, small groupings is better than one with only a few categories.

If the test is of appropriate difficulty there will be no concentration of cases except to some extent in the middle range of ability. A T-scale will give more concentration than a 0-100 scale. Increments on either are relative to the total range.

The increased increment scale mentioned above, provides for more concentration among the less skilled performers in order to provide for more spread at the upper levels. Such a scale is doubtless better if interpretation is solely on individual progress, with no attention to status within the group.

ACHIEVEMENT SCALES ARE SPECIFIC TO A GIVEN GROUP OR CLASS

A scale computed on a class of high school girls would have little or no value for high school boys. Likewise, no interchange of use is possible between groups with much and little background of training, marked differences in opportunities by virtue of facilities, instruction, age, etc. Nation-wide norms are not going to fit all schools, and scales on school A may not be suited to school B.

It is preferable to accumulate scores in a given school until a sufficient number become available; then these can be used to compute a scale for the local group of students. As long as circumstances and students in the school continue similar it can be assumed that the scale is applicable. If scales are borrowed from other sources, consideration should be given to comparison of the group on which it was established and the group for which it is proposed.

ACHIEVEMENT SCALES SHOULD
BE MOTIVATING TO STUDENTS

Interest in scale interpretation of test scores, or lack thereof, may be due to various factors. At least one is the nature of the scale. Understandability and recognition of improvement are important in this respect.

Achievement scales are an artificial device for interpretation. They might be considered somewhat like grades as a form of reward. If the student is interested in raw scores and they have meaning for him, there is no need to divert his attention. However, there should be scales available for those who do want such help.

CRITERIA FOR KNOWLEDGE TESTS

The use of knowledge tests is increasing not only at the college level but also at the secondary level. Since acquisition of information and use of information are important objectives of all of our physical education courses it seems pertinent to develop the ability of all teachers to construct good written tests.

The criteria of effective knowledge tests in physical education are much the same as in any other field. These criteria are not unlike those for skill tests. The separate questions in the examination may be considered parallel to the separate tests in a skill battery.

TEST ITEMS SHOULD DEAL WITH IMPORTANT
SUBJECT MATTER

This is a decision to be made by the test constructor and in light of the specific circumstances for which the test is built. This is usually achieved by working from an outline of content covered in class or through other experiences, and then determining the proportion of the examination to be devoted to each content area. In any case it can only be a sample of the total content which might be expected of the group.

TEST ITEMS SHOULD REQUIRE USE
OR INTERPRETATION OF INFORMATION

There are few instances in education when facts for
facts sake are considered the goal of learning. Instead it
is hoped that the learner acquires facts in order to be able
to do something or do it in a way he could not do before.
It has been demonstrated that learners frequently acquire
an ability for verbatim repetition of words, but they have
limited association of cues eliciting the quotation, little
or no knowledge of meaning, and no comprehension of consequences. This has frequently been true with respect to the
rules of a game. The words can be repeated, the penalty re-
called, but the student has no knowledge of how these situations occur, what the rules provide for the game, how to
acquire the ability to conform, how to observe another in
order to recognize the differences between legal and illegal
play, what the consequences are of infringement, how to distinguish one infringement from another, or other understandings affecting his behavior in a game.

The ability to construct questions which deal with use
of information, or with basic understandings rather than
with words or isolated facts, is usually hard to acquire.
Experience, analysis of the process of responding, analysis
of test results, listening to students' reactions on examinations can all be helpful steps in improving test items.

EACH TEST ITEM SHOULD DIFFERENTIATE
BETWEEN THOSE WHO KNOW
AND THOSE WHO DO NOT

The purpose of the total examination is to arrange the
class in rank order according to total knowledge and understanding. This can be accomplished only if each item contributes toward this purpose. Failure occurs most often if
the question is too difficult or too easy, if there are
grammatical clues or others not related to the content itself.

This ability to differentiate is closely related to
what is called the validity of a measure. In construction
of knowledge tests it is usually judged by an index of discrimination. There are shortcomings in this process of determining this capacity of the item. It can be supplemented
by discussion with students to find out how they arrive at
a decision on the test item.

THE TEST SHOULD ELICIT CAREFUL, THOUGHTFUL CONSIDERATION

There are many factors which affect the way in which the student goes about answering the questions. Some of these have nothing to do with the test itself. Distractions are known to exist as a result of lack of interest in the course, disturbances in the room, the way in which the test is presented and administered, and announcements relative to the use to be made of scores. The appearance of the test, its readability, its length, its vocabulary, its appropriateness to content expected by the student, and ability to succeed on the first few items, all affect students' work methods.

EACH ITEM SHOULD HAVE A DEFINITE ANSWER

Students become disinterested, frustrated, or even antagonistic if answering questions in an examination becomes a matter of trying to guess the answer that the teacher would make to the question. There should be some basis in fact, logic, and the framework created by the question that makes a specific answer the best answer. This is sometimes referred to as objectivity.

This does not mean that the student should see the answer as completely obvious. He should be required to think, to apply information and interpret situations. The process of answering an examination can be a learning process in which he acquires ability to reason and use his factual learnings.

The items are based on assumptions of face validity. They are written and revised carefully, frequently with several persons reading and suggesting possible defects in the items or ways of improving them. The writer tries to recall the kinds of questions which have worked well previously and procedures he has found necessary previously for revising items. Such a thoughtful approach to test construction should lead to assurance that the question is answerable, and assurance that a particular answer is correct.

THE TEST SHOULD BE COMPOSED OF ITEMS OF KNOWN VALUE AND DIFFICULTY

This is possible with a new test only to the extent of the care which is taken in its construction, and the skill of the test writer. When the test has been administered, the items should be analyzed for discrimination, difficulty, nonfunctioning foils, cues and other defects. Then items can be selected and used in the future with confidence.

Until such an item analysis has been done and files of questions built up, the teacher must construct items with as much care as possible and work always toward improvement of his own skill in writing items. This skill does improve if one studies success and failure in items used. Also, pending completion of an item analysis, questions which are completely misinterpreted or nonfunctioning can be detected and eliminated.

CRITERIA FOR SUBJECTIVE EVALUATION

Subjective evaluation may take the form of ratings, selection of team members, diagnosis for guidance and coaching, or sometimes grading. In each case a considered judgment is made which is a basis for future action affecting the student. This is an essential procedure in many instances. Frequently there is no other way of arriving at a basis for this action. Frequently it is an excellent supplement to objective measures or a further interpretation of a compilation of objective evidence relative to the student's abilities.

Certain basic assumptions must be tenable if subjective ratings are to be made. These can be stated briefly as follows:

1. the capacity or ability to be judged can be defined or described,

2. the capacity or ability is observable, can be demonstrated by each individual to the rater,

3. individuals differ significantly in the capacity in question,

4. individuals to be rated are relatively consistent in this ability and in their demonstration of it,

5. judges can differentiate between levels of this ability as it is demonstrated,

6. judges can differentiate this capacity from others.

In order for subjective evaluation to be well done, certain criteria should be met.

THE ABILITY AND GRADATIONS OF THAT ABILITY SHOULD BE DEFINED

The definitions of ability will help the rater to confine his thinking to the ability, and to avoid outside factors from influencing his decisions. The "halo effect" of acquaintanceship and extraneous factors is frequently present and should be avoided as much as possible. It may be such that it will either raise or lower the estimate made.

The definitions of the various levels of the ability will aid in consistency of judgment from one student to the next. The definitions should be explicit enough to be a guide but not so detailed that they handicap the actual decision.

THE JUDGE SHOULD BE TRAINED AND EXPERIENCED IN SUBJECTIVE EVALUATION

There is a certain degree of objectivity of working method, of detachment from personalities involved which does not always parallel the kind of training that the teacher has. For example, in grading it is not always possible to consider the whole child whereas in teaching from day to day that is essential.

The judge should be oriented to the descriptions of the ability as prepared for the rating and in relation to the group to which it is to be applied. He should be trained to think of the extremes of the group being rated as fitting the extremes of the rating scale. Other students can then be differentiated within that range.

The judges should be trained to observe carefully. This is one of the hardest capacities to develop in young teachers and some never become really skilled at seeing the important differences in performance.

THE RATING SCALE SHOULD MATCH
THE ABILITY LEVEL OF THE GROUP
TO WHICH IT IS APPLIED

This is a matter of adjusting our standards, or levels of expectations. Failure to define the levels of the ability in relation to the group can lead to shifting either up or down of the entire group, or a failure to use the extremes of the scale.

Failure to use the entire range of the scale usually results in inadequate differentiation in the group. The result of a rating on an unselected group should be approximately a normal distribution.

THE RATING SCALE SHOULD BE SIMPLE

Complexity of the system of rating can be a distracting factor to the judge. This is particularly true in motor performance where the skill must be observed as it occurs, judgment made and recorded. Many times this goes on in rapid succession for the various students and opportunity on a given student does not recur for a long time.

RATINGS SHOULD BE BASED
ON SUFFICIENT EVIDENCE
TO REPRESENT ABILITY OF THE STUDENT

There are two aspects to sufficient evidence. The first is duration of observation, and the second is number of observers.

Some abilities can be demonstrated much more quickly than others. If a given stunt or skill is to be performed, it can be staged by each student successively with a uniform number of trials. If ability to play tennis or badminton singles is needed, then a match can be watched for a relatively brief period of time and ability at least against that particular opponent can be determined. However, if rating of ability in a soccer or hockey game is desired, then opportunities for observing a particular player may be long in coming.

Different judges see a performance in a little different viewpoint both because of their actual position for observation, but also because of their training. Therefore, it is frequently desirable to have more than one rater observe a class.

There is also a question of day by day differences in demonstrating ability. In some cases it is desirable for the ratings to reflect these fluctuations. These daily changes affect the reliability of both objective tests and subjective ratings.

If subjective ratings are carefully done, they can be a real asset. They are an indispensable part of a comprehensive evaluation of educational outcomes.

SELECTED REFERENCES

1. Adkins, Dorothy C.: Construction and Analysis of Achievement Tests, Washington, D. C., U. S. Government Printing Office, 1947, Chapter 5.

2. Bovard, John F., Frederick W. Cozens, and Patricia E. Hagman: Tests and Measurements in Physical Education, ed. 3. Philadelphia, W. B. Saunders Company, 1949, Chapter 17.

3. Cassidy, Rosalind: New Directions in Physical Education for the Adolescent Girl in High School and College. New York, A. S. Barnes & Company, 1938, p. 124-139.

4. Clarke, H. Harrison: The Application of Measurement to Health and Physical Education. New York, Prentice-Hall, Inc., 1945, Chapter 2.

5. Feldt, Leonard S., and Mary Ellen McKee: Estimation of the Reliability of Skill Tests. Research Quarterly, 29, October 1958, p. 279.

6. Lindquist, E. F., Editor: Educational Measurement. Washington, D. C., American Council on Education, 1951.

7. McCloy, C. H.: The Measurement of Athletic Power. New York, A. S. Barnes & Company, 1932, Chapter 3 and Appendix.

8. McCloy, C. H., and Norma D. Young: Tests and Measurements in Health and Physical Education, ed. 3. New York, Appleton-Century-Crofts, Inc., 1954, Chapter 3.

9. Mathews, Donald K.: Measurement in Physical Education. Philadelphia, W. B. Saunders Company, 1958, Chapter 2.

10. Ross, Clay C.: <u>Measurement in Today's Schools</u>. New York, Prentice-Hall, Inc., 1947, Chapter 3.

Chapter III

BASIC STATISTICS FOR THE TEST USER

An understanding of elementary statistical procedures is helpful in selecting tests and essential if proper use is to be made of test scores. With this knowledge, the user of tests is able to assemble data, interpret test scores, read with understanding much of the literature in the field of physical education and evaluate new developments as they appear. It is not necessary to be a highly skilled mathematician to understand and use many of the statistical procedures. Addition, subtraction, multiplication and division are in common use; the only other mathematical ability required for the procedures outlined in this chapter is the ability to extract square root.

Many excellent textbooks are available which describe the mathematical derivations of formulas and presuppose college training in mathematics. Some which do not presuppose this advanced training are included in the bibliography and may well be used to supplement the materials presented in this chapter by giving a more detailed explanation.

THE FREQUENCY DISTRIBUTION

The first task in dealing with a large number of test scores is to assemble them in some logical way so that each test score will have a meaning. In statistics this logical arrangement is called a frequency distribution. As an illustration of this technique, the scores obtained from forty-three college women on the Badminton Clear Test are presented in Table I. (See page 148 for the test description.) The test was given at the end of seven periods of instruction. A perfect score on the test is 100.

The raw scores, as presented in Table I, are not very meaningful or helpful in evaluating the relative performance of any individual within the group. It is apparent that no student made a perfect score and that the highest

Table I.

Scores of Forty-Three Students
on the Badminton Clear Test

45	6	75	60	78	47	65	65	63
32	22	35	56	74	54	72	64	72
28	39	47	54	73	59	78	64	63
69	86	49	85	69	64	79	60	
60	80	52	80	84	61	66	62	

score was 86 and the lowest score 6. It is possible to obtain the range by subtracting the lowest score in the series from the highest score; therefore, the range is 80.
In other words, all of the scores fell between 86 and 6, a
difference of 80 points.

The scores can be interpreted better if all of the
possible scores within the range are listed in order of
size, and then the number of times each score was made is
recorded, as has been done in Table II in the column marked
f, or frequency column.

Table II.

Simple Frequency Distribution of Scores
on Badminton Clear Test
(Intervals of one unit)

S	f	S	f	S	f	S	f	S	f
86	1	69	2	52	1	35	1	18	
85	1	68		51		34		17	
84	1	67		50		33		16	
83		66	1	49	1	32	1	15	
82		65	2	48		31		14	
81		64	3	47	2	30		13	
80	2	63	2	46		29		12	
79	1	62	1	45	1	28	1	11	
78	2	61	1	44		27		10	
77		60	3	43		26		9	
76		59	1	42		25		8	
75	1	58		41		24		7	
74	1	57		40		23		6	1
73	1	56	1	39	1	22	1		
72	2	55		38		21			N=43
71		54	2	37		20			
70		53		36		19			

The more frequently occurring scores now stand out, the points of concentration are apparent, and the number of scores between any two points can be secured quickly by simple addition. (The frequency table is usually arranged in a linear form instead of the five columns as shown in Table II, an arrangement made to conserve space. When in linear form, the graphic distribution of scores is more apparent.) For convenience in handling, Table II needs to be condensed into classes or groups of scores. Each class or step-interval will include all the records of scores within the limits of that interval. The size of the step-interval will depend upon the use to be made of the data. There is seldom any need for more than twenty intervals or for fewer than twelve. A quick approximation of the size of the interval can be obtained by dividing the range by 15. For the data presented in Table I, the range of 80 when divided by 15 is 5.3, or, in round numbers, 5. For ease and accuracy in tabulation, an interval of 1, 2, 3, 5, 7, 10, 15, or any higher multiple of 5 is preferred. In this frequency distribution a step-interval of 5 units will yield seventeen classes which is within the suggested number of twelve to twenty. The increase or decrease in the number of classes by one or two is not important. Table III shows the grouped frequency distribution for the same data as that used in Tables I and II. Each score is tabulated in the column marked Tab. The total number of tallies has been added and transferred to the frequency column marked f. The total in this column is recorded as N (total number of cases). This table could be made more compact by increasing the size of the step-interval. By using an interval of 25 units, for example, only four classes would be needed. Such an increase in the size of the unit would mean a large loss in the identity of the original scores. This is sometimes referred to as "grouping too coarsely." Over one-half of the scores would fall in the interval of 63 to 87. A broad interval will prove satisfactory only when a very rough picture is needed. If higher precision in description is desirable, then the interval used should be small. If a detailed study is to be made of the data, the step-intervals should be small.

The steps in constructing a grouped frequency distribution are as follows:

1. Prepare a data sheet with the three headings as shown in Table III: S is for scores, Tab for tabulation of

tally marks, and _f_ for frequencies (the number of times that a score occurs within that interval).

2. Determine the range by locating the highest score and the lowest score and subtracting the lowest from the highest.

Table III.

Grouped Frequency Distribution of Scores
on Badminton Clear Test
(Intervals of five units)

S	Tab	f
83-87	///	3
78-82	////	5
73-77	///	3
68-72	////	4
63-67	//// ///	8
58-62	//// /	6
53-57	///	3
48-52	//	2
43-47	///	3
38-42	/	1
33-37	/	1
28-32	//	2
23-27		0
18-22	/	1
13-17		0
8-12		0
3- 7	/	1
		N=43

3. Divide the range (number obtained in Step 2) by 15. (Carry the results to one decimal place.)

4. Select from the following preferred list the number nearest the quotient secured in Step 3: 1, 2, 3, 5, 7, 10, 15, or any higher multiple of 5.

5. Write the limits of each interval, in descending order, in the first column, the S column, of the table. Begin at the top with the interval containing the highest score. Determine these limits as follows:

      a. When the number of units in the interval is an even number, the lower limit of each interval should be a multiple of this number.

46

b. When the number of units in the interval is an odd number, find the multiple of this number that is nearest to the highest score in the series. (In the example, using an odd number for the interval (5), since the highest score is 86, the nearest multiple is 85.) Select the limits of the interval so that this multiple is the middle score in the interval. (With the multiple 85 in the middle and two scores on either side, the top interval becomes 83-87. Continue to write the limits of each interval in descending order until the interval containing the lowest score is reached. The limits of the intervals will be determined automatically when those of the top interval are fixed. For the example, the bottom interval in the distribution will be 3-7.)

6. Tabulate the scores by placing a tally mark opposite the appropriate interval. The subsequent counting is facilitated if every fifth mark in a row is made slanting across the other four.

7. Count the number of tally marks in each interval and record the number in the frequency column opposite each interval.

8. Add the numbers in the frequency column as a partial check on the accuracy of tabulation; the result should agree with the total number of scores in the original list. (See $\underline{N}$, the symbol for the total number of cases, in Table III.)

Some students will be interested in the reasons for the procedures suggested in Steps 3, 4, and 5. They are as follows:

Step 3: If the range is divided by 15 it will result in approximately 15 classes or intervals. Experience has indicated that this number of intervals is adequate for many purposes. It is few enough not to be excessively laborious in further computations.

Step 4: The suggestion in step 4 is for convenience only, and has no bearing on the accuracy of results obtained from the frequency distribution. It seems to be easier for most persons to think in terms of multiples of 5 and 10 than in terms of such numbers as 6, 13, 16, 17, 19, and so forth. In general, the use of an interval containing an odd number of units results in a more convenient midpoint for each interval. In later computations, the midpoint is used to represent all of the scores in the interval. If the interval contains an even number of units, the midpoint will be a decimal and therefore inconvenient to use.

Step 5: The question of where to start an interval is bothersome and the answer debatable. The definite basis for settling this problem is suggested in Step 5 to secure uniformity. Like the suggestion made in Step 4, it is for convenience only.

The construction of a frequency distribution has been described in considerable detail because it is the basic step for practically all statistical procedures.

CONVERTING RAW SCORES INTO LETTER GRADES

Raw scores can be quickly transferred into grades when they have been placed in a frequency distribution. A sample of a percentage system used by many schools in determining the distribution of grades is as follows: 7 per cent, A; 24 per cent, B; 38 per cent, C; 24 per cent, D; and 7 per cent, E (or failure). The percentage system is intended to be used as a guide and it should not be applied to small and select groups; the total number of cases and the distribution of their abilities should be such that their performance can be considered representative of the performance of much larger groups. The number of cases in Table II is too few to be representative of a normal distribution but the data there will suffice for the purposes of illustration.

The limits of each grade for the scores in Table II can be determined by multiplying N(43) by each of the respective percentages and rounding the figures. Seven per cent of 43 is 3.01, so the value A is assigned to the top three scores. If a plus and minus system is used, the score of 86 would have the value of A + and the score of 84 the value of A -. Likewise, the lowest three scores receive a grade of E, or failure. Thus scores of 30 or below fall in this category. To find the number of scores that should be given the value of B, multiply N by 24 per cent (or 43 by 24 per cent) which is 10.32, or 10. The scores falling between 70 and 80 are given B grades. The ten scores above the failure category receive D. The

D range thus is 32 to 54. Thirty-eight per cent of 43 is
16.34 or 16. There are seventeen scores remaining between
the B and D grades. This extra case is the result of
rounding of numbers for the B and D categories. It seems
preferable to put the extra score into the C category
rather than in one of the grades at the end of the scale.
Placement at one of the extremes would result if grades
were assigned to consecutive categories working from either
the top or bottom of the distribution. The divisions and
frequencies are shown below:

		f
81 and up	A	3
72-80	B	10
55-71	C	17
32-54	D	10
31 and below	E	3

When the conversion of raw scores into grades is done
from a grouped frequency distribution, a few more complica-
tions occur. For example, try using the data as presented
in Table III, which contains the same scores as in Table II
but grouped in intervals of five units. The top division
(A's) becomes 83 and up; the number of frequencies happens
to remain the same. The B's will include the five recorded
in the 78-82 interval, the three in the 73-77 interval, and
in order to get at least ten B's, it is necessary to include
the four in the 68-72 interval. This results in twelve instead of ten B's. The three lowest scores should be assigned the E grade but a choice must be made between two or
four scores. In this case two would probably be selected
since there is a considerable difference between the value
of the second lowest score and the two scores next above it.
Ten scores plus the one case not receiving an E according
to the percentage should receive a grade of D. In order to
include the eleven cases it is necessary to include all of
interval 53-57. This makes a total of twelve cases. There
are fourteen cases remaining in the C category. The scoring table now is as follows:

		f
83 and up	A	3
68-82	B	12
58-67	C	14
28-57	D	12
27 and below	E	2

In the illustration on the preceding page the number of cases in C, 14, is below the desired percentage. The only alternative is to reduce the B category to 8 and the D and E categories to a combination of eleven cases. This would raise the C group to twenty-one, or considerably more than 38 per cent. However, in some cases this might be better procedure.

In order to avoid the difficulties outlined for the grouped frequencies, the scores should not be grouped in intervals of 5. If the number of scores is as small as in this illustration, they may be ranked or the interval may be reduced.

As stated previously, the percentage system is intended to be used merely as a guide. It is frequently necessary and desirable to modify it. If the scores fall below reasonable expectations, the teacher may reduce the number of A's or eliminate them entirely. If, on the lower end of the distribution, the scores represent performance that is satisfactory, the teacher would probably not give any E's but would increase the percentage of D's or C's.

If there are long gaps between scores in the distribution, they may form more natural and just divisions between categories than those defined by the percentage system. Working from Table III, the teacher would probably assign only two E's. A distribution with a larger number of cases would have fewer and shorter gaps between scores. If the frequency distribution shown in Table III is retained and scores are added to it for several classes or seasons, the gaps will tend to disappear. The limits will need to be adjusted each time data are added but gradually they will become more stable.

COMBINING NUMERICAL GRADES OR SCORES

Numerical grades or scores made by an individual should not be combined into a composite score by totalling them or averaging them in their raw score form. They must first be converted into a comparable value. For example, one student in a group made the following scores on some physical fitness tests: Bounce, 100; Sit-ups, 62; Chair Stepping, 112; Obstacle Race, 20.6 seconds; Pull, 72 pounds. In comparing these scores, it might appear that his performance was best in the bounce test. Actually, his best performance was in the obstacle race, but this cannot be determined from the raw scores alone.

If the raw scores were added, it would result in some tests receiving a higher proportion of importance in the total score than is their due. For the set of fitness tests in the illustration above, the top score for the bounce test was 325. If this score were added with the sit-ups for example, where the top score was 100, the bounce test would receive three times the importance or "weight" given to the sit-ups, or two times the value given to the top score in chair stepping, which was 165. Still another difficulty is encountered in adding raw scores in timed events such as the obstacle race, where the better performance results in a lower number as the score.

For some groups of tests, an equation will have been derived by the test constructor which will tell the test user how much weighting should be given to each test score. This is limited to tests within a particular battery (group of related tests). For example, in a three item battery of motor ability tests, the equation recommended by the test constructor is as follows:

2.0 basketball throw + 1.4 broad jump - 1.0 obstacle race

The raw score made by the student in the basketball throw for distance test would be multiplied by two, the broad jump score would be multiplied by 1.4. These two would be added together and then the score made on the obstacle race would be subtracted.

One method of converting raw scores into comparable values in order to permit combination is to convert the raw scores for each test into letter grades. This is frequently used, and is convenient particularly when some of the scores have already been converted into letter grades, as for example, for knowledge tests. Some tests can be weighted more (assigned more importance) than others if in the subjective opinion of the instructor, they deserve more weighting. For example, if you have two knowledge test grades and one skill test grade and wish to give equal importance to skill and knowledge, you could average the two knowledge tests grades before averaging that one grade with the one skill test grade. See later discussion on averaging letter grades.

If the scores are to be used to motivate the student to put forth greater effort, a scale of scores should be

51

developed which has many divisions. The divisions should be small enough to enable slight improvements in performance to be rewarded by an increase in score. The objections to scales limited to letter grade values or divisions is that the number of categories is too few (five if plus and minus signs are omitted; thirteen if they are used). The divisions or categories are too large to register small increases.

Raw scores can be converted into comparable values other than letter grades by converting them into what is known as "standard scores." There are two kinds of standard scores, those that are calculated on a percentage basis (percentiles, deciles, etc.,) and those that are calculated on the deviation basis (distance of each score from the mean). In the latter group there are several variations, such as the T-scale, the sigma scale, and the Hull scale. Since these all involve an understanding of the standard deviation, further explanation will follow after standard deviation has been discussed.

AVERAGING LETTER GRADES

Whenever it is desirable to average a number of letter grades, particularly when pluses and minuses are used, point values are assigned to each grade. Each letter grade is converted into a point value, the points are added, and these totals are either averaged by dividing them by the number of grades or the totals themselves are placed in a frequency distribution and grades determined, as described earlier under the heading Converting Raw Scores Into Grades.

If C is considered an average grade and D a passing grade, the point values are as follows:

Table IV

Point Value Table for Averaging Letter Grades

A+:12 A :11 A-:10	B+:9 B :8 B-:7	C+:6 C :5 C-:4	D+:3 D :2 D-:1	E:0

For example, if a student has A-, C+, D, B-, E, C, B+, and C-, these eight grades would be converted into the point

52

values of 10, 6, 2, 7, 0, 5, 9, 4 and added for a total of 43. The average would be obtained by dividing 43 by 8, which is the equivalent of a C grade.

Whenever four or more grades are averaged together to obtain a final grade, there is a tendency to have too many C's and too few A's and E's. To avoid this, the point totals should be placed on a frequency distribution. The conversion into grades is then achieved by the assignment of limits according to percentages. For example, if you have sixty students and wish to assign 7% A's, you would multiply N (in this case 60) by .07 and thus you would determine that the four with the highest totals would receive A's. If instead of giving A's to 7% of the class, you wished to give A's to say 25% of the class, you would multiply N, a symbol which always stands for the total number of cases, by .25. In this case, A's would be assigned to the top fifteen totals (fifteen obtained by multiplying 60 by .25).

MEASURES OF CENTRAL TENDENCY

In describing groups, it is easier to use a single measure representing all of the scores in a group than it is to try to describe the characteristics or scores of all of the individuals in the group. The single measure which is most familiar is the "average." There are two measures of central tendency which are commonly used in handling physical education test data, the mean, or average, and the median.

The mean is the arithmetical average; it is obtained by adding all of the scores and dividing by the number of individuals. It is based on every score in the distribution and since it is a mathematically derived value, it may be used in practically all statistical procedures. The symbol M is used in referring to the mean.

The median is the middle measure in a series in which all of the measures have been arranged in the order of their magnitude. It may quickly be computed from a frequency distribution by dividing N (total number of cases) by 2 and then counting that number of frequencies from either end of the distribution. When the number of cases is small and one or more cases deviate markedly from the others, the median will give a better representation of the typical than will the mean. The median is not affected by

one extremely high score or one extremely low score as is
the mean. The symbol for the median is M_{dn}.

The mean can be found by the laborious method of sum-
ming all of the scores and then dividing by N. When the
number of cases is small, such as for Table III, that can
be done without great effort. Frequently the mean must be
computed from a grouped frequency distribution containing
many cases. The steps to be followed in computing the
mean from a grouped frequency distribution are illustrated
in Table V using the same data as those presented in Table
III. Disregard for the time being the column headed cf
(cumulative frequency); it is used in computing the median
but not the mean.

Table V.

Computation of Mean and Median for Grouped Frequency
Distribution on Badminton Clear Test

	f	d	fd	cf	
83-87	3	5	15	43	$\Sigma fd = 60 - 56 = 4$
78-82	5	4	20	40	
73-77	3	3	9	35	Σfd
68-72	4	2	8	32	$\dfrac{\Sigma fd}{N} = \dfrac{4}{43} = .093$ or $.09$
63-67	8	1	8	28	(rounded)
			+60		
A.R. 58-62	6	0		20	.09 is the correction in interval units
53-57	3	- 1	- 3	14	Correction in score units:
48-52	2	- 2	- 4	11	$5 \times .09 = .45$
43-47	3	- 3	- 9	9	
38-42	1	- 4	- 4	6	Mean = A.R. + correction
33-37	1	- 5	- 5	5	in score units =
28-32	2	- 6	-12	4	$60 + .45 = 60.45$
23-27	0	- 7		2	
18-22	1	- 8	- 8	2	
13-17	0	- 9		1	
8-12	0	-10		1	
3- 7	1	-11	-11	1	
			-56		

The symbol Σ means summation or "the sum of."

The steps in computing the mean from a grouped frequency distribution are as follows:

1. Select as an arbitrary reference point the interval which appears most likely to contain the mean. (Some statisticians refer to this as the "guessed mean"; others call it the "assumed mean.")

2. Express each interval above and below the arbitrary reference point (A.R.) as a deviation, or d. These are numbered in the deviation column, as shown in the illustration, with all deviations below the A.R. preceded by a negative sign.

3. Multiply the frequency in each interval by the corresponding d value and record the products in the column headed fd. All those below the A.R. will have a negative sign.

4. Add the positive products, then the negative products, and add these sums algebraically. (For the illustration, the sum of the positive products is 60 and the sum of the negative products is -56. When they are added algebraically, the result is +4.)

5. Divide the result obtained in Step 4 by N. This represents the correction (symbol c) to the A.R. This quotient must be multiplied by the size of the interval in order to convert to score units. (In the illustration, 4 divided by N or 43 is .093 or .09 when rounded. The correction is obtained by multiplying .09 by the size of the step-interval 5. Thus, the correction in terms of score units is .45.)

6. The correction in terms of score units is added algebraically to the midpoint of the A.R. interval. (For the illustration, .45 is positive and will therefore be added; had it been negative, it would be subtracted. The midpoint of the interval containing the A.R. is 60, so the mean for the scores in the illustration is 60.45 as computed from the grouped frequency distribution.)

Formula for Mean:

$$\text{Mean} = \text{Arbitrary Reference Point} + \left(\frac{\text{Algebraic } \Sigma fd}{N}\right) \times$$

step interval

$\Sigma = \text{sum}$

The median can be computed from a simple frequency distribution as shown in Table II, by dividing N by 2 and finding that point on the scale above or below which half of the frequencies lie. In the example in Table II the median is 63. Computing the median from a grouped frequency distribution is more difficult than from a simple frequency distribution because of the loss of identity of the original scores within each step-interval. Since the median must frequently be constructed from grouped data, the steps are described:

1. Add a cumulative frequency column to the frequency distribution. (See the column headed cf in Table V.) This is done by totalling the frequencies interval-by-interval from the bottom up. As a partial check on accuracy, the top entry in the cf column should equal N.

2. If N is an even number, the median is located by the formula $\frac{N}{2}$. (If the N in the illustration had been 44, the median would be halfway between the twenty-second and twenty-third scores.) If N is an odd number, the middle point in the distribution is located by the formula $\frac{N + 1}{2}$. (In the illustration N is 43, an odd number, therefore the median is $\frac{43 + 1}{2} = 22$. The twenty-second score falls in the interval 63-67.)

3. The next step is to subtract from the quotient secured in Step 2 (22) the number in the cumulative frequency column just below (22 - 20 = 2).

4. Divide the result obtained in Step 3 by the frequency of the interval. $\left(\frac{2}{8} = .25.\right)$

5. Multiply this quotient by the size of the interval (.25 × 5 = 1.25).

6. Add the result obtained in Step 5 to the lower limit of the interval to obtain the median. (63 + 1.25 = 64.25, or, in round numbers, 64.)

The effect of the one extremely low score on the mean is now apparent when a comparison is made between the mean and the median. The mean is 60.45 and the median 64.25. In a normal distribution the mean and median would coincide. The one low score does not affect the median to any greater extent in its actual location in the distribution than it would have if it had varied several intervals in either direction from its actual location. The median in this case gives a better description of the typical individual's score for this distribution. The mean is important because of its use in other computations.

A third measure of central tendency is the mode. It is of so little value in the treatment of physical education data that it can almost be disregarded. The mode is the interval in which the greatest number of frequencies occurs. The mode, then, for the data in Table V is the interval 63-67, or more specifically, the midpoint of that interval, 65. The actual mode, as obtained from the simple frequency distribution, is the score that occurs the most often. (See Table II, actual mode is 64.)

Students should not be disturbed by slight discrepancies that occur between a measure of central tendency as computed from grouped frequency distributions and when computed from simple frequency distributions. These differences are due to loss of identity in original scores that occurs in grouped data and is of little consequence.

Measures of Distribution

Measures of central tendency indicate typical performance for a group but they give only a single value which is used to represent the total distribution. A single measure or value does not tell how much variation or concentration is present in the distribution. The variability within the distribution and the spread or scatter of scores around the measure of central tendency must be considered. For example, if a group of sixth-grade boys were tested in the standing broad jump and the average jump was found to be 66 inches, it might be erroneously assumed that many scored near that point. Very little is known about the performance of the entire group until some measure is available of the distribution of scores. Knowing the mean score only of the previous example of Badminton Clear Test scores, one would have no idea of the great variability in that distribution.

The four measures of variability that will be described are as follows: (1) the range, (2) the quartile deviation, (3) the standard deviation, and (4) the probable error.

The range is quite unreliable when used as a measure of variability if frequent or large gaps occur in the distribution, since it takes into account only the extreme scores. To avoid this condition, the other measures of variability consider only the scatter or spread of scores in the center of the distribution.

The quartile deviation, or Q, is used to describe the distribution of scores around the median. The quartile simply splits each half designated by the median. See Figure 3, page 29. The first and third quartile points are located by exactly the same process as was the median but using one-half of the distribution each time; the first quartile point is below the median for the entire distribution, the third is above. The first quartile point is the twenty-fifth percentile; the third quartile point is the seventy-fifth percentile. The median, or Q_2, by way of comparison, is the fiftieth percentile. The distance between Q_3 and Q_1 is known as the interquartile range, and one-half of this distance is the quartile deviation, or Q. The formula for calculating the quartile deviation is as follows:

$$Q = \frac{Q_3 - Q_1}{2}$$

No further description will be given, as the quartile deviation is not considered highly descriptive. Scores may be assigned their proper quartile as a quick means of interpreting scores to the students.

The distribution around the mean usually is interpreted by the standard deviation, or S.D. (It is also designated by the Greek sigma σ.) Since it is the most reliable of the measures of variability and for that reason is employed widely in research, it will be described in considerable detail. Although the standard deviation may be defined as the square root of the mean of the squared deviations taken from the mean of the distribution, such a definition means little to most persons. It is more easily understood when defined as the measure which indicates the scatter or spread of the middle 68.26 per cent of the scores taken from the mean of the distribution. (See Figure 4, page 30, for a graphic portrayal of a normal curve divided into six standard deviations. When measured off above and below the mean, the standard deviation will designate the limits of the middle two-thirds of the distribution.)

The standard deviation can be calculated from a grouped frequency distribution by means of a short method. Another column is added to the grouped frequency distribution presented in Table III, headed $\underline{fd}^2$. The values in this column are obtained by multiplying those in the $\underline{fd}$ column by those in $\underline{d}$. Do not square the $\underline{fd}$ column; such a procedure would be written $(\underline{fd})^2$. The computation proceeds as in Table VI.

Table VI.

Computation of Standard Deviation for Grouped Frequency Distribution on Badminton Clear Test

	$\underline{f}$	$\underline{d}$	$\underline{fd}$	$\underline{fd}^2$	
83-87	3	5	15	75	$\Sigma\underline{fd}^2 = 542$
78-82	5	4	20	80	
73-77	3	3	9	27	$\dfrac{\Sigma\underline{fd}^2}{N} = \dfrac{542}{43} = 12.6$
68-72	4	2	8	16	
63-67	8	1	8	8	$c = .09$ (computed in
58-62	6	0			Table XXV) $c^2 = .008$
53-57	3	- 1	- 3	3	
48-52	2	- 2	- 4	8	S.D. $= \sqrt{\dfrac{\Sigma\underline{fd}^2}{N} - c^2} \times$ size of
43-47	3	- 3	- 9	27	step-interval
38-42	1	- 4	- 4	16	
33-37	1	- 5	- 5	25	$\sqrt{} = 12.6 - .008 \times 5$
28-32	2	- 6	-12	72	
23-27	0	- 7			$= \sqrt{12.592} = 3.6 \times 5$
18-22	1	- 8	- 8	64	$3.6 \times$ size of step-interval
13-17	0	- 9			$= 3.6 \times 5 = 18.$
8-12	0	-10			
3-7	1	-11	-11	121	
				542	

The $\underline{fd}^2$ column is added ($\Sigma\underline{fd}^2 = 542$) and then divided by $N.\left(\dfrac{\Sigma\underline{fd}^2}{N} = 12.6\right)$. The correction in interval units computed for the arbitrary reference point in obtaining the mean is squared and then subtracted from the last quotient ($12.6 - .008 = 12.592$). The square root of this number is then determined to complete the last step in the formula $\left(\text{S.D.} = \sqrt{\dfrac{\Sigma\underline{fd}^2}{N} - c^2} = \sqrt{12.592} = 3.6\right)$. To interpret in terms of raw scores it is necessary to multiply by the size of the step-interval (3.6 × 5 = 18.0). Eighteen, then, is the standard deviation for the distribution of scores in Table VI.

The standard deviation may be interpreted in the following manner: roughly two-thirds of the cases in any normal distribution will fall within the limits of one S.D. below and above the mean. Thus, for the group data presented in Table VI, about two-thirds of the scores fall between 42 and 78. (Mean score, or 60.45 ± 18.) This gives an indication of how the scores are spread around the mean, and the large S.D. indicates that in this distribution there is a large amount of variability. The S.D. is small if the total range is small and the cases cluster around the mean. The S.D. becomes larger as the range increases and the cases spread. The proportion of cases between any two S.D. points in the distribution remains approximately the same as in the normal curve if the distribution closely resembles the normal curve. If the distribution becomes too dissimilar to the normal curve, the S.D. should not be used.

The probable error is used quite frequently as a measure of variability because it can be easily calculated from the standard deviation and because one probable error below and above the mean includes 50 per cent of the cases. The probable error is obtained by multiplying the S.D. by .6745. (The probable error for the distribution of scores in Table VI is 18 times .6745 or 12.14. It is now apparent that while two-thirds of the cases fall between 42 and 78, one-half of the cases fall between 60.45 ± 12.14 or between 48 and 73.) The probable error is expressed by the formula:

$$\text{P.E.} = .6745 \; \sigma$$

To summarize, the range is used as a rough but unreliable measure of variability when a knowledge of the entire spread of the scores is wanted. The quartile deviation is used when only the concentration of scores around the median is sought. The standard deviation should be used when the most reliable measure of variability is wanted. It considers equally all parts of the distribution; it is affected by the extreme scores in the distribution, as is the mean. If the number of cases is large, the effect of a few extreme scores is less. The probable error is similar to the standard deviation but uses a smaller proportion of the distribution.

ACHIEVEMENT SCALES

As mentioned earlier, if achievement scales are to be used for the purposes of motivation, a form should be selected which will best serve this purpose. Certainly all scores should be included on the scale. In selecting the variety of scale to be used, preference should be given to scales which will not require revision should a student come along who makes a better score than the previously highest score and conversely, should a student make a lower score than the previously lowest score. There should be room for expansion on both ends of the scale.

T-scales will be described in considerable detail here because they have been widely used in physical education and have several advantages.

1. T-Scales

The T-scale was discussed earlier as a means of converting raw scores on different tests into comparable values. This scale is best understood as a modification of the standard deviation proportions in the distribution. It is based upon a comparison of scores in terms of distances from the mean as measured in standard deviations. In the T-scale, the mean is expressed as 50 and each standard deviation above or below the mean adds or subtracts 10 points. The normal curve, of course, extends three standard deviations in each direction from the mean. By assigning ten T-scores to each standard deviation, the scale must then range from approximately 20 to 80 (in actual situations, T-scores are sometimes found extending from 15 to 85).

With a scale having so many divisions, small improvements in ability can easily be detected. McCall also devised a method of securing T-scores without having to compute the mean and standard deviation; that method will be described in detail later.

$$\text{T-score} = 50 + \frac{10 \ (X - M)}{\sigma}$$

where X = the test score (raw score)
M = the mean of the distribution (raw scores)
σ = the standard deviation (of the raw scores)

The T-scale can be constructed easily from raw scores collected on any class or group of similar classes. There should be a minimum of fifty students represented in the scale and preferably 100 or more. If there are two or three sections of the same age group working on the same activity in one school, it is better to combine the scores from all classes into a single distribution, instead of computing a separate one for each section. This combination puts the standards represented by the scale on a school basis rather than entirely on their particular group. Most of the T-scales presented in this book are based on several sections within the school, on similar classes for several schools, or on several years' accumulation of data. The number of subjects is always noted and usually other information concerning the subjects is given, such as age, sex, previous experience in the activity, and amount of time of instructional periods prior to testing.

The T-scale is based on the characteristic distribution of cases in a normal curve, hence separate T-scales must be computed for groups that are not homogeneous at least in age and previous experience. The teacher or person who constructs the scale should understand something about the normal curve. The two ends are symmetrical, the scores concentrate heavily at the center, the two extremes are at equal distance from the center, and the frequencies near the extremes fall off (diminish) very rapidly. See Figure 4, page 30, for the percentage of scores within each standard deviation in the normal curve. Since the scores are massed near the center, there will be many who receive a score between 40 and 60. There will be considerably fewer who receive scores in the 30's or 60's, and comparatively few who receive scores in the 20's and 70's.

Such a scale is easily explained to students. They are all familiar with the term "average." If it is explained that scores near 50 are about average, that a score above 50 is better than average (the higher, the better), and a score below 50 is poorer than average (the lower, the poorer), then such scores are meaningful to students. In addition to enabling the student to understand his relative ability on a single test, he may also make a comparison of his performance on several tests within the same activity. For example, see T-scales for field hockey, page 170. The player can detect at once the skills in which he is weak and can make use of this knowledge in distributing his practice time to the best advantage.

From the standpoint of the teacher or test administrator, another advantage of the T-score is the ease with

62

Table VII.

Computation of a T-Scale for 200 Cases
on a Motor Ability Battery

Step-interval	Tallies	f	t	1/2	t + 1/2	%	T-score
156-up	/	1	0	.5	.5	.250	78
154-155	/	1	1	.5	1.5	.750	74
152-153	/	1	2	.5	2.5	1.250	72
150-151	//	2	3	1.0	4.0	2.000	71
148-149	///	3	5	1.5	6.5	3.250	68
146-147	////	4	8	2.0	10.0	5.000	66
144-145	///	3	12	1.5	13.5	6.750	65
142-143	///	3	15	1.5	16.5	8.250	64
140-141	////	5	18	2.5	20.5	10.250	63
138-139	////	5	23	2.5	25.5	12.750	61
136-137	//// //	7	28	3.5	31.5	15.750	60
134-135	//// /	6	35	3.0	38.0	19.000	59
132-133	//// ///	8	41	4.0	45.0	22.500	58
130-131	//// ////	10	49	5.0	54.0	27.000	56
128-129	//// //// ////	14	59	7.0	66.0	33.000	54
126-127	//// //// ///	13	73	6.5	79.5	39.700	53
124-125	//// //// //// /	16	86	8.0	94.0	47.000	51
122-123	//// //// //	12	102	6.0	108.0	54.000	49
120-121	//// ////	10	114	5.0	119.0	59.500	48
118-119	//// ////	9	124	4.5	128.5	64.250	46
116-117	//// ////	10	133	5.0	138.0	69.000	45
114-115	//// //// /	11	143	5.5	148.5	74.250	43
112-113	//// ////	9	154	4.5	158.5	79.250	42
110-111	//// ///	8	163	4.0	167.0	83.500	40
108-109	//// //	7	171	3.5	174.5	87.250	39
106-107	//// //	7	178	3.5	181.5	90.750	37
104-105	////	5	185	2.5	187.5	93.750	35
102-103	///	3	190	1.5	191.5	95.750	33
100-101	//	2	193	1.0	194.0	97.000	31
98-99	//	2	195	1.0	196.0	98.000	29
96-97	/	1	197	.5	197.5	98.750	28
94-95	/	1	198	5	198.5	99.250	26
93-down	/	1	199	.5	199.5	99.750	22
	N = 200						

which a composite score may be obtained; T-scores may be
added to obtain a single score for a series of measures.
Those persons familiar with the use of a regression equation
for combining scores will be interested in knowing that the
sum of T-scores leaves relative standings almost unchanged
if the weightings of the respective tests are almost equal.

(Correlations by the authors on such comparisons range from .94 to .98.)

If the mean and standard deviation have not been computed, it is possible to construct a T-score table by using a table of percentile deviations of the normal curve. (See Table VIII, page 65.)

Steps in Construction of a T-Scale Table

1. Make a frequency distribution of the scores to be used. (This is the same procedure as outlined previously except that in this case the number of the step-intervals must be larger, resulting in a small-sized interval. It is probably best to have forty to fifty intervals when data permit. If intervals are too large, there will be too much massing of raw scores and the T-scale will be broken rather than continuous. Another way of saying the same thing is that the scale will fail to discriminate between the persons with quite similar scores.)

2. Total the frequencies in the column marked $\underline{f}$.

3. Count the total of all frequencies above each interval and put the total in the column $\underline{t}$. Since there are no frequencies above the top interval, the $\underline{t}$ column will always read 0 in the first interval; in the successive intervals of $\underline{t}$, the value will be the sum of $\underline{f}$ and $\underline{t}$ of the interval above. As a check on accuracy, the sum of the $\underline{f}$ and $\underline{t}$ of the last interval always should be equal to N.

4. Divide the $\underline{f}$ values for each interval by 2. Record in the 1/2 column.

5. Add the $\underline{t}$ and 1/2 columns for each interval; label the column $\underline{t}$ + 1/2. (The purpose of this step is to find the number of frequencies above the midpoint of each interval. This is done because the midpoint of the interval is always considered as representative of all cases in the interval and the frequencies are considered to be equally distributed in the interval. This is another reason for keeping the size of the step-interval small.) If values in successive intervals are the same because of zero frequencies in the interval, the same score is repeated.

6. Divide the $\underline{t}$ + 1/2 column by N and multiply by 100. This column is the per cent column. (Carry the percentages to at least three decimal places.)

Table VIII.
Conversion of Percentages into T-Scores

T-SCORES*	%	T-SCORES*	%	T-SCORES*	%	T-SCORES*	%
0	99.999971	25	99.38	50	50.00	75	0.62
0.5	99.999963	25.5	99.29	50.5	48.01	75.5	0.54
1	99.999952	26	99.18	51	46.02	76	0.47
1.5	99.999938	26.5	99.06	51.5	44.04	76.5	0.40
2	99.99992	27	98.93	52	42.07	77	0.35
2.5	99.99990	27.5	98.78	52.5	40.13	77.5	0.30
3	99.99987	28	98.61	53	38.21	78	0.26
3.5	99.99983	28.5	98.42	53.5	36.32	78.5	0.22
4	99.99979	29	98.21	54	34.46	79	0.19
4.5	99.99973	29.5	97.98	54.5	32.64	79.5	0.16
5	99.99966	30	97.72	55	30.85	80	0.13
5.5	99.99957	30.5	97.44	55.5	29.12	80.5	0.11
6	99.99946	31	97.13	56	27.43	81	0.097
6.5	99.99932	31.5	96.78	56.5	25.78	81.5	0.082
7	99.99915	32	96.41	57	24.20	82	0.069
7.5	99.9989	32.5	95.99	57.5	22.66	82.5	0.058
8	99.9987	33	95.54	58	21.19	83	0.048
8.5	99.9983	33.5	95.05	58.5	19.77	83.5	0.040
9	99.9979	34	94.52	59	18.41	84	0.034
9.5	99.9974	34.5	93.94	59.5	17.11	84.5	0.028
10	99.9968	35	93.32	60	15.87	85	0.023
10.5	99.9961	35.5	92.65	60.5	14.69	85.5	0.019
11	99.9952	36	91.92	61	13.57	86	0.016
11.5	99.9941	36.5	91.15	61.5	12.51	86.5	0.013
12	99.9928	37	90.32	62	11.51	87	0.011
12.5	99.9912	37.5	89.44	62.5	10.56	87.5	0.009
13	99.989	38	88.49	63	9.68	88	0.007
13.5	99.987	38.5	87.49	63.5	8.85	88.5	0.0059
14	99.984	39	86.43	64	8.08	89	0.0048
14.5	99.981	39.5	85.31	64.5	7.35	89.5	0.0039
15	99.977	40	84.13	65	6.68	90	0.0032
15.5	99.972	40.5	82.89	65.5	6.06	90.5	0.0026
16	99.966	41	81.59	66	5.48	91	0.0021
16.5	99.960	41.5	80.23	66.5	4.95	91.5	0.0017
17	99.952	42	78.81	67	4.46	92	0.0013
17.5	99.942	42.5	77.34	67.5	4.01	92.5	0.0011
18	99.931	43	75.80	68	3.59	93	0.0009
18.5	99.918	43.5	74.22	68.5	3.22	93.5	0.0007
19	99.903	44	72.57	69	2.87	94	0.0005
19.5	99.886	44.5	70.88	69.5	2.56	94.5	0.00043
20	99.865	45	69.15	70	2.28	95	0.00034
20.5	99.84	45.5	67.36	70.5	2.02	95.5	0.00027
21	99.81	46	65.54	71	1.79	96	0.00021
21.5	99.78	46.5	63.68	71.5	1.58	96.5	0.00017
22	99.74	47	61.79	72	1.39	97	0.00013
22.5	99.70	47.5	59.87	72.5	1.22	97.5	0.00010
23	99.65	48	57.93	73	1.07	98	0.00008
23.5	99.60	48.5	55.96	73.5	0.94	98.5	0.000062
24	99.53	49	53.98	74	0.82	99	0.000048
24.5	99.46	49.5	51.99	74.5	0.71	99.5	0.000037
						100	0.000029

*T-scores are S.D. values.

7. Read in Table VIII the standard deviation value corresponding to each percentage value. (Find the percentage value which is closest to the one obtained and read the figure in the column directly to the left.) This is the T-score and it should be inserted in the column so labeled. (Use the T-score to the nearest whole number, rather than recording it in decimals.) The five-tenth T-scores are in Table VIII merely as an aid in selecting the nearest whole T-score.

8. If a more permanent form is needed or the T-scale is to be posted, copy only the raw scores and T-score columns on another sheet. It may be desirable to include T-scales for several tests on the same sheet for greater convenience in comparing scores. (See page 308.) If possible, give each student a printed or mimeographed card with the scales so he can encircle his scores and draw lines between them representing a profile. Scores made on a repetition of the same tests at a later date can be marked with a different color if desired.

If the mean and standard deviation have been computed for the distribution of scores being used, T-scores can be found by substitution in the formula for T-scores,

$$\text{T-score} = 50 + \frac{10 \ (\text{raw score} - \text{mean score})}{\text{standard deviation}}$$

Convenient data for practice in converting raw scores into T-scores using this formula are available in Tables V and VI. The mean was computed in Table V and found to be 60.45. In Table VI, the standard deviation was computed and found to be 18. To find the T-score for the raw score of 65, substitute in the formula as follows:

$$\text{T-score} = 50 + \frac{10 \ (65 - 60.45)}{18}$$

$$= 50 + \frac{10 \ (4.55)}{18} = 50 + \frac{45.50}{18}$$

$$= 50 + 2.53 = 52.53$$

or the T-score for a raw score of 65 for this distribution is 53.

A graphic method for obtaining T-scores is usable as a "short cut" where time is at a premium and the use that is to be made of the scores does not require complete accuracy. This method cannot be used unless the mean and standard deviation of the raw scores are known.

66

To illustrate the method, use will be made of the data presented in Table V. The mean score for these data is 60.45 and the standard deviation is 18.

A sheet of graph paper is needed, preferably with ten divisions to each inch. The scores made on the test should be arranged down the left-hand side of the graph in descending order and in such a manner that the mean score will be placed slightly above the midway point on the paper. For the data in Table V, they extend from 86 to 6. Then, across the bottom of the page, T-scores starting with 20 at the left and extending to 80 should be marked. See the illustration in Figure 5.

Locate the point where the horizontal line opposite the mean for the raw scores (60) intersects the vertical line from 50, the mean of the T-scores and place a dot at this point.

Then, using the formula

$$\text{T-score} = 50 + \frac{10 \ (X - M)}{\sigma}$$

compute the T-score for one other score, preferably one fairly near the mean.

For example, 69. The computation follows:

For X, substitute the raw score (69)

For M, substitute the mean score (60)

For σ, substitute the standard deviation (18)

$$\text{T-score for raw score of } 69 = 50 + \frac{10 \ (69 - 60)}{18}$$

$$= 50 + \frac{10 \times 9}{18}$$

$$= 50 + \frac{90}{18}$$

$$= 50 + 5$$

The next step is to place a dot on the line opposite the selected score at the point where the vertical line intersects it that leads to the T-score obtained by use of the formula. (For the illustration, opposite 69 and above 55.) Then, using a steel edged ruler, draw a line between the exact center of the two dots extending diagonally across the page, from lower left to upper right.

T-scores for any given raw score can now be obtained by looking across from the raw score to the point where the diagonal line is reached and then going down to read the T-score.

Note that in Figure 5 only the heavy dividing lines are shown. Each square on the graph paper should have additional fine lines dividing it into one hundred smaller squares, ten each direction. This is essential to obtain even a fair degree of accuracy.

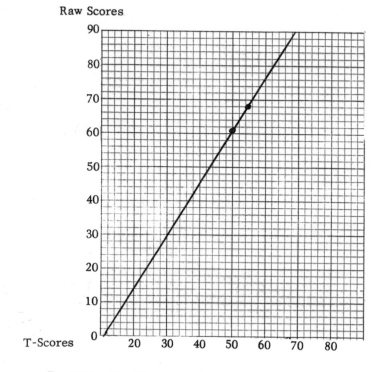

Figure 5. Graphic method for obtaining T-Scores.

Obviously, this is a method which is economical of time and one which would not be selected for use when the need for complete accuracy is great. When the number of cases is relatively small as in the illustration (N = 43), the results are likely to be less accurate than when the number is such that one can be assured of a normal distribution of abilities.

68

2. Other Achievement Scales

As stated before, there are other variations of standard scores into which raw data may be converted. The choice of method should be based upon the use that is to be made of the scores and the purposes for having given the test or other measuring device.

CORRELATION

The knowledge of how to compute a correlation is not absolutely necessary for a teacher to be able to make good use of tests. However, many teachers wish to have this information in order to be able to evaluate tests that they themselves have devised. Or they may wish to use a test that has not been studied for use in situations similar to theirs. For example, the test may have been constructed for a different age level as, for example, for college when you are teaching in a high school. Or, having administered two "duplicate forms" of the same test, they may have reason to doubt that the tests were of equal difficulty.

For most skill tests, reliability and validity coefficients* are given. These indicate that when the test was given to a particular group, it yielded that coefficient. Usually the group upon whom the study was conducted is described. A test does not have a reliability or a validity per se. The coefficient of correlation that is reported is in relation to a specified group. Similar results can be expected elsewhere or with other groups only to the extent that the group being tested is similar to the original group. For example, the very same test, administered in the same teaching facilities and by the same administrator, may yield different coefficients of correlation, if the groups being tested vary greatly in the ability being measured. For example, see the reliabilities for the Badminton Short Serve Test, page 145, where the variation was thought to be due to one group having had many more students to a class and a shorter playing season. Sometimes the groups vary in age as well as playing experience. Can a test having acceptable reliability and validity for a particular college group be expected to be sufficiently reliable and valid for use with a junior high school group, for example? Some tests will be, others will not.[1] The teacher may wish to

*For definitions of such terms as reliability and validity, see p. 19, Chapter II.

make certain modifications or alterations in a test which has been constructed for use with a different age level. For example, changes in distances or in length of test, such as in the number of trials or the amount of time. The teacher who knows how to compute a correlation can determine the reliability and validity for the test when given to his own group, and thus have a better idea of how much reliance he can place on the test scores.

The correlation coefficient is a numerical expression of the degree of relationship between two variables. In Chapter II the meaning of correlation coefficients was discussed. The range of the degree of relationship extends from a + 1.00 through 0.00 to a - 1.00, or from a perfect positive correlation through a zero correlation (no relationship) to a perfect negative correlation. These extremes, the ± 1.00, rarely happen because of the fact that in dealing with human characteristics there are many variables beside the two being studied which have a bearing upon the relationship.

The Pearson Product-Moment method of correlation is in common use when the number of cases exceeds fifty. While it is the method of correlation that should be learned by the average physical education teacher for use in most testing problems, it should be remembered that other methods exist and that there are times when it is better to use them. The calculation of a product-moment r will be illustrated by showing the computations involved. Data from Table IX will be used; the problem is to compute the degree of relationship existing between throwing ability in speedball as measured by the Throwing and Catching Test and kicking ability in speedball as measured by the Soccer Pass Test. Figure 6, called a scattergram, will be used in the illustration.

Steps in Computation of r from a Scattergram

1. Decide upon the intervals to be used for each of the two distributions or variables. These should be listed on the scattergram. One variable is designated as the Y variable and is arranged on the left of the diagram. The other variable is designated as the X variable and is placed across the top of the diagram. The scores should be so entered on the diagram that the low scores on the Y variable appear at the bottom and the low scores on the X variable appear at the left. For the sample problem the size of the

70

intervals happens to be the same for both variables, but
this is not necessary.

2. Starting with Case 1 in Table IX, make a tally in
the proper cell for each pair of performances. The cell of
Case 54 has been heavily ruled. The tallies are placed in
the upper left-hand corner of the squares.

Table IX.

Data for Calculation of Correlation Coefficient

CASE NO.	SPEEDBALL WALL PASS	SOCCER PASS	CASE NO.	SPEEDBALL WALL PASS	SOCCER PASS	CASE NO.	SPEEDBALL WALL PASS	SOCCER PASS
1	59	31	19	56	18	37	58	32
2	46	32	20	66	40	38	61	32
3	62	21	21	57	32	39	64	37
4	59	33	22	61	31	40	42	23
5	59	28	23	44	22	41	61	35
6	65	31	24	63	34	42	47	30
7	75	38	25	59	23	43	60	38
8	50	32	26	56	27	44	61	35
9	45	19	27	60	30	45	56	32
10	57	34	28	62	33	46	55	27
11	54	27	29	48	19	47	51	27
12	62	31	30	53	28	48	64	37
13	62	27	31	57	33	49	61	32
14	65	36	32	60	27	50	58	36
15	62	27	33	64	40	51	61	35
16	57	33	34	62	30	52	64	40
17	61	44	35	58	36	53	68	42
18	53	33	36	63	30	54	70	44

3. When the tallying has been completed, add frequency
columns in the scattergram, placing fy in the first column
on the right-hand side and fx in the first row across the
bottom of the scattergram.

4. Assume as a mean or arbitrary reference point for
each variable the midpoint of an interval approximately in
the middle of each distribution. Mark with heavy lines or
colored pencil the row where the assumed mean for the X
variable lies. Likewise, rule off the column where the assumed mean of the Y variable lies.

5. Record in the d column for the Y axis the deviation
of each interval above and below the mean. The first above

71

←------X VARIABLE -- (Soccer Pass)--------→

←----Y VARIABLE -- (Throwing and Catching)----→

	18-19	20-21	22-23	24-25	26-27	28-29	30-31	32-33	34-35	36-37	38-39	40-41	42-43	44-45	fy	dy	fdy	fd^2y	x' −	y' +
74-75											(32)				1	8	8	64		32
72-73													Case No. 54↓		0	7	0	0		
70-71														(42)	1	6	6	36		42
68-69													(30)		1	5	5	25		30
66-67												(20)			1	4	4	16		20
64-65										(27)		(30)			6	3	18	54		57
62-63		(-10)			(-8)			(2)	(4)						8	2	16	32	18	6
60-61					(-2)			(2)	(6)		(4)			(7)	10	1	10	10	2	19
58-59															7		67			
56-57	(6)				(2)			(-4)	(-2)						7	-1	-7	7	6	8
54-55					(8)										2	-2	-4	8		8
52-53						(3)		(-3)							2	-3	-6	18	3	3
50-51					(8)			(-4)							2	-4	-8	32	4	8
48-49	(30)														1	-5	-5	25		30
46-47								(-6)							2	-6	-12	72	6	
44-45	(42)		(28)												2	-7	-14	98		70
42-43			(32)												1	-8	-8	64		32
fx	3	1	3	0	7	2	8	12	5	5	2	3	1	2	54		-64	561	-39	365
dx	-6	-5	-4	-3	-2	-1		1	2	3	4	5	6	7		N				-39
fdx	-18	-5	-12	0	-14	-2		12	10	15	8	15	6	14	80					326
fd^2x	108	25	48	0	28	2		12	20	45	32	75	36	98	529		Check			
Σ xy	78	-10	60	0	8	3		-13	8	27	36	50	30	49	326					

(1). $c_y = \frac{3}{54} = .055$ or $.06$

(2). $c_x = \frac{29}{54} = .537$ or $.58$

(3). $\sigma_y = \sqrt{\frac{561}{54} - (.06)^2} = 3.22$

(4). $\sigma_x = \sqrt{\frac{529}{54} - (.58)^2} = 3.045$

(5). $r = \dfrac{\frac{\Sigma x'y'}{N} - c_x c_y}{\sigma_x \sigma_y} = .6133$

Figure 6. Calculation of product-moment coefficient of correlation.

is +1, second +2, first below -1; continue until all are counted. Do the same for the X axis, with those to the left of the mean being the negative deviations.

6. Compute the $\underline{fd}$ and $\underline{fd^2}$ products for each interval. This is the same procedure as outlined earlier for the computation of the S.D.

7. Add the columns $\underline{f}$, $\underline{fd}$, and $\underline{fd^2}$ on the right-hand side for the Y variable and at the bottom for the X variable. The sum of the $\underline{f}$'s must agree, otherwise an error has been made in counting tallies.

8. Compute the correction $\underline{c}$ for each variable, $\underline{c_x}$ and $\underline{c_y}$, and the standard deviation of each variable, X and Y, in terms of deviation units, that is, without multiplying by the size of the step-interval.

   a. In computing the correction for each variable, the $\Sigma\underline{fd}$ positive is added to $\Sigma\underline{fd}$ negative. (In the illustration, for the Y variable this is $67 - 64 = 3$. The correction for Y is obtained by dividing 3 by N or 54, which is .055 or .06. For the X variable, the sum of $\underline{fd_x}$ positive is 80; of $\underline{fd_x}$ negative, $- 51$; when added algebraically, the result is 29. Therefore, $\underline{c_x}$ is $\dfrac{29}{54} = .537$ or .58.)

   b. In computing the standard deviation for each variable, the $\Sigma\underline{fd^2}$ is used. (In the illustration, for the Y variable, the $\overline{\Sigma\underline{fd^2}}_y$ is 561. Using the formula for standard deviation $\sqrt{\dfrac{\Sigma\underline{fd^2}}{N} - c^2}$, the computation is shown in Step 3 at the right of the scattergram. The $\Sigma\underline{fd^2}_x$ is 529, and that number is used in the fourth step at the right of the scattergram.)

9. The final step in the problem is to compute $\Sigma\underline{x'y'}$. So far, in calculating $\underline{r}$, no new statistical work has been presented with the exception of the construction of the scattergram which is purely mechanical. The symbol, $\underline{x'y'}$ may be defined as the deviation of the various scores from the two assumed means. The product is obtained by multiplying the deviation of the scores from one assumed mean by the deviation from the other, in terms of deviation units. The procedure is as follows:

   a. The lines representing the assumed means divide the scattergram into four quadrants: upper right, upper left, lower left, and lower right, or quadrants I, II, III, and IV, respectively. The upper right is positive, upper left negative, lower left positive, and the lower right negative. Cell deviations in quadrants I and III will be positive and in quadrants II and IV negative. Case 54 is in quadrant I (the upper right) and will therefore be positive.

b. The cell deviation, or product deviation from the assumed means, is placed in the lower right-hand corner of each cell, as indicated in Figure 6. (The cell containing Case 54 deviates upward six and to the right seven; its "value," therefore, is forty-two.) Only the value of the cells containing frequencies need be entered on the scattergram; when commercially produced correlation charts are used, the values of all cells are printed on the chart for the convenience of the user.

c. The product-moment for each cell is obtained by multiplying the deviation value of the cell by the frequencies. This number can be written in the middle of each cell using colored pencil. In the illustration, the number has been encircled. (For case number 54, the product-moment is 42 × 1 or 42; if, however, there were two frequencies, the product-moment would be 42 × 2 or 84.)

d. When the product-moments of all of the squares have been computed, observing plus and minus signs, the entries in the x'y' columns can be made. Add the product-moments for each step-interval of the Y variable, placing the sum of the positive values under the plus sign and the sum of the negative values under the minus sign. The algebraic sum of this column for the problem in question is 326. This procedure is duplicated in the X variable columns as a check; the two answers must agree if there has been no mistake in computation. (In Figure 6, across the bottom of the scattergram, these have been summed algebraically and placed in one row, Σxy. In the fifth column from the left, -8 and -2 were added algebraically to +2, +8, and +8 to obtain Σxy or 8.)

10. Compute the coefficient of correlation by means of the formula

$$\underline{r} = \frac{\dfrac{\Sigma xy}{N} - c_x c_y}{\sigma_x \sigma_y}.$$

For the problem in question, the computation is as follows:

$$r = \frac{\dfrac{326}{54} - (.58 \times .06)}{3.045 \times 3.22} = \frac{6.0133}{9.805} = .6133$$

The coefficient of .6133 is large enough to indicate considerable relationship between the throwing ability in speedball as measured by the Throwing and Catching Test and kicking ability in speedball as measured by the Soccer Pass Test.

SUMMARY

It is not necessary to be "research-minded" to understand and use the procedures described in this chapter. More techniques are included than in the usual tests and measurements texts for physical education students because it is the belief of the authors that all teachers of physical education need this information and that it is not beyond the grasp of the majority of them.

SELECTED REFERENCES

1. Broer, Marion R.: Reliability of Certain Skill Tests for Junior High School Girls. Research Quarterly, 29, 2, 139-145, 1958.

2. Garrett, Henry E.: Statistics in Psychology and Education, 4th ed. New York, Longmans, Green and Company, 1953.

3. Smith, G. Milton: A Simplified Guide to Statistics for Psychology and Education. New York, Rhinehart and Company, Inc., 1946.

4. Snedecor, George W.: Statistical Methods. Ames, Iowa, The Iowa State College Press, 1956.

5. Walker, Helen M.: Elementary Statistical Methods. New York, Henry Holt and Company, 1943.

6. Walker, Helen M.: Mathematics Essential for Elementary Statistics. New York, Henry Holt and Company, 1934.

Chapter IV

CONSTRUCTION OF SKILL TESTS AND BATTERIES

The methods used in constructing skill tests, in analyzing them, and in combining such tests into batteries will be described in this chapter. New tests need to be developed. Little work has been done in some areas. The steps in the construction of a skill test battery are essentially the same for all activities. These steps will be outlined here and illustrations will be given. It will be noted that the test constructor relies both upon logic and upon statistical analysis; each supplements the other. A few statistical procedures will be added in this chapter which are not essential to the test user.

STUDY THE PROBLEM OR NEED FOR THE TEST

The test constructor usually starts with a recognized need. Frequently there are no tests available for the particular purpose or those that are available do not appear satisfactory. Sometimes there is no statistical evidence of the value of the tests or the data were gathered on a group which is not comparable, perhaps in age level, sex, amount of experience, general intelligence, or a combination of such factors. The present tests may not be practical to use in the space and time available or they may require equipment which is lacking.

The available tests for some sports activities measure skill in only limited aspects of the activity. In certain team sports such as basketball, field hockey and football, there is a dearth of tests measuring defensive tactics. The tests for many sports activities present an artificial situation or one that is not frequently encountered in the game situation. A number of tests have been developed to measure the ability to throw accurately. If the throw is made while standing still with an unlimited amount of time to aim and to get set, and if the target is in a stationary

76

position, the tests are not measuring exactly the same skill as that needed in a game situation where there are time pressures. In baseball and softball, the fielder's throw must beat the runner to the base. In football, the problem is more complex. Not only must the passer hit the moving receiver at precisely the right split second but he must avoid an interception. He is also under great pressure to get the pass off quickly.

Some skills are more easily measured than others. For example, there are more tests of the ability to serve in tennis than there are of ability to make returns. But even for the serve, one might ask if the tests measure speed as well as accuracy of placement; variety as well as form. Are the most important skills being tested? Does having ability in the skill or skills with which you are concerned matter?

ANALYZE THE ABILITY TO BE MEASURED

Careful consideration should be given to the skill or skills to be measured. The frequency with which each skill is used can be determined by tabulating the occurrences of use in several regulation games. It is advisable to chart games between groups of beginners as well as games between highly skilled players, if concerned with skill tests for a team activity. It may also be helpful to watch teams which employ different types of offensive and defensive strategy as this is known to influence the frequency of usage of certain skills. For example, against a player-to-player defense in basketball, one can expect a higher proportion of short length shots than against a zone type of defense.

The manner in which the skill is used is of concern as well as the amount of use. Observation and analysis should reveal space relationships, timing, force of the movement, and the manner of execution. For example, if the successfully executed smash stroke in badminton is usually made from near the net and with great force, then the test should make similar requirements. If the test permits the player to "lob" the shuttlecock across the net, then some other ability is apt to be measured in the test. Unless the test constructor is able to analyze the ability to be measured and thoroughly understands the activity, the tests are not likely to be good.

77

If concerned with the development of a battery of tests for an activity, it may be helpful to start by listing the principal skills and then rate their importance in relation to successful performance in the activity. As an illustration, if volleyball tests are under consideration, the listing and ratings might resemble the following:

Skills Involved	Rating of Importance*
1. Receiving the ball	
a. From service	3
b. From a teammate's pass	1
c. From across the net	2
d. From a teammate's setup	2
2. Playing the ball	
a. Service	3
b. Pass of Teammate	3
c. Volley across net	2
d. Spike	1
e. Block	1
f. Setup	3
3. Footwork	
a. Getting under the ball	2
b. Jumping	2
c. Following into court after service	1
d. Filling opening left by teammate	2

Obviously the listing of skills as well as the ratings will vary with the level of skill and type of game played, and the above is merely an illustration. The chart should assist in the decision as to which skills are important enough that tests should be devised to measure them. Perhaps certain of these skills already have tests that have been proven useful and valid and can be used to supplement the tests you plan to devise.

DEVISE THE EXPERIMENTAL ITEMS

One's ingenuity constitutes the chief source of ideas. Considerable experimentation is necessary and the good skill test usually undergoes a number of changes before it is

---

*3 high, 1 low.

developed to the extent of collecting a considerable amount of data. The test in its various forms should be tried out on small groups until one is quite sure that the dimensions, markings, and time allotments are satisfactory and the scoring scheme feasible. The players known to be better performers should score considerably higher on the test than do those with less skill and the range of scores should be fairly wide. If the test as devised is too difficult for some of the players to register a score, or conversely, if the amount of skill required is so little that many register high scores, obviously some adjustment must be made since differentiation between all levels of ability is essential.

Practicality must also be considered in devising or constructing tests. Most school budgets are not adequate to justify the expenditures of funds for expensive equipment to be used solely for testing purposes. If use can be made of equipment commonly on hand in physical education departments or inexpensive to acquire, the test will be of use to more persons.

These suggestions are based upon the assumption that the skill tests are being devised to serve the purposes usually found in school situations, and some of them do not apply to other purposes. If developing tests for use in selecting performers from a group of highly skilled athletes, as, for example in Olympic trials, concern would not need be felt for having tests that would permit those persons with low motor ability to score. It is also conceivable that in such a situation one might be able to afford some specialized equipment.

In the early stages of test development much time will be saved if a single test can be given and the results recorded in such a manner as to permit scoring in different ways to represent different tests. It is essential in this case to be definite on the point of aim. For example, if the area A (Figure 7) just in front of the baseline is considered the most desirable area for service, then all students aim for that area. By use of a scoring chart showing the actual court, each serve may be marked for its exact point of contact. It is then possible to score the test in as many ways as seem desirable. The shaded area may be subdivided into corners and center (b) or left as an undivided area (a); the space in front may be divided into zones parallel to A (c), or subdivided into zones by lines at right angles to A (d); the space behind A (e) may be

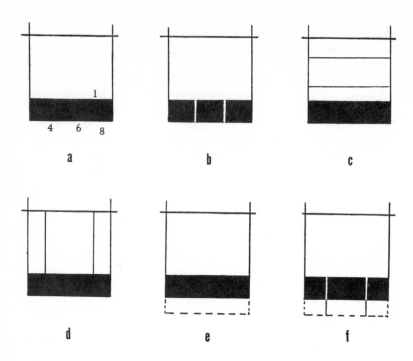

Figure 7. Suggested target areas for volley ball serve test.

scored as zero, or the whole area scored a little less than
A, or subdivided into zones the same as those in front of
A (f). Each player would have a score sheet in the form of
a court outline. The scorer records the number of the trial
as indicated in (a). It is then possible to construct new
markings on the chart and score in any way desired. Later
correlations will reveal which scoring method is best.

The scoring plan for the Badminton Short Serve Test
(Chapter VI) was devised in this way. The test was designed
to test ability for a short service into the front left
corner of the right service court. The scoring chart was
identical with the floor markings. The student knew he was
aiming for the corner of the court but knew nothing of how
it was to be scored. Each service was recorded on the
chart. A series of scoring schemes was tried with the even-
tual selection of the one given in Chapter VI, since it
correlated the most highly with the criterion.

PREPARE WRITTEN DIRECTIONS
FOR THE TEST

After the test has been tried in various forms with a small group, the test directions should be prepared. These should include all of the information needed to assure the test being given in the same manner to all subjects to be used in the study. See Chapter VI for a form that may prove useful in indicating what should be included.

In addition to uniformity in such things as equipment (including field or floor markings, etc.,), uniformity is needed in the presentation of the test. See Chapter XIV.

Careful planning at this stage is most essential. If after having administered the test to about half of the group, a better way is discovered in administering it or an idea develops for improving the test, it is necessary to either stay with the original plan or repeat the testing. The "kinks" should be removed during the preliminaries, not after the collection of data has started.

SELECT AND OBTAIN THE CRITERION

Every test may be compared with some criterion which is used as a yardstick against which the new test is measured. If a test of proven worth exists but for some reason it is not desirable for use, (as for example, too time-consuming or requiring too much space), this measure could be used as the criterion, if it is otherwise acceptable. Many of the mental abilities tests have been validated in this manner. This of course requires that both tests be given to each subject but if the new test proves to be highly related to the longer test, it can be used alone in the future.

It frequently happens that the available measures are inadequate for use as a criterion. Judges' ratings can be a satisfactory criterion if opportunities for observation are adequate and the judges are well-trained and competent. (See pages 38 to 41 for rating procedures.) It is essential that these judges see the subjects in action in the activity, not in tests, though the ratings should be done at a time not too remote from that in which the tests are given. The scale to be used usually contains five categories, each carefully defined. The judges should be instructed to use all categories and not just the middle three. Some raters seem timid about using the top and the bottom categories. Stalter,[8] in an attempt to secure a wider range in ratings, made use of a percentage scheme and asked the judges to assign the top rating to a specified per cent of the subjects and the lowest rating to a similar per cent.

In conducting ratings which are to be used as a criterion in evaluating tests, it is necessary that the ability to be rated be carefully defined. If it is playing ability in general, then the raters need to discuss what they consider excellent playing ability, what good, what average, and so on through the range. The size of the range depends upon the amount of discrimination that appears possible and desirable. After the raters have met and discussed the various points on the scale, they should have time to become familiar with the chart that they are to use before the actual rating begins. The code for marking should be placed on the chart. The rating form may be subdivided into skills if playing ability in general is being rated. The raters should have a practice period where they will become aware of the problems involved and familiar with the length of time that can be spent in watching each player, the procedure to be followed either in rotating the players into positions to facilitate observation or be better able to anticipate what movement will be helpful on their part. An additional device, called a player-to-player comparison, has been used to aid the raters to gain a picture of the various levels of skill. Players were observed who were identified as fitting each of the described categories. This took place during a practice rating session, with a different group from that used in the actual study.

The rating forms should have some identification of players already recorded upon them. Colored pinnies with numbers on both front and back are helpful. As soon as attendance has been checked, the raters should be informed of absentees, if any.

The raters should work independently. The length of time that they watch the players will vary with the activity but they should see each player active for a long enough time to be able to rank him in each of the units or skills and to give him a composite score. If the play is affected by the abilities of the opponents or of teammates, or if the physical setup is not uniform (position of the sun, condition of playing court, etc.,), the person in charge of the ratings must make the necessary adjustments. In team sports, ratings should usually extend over several consecutive class periods.

In utilizing the ratings secured from the various judges, it is better to use the sum of the judges' ratings rather than the average as the criterion. When the sum is used, the range is greater. On a five point scale with three judges, the range is 3 to 15, with four judges, 4 to 20. This gives a range of rating scores more nearly comparable to the test score range for computation of a correlation.

Sometimes these ratings are weighted by giving extra value to one judge's opinion, as, for example, the instructor of the class, who has had more opportunity to see the players in action. His ratings might be multiplied by a constant such as 2.

Agreement of the judges can be determined by the correlation technique. If the judges are well-trained and the length of time for observation is sufficient, the coefficient should be high (at least .80). Agreement between three judges as determined by correlation of their ratings might read as follows: Judges 1 and 2, .81; Judges 1 and 3, .90; Judges 2 and 3, .87. These could be considered satisfactory. The sum of the three judges' ratings would then be used for the player's score on playing ability, which is the criterion for evaluating the experimental items. Occasionally an error is made in selecting judges and some one thought to know a great deal about the activity, to be highly objective, and to be highly competent in such procedures does not prove to have all of these qualities. This will be revealed by the correlation between the ratings of judges. For example, if there were four judges and the correlations were as follows, one judge is obviously not in agreement with the others: 1 and 2, .76; 1 and 3, .89; 1 and 4, .88; 2 and 3, .63; 2 and 4, .71; 3 and 4, .91. In this case, the ratings made by judge 2 would not be used.

It should be kept clearly in mind that the work connected with establishment of a criterion measure is necessary only in a project to evaluate or develop a new or comparatively unknown test or battery of tests. It is not a part of the regular testing program. Previously validated tests and ratings by judges have been described in relation to their use as a criterion. Standings following competition are not feasible in most cases but have been used in a few studies where class size and length of season made it possible to carry on a ladder tournament until stability was obtained.

SELECT THE SUBJECTS TO BE USED

The subjects used in the development of a new test or battery of tests should be representative of the population for which the instrument is designed. Validation on a college group would indicate similar results with comparable college groups, for example. The experience of the group must be considered, too, since different results may be obtained on beginners and advanced groups of the like age and sex.

There is no magical number which can be given as the one which will give satisfactory results in all studies. However, as a generalization it can be said that approximately 100 should be considered a minimum. The number increases with the variability of the skill demonstrated, the lowered reliability of the measures, and the confidence which you wish to place on the results. If the group consists of physical education majors or other experienced players, the total number could be considerably less than if the group is made up of junior high school players, with the majority being beginners.

If you had your choice of ten high school sections, averaging forty to a section but ranging in size from 17 to 125, and all were a grand mixture of skills and year in high school, it would be advisable to select the smaller sections if ratings are to be used as the criterion. However, if previously validated tests are to be used as the criterion and there is ample space and equipment available for testing the larger classes, the selection might be made by drawing class hour numbers by chance until a sufficiently large total was reached.

If the test being developed is intended for use with beginning players in college and there are available 98 such players in four classes, then all would be used except the few who may be absent during the testing and rating periods.

DETERMINE THE RELIABILITY
OF THE EXPERIMENTAL TEST ITEMS

The ideal method of ascertaining the reliability of
the separate items (tests) is to administer each in identical form on two successive days and then to correlate the
results. If the test is measuring consistently, it should
yield a very high coefficient (in the .90's). Administration on two successive days is preferable to permitting a
day or more to intervene because there is less likely to be
an opportunity for practice and more likely that the physical status will be similar. In general, this procedure of
consecutive days is better than two repetitions of the test
on the same day because some will be affected more than
others by fatigue. The length of the test rather than its
strenuousness may be the determining factor.

It is not always possible to give two complete repetitions of the same test, especially when it is a long one.
The score for half of the test can be correlated against the
score for the other half. If the test consists of ten trials, for example, the score for the odd-numbered trials
(1,3,5,7, and 9) would be correlated against the score for
the even-numbered trials (2,4,6,8,10); this is preferable
to correlating the score for the first half against the
score for the last half since in the odds-evens method,
practice effects and fatigue tend to cancel out.

When the odd-even method is used it is permissible to
use the Spearman-Brown Prophecy formula to step up the coefficient to the actual length of the full test. The procedure for this will follow on pages 86 to 88.

If at this stage it is discovered that the test is decidedly below the desired reliability (usually .80 minimum), it is discarded. However, if the reliability is in
the high .70's and the test appears to have many good qualities, the number of trials might be increased. The Spearman-Brown Prophecy formula may be used to predict the like-
lihood that an increase in trials will raise the reliability
sufficiently. See page 87. If this proves favorable, then
the additional trials should be administered.

It will be seen, then, that the reliability of the test
is partially a function of the length of the test. For that
reason it is well to plan on several trials of any test
where there is considerable variation in performance and

any element of chance involved. Chance variations and the erratic performances characteristic of beginners explains why beginners frequently require more trials than advanced players on the same test. Tests involving an all out performance such as a baseball throw for distance usually require fewer trials than do tests where the element of chance plays a greater part, such as accuracy tests, particularly if the latter are scored on a success or failure basis. Basket shooting is an example; if this could be scored according to how close one came to hitting the basket, as in a concentric circles target type test like in archery, then the number of trials could be reduced. Thus it is seen that the type of scoring as well as the length of the test affects the reliability.

It must be kept in mind that there is no such thing as the reliability of a test. The reliability found is always for the group and under the circumstances stated. In studying a number of tests in a selected activity with the intended purpose of developing a battery, the tests should all be administered to the same subjects. Reliabilities are computed first and all experimental items with very low reliabilities can be dropped before attempting correlation with the criterion. This saves time and such tests would be dropped later, anyway, as tests with low reliabilities invariably yield low validity coefficients.

APPLICATION OF THE SPEARMAN-BROWN PROPHECY FORMULA

This statistical technique is used to estimate the reliability of a test when the test is of such nature that it can be scored in halves. For example, if the test consists of twenty trials and it is impossible or inadvisable to repeat the entire test, the sum of the odd-numbered trials can be correlated against the sum of the even-numbered trials. (See page 85 for an explanation of why this method of splitting the test into halves is preferable to correlating the sum of the first half against the sum of the second half.)

Whenever the split halves method of determining reliability has been used, the coefficient obtained is the reliability for half the length of the test. In order to obtain an estimate of the reliability of the full number of trials, the Spearman-Brown Prophecy Formula is used:

$$r_x = \frac{nr}{1 + (n-1)r}$$

when r_x is the coefficient to be estimated

n equals 2 (or the proportion of increase in length)
r is the correlation coefficient obtained on the halves.

To illustrate, assume a reliability of .80 for half the length of the test. The estimate of the reliability for the full length of the test is obtained by substituting in the formula as follows:

$$r_x = \frac{2 \times .80}{1 + (2-1) \times .80}$$

$$= \frac{1.60}{1.80} = .89$$

Many students have difficulty in substituting correctly in formulas. In the denominator for this formula, observe the plus sign and solve everything to the right before adding it to 1.00. Two minus one is of course one, and one times .80 is .80. Add .80 to 1.00 to obtain 1.80.

The same value could have been obtained from Table X.

Table X.

Coefficients Stepped Up
by the Spearman-Brown Prophecy Formula
as an Estimate for Twice the Number of Trials

ODD-EVEN	SPEARMAN-BROWN	ODD-EVEN	SPEARMAN-BROWN	ODD-EVEN	SPEARMAN-BROWN
.60	.75	.70	.82	.80	.89
.61	.76	.71	.83	.81	.90
.62	.77	.72	.84	.82	.90
.63	.78	.73	.84	.83	.91
.64	.78	.74	.85	.84	.91
.65	.79	.75	.86	.85	.92
.66	.80	.76	.86	.86	.93
.67	.80	.77	.87	.87	.93
.68	.81	.78	.88	.88	.94
.69	.82	.79	.88	.89	.94

Values not included in this table may be computed by use of the formula. The Spearman-Brown Prophecy Formula can be simplified for use in estimating double the number of trials as follows:

$$r_x = \frac{2\ r}{1 + r}$$

The more complex formula is included for use in those situations where an estimate is needed of the reliability of an increased number of trials. For example, if the number of trials given in a skills test appears to have been too few and the reliability found by correlating odds versus evens is unacceptably low, the effect of increasing the number of trials can be predicted by substituting a different number than 2 for "n" in the original formula. This number should represent the proportion of the increase in the number of trials.

To illustrate, if the test consisted of four trials and the odds were correlated against the evens yielding a reliability coefficient of .50 for half the length of the test, application of the formula using two for "n" gives an estimated reliability of .66 for the four trials. This is too low. What effect would increasing the number to 6 trials have? To determine this, substitute 3 rather than 2 for "n" since three is the same proportion to six trials that two is to four trials. The computation:

$$r_x = \frac{n\ r}{1 + (n-1)\ r}$$

$$= \frac{3 \times .50}{1 + (3-1) \times .50} = \frac{1.50}{1 + 2 \times .50}$$

$$= \frac{1.50}{1 + 1.00} = \frac{1.50}{2.00} = .75$$

It would appear that the test is inconsistent in measuring whatever it is measuring.

DETERMINE THE VALIDITY OF THE TEST ITEMS

The validity of the test is determined by correlating the scores of each subject with his criterion score. If previous work has been well done and the experimental items are of the right type, these coefficients will range from about .60 to .80 or .85. If the criterion used was judges' ratings of general playing ability in an activity and a single item (test) was found with a coefficient in the .80's, this may be considered satisfactory alone. In general, tests are found to be well below the .80's and at a level which is not high enough for individual prediction or evaluation. For that reason, it is usually necessary to combine two or three of the better tests for a battery. Those with low validity coefficients are not considered further.

The validity of a test, as well as the reliability, is in terms of the group and the circumstances under which it is established. A description of the group and an explanation of the circumstances should accompany the statement of validity; this should include a description of the criterion used.

Perhaps some mention should be made of "face validity." Some activities are played under conditions which yield a score. This is true of archery, bowling, and golf, for example. The scores themselves can be used as valid measures of playing ability, provided enough scores are used to obtain acceptable reliability. When this occurs, there is no need for further validation. It is important to note that this concept of face validity should be applied only to activities in which individual performance is not affected by the ability of an opponent.

COMPUTE THE INTERCORRELATIONS OF THE EXPERIMENTAL TESTS

During the successive steps, the number of experimental items is gradually reduced. Those tests of low reliability and low validity have already been discarded. It is not helpful to have two tests which are measuring exactly the same skill. In order to determine the extent to which the tests measure the same thing, each item retained at this stage is correlated with every other item.

In the example on the following page, the intercorrelations for four volleyball skill tests are shown. As would be expected, the two service tests correlate rather highly. The other tests show low but varying degrees of relationship.

	1	2	3	4
1. Service test #1				
2. Service test #2	.70			
3. Volleying test	.25	.40		
4. Setup test	.50	.45	.30	

THE LOGIC FOR COMBINING TESTS

The logic for combining tests should now be clear.
Each test to go into a battery should have a relatively high
validity coefficient, but it should have a minimum relationship to the other tests in the battery. This would mean
that each test measures the desired ability but that each
measures some element of the total which is not measured by
the other tests.

MULTIPLE CORRELATION

The multiple correlation is used to determine the influence of adding an item to a test battery, or to tell the
test user which combination of tests will yield the higher
validity. For example, see the various combinations tried
with badminton skill tests, page 158. The multiple correlation tells you <u>which</u> tests to use but it does not give information concerning weightings; such information is obtained from regression equations.

The multiple correlation may be computed by any one of
the usual methods referred to in any text on statistics
which covers advanced correlation techniques. Some of the
explanations are helpful to persons who have studied matrix
algebra and incomprehensible to most others. A short cut
method which is considerably simpler and which consolidates
several of the intermediate steps is presented here, without
explanation as to the underlying rationale. It requires
careful reading and following of directions, combined with
the willingness to take the routine more or less on faith.

The process of multiple correlation yields the information as to which tests when combined correlate the highest
with the criterion. The symbol R is used to indicate the
multiple correlation coefficient and 0 to indicate the criterion. The tests are numbered consecutively.

If it is reported that $R_{0.124} = .86$ and $R_{0.14} = .70$, the reader would know that the first combination yielded the higher coefficient of correlation and that three tests were combined and correlated against the criterion. He would also know that the tests that yielded the higher correlation were tests numbered 1, 2, and 4.

The computation of a multiple correlation (R) between two tests (1,2) and the criterion (0), or $R_{0.12}$ is shown in the sample computational sheet in Table XI. The work sheet is arranged for combining as many as six tests. The **bolder** figures are the ones that have been filled in on the printed work sheet to illustrate the computations for the sample problem.

Sample Problem

The criterion, or 0, is general volleyball ability, as measured by ratings made by judges. We are attempting to find the degree to which the two selected tests (#1 and #2) when combined correlate with the criterion. Also given is the following information:

Test #1 has a validity of .780 (r_{01})
Test #2 has a validity of .611 (r_{02})
The intercorrelation between the two tests is
.250 (r_{12}).

The parts of the work sheet which are not needed are simply ignored. This is a two-item sample problem and as stated before, the work sheet is arranged for combining as many as six tests.

The instructions appear in a column on the left side of the work sheet and should be followed step by step. Note that the rows or lines are numbered and the columns carry letter headings. Line 1 says "Insert values for r's." Therefore, r_{12} is inserted in the top of the cell <u>1b</u>. Also r_{01} is inserted in the top of cell <u>1x</u>, bearing a negative sign according to the code $-r_{01}$ in that cell. Line 2 says, "Divide line 1 by -1." That results in changing the sign and inserting the same numbers in the bottom of each of the two cells. Instructions are followed exactly, giving attention to signs, as far as necessary. In combining two tests work will proceed through line 6, for three tests through line 11, for four tests through line 17, and so through the sheet.

91

Table XI.
Sample Doolittle Sheet with Computation
of Multiple Correlation for Volleyball Battery

Directions	a	b	c	d	e	f	x
1 Insert values for r's	1.000	r_{12}	r_{13}	r_{14}	r_{15}	r_{16}	$-r_{01}$
		.250					-.780
2 Divide line 1 by -1		-.250					+.780
3 Insert values for r's		1.000	r_{23}	r_{24}	r_{25}	r_{26}	$-r_{02}$
							-.611
4 Multiply items in line 1, b to x, by b2		-.063					+.195
5 Add algebraically lines 3 and 4		+.937					-.416
6 Divide line 5 by negative b5							+.444
7 Insert values for r's			1.000	r_{34}	r_{35}	r_{36}	$-r_{03}$
8 Multiply items in Line 1, c to x, by c2							
9 Multiply items in Line 5, c to x, by c6							
10 Add algebraically Lines 7, 8, 9							
11 Divide Line 10 by negative c10							
12 Insert values for r's				1.000	r_{45}	r_{46}	$-r_{04}$
13 Multiply items in Line 1, d to x, by d2							
14 Multiply items in Line 5, d to x, by d6							
15 Multiply items in Line 10, d to x, by d11							
16 Add algebraically Lines 12, 13, 14 and 15							
17 Divide Line 16 by negative d16							
18 Insert values for r's					1.000	r_{56}	$-r_{05}$
19 Multiply items in Line 1, c to x, by e2							
20 Multiply items in Line 5, e to x, by e6							
21 Multiply items in Line 10, e to x, by e11							
22 Multiply items in Line 16, e to x, by e17							
23 Add algebraically Lines 18, 19, 20, 21, 22							
24 Divide Line 23 by negative e23							
25 Insert values for r's						1.000	$-r_{06}$
26 Multiply items in Line 1, f to x by f2							
27 Multiply items in Line 5, f to x, by f6							
28 Multiply items in Line 10, f to x, by f11							
29 Multiply items in Line 16, f to x, by f17							
30 Multiply items in Line 23, f to x, by f24							
31 Add algebraically Lines 25, 26, 27, 28, 29, 30							
32 Divide Line 31 by negative f31							

Substitute values from above table for symbols in following equations (B's for each equation found when each variable in turn is solved for) and solve equations for the regression coefficients, B_1, B_2, B_3, $-B_n$.

$(B_6) = x32$

$(B_5) = (B_6)f25 + x24$

$(B_4) = (B_6)f17 + (B_5)e17 + x17$

$(B_3) = (B_6)f11 + (B_5)e11 + (B_4)d_{11} + x11$

$(B_2) = (B_6)f6 + (B_5)e6 + (B_4)d6 + (B_3)c6 + x6 = +.444$

$(B_1) = (B_6)f2 + (B_5)e2 + (B_4)d2 + (B_3)c2 + (B_2)b2 + x2 = (.444 \times -.250) + .780 = +.669$

FORMULA FOR MULTIPLE CORRELATION

Having found the several regression coefficients, the multiple R is to be found by the following formula:

$$R_{0.123\ldots,n} = \sqrt{B_1 r_{01} + B_2 r_{02} + B_3 r_{03} + \ldots + B_n r_{0n}}$$

$$B_1 r_{01} = .669 \times .780 = .522$$

$$B_2 r_{02} = .444 \times .611 = \frac{.271}{.793}$$

$$R = \sqrt{.793} = .891$$

92

The next step is to solve for the beta weightings, listed as B_6 to B_1, near the bottom of the work sheet. The full formula given there for each B is used only if six tests have been combined. In this case, with only two tests in the multiple, only two B's, B_2 and B_1 are used. Only the parts of the formula which apply to the two tests can be employed. For example, B_2 is simply X_6 (+.444) from the work sheet above since there is no B_6, B_5, B_4, or B_3. B_1 employs only the part of the formula beginning with the product of B_2 and b2, to which is added X2 from the work sheet.

The next step in this computation is the sum of the products of B and the validity r of the respective tests. Formula $= \sqrt{B_1 r_{01} + B_2 r_{02}}$. In this example that sum is .793. (See work sheet.)

The final step is finding the square root of the sum obtained. In this example $\sqrt{.793} = .89$. This is the multiple coefficient, and is represented by the symbol R. This would be interpreted as indicating good prediction of the ability represented by the criterion, in this case general volleyball playing ability.

A similar procedure should be used in determining the multiple correlation for various other combinations. A separate work sheet similar to that shown in Table XI will be needed for each combination tried.

REGRESSION EQUATIONS

Having decided upon the tests to be combined, the method of combining them must be determined. This can be likened to a recipe for a cake. Just as it is necessary to know how much of each ingredient to use in the cake, so it is necessary to know what weighting to give to each test in the battery. The regression equation takes into account the variability of the raw scores on each test and the relative value of each test in the total battery. The formula for this computation reads:

$$B_1 \left(\frac{\sigma_0}{\sigma_1} \right) \text{ test } 1 + B_2 \left(\frac{\sigma_0}{\sigma_2} \right) \text{ test } 2 + \text{------} B_n \left(\frac{\sigma_0}{\sigma_n} \right) \text{ test } n$$

Before substituting in this formula to determine the weightings for the sample problem, the standard deviation information needs to be given. The standard deviation for the criterion (σ_0) was 2.5, for test #1 (σ_1) 7.0, for test #2 (σ_2) 10.0.

As applied to $R_{0.12}$ in the volleyball illustration, it reads

$$.669 \left(\frac{2.5}{7.0}\right) \text{ service test} + .444 \left(\frac{2.5}{10.0}\right) \text{ volleying test} =$$

.240 service test + .111 volleying test.

Since weightings such as these for the sample problem would be time consuming to use, it is suggested that either one of two things be done:

1. Prepare multiplication tables for each set of weightings. For example, for test #1, if the range of scores extends from 40 to 7, multiply 7 × .240, then 8 × .240, etc., to 40 × .240.

OR

2. Compute the relationship between the weightings and substitute in the equation. For example,
.240 serving test + .111 volleying test would be changed to
2.2 serving test + 1.0 volleying test.

This computation is then simple enough to be done without paper and pencil or tables. The advantage over simple addition is that it keeps the scores on the two tests in proper proportion.

PROVIDE STANDARD SCORES

Raw scores are not very meaningful to either the teacher or the student. Therefore, it is considered an essential part of any project in which tests have been developed to provide the means for translating raw scores into standard scores.

The provision of norms is not listed as a step in the process of constructing tests as they cannot be prepared until an adequate, random and representative sample of the population has taken the tests.

SUMMARY

The procedure for constructing skill tests and test batteries is considerably longer and more laborious than the procedure for using established tests in connection with teaching. The labor involved in the development of new batteries or tests becomes profitable as it results in improved teaching aids and as these in turn help to place physical education on a firmer scientific basis.

Once an understanding of the procedures is gained, use can be made of labor saving devices, such as machines. Very few research workers do correlations, for example, by the method described herein. After the method is understood, machines can be used to substantially reduce the amount of labor involved. Test constructors who do not have the use of such mechanical aids may wish to avail themselves of the services of test agencies.

The process outlined in this chapter for the construction of skill tests and batteries applies to motor tests in general. The procedures differ in the content of the criteria and in the test variables but the methods are the same.

SELECTED REFERENCES

I. DISCUSSION OF METHODS

1. American Association for Health, Physical Education and Recreation: Research Methods Applied to Health, Physical Education and Recreation. Washington, D. C., 1949, Chapter XVI, or 1959 Edition, Chapter 8.

2. Peters, Charles C., and Wykes, Elizabeth Crossley: Simplified Methods for Computing Regression Coefficients and Partial and Multiple Correlations. Journal of Educational Research, 23: 383, 1931.

3. Walker, Helen M., and Lev, Joseph: Statistical Inference. New York, Henry Holt and Company, 1953.

II. EXAMPLES OF STUDIES ILLUSTRATING METHODS

1. Bassett, Gladys, Glassow, Ruth, and Locke, Mabel: Studies in Testing Volleyball Skills. Research Quarterly, 8: 60, 1937.

2. Brace, David K.: Validity of Football Achievement Tests as Measures of Motor Learning and a Partial

Basis for Selection of Players, Research Quarterly, 14: 372, 1943.

3. Cornish, Clayton: A Study of Measurement of Ability in Handball. Research Quarterly, 20: 215, 1949.

4. French, Esther, and Cooper, Bernice: Achievement Tests in Volleyball for High School Girls. Research Quarterly, 8: 150, 1937.

5. Friedel, Jean: Development of a Field Hockey Skill Test for High School Girls. Master's thesis, Illinois State Normal University, Normal. 1950. Microcards,* P E 289.

6. Lockhart, Aileene, and McPherson, Frances A.: The Development of a Test of Badminton Playing Ability. Research Quarterly, 20: 402, 1949.

7. Schmithals, Margaret, and French, Esther: Achievement Tests in Field Hockey for College Women. Research Quarterly, 11: 84, 1940.

8. Stalter, Evelyn, and French, Esther: A Study of Skill Tests in Badminton for College Women. Research Quarterly, 20: 257, 1949.

*Available in microcards from University of Oregon, Eugene.

Chapter V

CONSTRUCTION OF KNOWLEDGE TESTS

The acquisition of knowledge is recognized as one of the objectives of physical education but many teachers are not able to measure the extent to which this objective is being met. Some teachers, even on the college level, use tests which have been so poorly constructed that they serve very little purpose. Unless teachers know how to construct and to revise their own tests, pupils are handicapped because full use of this excellent tool in teaching cannot be made by teachers who are limited to the use of published tests or to poorly constructed homemade tests.

Relatively few knowledge tests have been published in our field. However, even if the number available were greatly increased, teachers would still need to know how to construct some of their own tests. The use of knowledge tests should not be limited to examinations given at the end of each course, as was indicated in Chapter I. It is unlikely that tests will be published for all uses or for all situations. The same test cannot be expected to serve a high school group and a college group, a beginners class and an advanced class, a group of slow learners and a superior group. In some situations, the time allotment will be longer than in others as for example in activity classes, some meeting daily and others but two times weekly. The selection of content varies; some teachers include more than others and emphasize different aspects or concepts. Teaching method also plays an important part in determining what should be tested and the same test will not serve all teachers adequately.

Distribution of Content

The first step in the construction of tests is to determine the use to be made of the examination. When a test is to be given as a final examination or for classification, it must be comprehensive. The course outline should be consulted, and if it is brief, the test constructor will need to develop it, listing all of the important concepts. In general, the larger number of questions should be devoted to the concepts that are considered important. Overweighting the examination with questions covering just one phase of instruction, as the rules of a sport, should be avoided. Following the course outline rather than the text or rule book will result not only in better distribution of items but in the desired elimination of textbook language.

The teacher who plans to use a ready-made test should consult the content distribution to see if it coincides with the emphases he has made in his course. An example of an attempt to distribute the number of questions according to content is found in a soccer knowledge test prepared for professional students. See Table XII.

Table XII.

Distribution of Questions According to Content

Soccer Knowledge	Number of Questions	Approximate Per cent
Analysis of individual techniques and form	3	5
Analysis of game situations and use of skills	8	13
General knowledge (history, selection, and care of equipment, safety precautions)	3	5
How to avoid fouling	3	5
Placement of passes and kicks for goal	2	4
Tactics and areas of play	22	37
Rules essential to intelligent play	15	25
Terminology	4	6
Total	60	100

The number of questions concerning each aspect of subject matter covered does not need to be in exact proportion to the amount of time devoted to teaching the content. Obviously, not all of the important concepts are equally difficult to master. The thing to be observed in planning the distribution of content is to include questions on all of the important points and to avoid having an undue proportion of the test concerned with trivial or relatively unimportant details. Essay type examinations as well as objective type tests may err in this respect unless the distribution of content is well thought out in advance. Because the number of questions that can be asked in an essay type examination is quite limited, the distribution of content in such a test is of utmost importance if the examination is to be a fair test of the student's knowledge.

Selection of Type of Item

After deciding the proportions and having gained some familiarity with content emphasis, the next step is to select the type of test exercise most appropriate to the content and to the purpose for which the test is being given. For example, if you wish to measure the student's ability to organize his thoughts and to express himself, you may prefer to use the essay type question. If, because of the large number of students to be tested or for other valid reasons, you have decided to prepare an examination that can be scored objectively, you still have to select the form and there are approximately fifty varieties. Four of the more commonly used types will be discussed and the use, rules for construction and scoring will be given for each type. Much that has been written on the construction of knowledge tests in such subject matter fields as history, English, and mathematics is applicable to tests in physical education. Assistance can be gained by consulting some of the texts to which reference is made in the bibliography for this chapter.

1. Multiple Choice

This type of an item consists of a statement, usually in the form of a direct question, followed by a number of responses from which the student is to select the answer. Some of these questions may require the students to differentiate between closely related points, several of which may be acceptable to some degree but some basis should exist for the superiority of one of the answers. Other questions of this same type (multiple choice) may have a number of responses only one of which is correct and all others

99

definitely incorrect. For an example of the latter type, in a test in a specified sport, you could ask what should be the official's decision when the ball is sent over the end line, last touched by a member of the attacking team. You could have a number of responses, only one of which is correct and all others definitely incorrect.

The question portion of the test exercise is known as the "stem" and the answer portions are referred to as responses, foils, distractors, alternatives. There is no particular advantage in having a fixed number of responses. The test may look neater if all the questions have five responses, but the test constructor would be forced to include some responses that would not function (be selected) and thus the test would contain superfluous material. If only three plausible responses can be contrived, then three are sufficient, but three is the minimum and seldom is there any advantage in having more than five. The chief disadvantage in including nonfunctional material in a test is that it wastes the student's time in having to read it and thus reduces the number of questions that can be asked in a given amount of time.

a. Uses

The multiple choice type of test item seems to fit the content of the majority of the subject matter in physical education and is preferred by the authors for the following reasons:

1. It can be adjusted to test for various depths of understanding.

2. It can be made completely objective in scoring and adapts easily to answer sheets. (See sample of answer sheet, page 483.)

3. It makes possible the detection of nonfunctional responses, thus facilitating the revision of questions for later use. (A nonfunctional response is one which is seldom, if ever, selected.)

4. It tests the student's ability to eliminate incorrect responses as well as to select the correct response directly.

5. It does not require correction for guessing.

6. It seems to have fewer disadvantages than the other commonly used forms: alternate response (true-false,

yes-no, etc.,), matching forms, and recall (completion, analogy, definitions).

b. Rules for construction

1. Use a short, simple, direct question statement for the stem. This is preferred to an incomplete sentence because the student knows from the outset what problem is being presented and does not have to reread the stem in connection with each response. Too, the use of a complete question avoids the use of such words as "a" or "an" immediately preceding the group of choices, which could serve as clues.

2. Avoid choices which are not plausible or which are too obvious.

3. Avoid having more than one correct response if the directions call for selecting the one correct answer. State in the directions that the one best response is to be selected for each question, that there may be more than one suitable response but that one response will be superior to all others.

4. Avoid answering one question with another.

5. Avoid unintentional clues, such as: placement of the correct answer in a certain pattern; word matching between the stem and the response; making the correct response consistently longer or shorter than the incorrect ones; the grammatical clue of a singular expression in the stem and plural ones in all but the correct response; and the grammatical clue of using an incomplete statement in the stem, ending in "a" or "an."

6. Avoid use of textbook language and of stereotyped phrases if the purpose is to test for ability to use information and for understanding rather than memorization. The occasional use of familiar or stereotyped phrases in an incorrect response to deliberately mislead the shallow thinker is sometimes defensible.

7. Avoid the negative approach whenever possible, particularly if the students being tested include many slow learners. A negative approach may be used when the test constructor can find many more correct responses than incorrect ones or when one best answer cannot be determined. When questions in the negative form are used, the negative portion of the stem should be underlined or capitalized so that the student will be sure to see it.

101

c. Scoring

Multiple choice questions can be scored by machine or by superimposing a homemade punched cardboard key directly on the answer sheet. The number of correct answers is the score. This can be quickly obtained by counting the errors as you mark them and then subtracting that number from the total number of items in the test.

d. Comments

It probably requires more ability to construct good multiple choice questions than it does to construct some of the other forms but it is a skill that can be acquired through practice. Students in tests and measurements courses should be given definite assignments such as the following:

1. Prepare a multiple choice item for a softball test which will test whether the student knows where basemen should play when anticipating a bunt.

2. Prepare a multiple choice item for a test in body mechanics using a negative approach in the stem and then revise it, testing the same information but using a positive approach.

Learning can also be accelerated by having students criticize the test questions constructed by classmates and placed on the board. They soon learn to detect common errors such as wordiness, lack of sufficient information, no one best answer, more than one correct answer, and grammatical errors. They will start asking the ever important questions, just what is this item intended to measure, and is it important that it be included.

In constructing multiple choice items, a variety of approaches may be used in the stem. For example, questions can start with such words as who, what, when, where, and which -- or they can start with a statement, describing the situation and giving all of the essential knowledge, followed by a second statement, asking the question. It is easy to fall into habitually using just one or two approaches in preparing the stem and then when they fail to fit a certain bit of content, to become discouraged and decide not to include it. If the content is important, try other approaches, starting with words such as in, if, to, does, and is, or the two sentence form. Ask yourself precisely what knowledge you are testing and then try to state the question as if you were asking someone else for information. Read test questions in published tests to gain ideas for additional approaches. Diagrams can also be used and will be discussed later.

2. Alternate Response

Test items or exercises falling within this category usually call for selecting one of two possible alternatives: True or false, yes or no, right or wrong. One of these variations, the true-false, was widely used when objective tests were in the infancy of their use. Probably the fact that it has been misused and at times poorly constructed is responsible for much of the resistance to all objective type knowledge tests. No one test can serve all purposes and certainly any poorly constructed test, regardless of its form, yields disappointing results.

Another variation of alternate response is the multiple responses or multiple true-false, where a statement is followed by three or more responses and the directions call for selecting all of the answers which are true or correct. There may be none; there may be any number of correct answers. At first glance, it appears similar to multiple choice but it is actually a set of related true-false items rather than a variant of multiple choice. Other names for the multiple responses form are as follows: plural responses, plural multiple answers, and plural choice.

a. Uses

The alternate response type of item can be used advantageously when large amounts of information must be covered and the content is such that there are only two possible responses. This form has the advantage of requiring less time to construct than the multiple choice form but it requires more care in construction than it frequently receives. If the test constructor habitually lifts sentences or headings from the text or rule book, students soon rely upon memorization. Ability to memorize is tested rather than understanding and the ability to make applications. It is more economical of paper and stencils than the multiple choice form.

b. Rules for Construction

1. Make the statements or questions brief and direct.

103

2. Avoid ambiguities (statements that are open to more than one interpretation, that have double or dubious meanings).

3. Avoid frequent use of "always" or "never" which should clue the student who is completely in doubt to guess "false."

4. Make original statements which call for understanding or which require the student to apply what he has been taught (or has read) to a new situation.

5. Have an approximately equal number of each alternative, with no regular pattern to the responses.

6. Make the directions clear regarding the scoring of omissions.

7. Be sure that the test is lengthy; a minimum of seventy-five questions is recommended.

c. Scoring

The scoring of alternate-response form of test exercises depends upon the test directions. If the student has been told not to guess, then errors should be penalized more than omissions. Customarily this is done by subtracting one point for each omission and two for each error from the total number of test items. Another way of arriving at the score is to subtract the total number of errors from the total number of correct responses, ignoring the number of omissions.

The disadvantage of having directed the students not to guess is that the reliability of the scores is reduced by the fact that the test is shortened in length by those students who prefer to omit a large proportion of the questions.

Some knowledge testing authorities maintain that it is better to tell students that all omissions will be scored the same as errors. This encourages them to respond to all questions and does not shorten the test or cause the scores to be dependent upon the student's judgment as to the advisability in each instance of guessing. Students frequently state that they didn't know the answer so they just took a guess. Usually these "guesses" are based on some information or hunch if the student has been exposed to the content being tested and it would seem preferable to measure how much he knows about all of the questions asked rather than having him respond only to those questions about which he is reasonably certain. It is true that guessing is encouraged by scoring omissions the same as errors, but this is not necessarily bad.

The scoring of multiple responses (or multiple true-false) is time consuming. Here an omission has to be scored as an error.

Correction for guessing does not seem to be worth the time that it takes in scoring papers and it is recommended that students be told that omissions will be counted as errors and that one point be deducted from the total number of items for each error and also for each omission, if any.

d. Additional Comments

Answer sheets are more economical if the examination extends over several pages. This permits the examination forms to be used again and saves much time in scoring, as well as adding to the accuracy in scoring. The answer sheet illustrated on page 483 can be adapted for either multiple choice or alternate response questions and can be scored with a superimposed key. If the student considers the statement to be true, he places an X in the first row of brackets; if false, in the second row of brackets.

The test constructor may want to give a test consisting of both multiple choice and alternate response forms, in which case he should group all of one type together. The directions may indicate, for example, that the first twenty-five questions are of the multiple choice type and questions twenty-six through seventy-five are of the true-false type. The same answer sheet can be used.

Every attempt should be made to use the form that best meets the objective of the examiner in giving the test, but it is not the form of test item alone that controls the results. The multiple choice form is favored over the alternate responses form. However, if the multiple choice questions are quite poor or too few in number and the alternate responses questions are good and you have about double the number, then the choice of the latter test might be defensible.

3. Recall

A third category of objective test forms is the recall, or "completion." One variant of this is sentence completion where the student must supply the missing word. Another form consists of a stimulus word or phrase, with a blank space provided for the student's answer.

Example: National physical education organization:

_____.

Still another is the short essay or listing.

Example, from a basketball test, is as follows:

What are the advantages of shifting zone defense over player-to-player defense? List four.

(1)

(2)

(3)

(4)

Sentence completion and the second form are both poor devices in that they tend to test for trivial information and may be unfairly scored. Unless the student can guess the exact phrase or word that the instructor had in mind, it is likely to be scored as an error. Hence, such tests have become known as guessing contests. The short essay or listing type of recall question is difficult to score. In the example given, the student may list four items but they may not be the four most important ones or he may make the mistake of combining two related items, in this case "advantages," under one number, leaving a space blank or filling it with an incorrect answer.

a. Uses

The recall question is better for instructional purposes than for testing purposes. Their use should be limited to identification of terms or for purely factual information. They could be used advantageously for anatomy and kinesiology quizzes, asking for information concerning insertions and origins of muscles, for example. Extensive use of this form encourages rote learning.

b. Rules for Construction

1. Be sure only one word or phrase can answer it correctly.

2. State questions in such a manner as to elicit brief answers.

3. Provide spaces of uniform length, long enough for the longest reply, to avoid unintentional clues.

4. Provide spaces for answers in or near a margin, to facilitate scoring.

c. Scoring

Recall questions should be scored according to the number of correct responses. They cannot be scored by machine or by use of a punched key.

4. Matching

This type of objective test has two commonly used forms, both consisting of two columns which must be paired or matched. One form has two columns of single words while the other has one column of phrases or explanations and one of words or names.

a. Uses

Matching forms may be used satisfactorily for the "who, when, and where" type of information, if properly constructed. They are obviously weak in measuring the ability to make applications and interpretations.

b. Rules for Construction

1. The right-hand column should contain the responses and should always have at least two more items than the left-hand column, to prevent answering the difficult ones on the basis of elimination alone.

2. The items in the responses column should be numbered or identified by letters. Place blank spaces for recording the number or letter of the matching item in front of the items in the left-hand column.

3. Avoid clues in grammatical form or in the use of proper names or in capitalization.

4. The content of each list should be homogeneous.

5. State in the directions whether items in the right-hand column may be used more than once.

6. Arrange the columns in sequence, alphabetically or numerically. This is not absolutely essential but sometimes is advantageous in avoiding clues.

Example of matching forms question:

_____ Constance Applebee   a. Baseball

_____ Matt Mann   b. Basketball

_____ Casey Stengel   c. Football

_____ Alonzo Stagg   d. Golf

_____ Eleanor Tennant   e. Hockey

                      f. Swimming

                      g. Tennis

c. Scoring

The score is the number of correct responses, not the number of entirely correct questions. Omissions are scored as errors.

SUPPLEMENTARY DEVICES

There are a number of devices that can be used to save lengthy descriptions. Among these are visual aids such as diagrams, charts, and symbols. A few are illustrated here and the ingenious person will doubtless be able to think of additional ones. Perhaps a word of warning should be inserted. Don't become so intrigued with the devices themselves that they are over used.

1. Diagrams

Diagrams should be used when questions involve spatial relations, or whenever they can clarify the situation. Sometimes they actually save space. The examination should be arranged so that all the questions making use of a certain diagram are placed on the same page with it; or the diagram may be placed on a separate sheet of paper having each diagram labeled with the corresponding question numbers.

The use of diagrams in connection with questions which involve flight of an object is illustrated with questions from a golf examination.

1. Which of the flights shown in the diagram most closely approximates that of the midiron?

   (1) a.
   (2) b.
   (3) c.
   (4) d.
   (5) e.

   Correct answer: (5)

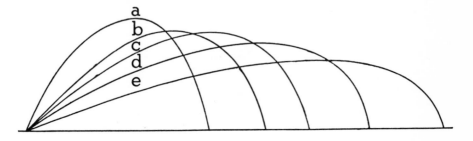

Figure 8.   Diagram of flight of ball with iron clubs.

2. To make a stroke with a flight similar to a, what should you do?

   (1) Stand farther from the ball than for a stroke made with a wooden club.

   (2) Check the follow-through in the direction you want the ball to go.

   (3) Take a stance with the ball nearer the rear foot than the front one.

   (4) Keep the face of the club closed.

   (5) Aim just above the center of the ball.

   Correct answer: (3)

   Sometimes a diagram can be used to save words in the test items as well as to save the time required by the student visualizing the situation. It has the added advantage of providing the player with a more natural situation. An example of such a diagram is taken from a basketball test for girls.

27. In the diagram for question 27, G6 has the ball out-of-bounds at the end line. The "small letter"

109

team is employing a shifting zone defense. If the
ball is passed from G6 to G5 to G4, what should f5
do?

(1) Move toward G5.

(2) Remain where she is.

(3) Move toward f4.

(4) Move closer to center of division line.

Correct answer: (3), depending on style of defense
taught.

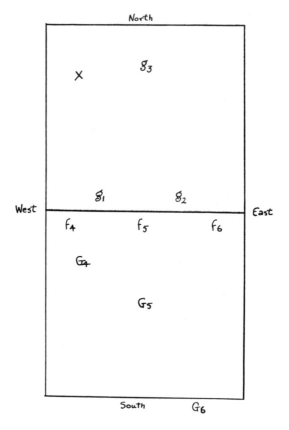

Figure 9. Basketball diagram.

28. If the ball is passed above the reach of g1 to a forward at the spot marked X, what should g2 do?

(1) Move toward the forward at spot X.

(2) Remain where she is.

(3) Move toward the northeast corner.

(4) Move toward g1.

Correct answer: (1), depending on style of defense taught.

2. Charts

In the illustrations below for bowling, note that the question precedes the chart. This enables the student to know what he is looking for and at.

Examples from a test on bowling:

22. What is the score at the end of the third frame in the following game?

Frame	1st Ball	2nd Ball
1	6	4
2	5	2
3	8	1

(1) 26.

(2) 31.

(3) 33.

(4) Correct answer not listed.

(5) Incomplete.

Correct answer: (2).

23. What is the score at the end of the third frame in this game?

Frame	1st Ball	2nd Ball
1	6	4
2	1	9
3	8	2

(1) 30.

(2) 31.

(3) 39.

(4) Correct answer not listed.

(5) Incomplete.

Correct Answer: (5).

24. At the end of the seventh frame the score was 100. What is the score at the end of the tenth frame?

Frame	1st Ball	2nd Ball
8	9	1
9	10	0
10	8	0

(1) 128.

(2) 138.

(3) 146.

(4) Correct answer not listed.

(5) Incomplete.

Correct answer: (3).

3. Symbols

Symbols can appear in the stem part of the question or in the foils. The test constructor should limit the use to those symbols that every one can be expected to know, unless purposely testing to see if they have this knowledge.

Examples from a test in rhythmical form and analysis:

19. How many beats has the primary rhythm of this measure?

♩ ♫ ♫ ♩

(1) 1.

(2) 2.

(3) 3.

(4) 4.

(5) 5.

Correct answer: (5).

20. How many steps are required to walk the secondary rhythm of the measure in question 19?

(1) 10.

(2) 6.

(3) 3.

(4) 4.

(5) 5.

Correct answer: (2)

21. Which note represents the unit of measurement for the pattern illustrated in question 19?

(1) ♪

(2) 𝅗𝅥

(3) 𝅝

(4) ♩

(5) ♫

Correct answer: (4).

22. What is the correct meter for the waltz?

(1) 2/4.

(2) 3/4.

(3) 6/8.

(4) 4/4.

(5) 5/4.

Correct answer: (2).

23. Which rhythmical pattern is syncopated?

(1) ♩ ♪ ♪

(2) ♫♩ ♫♩

(3) ♪ ♩ ♪

(4) 𝅗𝅥 ♩ ♫

Correct answer: (3).

Check List for Evaluating Items

After the items have been prepared, the use of the following check list* will prove helpful in evaluating them.

1. Form and Function:

(a) Exactly what is this item intended to measure?

(b) Is the intended purpose of the item acceptable? Is the inclusion of the item important? Does it test something significant?

(c) Is there any ambiguity in the item? Will the student recognize the purpose of the item? Can it be made more clear? Are there any qualifying phrases that might start the student to thinking along irrelevant lines?

(d) Does the item contain any unintentional clues to the correct response?

(e) Will authorities agree on the correct response? Are the responses which are intended to be wrong really less acceptable than the correct ones?

(f) In multiple choice items will any of the wrong responses appear more plausible than the correct answers to the best of the students to be tested? Is the item too difficult for the best students in the group?

(g) Is the item phrased as economically as possible? Is it straightforward and direct?

(h) Is the form of the item well adapted to its intended purpose? Would a diagram help?

(i) Would the rote learner have any undue advantage in responding to the item? Has textbook language been avoided?

Another method of evaluating questions before using them with a group is to have some other person read them critically. Rereading the questions yourself after the lapse of a few days is a good procedure.

For help in the technical problems involved in setting up the examination and administering it, see pages 116 to 118.

---

*Check list adapted from class notes, Improvement of the Written Exam..... tion, taught by Dr. E. F. Lindquist, University of Iowa.

2. Administration:

(a) Is the provision for the student's response as economical of his time as possible?

(b) Are the directions to the student as simple and understandable as they can be?

(c) Does the provision for the student's response provide for convenient, accurate, and economical scoring?

(d) Can the typographical arrangement of the items be improved?

(e) Is the spread of estimated difficulty of items adapted to the spread of ability in the group to be tested? (See page 122.)

(f) Are the time limits adequate?

(g) Are the questions placed in the test in an order progressing from easy to difficult? Will the slow student be prevented from spending an undue amount of time on items that are too difficult for him?

3. Validity:

(a) Are any important objectives or outcomes of instruction seriously neglected in the test as a whole?

(b) Is the emphasis on functional value and not on content objectives?

(c) Is there any unwarranted testing of isolated details or unimportant items of information, such as terminology or definitions?

(d) Are test situations suggestive of the actual situations in which the student may make use of what he has learned?

(e) Would this test be less satisfactory if it were used as an open book test? Are there a sufficient number of questions which require drawing of inferences and making of applications?

Obviously, these are rigid criteria and it is doubtful whether any test could meet all of them; but they are goals toward which the conscientious test constructor may strive. Some criteria may have to be sacrificed for the sake of others, for example, Administration. (a). The use of an answer sheet requires slightly more of the student's time than writing on the test form itself. An estimate has been made that the students can answer about 10 per cent fewer items when using an answer sheet than when writing directly on the test forms. This percentage is reduced when students become accustomed to using answer sheets. Administration, (a), then might be sacrificed somewhat for the sake of Administration, (c). Form and Function, (e), "Will the authorities agree on the correct response?" presents difficulties. Complete agreement on any complex mental ability is impossible to secure. Even in a field as objective as the correct usage of English, absolute agreement on the proper use of a comma cannot be found. The questions on rules and other factual material offer less opportunity for disagreement, which probably accounts for the tendency among constructors of knowledge tests to overweigh these items. Taking Form and Function (e) too seriously and attempting to secure 100 per cent agreement from a large number of authorities would probably materially lessen the discriminatory value of test items. In other words, the questions would be so easy that they would not discriminate between students of varying abilities. Consultation of the textbooks in physical education shows the wide variance in the opinion of authorities, particularly on strategy and on the performance of skills. The discrepancy of opinion occurs frequently in tennis and golf, fields in which professional players and those who write under their names tend to dominate the literature. Their mechanical analysis may sometimes be faulty.

Planning the Total Examination

The steps in constructing an examination have been described. They include planning the distribution of content, choosing the type of item that best fits the purpose and the content, preparing the items, making use of diagrams if needed, and then using a check list for evaluating items. A tally of prepared items according to content may now be needed to insure correct proportions. Questions which fail to meet the criteria set up in the check list will need to be rewritten or eliminated. At this point in the process it is helpful to have some other person or persons study and evaluate the questions.

Directions or instructions are needed. These can be placed directly on the testing form or can be written on a separate sheet if the set of directions can be used for more than one examination. See page 484 for a sample of the latter method. Instructions should include the mechanics, with important parts underlined and directions concerning guessing. Sample questions for each section should be included unless the students are familiar with the form. The sample question should be a simple one that all are sure to know. It should be clearly indicated that it is a sample. Example of a sample question from a multiple choice section:

0. Sample

How many players are there on a girls' basketball team?

(1) Eleven.
(2) Nine.
(3) Six
(4) Five.

The sample question should be filled in on the answer sheet, or checked on the test form itself, in compliance with the instructions.

Using a large variety of types or forms of test items in the same examination only confuses the student and wastes time and space, since instructions must be repeated. Nothing is gained by great variety. To change a question from one form to another is usually easy, provided the intended purpose of the item is clear. Example: a true-false question concerning the direction of applied force in swimming can easily be changed into a multiple choice question.

T F   The direction of the force that is applied with the arms in the crawl stroke should be toward the feet.

Change to:

In which direction should force be applied with the arms in the crawl stroke?

(1) In the direction in which the swimmer is moving.
(2) At right angles to the side of the body.
(3) Toward the feet.
(4) Toward the surface of the water.
(5) Diagonally across and under the face.

The examination now needs to be prepared for the typist. The test constructor should plan to construct the diagrams on the stencils himself since most typists are not familiar with the details and spatial relations of the material. The form to be used in placing the materials on the page must be decided. The columnar form, which splits the page in half lengthwise, is more economical of space than the continuous form when items are short. The columnar form may be used only when answer sheets are used; otherwise scoring is too difficult. The questions should be arranged in order of estimated difficulty, ranking from easy to hard. The copy given to the typist should be readable and, as nearly as possible, in the exact form wanted. Suggestions:

1. Provide a space for the student's name and other essential data, either on answer sheets or on test forms if answer sheets are not used.

2. Indicate the amount of space to be left for diagrams.

3. Ask that the questions be arranged so that the diagrams can appear on the same page with the questions that refer to them.

4. Ask that no questions be split; all of the items should appear on the same page with the stem.

5. When abbreviations or symbols are used, ask that they be repeated at the top of each page.

6. Ask to proofread the stencils before the examination is mimeographed.

EVALUATION OF KNOWLEDGE TESTS

The steps in constructing a knowledge test that have been discussed up to this point include the following:

1. Determination of the use to be made of the test.

2. Consultation of the course (or unit) outline and the listing of the important concepts that the student should have gained.

3. Development of a plan to distribute the number of questions somewhat in proportion to the importance given to each phase of instruction or content.

4. Selection of type of item which is most appropriate to the content and most likely to give the desired results according to the choice made in step one.

5. Preparation of items, the most time-consuming step.

6. Application of check list for evaluating items.

7. Planning the total examination.

8. Preparation of copy for the typist. The next step is obvious, the administration of the examination. Since the manner in which this is done affects the value of the test, consult the section on administration of knowledge tests in Chapter XIV.

JUDGING THE QUALITY OF THE TEST

The teacher who has devoted time and thought in constructing a knowledge test worthy of the name will want to retain it for future use and will be interested in knowing how well the examination functioned.

The following criteria may be used in determining subjectively a general estimate of the worth of the examination in its entirety:

1. Did it provide a wide range of scores, with no undue massing of scores at any one point?

2. Does the rank order of scores coincide roughly with a previous estimate of the abilities of the individuals within the group?

3. Was·the examination of the right length? Would students have had time to answer more questions? Was it so long that more than 10% of the students did not complete it?

4. Did the discussion of papers reveal any ambiguities or lack of clarity in the questions or directions?

5. Did the examination reveal areas of content which need no further instruction? Did it indicate inadequate understanding of certain phases of subject matter?

Ebel[5] has listed ten criteria for judging the quality of a classroom test.

1. Is the test fair to the course, in view of the things the course is supposed to teach?

2. Is the test fair to the students, in view of the instruction given them?

3. Is the test administered under conditions which give each student a good and equal chance to demonstrate his achievements?

4. Does the test emphasize important, long run achievements more than incidental, quickly forgotten information?

5. Are the questions individually effective in distinguishing between good and poor students?

6. Is the test of appropriate difficulty, neither too hard nor too easy?

7. Does the test as a whole distinguish clearly between students at different levels of ability?

8. Are the scores reasonably reliable, so that they would agree closely with those from another equivalent test?

9. Are the scores reasonably accurate, so that they closely approximate the students' true scores?

10. Is the length of the test appropriate for the time available -- long enough to give reliable scores but short enough so most students have time to attempt all items?

In discussing fairness to the course, Ebel[5] comments that any course is expected to make some permanent changes in the students who take it -- to leave them with new knowledge and understanding, improved and extended abilities, new attitudes, ideals and interests. These are long range goals which often are neglected when tests are constructed. Frequently the student is judged by his memory of what went on from day to day in the class or what he read in preparation.

As to fairness to students, instructors are in the best position to judge this. On the other hand, student comments on a test's fairness are often worth securing and considering. A student may call attention to ambiguity in a question, to the omission of questions on matters which were stressed, or to the presence of questions dealing with material not covered in the class.

As to the conditions of administration, again, the instructor who administered the examination is in position to answer this but student comments can be helpful. Were all examinees on an equal footing so far as prior knowledge of the examination was concerned? Did they have enough prior information to be able to prepare properly? Was cheating prevented?

Some type of test analysis is needed in order to apply the remainder of the criteria listed by Ebel. Several institutions of higher education now offer this service and teachers are invited to make use of it. Usually, all they need to do is to mail in the answer sheets and request an item analysis. Test analysis does not in itself improve a test but it furnishes valuable information to the teacher to use in improving his tests.

All teachers should have the experience of analyzing at least one test themselves. This experience is an aid to understanding not only the information accompanying published or standardized tests but the information supplied by test agencies, should they have such service available. In revising one's own test based upon an item analysis, one is able not only to improve the test but also to detect where improvements can be made in instruction.

Item Analysis

Item analysis is a process of determining the merits of the individual questions which constitute the examination. The purpose is to select the best questions and discard or rewrite the poor ones. If the test has not been carefully constructed and the teacher realizes that the scores do not reflect the true abilities of the students, nothing much can be gained by making an item analysis. Limit item analysis to tests which have been well constructed and which meet the first three criteria listed on page 120. The total scores must reflect what is known of the students' ability or the validity (index of discrimination) revealed in the analysis for the individual questions will be misleading. This will become clearer when the method of determining the index of discrimination is explained.

1. Difficulty Rating and Functioning of Responses

The teacher first wants to know how difficult each question proved to be for the group. If this information can be obtained before going over the examination with the students in class, sometimes time can be saved as only those questions on which errors were made need be discussed. The percentage answering the question correctly is the difficulty rating. This is obtained by dividing the number of correct responses by the number who took the test. Thus, a question with a difficulty rating of 40 is more difficult than a test with a difficulty rating of 50. In other words, the lower the rating the more difficult the question. Items which are too difficult or too easy are likely to have low discriminating power. In other words, they do not serve to help discriminate between various levels of ability in the class. Teachers have to decide for themselves what limits they will use, but they probably should not retain many questions with a difficulty rating above 90 (too easy) or below 10 (too hard).

The formula for difficulty rating is as follows:

$$D.R. = \frac{R}{N}$$

When R represents the total number of persons answering correctly (rights) and N represents the total number taking the test.

For example, if 50 persons took the test, the difficulty ratings for the first five questions might read as follows:

Question #	# R	D.R.
1	25	50%
2	40	80%
3	41	82%
4	49	98%
5	1	2%

Question 4 is too easy and question 5 too difficult, if the 90 to 10 limits are used. For most purposes, it is desirable to have a fairly wide range of difficulty ratings between the limits of 90 and 10, with more questions concentrated around 50%. A test which has many very easy items gives a concentration of cases on the higher scores and works to the disadvantage of the superior students, and to

the teacher, who must distinguish between several making
the same score. In the same way, an examination which is
too difficult will provide a massing of low scores and
makes it impossible for the poor students to be distinguished from those who are a little better.

The teacher will want to know how the responses functioned in each question. Did any of the students select
that foil which he thought of in the middle of the night?
If not, then it did not function. Responses which were not
selected by any of the students taking the test should be
dropped, providing the total to whom the test has been
given is sufficient in size to be considered an adequate
sampling of student abilities in general. It may be advisable to set a limit or minimum, such as 3 per cent, and
drop from further use any response not selected by at least
3 per cent of the total number of persons taking the test.
The limits should be determined according to the uses to be
made of the test. Accordingly, in the table below, data
for three different percentage minimums are provided.

Table XIII

Percentage Minimums for Functioning of Items					
Table for 3%		Table for 4%		Table for 5%	
N	Minimum	N	Minimum	N	Minimum
Below 50	1	Below 38	1	Below 30	1
50 - 83	2	38 - 62	2	30 - 49	2
84 - 116	3	63 - 87	3	50 - 69	3
117 - 150	4	88 - 112	4	70 - 89	4
151 - 183	5	113 - 137	5	90 - 109	5
		138 - 162	6	110 - 129	6
		163 - 187	7	130 - 149	7
		188 - 212	8	150 - 169	8
Note: N = total number				170 - 189	9
of test papers being				190 - 209	10
used in the analysis.					

An example of the difficulty rating and functioning of responses follows, taken from a soccer test. A negative

123

approach is used which may account for some of the difficulty students encountered in answering it.

The following statements concern trapping the ball with
the sole of the foot. Which one is <u>false</u>?

(1) Keep your eyes on the ball rather than on the opponent.

(2) Use this trap for balls that are rolling slowly on
smooth ground.

(3) Put your weight on the foot which is over the ball,
clamping the ball between the foot and the ground.

(4) Place the middle of the sole on the ball, lowering
the heel slightly.

(5) Get your body in line with the oncoming ball, so
that you face it squarely as it approaches.

Correct answer: (3), since it is a false statement and
therefore the correct response. Seventeen of the 48 students taking the test selected the correct answer so the
question had a difficulty rating of 35%, obtained by dividing 17 by 48. Four of the 48 chose foil one, an adequate
number on any of the percentage levels listed in the chart.
Eight chose response two; twelve part four, while four selected response five. Three of the 48 omitted the question.
Therefore, regardless which of the percentage minimums
listed in the chart were used, all five responses would be
retained.

2. Validity

Validity is the prime consideration in test construction. Actually, there are two types of validity to be considered in knowledge testing but the first type, termed
curricular validity, is judged more or less subjectively
and is not the type with which the item analysis is concerned. Curricular validity uses the opinion of the teacher
or perhaps a committee of teachers as to the content and
particularly the importance of the respective questions.
This has definite merit as a step in the development of the
test as was explained earlier. A check list was provided
on pages 98 to 99 for this purpose. The type of validity
that is measured in an item analysis is the power of each
item (or question) to discriminate between students of high

and low levels of general achievement in the subject matter involved. A question is said to have perfect discriminating power when every student who answers the question correctly ranks higher in the scale than all students who answer it incorrectly. The scale referred to here is the rank order of students according to total scores made on the examination. A question in which more students of low ability succeed than do students of high ability may be said to have minus discriminating power and is obviously a very poor question. Between the extremes of perfect and minus discriminating powers, questions of all degrees of discrimination are found. An inspection of the tabulation sheet for item analysis of each question will give a vivid picture or estimate of how well the questions discriminate between various levels of ability, as well as how the various items functioned.

A single quantitative measure can be computed for each item which makes comparison possible. Such a measure is referred to as the index of discrimination. Various methods for obtaining this index figure have been developed and have had extensive study. Every method has its proponents. Long and Sandiford,[16] discussing the problem of selecting an index of validity, stated that the better indices differ so little in effectiveness that the selection might justifiably be made on the basis of ease of computation. Two such methods will be described here to provide some choice.

3. Flanagan Method

First, the papers are scored, with the total number of questions answered correctly being recorded on the answer sheet. If answer sheets similar to those shown on page 483 are used, the score will be recorded in the upper right-hand corner of each answer sheet. If the key is punched with a hole where the answer should appear and is superimposed on the answer sheet, and the errors are marked by placing a colored dot wherever there is an empty space appearing through the key, the work is facilitated.

Next, the answer sheets are arranged in order according to total scores. Then, the papers to be used in the analysis are determined. According to the Flanagan method, two groups of papers are selected, usually the 27 per cent making the highest scores and the 27 per cent making the lowest scores, out of the total number taking the examination.

These are known as the "high" and "low" groups. The percentage may be slightly more or less than 27. From the standpoint of economy of time involved in later computations, it is desirable to use 25, 33, 50, or 100 cases in each group. Choice would be made of one of these numbers if it is near 27 per cent of the total group, rather than some intermediate number.

There is disagreement concerning the minimum number of papers needed before an analysis should be made. If you have 100, then use 25 "highs" rather than 27. To accumulate a sizeable number, either the same test will have to have been given to several sections or the analysis will have to be postponed until a sufficient amount of data has accumulated. In large schools with many sections, the only problem is deciding the maximum number to use as it is wasteful of time to use as many as several thousand cases. If confronted with that amount of data, it would be well to limit the analysis to data from classes selected randomly. There are definite advantages to having the item analysis done on classes taught by the same teacher or at least in classes where the instructional methods have been similar.

Next, tabulation sheets should be prepared. See Figure 10 on page 127 for a sheet prepared to accommodate data for ten questions. These may be mimeographed or the six or seven sheets necessary for an entire examination may be prepared simultaneously by using carbon paper.

The question numbers should then be filled in on the tabulation sheets, using the column to the left, headed "Q." If the examination being analyzed is a multiple choice form, some of the questions will have fewer than five foils. The superfluous squares or cells on the tabulation sheet should be crossed out. A diagonal line or an X will suffice. Information regarding the number of foils for each question is provided on the test itself. Then, the cell which corresponds with the correct answer for each question should be outlined. See sample, Figure 11.

All of the high papers should be recorded first, using the upper half of each cell. In the sample, the record is shown for the first three questions in an item analysis made with twenty-five papers in each group. The recording is facilitated by two persons working together, one reading and the other recording. The record is made as follows: Answer sheet of Student A reads 1-3, 2-1, 3-4, etc., meaning

KNOWLEDGE TEST TABULATION

Name of Test

Q	1	2	3	4	5	Omit	D.R.	I.D.	Rev.

Figure 10. Knowledge test tabulation sheet.

Q.	1	2	3	4	5	Omit	D.R.	I.D	Rev.
1	THN	THN I	⟨THN THN THN / THN IIII⟩ / THN I		THN III		60	75	
2	⟨THN THN THN THN / THN THN II⟩	II / (II	THN	I / (II	II		64	35	
3		THN THN II / THN THN THN / IIII		THN THN III / THN I	✕		38	30	✓

Figure 11. Sample tabulation.

that on question 1, Student A selected foil 3, on question
2, he selected foil 1, and on question 3, foil 4. A's entire sheet is recorded. Then, B's, etc., until the entire
high group has been recorded. Before proceeding in a similar manner with the "lows," it is well to check that you
have twenty-five tallies for each question. This serves as
a partial check on accuracy but does not reveal errors made
by the reader or errors made by the recorder in placing the
tally mark in an incorrect cell. Great care is needed.

The low papers should be recorded in a similar manner
except that the tally marks are made with a colored pencil
and should be placed in the bottom half of each cell. Some
persons prefer to draw a pencil line between the tallies
recorded for each group.

After the data are recorded, difficulty ratings are
computed by adding all of the tallies in the correct cell
and dividing by the total number of papers. For the sample
tabulation, the total number of papers was 50. Twenty-four
of the high group and six of the low group answered question 1 correctly; the difficulty rating is $\frac{24 + 6}{50} = 60$.

This is recorded in the column headed D.R., or difficulty
rating. For this test, the difficulty rating limits were
set as between 90 and 10. Any question with a difficulty
rating above 90 or below 10 should be checked in the column
to the far right, headed Rev. or revise. The cells which
are empty represent the nonfunctioning foils and stand out
clearly on the page. If there are fewer than three functioning choices in a multiple choice test, the question

128

should be revised. This was true for question number three, which had only four foils. Note that the cell for foil 5 has been crossed out. Also note that question one had one nonfunctioning foil, number four, but was not checked for a complete revision.

In computing the index of discrimination, two steps are necessary. First, compute the percentage of the "highs" who answered the item correctly and the percentage of "lows" who answered it correctly. This can be done mentally if the number of cases in each group is 25. 33, 50, or 100. For example, in the sample, there are twenty-five cases in each extreme. Therefore, each case represents 4 per cent of the group. Question 1 was answered correctly by twenty-four or 96 per cent of the "highs" and by six or 24 per cent of the "lows."

The final step in the calculation is to translate the percentages who answered the question correctly into a single index of discrimination figure. This is done by means of Table XIV. The proportions of the "high" group are found on the horizontal axis of the table (across the top); figures may be located by reading from left to right. The low group is on the vertical axis with numbers in the left-hand margin, reading downward. Question 1 had 96 per cent of the "highs" correct. Locate this column on Table XIV (third column from the right-hand side). 24 per cent of the "lows" succeeded on Question 1. Locate this in the left-hand margin, the thirteenth row down. The index is found at the point where the designated column and row intersect. The same procedure is followed for the next question. Because the table is set up in step intervals of two to save space, it is sometimes necessary to obtain the index by interpolation.

Questions which do not discriminate are marked for discard or revision. The point at which items are retained or discarded is located according to how critical one wishes to be and the significance that is to be placed on test scores in the future use of the examination. As a general rule, it might be well to retain all items with an index of 20 or above if they are satisfactory with respect to difficulty level and have an adequate number of choices remaining after the nonfunctioning foils have been removed. Those with an index below 15 might as well be discarded. Those with indices of 15 to 20 might be retained if their difficulty level is suitable and in the opinion of the instructor there are no other items of known worth available to replace them in the content they represent.

Some persons prefer to make this decision as to the cutting point in size of the index of discrimination by means of proportions within the entire test. For example, the Test Analysis Report Form of the University Examinations Service at the State University of Iowa, indicates that they consider an item to be high in discrimination if .41 and up. They set as a standard that more than 25 per cent should be high. They consider .21 to .40 to be moderate and that more than one-fourth of the total number of questions should fall in that range. They list as low .01 to .20 and 15 per cent as standard. For questions with zero or negative discrimination, less than 5 per cent is considered as being standard, according to their report form.

4. Newer Method

A variation of the Flanagan technique is now being used by some of the testing services and appears to have some advantages. It avoids the transfer into percentage figures, an operation which is somewhat time consuming if the number in each group (highs, lows) is some figure between the convenient four: 25, 33, 50, 100. The formula is as follows:

$$I.D. = \frac{\#R_H - \#R_L}{N}$$

When $\#R_H$ is the number of cases correct in highs and $\#R_L$ is the number of cases correct in the lows and when N is the number of cases in one extreme (N = 27%).

For example, if there were fifty in each extreme and all the higher groups answered the question correctly and none of the lower group, it would be

$$I.D. = \frac{50 - 0}{50} = 1.0$$

Computing the index of discrimination for question 1 in the sample tabulation,

$$I.D. = \frac{24 - 6}{25} = 72$$

as compared to 75 when percentages were computed and the Flanagan table used. For question 2, the I.D. by the newer

method is 32 as compared to 35 when percentages were computed and the Flanagan table used. Likewise, for question 3, 28 as compared to 30.

The two methods described above yield a measure of the validity of each individual item or question in the test. The statistical validity of a classroom test in its entirety cannot ordinarily be determined. One would need an external criterion of achievement that is a better measure than the test scores themselves and this is seldom available.

5. Reliability

Mention should be made of reliability since it plays such an important role in evaluating skill tests. It plays a lesser role in the evaluation of knowledge tests but this is not to say that it is of less importance that a knowledge test be reliable. According to Ebel,[5] "The reliability of a knowledge test depends upon how sharply the items discriminate between good and poor students, how many items there are, how similar the items are with respect to the ability measured, and how much the students differ from one another in the ability measured. Thus it is easier to get a high reliability of scores in one subject than in another, and with one group of students than with another. The other two factors of reliability, quality and the number of items, are under the instructor's control. If the coefficient is too low it can almost always be raised by improving the items used, or adding more items, or both."

In sixteen carefully constructed tests[8] designed to meet the criteria set up in Lindquist's Check List for Evaluating Items, eleven had reliabilities above .80 with five exceeding .85; none fell below .70. The average number of questions was 53. The reliability coefficients were obtained by the correlation of scores for each subject on the odd numbered questions with the correlation of scores for each subject on the even numbered questions, corrected by the application of the Spearman-Brown formula. See pages 86 to 88 for a discussion of this technique.

When these same tests were reduced to shorter forms averaging twenty-five questions in length and rescored using the same answer sheets as previously (the students did not repeat the tests; new keys were punched), ten of the sixteen tests had lowered reliabilities in the short forms.

Gulliksen[10] has pointed out that reliability can be raised by including items with high intercorrelations and all on the same difficulty level, preferably 50 per cent. It seems to your authors that the test constructor need have little concern with reliability if care is taken to develop a test which contains items that discriminate well between the upper and lower ability groups and is sufficiently long. The number of items (questions) needed is related to the type of question form used with 50 being recommended as the minimum for multiple choice tests and 75 for alternate responses.

6. Test Analysis Report Form

A form similar to that provided on the following page is useful to the instructor in gaining an overall look at the test once it has been analyzed. The standards are adapted from a number of sources.

Ebel[5] has stated that generally the average score on an objective test should be slightly higher than half the maximum possible score. For the test reported on the Test Analysis Report, this would have been 32 (31.5 rounded). The mean score obtained of 43 indicates that this test was a bit too easy for the group to which it was administered.

Ordinarily, the larger the standard deviation, the better the test. A test that is too hard, too easy, or composed of too many items lacking in discriminating power, yields scores having less spread (smaller standard deviation).

Statistical evidence of the value of a test can be misleading, if the test does not fit your course or if the group on which the data were gathered varies decidedly from your group. Beware of judging the value of a published test by the reliability report. It is possible to obtain a high coefficient of correlation between two forms of the same test even though both forms may be poor. When the reliability of a single form of a test is computed by the odd-even method, the correlation coefficient expresses the degree to which the more difficult questions have been distributed by chance to odd- and even-numbered questions. Since the chances for an equal distribution are better with longer examinations, the length of the test largely determines the reliability.

TEST ANALYSIS REPORT

Test Title: Badminton Knowledge Test for Major Students

Group Tested: Major Students   N = 117   Date:

Time Limit: 50 minutes   Number of Questions:

Characteristics

I. Difficulty

D.R.'s	Standard Value	Obtained f	%	Rating
90 - 100	5% or less	5	7.4	Too many
10 - 89	90% or more	57	90.4	O.K.
0 - 9	5% or less	1	1.5	O.K.

II. Discrimination

A. Item

1. High (.41 and up)	more than 25%	19	30	O.K.
2. Moderate (.21 to .40)	more than 25%	29	46	Good
3. Low (.01 to .20)	more than 15%	15	23	Too many
4. Zero or negative	less than 5%	0	0	O.K.

B. Score

1. Mean (a)*	40	43		O.K.
2. Standard deviation(b)**	8	7.92		O.K.

III. Time Limitation

A. Per cent of Completed
   Papers   more than 90%   112   96   Good

Teachers should learn not only to construct tests for
use with their own classes but to analyze their carefully
constructed tests. It is only through these procedures
that they can be assured of having tests which are highly
valid for use in their own classes.

SELECTED REFERENCES

1. American Association for Health, Physical Education,
   and Recreation: Research Methods Applied to Health,
   Physical Education and Recreation. Washington, D. C.,
   1952, Chapter 16.

---

*(a) Midpoint of range between highest possible score and the expected
      chance score.
**(b) One sixth of the range between highest possible score and expected
       chance score.

135

2. Adkins, Dorothy C.: Construction and Analysis of Achievement Tests. Washington, D.C., U.S. Government Printing Office, 1947.

3. Brogden, Hubert: Variations in Test Validity with Variations in the Distribution of Item Difficulties, Number of Items, and Degree of Their Intercorrelation. Psychometrika, 11: 197, 1946.

4. Broer, Marion, and Miller, Donna Mae: Achievement Tests for Beginning and Intermediate Tennis. Research Quarterly, 21: 303-313, 1950.

5. Ebel, Robert L.: How to Judge the Quality of a Classroom Test. The Examinations Service of the State University of Iowa, Technical Bulletin No. 7, January 1954.

6. Fox, Katherine: Beginning Badminton Written Examination. Research Quarterly, 24: 135-146, 1953.

7. Flanagan, John C.: General Considerations in the Selection of Test Items and a Short Method of Estimating the Product-Moment Coefficient from Data at the Tails of the Distribution. Journal of Educational Psychology, 30: 674, 1939.

8. French, Esther: The Construction of Knowledge Tests in Selected Professional Courses in Physical Education. Research Quarterly, 14: 406-424, 1943.

9. *Goll, Lillian M.: Construction of Badminton and Swimming Knowledge Tests for High School Girls. Unpublished master's thesis, Illinois State Normal University, Normal, Illinois, 1956. Microcards P.E. 292.

10. Gulliksen, Harold: Relation of Item Difficulty and Inter-Item Correlation to Test Variance and Reliability. Psychometrika, 10: 79, 1945.

11. Hawkes, Herbert E., Lindquist, E.F., and Mann, C.R.: Construction and Use of Achievement Examinations. Boston, Houghton Mifflin Company, 1936.

12. Hennis, Gail M.: Construction of Knowledge Tests in Selected Physical Education Activities for College Women. Research Quarterly, 27: 301-309, 1956.

---

*Also available on microcards from University of Oregon, Eugene.

13. Kelly, Ellen Davis, and Brown, Jane E.: The Construction of a Field Hockey Test for Women Physical Education Majors. Research Quarterly, 23: 233-239, 1952.

14. Langston, Dewey F.: Standardization of a Volleyball Knowledge Test for College Men Physical Education Majors. Research Quarterly, 26: 60-68, 1955.

15. Lindquist, E. F. (Editor): Educational Measurement. Washington, D. C., American Council on Education, 1951.

16. Long, John A., and Sandiford, Peter: Validity of Test Items. Bulletin of Department of Educational Research, University of Toronto, 3: 1935, p. 118.

17. Miller, Wilma K.: Achievement Levels in Tennis Knowledge and Skill for Women Physical Education Major Students. Research Quarterly, 24: 81-90, 1953.

18. Mosier, Charles I., Myers, M. Claire, and Price, Helen G.: Suggestions for the Construction of Multiple Choice Test Items. Educational and Psychological Measurement, 5: #3, 261, 1945.

19. Mosier, Charles I., and Price, Helen G.: Arrangement of Choices in Multiple Choice Questions and a Scheme for Randomizing Choices. Educational and Psychological Measurement, 5: #4, 379, 1945.

20. Phillips, Marjorie: Standardization of a Badminton Knowledge Test for College Women. Research Quarterly, 17: 48-63, 1946.

21. Ross, C. C., and Stanely, Julian C.: Measurement in Today's Schools, 3rd ed. Englewood Cliffs, New Jersey, Prentice-Hall, Inc., 1954.

22. Scott, M. Gladys: Achievement Examinations for Elementary and Intermediate Swimming Classes. Research Quarterly, 11: 100-111, 1940.

23. Scott, M. Gladys: Achievement Examinations for Elementary and Intermediate Tennis Classes. Research Quarterly, 12: 40- , 1941.

24. Scott, M. Gladys: Achievement Examinations in Badminton. Research Quarterly, 12: 242-253, 1941.

25. Waglow, I. F., and Stephens, Fay: A Softball Knowledge Test. Research Quarterly, 26: 234-243, 1955.

26. Waglow, I. F., and Rehling, C. H.: A Golf Knowledge Test. Research Quarterly, 24: 463-470, 1953.

Chapter VI

SPORTS SKILL TESTS

The measurement of sports skills has become an integral part of a well-conducted program. Teachers are interested in determining the skill abilities of each student in order to place students into groups of like ability and thus facilitate teaching. They are also concerned with discovering how much skill improvement has taken place, not only to serve as a partial basis for grading but also to evaluate the effectiveness of their instructional methods. Skill tests are used to assist the student in analyzing his own abilities. They also serve to motivate students to put forth greater effort and to take advantage of opportunities for additional practice and instruction.

Skill tests have been in use for a considerable length of time but many of the early tests were of dubious quality. Their reliability and validity were not known nor was the extent to which they duplicated one another known. Many of the present day tests have weaknesses; some, for example, appear to be measuring general motor ability to too great an extent, rather than ability in the activity itself.[37]

It is not the purpose of the authors to duplicate the work of other writers in presenting a review of skill test studies. The reports of many of these studies are not readily available to teachers, being scattered in the literature or in unpublished form. For inclusion in this chapter, tests which have proved valuable in a number of teaching situations have been selected. They are the tests which also come the nearest to meeting the criteria for effective tests listed in Chapter II. Enough information is supplied concerning each test to make it usable. Tentative standards for many of the tests are included as well as a description of the group or groups providing the test score data. Statistically derived evidence of the worth of each test is presented. For interpretation of such information, see Chapters II, III, and IV.

For some sports activities, no tests are included. Either there were no objective measures available or those available failed to meet a majority of the criteria for effective tests. For many sports activities, only a few of the skills involved in the sport have suitable tests. The tests included here may need to be supplemented with ratings (see Chapter X), performance analysis charts (see Chapter XI) and achievement progressions (Chapter XI). The selected references presented at the end of this chapter are provided for those persons looking for more information.

ARCHERY

In the target shooting form, archery is a test in itself. When the Columbia Round is used as a measure of achievement in archery, Hyde[26] has found that the scores at 40 yards are the best measure of the ability of beginners and the scores made at 50 yards are the best measure of the ability of advanced archers.

Equipment:

1. Perfectly matched arrows and standard 48-inch targets, so placed that the center of the gold is 4 feet from the ground.

2. Field markings
Three lines are marked parallel to the target line at distances of 50, 40, and 30 yards.

Test:

Twenty-four arrows are shot from 50 yards distance, twenty-four from 40 yards distance, and twenty-four from 30 yards distance. The arrows should be shot in ends of six arrows each, one practice end only being allowed at each distance. The entire round need not be completed on the same day; however, at least one distance should be completed at each session.

Scoring:

The target values are: gold, 9; red, 7; blue, 5; black, 3; white, 1; outside the white or missing the target, 0. An arrow cutting two colors counts as having hit the inner one; an arrow rebounding from or passing through the scoring face of the target counts as one hit and scores 5 points.

Scales:

See Table XV. The scores in this table are sigma values; 0 in the sigma table is 5 sigma deviations below the mean and the 100 in the sigma table is 5 sigmas above the average. These scales were constructed on data from twenty-seven colleges in sixteen states and include over 1,400 scores.

TABLE XV.

ACHIEVEMENT SCALES IN ARCHERY FOR WOMEN*

SCALE	FIRST COLUMBIA TOTAL SCORE (TARGET SCORE)	FINAL COLUMBIA RECORD (TARGET SCORE)			
		TOTAL SCORE	50 YARDS	40 YARDS	30 YARDS
100	436	466	150	176	194
99	430	460	148	174	192
98	424	455	146	171	190
97	418	449	143	169	187
96	412	443	141	167	185
95	406	438	139	164	183
94	400	432	137	162	181
93	394	426	135	160	179
92	388	420	132	157	176
91	382	415	130	155	174
90	376	409	128	153	172
89	370	403	126	150	170
88	364	398	124	148	168
87	358	392	121	146	165
86	352	386	119	143	163
85	346	381	117	141	161
84	340	375	115	139	159
83	334	369	113	136	157
82	328	363	110	134	154
81	322	358	108	132	152
80	316	352	106	129	150
79	310	346	104	127	148
78	304	341	102	125	146
77	298	335	99	122	143
76	292	329	97	120	141

141

Table XV. (Cont.)

SCALE	FIRST COLUMBIA TOTAL SCORE (TARGET SCORE)	FINAL COLUMBIA RECORD (TARGET SCORE)			
		TOTAL SCORE	50 YARDS	40 YARDS	30 YARDS
75	286	324	95	118	139
74	280	318	93	115	137
73	274	312	91	113	135
72	268	306	88	111	132
71	262	301	86	108	130
70	256	295	84	106	128
69	250	289	82	104	126
68	244	284	80	101	124
67	238	278	77	99	121
66	232	272	75	97	119
65	226	267	73	94	117
64	220	261	71	92	115
63	214	255	69	90	113
62	208	249	66	87	110
61	202	244	64	85	108
60	196	238	62	83	106
59	190	232	60	80	104
58	184	227	58	78	102
57	178	221	55	76	99
56	172	215	53	73	97
55	166	210	51	71	95
54	160	204	49	69	93
53	154	198	47	66	91
52	148	192	44	64	88
51	142	187	42	62	86
50	136	181	40	59	84
49	133	178	39	58	82
48	131	174		57	80
47	128	171	38	56	79
46	125	167	37	55	77
45	122	164	36	53	75
44	120	160	35	52	74
43	117	157		51	72
42	114	153	34	50	70
41	111	150	33	49	69
40	109	146	32	47	67
39	106	143	31	46	65
38	103	139		45	64
37	100	136	30	44	62
36	98	132	29	43	60

Table XV. (Cont.)

SCALE	FIRST COLUMBIA TOTAL SCORE (TARGET SCORE)	FINAL COLUMBIA RECORD (TARGET SCORE)			
		TOTAL SCORE	50 YARDS	40 YARDS	30 YARDS
35	95	129	28	42	59
34	92	125	27	40	57
33	89	122		39	55
32	87	118	26	38	54
31	84	115	25	37	52
30	81	111	24	36	50
29	78	108	23	34	49
28	76	104		33	47
27	73	101	22	32	45
26	70	97	21	31	44
25	67	94	20	30	42
24	65	90	19	28	40
23	62	87		27	39
22	59	83	18	26	37
21	56	80	17	25	35
20	54	76	16	24	34
19	51	73	15	23	32
18	48	69		21	30
17	45	66	14	20	29
16	43	62	13	19	27
15	40	59	12	18	25
14	37	55	11	17	24
13	34	52		15	22
12	32	48	10	14	20
11	29	45	9	13	19
10	26	41	8	12	17
9	23	38	7	11	15
8	21	34		9	14
7	18	31	6	8	12
6	15	27	5	7	10
5	12	24	4	6	9
4	10	20	3	5	7
3	7	17		4	5
2	4	13	2	2	4
1	1	10	1	1	2

*Scale constructed by F. W. Cozens, University of California at Los Angeles. Reproduced from Hyde, Edith I.: An Achievement Scale in Archery, Research Quarterly, May 1937, 7: No. 2, p. 109, by permission of the publishers.

BADMINTON

Six tests have been selected for inclusion, two for each of the following skills: serve and clear. The other two tests are wall volley tests and are thought to measure a number of elements such as coordination, wrist strength, and footwork. These tests have been selected from several studies, namely French,[48] Lockhart and McPherson,[35] Miller,[39] Scott and Fox* and Stalter.[52]

1. Short Serve (French)

Equipment:

1. A clothesline rope stretched 20 inches directly above the net and parallel to it, attached to the same standards as the net. New shuttles and tightly strung rackets.

2. Floor markings
    Using the intersection of the short service line and the center line as a midpoint, describe a series of arcs in the right service court at distances of 22 inches, 30 inches, 38 inches, and 46 inches from the midpoint, the measurement including the width of the 2-inch line. Extend these arcs from the short service line to the center line, as indicated in the diagram (Figure 12). The lines should be painted in different colors to increase accuracy in scoring. Showcard paint, which can be washed from the floor, is suggested.

Test:

The player being tested stands any place in the right service area diagonally opposite the target, and serves twenty times, attempting to send the shuttle through the space between the rope and the net in such a manner that it lands in the right service court for the doubles game. The scorer stands near the center of the left service court on the same side of the net with the target and facing the target. The corner of the target nearest the intersection of the short service line and center line counts 5 points, next space 4 points, the next 3, then 2, and any shuttle off the target but in the service area for the doubles games counts 1 point.

---

*Scott, Gladys, and Fox, Margaret: Unpublished studies.

144

Scoring:

No score is given for any trial which fails to go between the rope and the net or which fails to land in the service court for the doubles game. Any shuttle landing within an area or on the line surrounding an area is scored as shown in the diagram. Any shuttle landing on a line dividing two scoring areas receives the score of the higher area. The score for the entire test is the total of twenty trials. It is considered a foul and the trial is repeated if the serve is illegal. (For definition of legal serve, see American Badminton Association rules.)

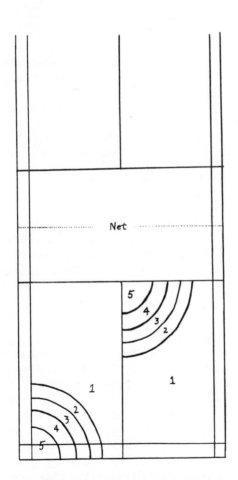

Figure 12. Floor markings for badminton serve test. 1-5 = scores for respective areas, right court for short serve, left court for long serve.

145

Reliability:

For twenty-nine majors in physical education, State
University of Iowa, the coefficient was .88 using the odd-
even method of reliability, stepped up by application of
the Spearman-Brown Prophecy Formula. (See pages 85 to 88 in
Chapter IV.) For other group of 268 freshman and sophomore women the coefficient was .68 by this method.* For
fifty-nine majors in physical education at Illinois State
Normal University (players with less experience), a reliability of .51 was obtained using the same method.[40] The
difference in amount of playing experience doubtless explains the difference in coefficients.

Validity:

The validity of the test was found to be .66 when
correlated with a criterion of tournament rankings (ladder
tournament carried on throughout twenty class periods) at
the State University of Iowa. For the fifty-nine students
at Illinois State Normal University, a coefficient of .41
was found with a criterion of subjective ratings. For the
group of 268 players, the coefficient between their test
score and judges' ratings of playing ability in the game
was .51.

T-Scales:

A scale is presented in Table XVI from data obtained in
college classes, most students being freshmen. The students
were in their first term of badminton instruction and the
test was given at the end of about twenty-five hours of instruction.

Comments:

This test is intended as a measure of accuracy of
placement and the ability to serve the shuttle in a low
flight. It is easy to administer but unless testing stations can be set up off the courts so that it does not
interfere with play on the courts, it is time-consuming.
(See Chapter III for suggestions.) The test should not be
administered until the majority of players are quite skillful in making short, low serves; in fact, it is highly unreliable before that time. The serve is probably a more
important skill for advanced players than for beginners.

---

*Scott, Gladys, and Fox, Margaret: Unpublished studies.

2. Long Serve (Scott and Fox)

Equipment:

    1. A clothesline rope stretched across the court 14 feet from the net and parallel to it, at a height of 8 feet from the floor.

    2. Floor markings
    Using the intersection of the long service line and the left side boundary line for singles as a midpoint, describe a series of arcs in the left service court at distances of 22 inches, 30 inches, 38 inches, and 46 inches from the midpoint, the measurement including the width of the 2-inch line. Extend these arcs from the long service line to the side line, as indicated in the diagram. (Figure 12) The lines should be painted in different colors to increase accuracy in scoring. Showcard paint, which can be washed from the floor, is suggested.

Test:

    The player being tested stands any place in the service area diagonally opposite the target, and serves twenty times, attempting to send the shuttle over the rope in such a manner that it will land in the target at the rear of the left court. The corner of the target nearest the intersection of the service line and the side line counts 5 points, the next space 4 points, the next 3, then 2, and any shuttle (over the rope) in the service area outside the target counts 1 point.

Scoring:

    No score is given for any trial which fails to go over the 8-foot rope or which fails to land in the service court. Any shuttle landing within an area or on the line surrounding an area is scored as shown in the diagram. Any shuttle landing on a line dividing two scoring areas receives the score of the higher area. The score for the entire test is the sum of twenty trials. It is considered a foul and the trial is repeated if the serve is illegal.

Reliability:

    Coefficients have been computed on two different groups of freshman and sophomore women at the University of Iowa. For a group of forty-five the r was .62 on odd-even trials,

.77 when corrected by the Spearman-Brown formula. On a much larger group of 332 players the coefficients were .52 and .68 on the respective computations.*

Validity:

The validity computed on the forty-five subjects at the University of Iowa was .54 when correlated with subjective ratings made by three judges during play.*

T-Scale:

The T-Scale on this test is on ninety-one freshman and sophomore women at the University of Iowa. The test was taken after about twenty-five hours of instruction.

Comments:

This test is designed to measure ability to place the serve high and to the rear of the court. From the standpoint of logic concerning different abilities involved in the two serve tests, it might seem desirable in some instances to use both tests. The dissimilarity is further borne out by the intercorrelation (r = .31) between the two tests.

3. Clear Test No. 1 (French)

Equipment:

1. A clothesline rope stretched across the court 14 feet from the net and parallel to it, at a height of 8 feet from the floor.

2. Floor markings
   a. Construct a line 2 feet nearer the net than the rear service line in the doubles game and parallel to it. Measure from the exact center of the line. Extend this line from one outer alley line to the other outer alley line.

   b. On the same side of the net, construct a line 2 feet farther from the net than the rear service line in the singles game and parallel to it. Measure from the exact center of the line. Extend this line from one outer alley line to the other outer line. The lines should be painted different colors to increase accuracy in scoring.

---

*Scott, Gladys, and Fox, Margaret: Unpublished studies.

148

c. On the opposite side of the net, draw marks 2 inches square at spots indicated on the diagram as <u>X</u> and <u>Y</u>. The center of <u>X</u> should be 11 feet from the net and 3 feet from the center line toward the left side line. The center of <u>Y</u> should be 11 feet from the net and 3 feet from the center line toward the right side line. In measuring from the center line, use the exact center of the line.

Test:

The player being tested stands between the two square marks on the court opposite the target. The person giving the tests (player with considerable experience) stands on the intersection of the short service line and the center line on the same side of the net as the target and serves the shuttle to the player being tested. The shuttle must cross the net with enough force to carry it as far as the two squares before it touches the floor. If it does not go that far or is outside the space between the two squares, the player being tested should not play it. The player

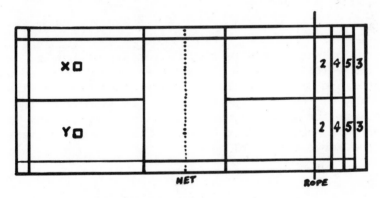

Figure 13. Floor markings for badminton clear test.

2 - 5 = scores for respective areas.
X-Y = limits of set-up for clear stroke.

being tested may move any place he wishes as soon as the shuttle has been hit to him. Only shuttles played by the player being tested count as trials. The player attempts to send the shuttle by means of a clear stroke above the rope so that the shuttle lands on the target. Twenty trials are allowed. The person giving the test should call out the score of each trial, to be recorded by an assistant. The area between the two rear lines of the regulation court

149

counts 5 points, the space just behind it counts 3 points, and the space just in front of the two rear lines of the regulation court counts 4 points. Any shuttle going over the rope but failing to reach the target counts 2 points. This test can be given to two players at once on the same court, placing the squares 6 feet from the center line, and each player taking one side of the court.

Scoring:

No score is given for any trial failing to go over the rope or failing to land in the court in the space behind the rope and on the target, as indicated on the diagram. Any shuttle landing within an area or on the line surrounding the area is scored as shown in the diagram. Any shuttle landing on a line dividing two scoring areas receives the score of the higher area. The score for the entire test is the total of twenty trials. It is considered a foul and the trial is repeated if the stroke is "carried" or "slung." (See official American Badminton Association rules for interpretation of terms.)

Reliability:

For the same subjects from University of Iowa as in the Short Serve Test, r was .96 by odd-even method, stepped up with Spearman-Brown formula. For the other group at the University of Iowa, forty-five cases, it was .77 by the same method; and for a third group, forty-five cases, r was .83. For the same subjects from Illinois State Normal University as in the serve test, .70.

Validity:

At Iowa, with criterion of tournament rankings the validity was, .60; with subjecting ratings of playing ability, .40; at Normal, with the criterion of subjective ratings, .50.

T-Scale:

The scale is presented in Table XVI. It was constructed from combined data from Illinois State Normal University and University of Iowa. The subjects were freshman and sophomore college students.

Comments:

This test is intended as a measure of power. After the players have practiced the test, the markers $\underline{X}$ and $\underline{Y}$ can be ignored and two players can be tested at the same time on the same court. This test is well liked as a practice device. Since power is a factor in general motor ability, scores made on the Badminton Clear Test were correlated with the scores made on Scott General Motor Ability Test, Battery $\underline{A}$ (see page 356) to determine the extent of relationship. The low correlation of .36 was obtained for the ninety-four cases in the study.[37]

4. Clear Test No. 2 (Miller)

Equipment:

1. Tightly strung rackets, new shuttlecocks, stop watch.
2. Floor markings
A straight line 10 feet from the wall is extended the length of the wall distance and parallel to the wall.
3. Wall markings
A 1-inch line is extended across the wall 7 1/2 feet from the floor and parallel to the floor. The width of the wall space should be at least 10 feet and the height preferably 15 feet or higher.

Test:

The subject is permitted a one-minute practice period before the first trial. On the signal "ready, go" the subject serves the shuttlecock in a legal manner against the wall from behind the 10-foot floor line. The serve puts the shuttlecock in a position to be rallied with a clear on each rebound. If the serve hits on or above the 7 1/2-foot wall line, that hit counts as one point and each following rebound hit made on or above the 7 1/2-foot wall line, when the subject is behind the 10-foot floor line, counts as one point. The hit is not counted if any part of a foot goes over the 10-foot restraining line. The scorer should say "back" whenever the subject consistently goes over the line. The hit is not counted if the shuttlecock goes below the 7 1/2-foot wall line. However, if either the foot goes over the 10-foot line or the shuttlecock hits below the 7 1/2-foot line, the subject is permitted to keep the shuttlecock in play. The bird may be stopped at any time and restarted

151

with a legal service from behind the 10-foot line. If the shuttlecock is missed and falls to the floor, the subject picks it up quickly as possible, gets behind the 10-foot line, and puts the shuttlecock into play with a legal service.

Scoring:

Three trials of 30 seconds each are given, and the score consists of the sum of the three trials.

Reliability:

By test-retest method, .94. A week or less intervened between tests. One hundred college women subjects of all ranges of ability were tested and included in the reliability study.

Validity:

To determine the validity, the scores of twenty players on the clear test were correlated with the results of a round-robin tournament. The resulting coefficient was .83.

Comments:

To compare the validity of this test to the validity of Clear Test #1, it would be necessary to use the same criterion and administer both tests to the same subjects.

Miller made a careful study of the number of times services, drop shots, clears, smashes, drives, and half-court drives were used during an amateur badminton tournament finals in both men's and women's singles and found that the finalists used clears more often than any other stroke. A cinematographical analysis of the clear shot was made to ascertain the proper distance from the wall.

5. Wall Volley No. 1 (Stalter)

Equipment:

1. New shuttles, tightly strung rackets, stop watch.
2. Floor markings
   Construct a restraining line parallel to and 6 feet from the wall, including the width of the line in the 6-foot distance from the wall.

3. Wall space
   Use an unobstructed wall with smooth brick construction with a space of from 12 to 15 feet in width for each testing station and a height of at least 15 feet.

Test:

The player to be tested stands behind the 6-foot restraining line facing the wall with racket and shuttle in hand. On signal, he sends the shuttle with an underhand serve against the wall and volleys it on each rebound for a period of thirty seconds. Strokes made while the player is touching the floor nearer the wall than the restraining line do not count. The player may cross the restraining line to recover the shuttle but he must return to behind the line before putting the shuttle into play again with an underhand motion. Any stroke may be used; hard driven forehands or backhands with good wrist action seem to produce the best results. The test should be demonstrated and a practice period should be allowed before any data are collected. (This wall practice can be used advantageously throughout the season by players waiting turns to get on the courts; if this has been done, the practice period on the testing day need not exceed one trial for each player.) The scorer stands behind the player and slightly to one side. The need for repeating trials due to foot faults can be minimized if the scorer immediately corrects the position of any player who steps on or over the restraining line. Twenty or more players can be tested at one time along the four walls of the usual sized gymnasium. Four trials are allowed for each player, recording all scores. The scorer and player to be tested should alternate to assure each of a rest period between trials.

Scoring:

One point is scored for each volley against the wall. Putting the shuttle into motion with an underhand serve is not to be considered a volley. The score for the test is the total of the four trials.

Reliability.

Correlation by the odd-even method was .71; .83 when stepped up with the Spearman-Brown formula. The subjects were fifty-nine women major students at Illinois State Normal University. Correlation of first and second trials

153

yielded an $\underline{r}$ of .75 stepped up to .90; subjects were 368 freshman and sophomore women at the University of Iowa. In another group of forty-five students the coefficient was .92 by the above computations.

Validity:

The validity was .52 with a criterion of combined subjective ratings at Illinois State Normal University; .78 with the forty-five Iowa students when scores were correlated with a subjective rating of playing ability.

T-Scale:

See Table XVI. The scale was constructed on data obtained from ninety-one freshman and sophomore college women at the end of about twenty-five hours of instruction.

Comments:

This test is believed to measure wrist strength. It provides a wide range of scores and is economical of time for administration. The intercorrelation with the clear test administered to the same groups was .36 in each case. While the validity is not high, this test contributes enough to be included in the recommended batteries as will be shown later.

6. Wall Volley No. 2 (Lockhart and McPherson)

Equipment:

1. New shuttlecocks (birds), tightly strung rackets, stop watch.
2. Floor markings
   Construct a starting line on the floor 6 1/2 feet from the base of the wall and parallel to the wall; a restraining line three feet from the wall and parallel to the starting line.
3. Wall markings
   Construct a 1-inch wide net line on the wall 5 feet above and parallel to the floor. The wall space should be 10 feet high and 10 feet in length.

Test:

The player taking the test stands behind the starting line holding the badminton racket in one hand and the

154

shuttlecock in the other. On signal, he serves the shuttlecock in a legal manner against the wall on or above the net
line. The shuttlecock is played as many times as possible
against the wall in thirty seconds. Three trials are given
to each player, with rest permitted between trials and a
practice period of fifteen seconds is given before the first
trial. Only hits on or above the net line are considered
good. After the shuttlecock has been served, the player may
move up to the restraining line if he wishes. If the restraining line is crossed the hit is not counted, but the
shuttlecock is still in play. If the bird is missed or gets
out of control, the player must retrieve it and continue by
putting it in play with a serve from behind the starting
line.

Scoring:

The score is the number of legal hits made on or above
the backboard net line in the three trials.

Reliability:

By the test-retest method, the correlation was .90 in
administering the test twice to fifty players, within an
interim of three days.

Validity:

The validity was .71 with a criterion of combined subjective ratings made by three judges of the badminton playing ability of sixty-eight women players. The validity was
.60 when the percentage of total games won in a twenty-seven
player round robin tournament was correlated with the test
scores.

Comments:

The relationship between the two criteria was determined by correlating the total games won by each player in
the round robin tournament with the combined ratings of the
judges. The resulting r equalled .90.

BATTERY OF BADMINTON TESTS

The short serve test and the clear test (#1) when
combined into a battery yielded a multiple correlation of

Table XVI.

T-Scales for Badminton Tests

T-SCORE	SHORT SERVE*	LONG SERVE†	CLEAR‡	VOLLEY§	VOLLEY¶ #TWO	T-SCORE
80	68		94			80
79						79
78					148	78
77	67		92			77
76						76
75		35	90	148		75
74	66				143	74
73	64		88	138		73
72	61				138	72
71	60			128	136	71
70	59		86		128	70
69	58		84	114	127	69
68	57	34		110	123	68
67	55	33	82		120	67
66	54		80		115	66
65	53	32		108	114	65
64	52	31	78		112	64
63	49	30	76	106	110	63
62	48	29		104	107	62
61	46	28	74	102	104	61
60	44	27	72	100	101	60
59	43	26		98	97	59
58	42	25	70	94	95	58
57	41	24	68	92	91	57
56	39	23	66	90	89	56
55	37	22	64	88	87	55
54	36	21		86	86	54
53	35	20	62	84	83	53
52	34	19	60		81	52
51	31		58	82	76	51
50	29	18	54		73	50
49	28	17	52	80	72	49
48	26	16	50	78	71	48
47	25	15	48	76	69	47
46	23	14	46	74	67	46

156

Table XVI. (Cont.)

T-SCORE	SHORT SERVE*	LONG SERVE†	CLEAR‡	VOLLEY§	VOLLEY¶ #TWO	T-SCORE
45	22		44	72	64	45
44	21	13	42	70	62	44
43	19	12	40	68	61	43
42	17	11	38	66	57	42
41	15	10	34	64	54	41
40	13	9	32	62	52	40
39	12	8	30	60	50	39
38	11	7	26		49	38
37	10	6	24	58	47	37
36	9		22	56	45	36
35	8		20	54	44	35
34	7	5	18	52	43	34
33	6		16		42	33
32	5		12		39	32
31	4	2	10	50	38	31
30			8	48		30
29			6	46	37	29
28	3		4			28
27	2					27
26					32	26
25	1		2			25
24		1		40		24
23						23
22						22
21					29	21

*Scale constructed on data obtained on 385 freshman and sophomore women at the University of Iowa.
†Scale constructed on data obtained on 91 freshman and sophomore women at the University of Iowa.
‡Scale constructed on data obtained on 429 freshman and sophomore women at Illinois State Normal University and the University of Iowa.
§Scale constructed on data obtained on 91 freshman and sophomore women at the University of Iowa.
¶Scale constructed on 178 college women players, University of Nebraska.

.85 with the criterion of tournament rankings. Various combinations were tried in the State University of Iowa study where the criterion was subjective ratings of three judges during tournament play. Multiple coefficients and weightings were as follows:

R

2.0 wall volley + 1.0 clear + 1.0 short serve 91
5.0 wall volley + 3.0 clear + 1.0 long serve 88
2.5 wall volley + 1.0 short serve 87
2.0 wall volley + 1.0 clear 84
5.0 wall volley + 1.0 long serve 83
2.0 clear + 1.0 short serve 73
3.0 clear + 1.0 long serve 71

Wall Volley Test #1 and Clear Test #1 were used. Any of these combinations could be used satisfactorily, the choice being made according to time available and the skills which have been emphasized.

BASKETBALL

Numerous basketball skill tests have been devised but very few are substantiated by statistical evidence of their worth. The two selected for inclusion have been proven valuable and can be used for both boys and girls.

1. Half-Minute Shooting (Johnson[28])

Equipment:

No special equipment. Balls should be well inflated. Stop watch.

Test:

The player stands at any position he selects near the basket, with a ball in his hands. On the signal, Ready, Go! he starts shooting and continues until the signal to stop, attempting to make as many baskets as possible within the thirty seconds. If the ball has left his hands when the signal to stop sounds, the basket counts, if made. Two trials are given each player.

Scoring:

The number of baskets made in thirty seconds is the score for each trial. The better of the two trials is recorded.

Reliability:

r = .58 on trials 1 and 3 versus trial 2; stepped up by the Spearman-Brown formula, .68, for 107 girls in Proviso Township High School, Maywood, Ill.
r = .73 on 190 high school boys.
r = .54 on first and second trials; subjects were 209 freshman and sophomore women.
r = .70 on first and second trials, .82 stepped up by Spearman-Brown formula; subjects were 233 freshman and sophomore college women.*

Validity:

r = .58 for the sum of three trials for high school girls with a rating criterion.
r = .71 on 190 high school boys.
r = .60 with a sports tests criterion, 155 college freshman women.

T-Scales:

Three scales are presented for the Basket Shooting Test in Table XVII. Two are for college students, one uses the average of three trials, the other uses the best of three trials. The third is for high school girls and uses the best of two trials.

Comments:

This test measures the ability to hit the spot at which one is aiming, and also the ability to judge rebounds, to move quickly to get to the ball and to put it in play. This makes it a good test for all players regardless of position. If there are as many as six baskets available, the test can be administered in a very few minutes to the usual class. Since no two backboards are exactly alike, the conditions for all can be somewhat equalized by having players rotate to a new basket for the second trial. A minimum of three trials is recommended for relatively inexperienced players.

---

*Scott, Gladys: Unpublished studies.

159

Table XVII.

T-Scales for Basketball Tests

T-SCORE	BASKET SHOOTING*	BASKET SHOOTING†	BASKET SHOOTING‡	PASSING§	T-SCORE
81		20			
80					80
79	16		15	50	79
78		19			78
77				48	77
76				47	76
75		18	14		75
74					74
73	15	17			73
72			13	46	72
71			12		71
70	14	16			70
69	13			45	69
68			11		68
67	12	15			67
66			10	44	66
65	11			43	65
64		14	9		64
63	10			42	63
62					62
61		13	8	41	61
60	9			40	60
59					59
58		12	7	39	58
57					57
56	8			38	56
55		11			55
54			6	37	54
53	7	10		36	53
52					52
51				35	51
50	6	9			50
49			5	34	49
48				33	48
47		8			47
46	5			32	46

Table XVII. (Cont.)

T-SCORE	BASKET SHOOTING*	BASKET SHOOTINGt	BASKET SHOOTINGt	PASSING§	T-SCORE
45					45
44		7		31	44
43			4	30	43
42					42
41		6		29	41
40	4			28	40
39					39
38		5		27	38
37			3		37
36				26	36
35	3	4		25	35
34					34
33		3		24	33
32					32
31				23	31
30		2		22	30
29			2		29
28	2			21	28
27		1		20	27
26				18	26
25				17	25
24					24
23					23
22				16	22
21	1		1		21

*Scale constructed on 307 freshman and sophomore students at the University of Iowa. Score is the average of three trials.
tScale constructed on 1812 women physical education majors, from Wilma K. Miller Study. [40]
‡Scale constructed on data obtained from girls in the ninth grade in Blue Island Community High School, Blue Island, Ill., and eleventh grade in Proviso Township High School, Maywood, Ill. The score was the best one out of two trials.
§Scale constructed on 233 freshman and sophomore students at the University of Iowa. The score was the sum of three trials.

2. Passing (Modification of Edgren[16])

Equipment:

    1. A flat, unobstructed wall space at least 15 feet long and 7 feet high. Official basketball; properly inflated. Stop watch.

    2. Floor markings

    Draw a line on the floor parallel to the wall and 7 1/2 feet from it. Then draw two parallel lines on the wall 3 feet apart (width of lines included in 3 feet) in the center of the wall space. Draw a line on the floor 15 inches to the outside of each line on wall (these are 5 1/2 feet apart, lines included) so that they intersect first line drawn. Mark corners on floor diagram A and B and opposite wall areas A and B (See Figure 14).

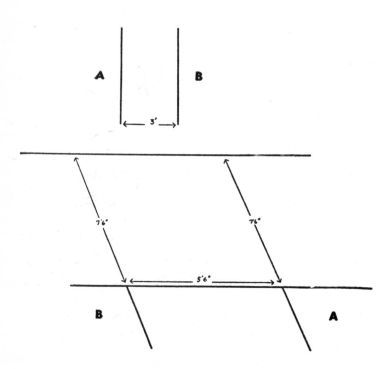

Figure 14. Wall and floor markings for basketball passing test.

A on floor = starting zone for first and alternate throws.
A on wall = target for first and alternate throws.
B on floor = starting zone for second and alternate throws.
B on wall = target for second and alternate throws.

Test:

The player stands in area <u>A</u> with basketball in hands. On signal <u>Ready, Go</u>! he throws the ball to area <u>A</u> on the wall, runs forward to corner <u>B</u> or beyond so that he catches the ball on the rebound. He repeats from <u>B</u>, throwing to <u>B</u> on the wall, and continues as rapidly as possible. He must stay behind the 7 1/2-foot line at all times, and the throws must be made while behind the proper parallel line. The ball may not hit in the 3-foot zone on the wall. He may use any type of pass, and any type of pivot or turn; he is not penalized for traveling. The ball may bounce on the floor one or more times before being caught. Three trials are given.

Scoring:

The score on each trial is the number of successful hits made in the proper wall area (without line violations being made in the recovery) in the twenty seconds allowed. Scores for the three trials are added.

Reliability:

The reliability was .70 for first and second trials, .82 by the Spearman-Brown correction for the sum of two trials; subjects were 233 freshman and sophomore women at the University of Iowa.*

Validity:

The validity was .51 when correlated with judges' ratings of ball handling ability for 154 freshman and sophomore women at the University of Iowa.*

T-Scales:

The scales appearing in Table XVII were constructed on the group described under reliability.

Comments:

This is a combination of agility and ball handling. It can be administered to as many players at one time as the wall space and the number of balls permit. Each person should be allowed three or four practice throws before taking the test. If four persons are assigned to each testing

---

*Scott, Gladys: Unpublished studies.

station, and they take turns, each participant will be assured sufficient rest between trials. If this test is given
to boys, the line parallel to the wall should be 8 feet from
the wall and the lines at right angles to the wall should be
6 feet apart.

This test is essentially the same as that of Edgren.[16]
Time and distance have been adjusted, and statistical evidence is here presented but was lacking in the Edgren report.

BATTERY OF BASKETBALL TESTS

Apparently there is some overlap in the element of
agility in each test as evidenced by an r of .45 on 233
first-term students taking both tests. As with almost any
agility test, there is some relationship with general motor
ability scores. On these same students the correlation also
was .45. If time permits the administration of just one
test, the half-minute shooting test probably is the one that
should be given.

If only two baskets are available, the shooting test
will take considerable time to give. In that case only part
of the class should be assigned to tests at a given time and
the rest of the class can practice on other techniques in
the center of the floor. Or if there is additional wall
space not interfering with the basket shooting test, both
tests may be given at once. When the two tests are run simultaneously, it is preferable to give thirty seconds instead of twenty for each trial of the passing test and to
have one central timer for all testing stations.

BOWLING

There are no published tests of skill in bowling but
the bowling score itself serves as an adequate measure of
the relative ability of players, and if a record of scores
is kept, they serve as a measure of improvement. See Chapter XI, page 437 for a description of a chart that can be
used to diagnose difficulties.

The following items have been found by experience to
discriminate between levels of ability, and are brief enough
to be completed in one or two lessons, depending upon the
number of players on each alley: (1) score on a complete
game; (2) sum of first balls in each frame for an entire

game; (3) score made on four common spare setups, bowling five balls at each setup.

No scoring method appears to correlate too closely with form of bowling. This is probably because very slight variations in some detail of form may make great differences in score and because many players learn to compensate for known errors.

CANOEING

Very little objective testing has been done on canoeing. Most schools or camps evaluate ability by means of subjective ratings on skills such as ability to keep a straight course, to execute certain turns or approaches to the dock. Such ratings have value, but objective evidence can be obtained, thus supplementing the ratings and also saving time.

No single test can be established which can be uniformly followed with respect to length and condition of the course in the way that tests are usually set up in the gymnasium. However, the following test should serve as a model from which others may be designed.

Equipment:

Two buoys, rafts, or other obstacles are placed about 525 feet apart to establish a course according to Figure 15; a canoe and paddle; stop watch.

Test:

The person being tested takes the stern position; he may paddle on either port or starboard side, but must paddle the entire course on the side chosen. Another person occupies the bow seat but does not paddle; weight of this person keeps the canoe on a more nearly even keel. The canoe is started far enough from the starting line that the canoe is in motion when it crosses the line. The figure eight path is followed with an attempt to cover the course as rapidly as possible.

Score:

The score is the time (minutes and seconds) required to cover the course. (Watch is started when the bow crosses starting line, stopped when bow again crosses starting line after covering course.)

Figure 15.   Diagram of canoeing course.

A = starting line and finish line.

■ = rafts or piers.

Reliability:

The reliability was .92 for twenty-three college women repeating the test on successive days with similar state of wind and current.[10]

Validity:

The validity was .64 when correlating the T-score on the test time with judges' ratings on form of strokes and general ability to handle the canoe. Subjects were 104 freshman and sophomore women at the University of Iowa.

Comments:

The course may be shortened a little. However, it should not be too short as there is no opportunity for the poorer canoeist to get off course, or for the best ones to get up speed on the straightaway. Too short a distance results in inadequate distribution of scores. It was found that variations in current or wind (within the range where canoes would be on the river) had little effect on value of the test or on actual scores.

After a course is established and a group of canoeists of various skill levels has taken the test, it should be possible to determine standards of performance on the course. The time required for each member of the group may be put into a T-scale, thus indicating relative ability for those tested in the future. Or the scores may be ranked in categories according to some plan such as this:

4'	to 5' 29"	excellent
5' 30"	to 6' 59"	good
7'	to 8' 29"	average
8' 30"	to 9' 59"	fair
10'	or slower	poor

FIELD HOCKEY

Four tests have been selected as the best available measures of field hockey skill. They need to be supplemented with ratings of such important phases of the game as tackling and timing the execution of passes.

1. Ball Control Test (Schmithals and French[47])

Equipment:

1. Hockey stick for each participant; stop watch; one or two balls; two high-jump standards (or other portable posts) with round bases.

2. Field markings

(a) A line 20 feet long to be used for a starting line.

(b) A line perpendicular to the midpoint of the starting line and extending 35 feet from it. This is the foul line.

(c) A line 10 feet long, perpendicular to and bisected by the foul line at a point 30 feet from the starting line. This is the restraining line.

(d) A line one foot long, perpendicular to and bisected by the foul line at a point 35 feet from the starting line.

(e) Two lines, each one foot long, bisecting each other at a point which is 45 feet from the starting line and in a straight line with the foul line. See Figure 16.

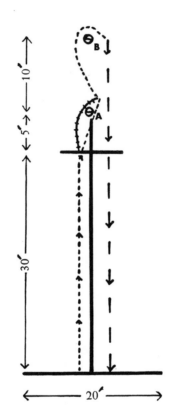

Figure 16. Field-markings and action sequence for field hockey ball control test.

A, B = jump standards (obstacles).
- - - - = dribble.
–|–|–|–|--|-- = path of player in dodge.
→ – – = drive.

168

3. Position of standards

(a) One standard is placed so that the middle of the base of the standard is directly over the point where the foul line and the line described in 2(d) bisect each other.

(b) The other standard is placed in a similar fashion over the point formed by the two lines described in 2(e).

Test:

The player being tested stands behind the starting line with the hockey ball placed on the starting line at any point to the left of the foul line. At the signal, Ready, Go! the player dribbles the ball forward to the left of and parallel to the foul line. As soon as the restraining line is reached, the ball is sent from the left side of the foul line to the right of the first obstacle (from the player's point of view), and the player runs around the left side of the obstacle and recovers the ball. (This is analogous to the dodge.) Next, the player executes a turn toward his right around the second obstacle, still keeping control of the ball. (This is analogous to the circular tackle.) As soon as possible after that the ball is driven toward the starting line. If the drive is not hard enough to reach the starting line, the player must follow it up and hit the ball again. This procedure is repeated until six trials have been given; players are alternated on trials to avoid their becoming fatigued.

Scoring:

The score for one trial is the time it takes from the signal Go until the player's ball has again crossed the starting line. The score for the entire test is the average of the six trials. It is considered a foul and the trial does not count if:

(a) The ball or player crosses the foul line before reaching the restraining line.

(b) In executing the dodge, the ball is not sent from the left side of the foul line.

Reliability:

$r = .92$ when computed by the odd-even method and stepped up by the Spearman-Brown formula. The subjects were

51 players in college classes and hockey club, University of Iowa.[35] On another 199 college players the reliability was 82 by the same method.*

Validity:

r = .44 when correlated with a criterion determined by ratings made by three nationally rated umpires with experience on selection committees. On the latter group of 199 cases the correlation between judges' ratings and test performance was .56.

T-Scales:

See Table XVIII. Two scales are presented for the Ball Control Test. The first is on combined data from 310 freshman and sophomore women at Illinois State Normal University

Table XVIII.

T-Scales for Field Hockey Tests

T-SCORE	BALL CONTROL*	BALL CONTROL†	GOAL SHOOTING‡	FIELDING AND DRIVE‡	T-SCORE
76	9.1–9.5				76
75		9.6-10.0			75
74					74
73	9.6-10.0		19.4-19.6	4.1	73
72					72
71		10.1-10.5	19.7-21.4	4.3	71
70	10.1-10.5				70
69					69
68			21.5-21.7	4.4	68
67					67
66	10.6-11.0				66
65				4.5	65
64		10.6-11.0	21.8-22.0	4.6	64
63	11.1-11.5				63
62				4.7	62
61	11.6-12.0		22.1-22.3	4.8	61

*Scott, Gladys: Unpublished studies.

170

Table XVIII. (Cont.)

T-SCORE	BALL CONTROL*	BALL CONTROL†	GOAL SHOOTING‡	FIELDING AND DRIVE‡	T-SCORE
60		11.1-11.5	22.4-22.6		60
59	12.1-12.5		22.7-22.9	4.9	59
58			23.0-23.2		58
57		11.6-12.0	23.3-23.8	5.0	57
56	12.6-13.0		23.9-24.1	5.1	56
55			24.2-25.0	5.2	55
54	13.1-13.5		25.1-25.3	5.4	54
53		12.1-12.5	25.4-25.6	5.6	53
52				5.8	52
51	13.6-14.0		25.7-25.9	5.9	51
50		12.6-13.0	26.0-26.5	6.0	50
49	14.1-14.5		26.6-26.8	6.1	49
48			26.9-27.1	6.2	48
47			27.2-27.4	6.4	47
46	14.6-15.0	13.1-13.5	27.5-28.0	6.5	46
45			28.1-28.3		45
44	15.1-15.5				44
43			28.4-28.6	6.6	43
42	15.6-16.0	13.6-14.0	28.7-28.9		42
41			29.0-29.5	6.7	41
40	16.1-16.5		29.6-29.8	6.9	40
39	16.6-17.0	14.1-14.5	29.0-30.7	7.2	39
38			30.8-31.0	7.3	38
37	17.1-17.5		31.1-31.9		37
36		14.6-15.0	32.0-32.8	7.4	36
35	17.6-18.0			7.6	35
34			32.1-33.1		34
33	18.1-18.5	15.1-15.5		7.7	33
32	18.6-19.0		33.2-33.4	8.0	32
31	19.1-19.5		33.5-33.7	9.0	31
30					30
29	19.6-20.0		33.8-34.3	9.2	29
28		15.6-16.0			28
27	20.1-20.5		34.4-34.6	10.7	27
26					26

171

Table XVIII. (Cont.)

T-SCORE	BALL CONTROL*	BALL CONTROL†	GOAL SHOOTING‡	FIELDING AND DRIVE‡	T-SCORE
25	20.6-21.0				25
24					24
23	21.1-25.5				23
22					22
21	25.6-26.0				21

*Scale constructed on data obtained on 310 freshman and sophomore students at Illinois State Normal University and the University of Iowa.
†Scale constructed on data obtained on 79 sophomore major students in their first term of hockey at Illinois State Normal University.
‡Scales constructed on data obtained on 51 students at the University of Iowa.

and the University of Iowa. The score is the average of three trials. The other scale was obtained from scores of seventy-nine sophomore major students at Illinois State Normal University. This score is the average of six trials.

Comments:

This test has been used for several years, in combination with a test of knowledge, for early season classification, and serves adequately. It calls for the use of a variety of skills, the ability to control the ball while moving rapidly, and the ability to make quick changes of direction. It can be administered along the edges of the field and requires no special equipment other than a stop watch and jumping standards. The test authors think that the low validity may be partially due to the difficulty in making discriminations in ratings. Field hockey presents a very difficult rating problem, with so many players and the small number of times that the ball is played by some players. The judges rated the players on two successive playing periods, which was not adequate to secure discrimination between all levels of ability.

2. Goal Shooting: Straight, Right, Left (Schmithals and French[47])

Equipment:

1. Target, 9 inches wide, 12 feet long, and at least 1/2 inch thick, made of hard wood. The board is painted

according to the following specifications: The length of the board is divided into eleven equal spaces, alternate space starting from either end being painted black and the other remaining the natural color of the wood. Numbers are painted in the spaces in contrasting colors (black on light background and white on black background) in the following order starting from either end: 1-2-3-4-5-6-5-4-3-2-1 (see Figure 17). A base made of board at least 3 inches wide, exactly 12 feet long, and at least 1/2 inch thick is nailed on the bottom of the target so that 2 1/2 inches extend beyond the back of the target. The board, in order to stand upright securely, may be anchored with an ice pick or other similar device. Hockey stick for each participant; four to ten balls; stop watch.

Figure 17. Target for field hockey goal shooting test. Insert above shows side view of board anchored with an ice pick.

2. Field markings

(a) A line 6 1/2 feet long to be used as a starting line.

(b) A rectangle, 11 feet long and 6 1/2 feet wide, 15 feet from the starting line. Point A is the midpoint of the side opposite the starting line.

(c) A line 12 feet long, called the center target line, parallel to and 60 feet from the starting line.

(d) A line 12 feet long, called the right inner target line.

(e) A line 12 feet long, called the left inner target line.

(f) The target is placed directly on the specified line with the numbers facing the starting line and the board anchored with ice picks. For the straight drive, it is

173

placed on the center target line, for the drive from the
right and left inners' positions, the right and left inners' target lines, respectively (see Figure 18).

Test:

    1. Drive from center's position. The player being
tested stands behind the starting line with the hockey ball
placed on the starting line. At the signal, <u>Ready, Go!</u> the
ball is dribbled to the rectangle, from within which area
it must be driven toward the board (placed on the center
target line). The procedure is repeated until ten trials
have been given.

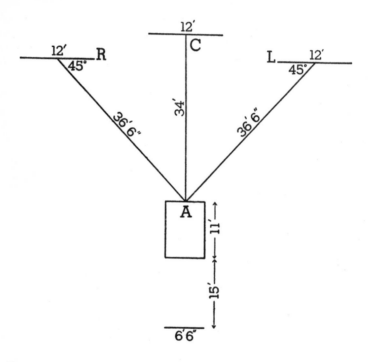

Figure 18. Field markings for field hockey goal shooting test.

    A = center of front line of rectangle, from which target
        lines are measured.
    R = right inner target line.
    C = center target line.
    L = left inner target line.

2. Drive from right inner's position. The same
procedure is repeated, the only difference being the position of the target, which is placed on the right inner target line.

3. Drive from left inner's position. The same procedure is repeated, the only difference being the change in
position of the target to the left inner target line.

Scoring:

The score for one trial constitutes the time elapsing
from the timer's signal, Go! until the ball strikes the target. The score for the entire test is the sum of the two
best odd-numbered trials and the sum of the two best even-
numbered trials made on the center drive, the right inner
drive, and the left inner drive. The score counts if the
ball bounces over the top of the target; in this case, the
time is taken until the instant the ball clears the target.
The score is zero if the ball is not driven from within the
rectangle, or if the driven ball fails to reach the target
or misses it at either end. The attempt is not counted as
a trial if "sticks" are made, or if the player raises the
ball so that it fails to touch the ground before passing
above the target.

Reliability:

r = .92 when the Spearman-Brown Prophecy Formula is
applied. The subjects are the same fifty-one included in
the report for Test 1.[35]

Validity:

r = .48 with the same criterion and for the same
group as Test 1.

T-Scales:

See Table XVIII, page 170. The scale for this test
was constructed from data on fifty-one subjects at the University of Iowa. Ten trials were given from each of the
three positions; the score was the sum of the two best odd-
and two best even-numbered trials as recorded in time from
each position, or a total of twelve trials out of the thirty
administered to each player. Only the time records were
used in computing the scale. Since field conditions affect
scores in this test, it may be necessary to construct scales
for local conditions.

Comments:

This test is designed to measure the ability of the player to adjust footwork, to judge space while moving, and to drive with accuracy and force while running. It is an excellent practice device and can be divided into parts, so that just one can be administered (goal shooting left) if time is limited. The reliability on goal shooting left is adequate (.87) and the validity is substantially the same as for the entire test (.44). The accuracy score is used to make the situation somewhat analogous to the game in that the player has to decide how much speed he can afford to sacrifice for the sake of accuracy. The player is given two scores for this test, a speed score and an accuracy score. The time score is the only one that actually is used in combining this test with others in a battery.

3. Fielding and Drive (Schmithals and French[47])

Equipment:

1. Hockey stick for each participant, three to seven balls, two ice picks with brightly colored tops, regulation hockey goal, stop watch.

2. Field markings (see Figure 19).

(a) Goal line extending across the area between goal posts.

(b) Foul line, 12 feet long, parallel to and 10 feet from the goal line, located directly in front of the goal area. The ice picks are placed on the foul line at points directly opposite each goal post.

(c) Restraining line, 30 feet long, parallel to and 10 feet from the foul line.

(d) Regulation striking circle in front of the goal.

Test:

The player being tested stands behind the goal line. The examiner stands at the edge of the striking circle directly in front of the goal with a hockey ball in one hand and a stop watch in the other. At the examiner's signal, Ready, Go! the hockey ball is rolled toward the goal. Simultaneously, the player runs forward and attempts to field the ball before it reaches the foul line, taps it once, and

176

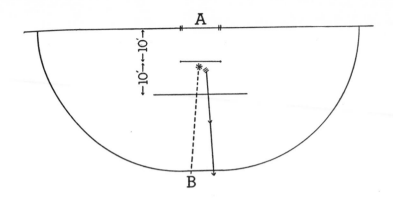

Figure 19.   Field markings for field hockey fielding and drive test.

A = player in position to start the test.
B = examiner in position to roll the ball.
---- = rolled ball.
* = field or stop.
≡ = tap.
➤ ➤ = drive.

drives it out of the striking circle from within the area
between the restraining line and the foul line. This procedure is repeated until sixteen trials have been given.
Instructions to the examiner: The ball should be rolled as
uniformly as possible for all trials and for all players.
Through a little practice a roll may be achieved which is
approximately 45 feet in 1.7 seconds.

Scoring:

      The score for one trial is the time from the instant
the player first touches the hockey ball to the instant the
ball reaches the edge of the striking circle. The score on
the entire test is the sum of the average of the three best
even- and the three best odd-numbered scores of the sixteen
trials. The attempt does not count as a trial if the
rolled ball does not pass between the two ice picks or if
the ball is not delivered at approximately the designated
speed. The player receives a zero score on a trial if the
ball is advanced illegally or if it rolls wholly over the
foul line before or after it is touched by the player's
stick. The zero score is assigned, too, if the ball is not
driven out of the striking cricle from within the area
bounded by the restraining line and the foul line, or if the

177

ball is not controlled, that is, stopped and tapped, before being driven.

Reliability:

r = .90 by the odd-even method, stepped up by the Spearman-Brown formula. The subjects were the same fifty-one as for Test 1.

Validity:

r = .48 with the same criterion as described for Test 1.

T-Scales:

See Table XVIII, page 170. The data were collected on the same subjects as for Test 2.

Comments:

The effect on the score of having the ball put in play by another person than the one being tested appears to be very slight, as the procedure is well standardized. This test is rather costly in time and impractical if classes are large.

4. Fielding, Control and Drive While Moving (Friedel[22])

Equipment:

1. Hockey stick for each participant; stop watch; two or three hockey balls for each testing station.

2. Field markings:

(a) Rectangular area 25 yards long and 10 yards wide.

(b) A restraining line marked 15 yards from and parallel to the starting line.

(c) A target 2 yards in length and 1 yard in width shall be marked in the center of the restraining line, half way between the two side lines of the rectangular areas.

(d) A line 1 yard in length is marked at the left and right corners of the starting line, at a right angle to the target. The ball is rolled into the testing area from these corner markers. See Figure 20.

178

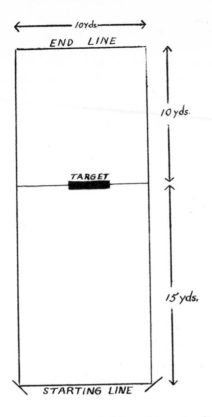

Figure 20. Diagram of field markings for fielding,
control and driving while moving hockey test.

Test:

    The player being tested stands behind the starting
line, with hockey stick in hand. On the signal "Ready, Go!"
the player moves forward into the area between the starting
line and the restraining line, receives the ball which has
been rolled to him from his right, carries the ball by dribbling to the end line, reverses his direction and drives
the ball back to the starting line. If the ball is not
driven hard enough to reach the starting line, the player
must follow up his first drive with a second.

    To test the ability to receive the ball from the left,
the procedure is the same as that described above except
that the ball is rolled in from the left. Players are rotated in taking trials to avoid fatigue.

The ball shall be rolled in from the area where the sideline meets the starting line, on either side. The roll-in should be aimed at the target. If the player being tested is unable to play the ball because of inaccuracy of the roll, the turn shall not count. (If the ball which was missed does not pass through the target, the roll-in is judged inaccurate.) It is important that a uniform speed be maintained in rolling the ball. If the return drive is driven out of the marked area, the trial does not count and is repeated.

Scoring:

The test is timed from the signal until the ball re-crosses the starting line at the completion of the drive. A total of 10 trials is given from the left and 10 from the right. The time is totalled separately for each side.

Reliability:

$r = .81$, stepped up to .90, for trials from the left;

$r = .62$, stepped up to .77, for trials from the right.

The subjects were 68 high school girls from Normal Community High School, Normal, Illinois. The majority were in their first season of play.

Validity:

$r = .87$ when scores were correlated against scores made on the Schmithals-French Ball Control Test.

Comments:

This test has considerable value as a practice device. It needs further study in regard to validity; it was impossible in this situation to use subjective ratings of playing ability as the criterion. There is no doubt about the importance of the skill being measured. Friedel experimented with many methods of putting the ball into play, including the use of an inclined plane, having the ball hit in with a hockey stick, and the roll-in. The inclined plane did not give enough momentum to the ball to have it carry the required distance at a speed comparable to that in the game situation. Greater consistency was secured with the roll-in than with the stick. This test is costly in time unless a number of testing stations are used.

BATTERY OF FIELD HOCKEY TESTS

The best single test for classification of college students is the Ball Control Test. The best combination of two tests, as determined by multiple correlations, is the Goal Shooting Left (one portion of Test 2) and the Fielding and Drive Test. They measure quite different things as is indicated by the low intercorrelation of .22. The two tests together yielded a correlation coefficient of .60. The addition of Test 1 to this battery raises the correlation only slightly (.62). The equation for combining scores on the two tests (Goal Shooting Left and the Fielding and Drive) to insure proper weighting is as follows:

1.0 goal shooting left + 1.2 fielding and drive.

GOLF

Golf, like archery and bowling, is individually scored and the game score may be used as a test score. Score on nine holes would be desirable but a minimum of five might be used satisfactorily if the players are not complete beginners. The game score should be supplemented by ratings during play.

Mechanical devices have been used in measuring driving ability but they are too expensive for most schools. Several tests[38] have been developed to measure length of drives, but problems have been encountered in attempting to penalize for inaccuracies. Tests which require measurements of velocity, angle of impact, and amount of deviation appear to be too time-consuming and complicated for use in most situations. Both indoor and outdoor tests which have been attempted agree on needing 30 or more trials per club tested to obtain adequate reliability. Validity has not been computed in every case but the coefficients have been low when it has been done.

One study using practice balls has yielded results better than other studies. Two tests nave been selected from that study. These were designed for indoor testing.

1. Drive test (Vanderhoof[53])

Equipment:

A #2 wood club; cocoa mat, preferably with a permanent tee inserted rather than the usual tee; plastic practice balls; standards placed 14 feet from a line at which the balls are hit, with a rope at 8 foot height between standards; a ten pin or other small object, placed at the opposite end of the gymnasium as a target.

Test:

The player being tested shall take as many practice swings as he desires; then hit two or three balls for warm-up. When he is ready, he will drive the ball from the tee toward the target, a total of 15 drives.

Scoring:

Score each trial from 0 to 3 points according to the area in which the ball lands. (See Figure 21.) Record two "topped" balls in succession as a trial with 0 score. Score is the sum of scores for the 15 trials.

Reliability:

The r was computed on odd-even sums for 110 players. This r was .82 or .90 when the Spearman-Brown formula was used.

Validity:

The validity was .71 compared with a rating of form.

2. Five Iron Approach (Vanderhoof)

Equipment:

A #5 iron club; plastic practice golf balls; cocoa mat; standards placed 14 feet from a line at which the balls are hit, with a rope at 8 foot height between standards; a ten pin or other small object, placed as a target at the opposite end of the gymnasium.

Test:

The player being tested shall take as many practice swings as he desires; then hit two or three balls for

182

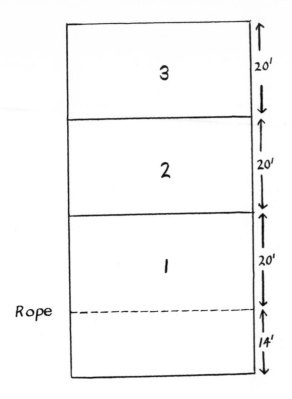

Figure 21. Scoring areas for Vanderhoof golf test.

warm-up. When he is ready he will hit the ball with a full swing toward the target, a total of 15 trials.

Scoring:

Score each trial from 0 to 3 points according to the area in which the ball lands. (See Figure 21.) Record two "topped" balls in succession as a trial with 0 score. Score is the sum of scores for the 15 trials.

Reliability:

The r obtained on the sum of odd and even trials was .73 for the 110 players. The Spearman-Brown formula raised it to .84 for the total.

Validity:

The r was .66 with the rating of form.

The driving test only might be used. The two tests have an intercorrelation of .55 but the R for the combination is .78. If the two tests are given the formula to be used is

1.3 drive + 1.0 five iron approach.

HANDBALL

Several studies[17] are known to have been made in constructing skill tests for handball but in only one study were attempts made to find the validity or reliability of these tests. Cornish[9] developed five tests and two of his tests have been selected for inclusion.

1. Power Test (Cornish)

The floor of the court is divided into areas as shown in Figure 22. One point was scored if the ball struck the floor in front of the service line. Standing in the service zone the player tossed the ball to the front wall, allowing it to bounce before playing it. The ball, after being stroked, must strike the front wall below a line six feet above the floor and parallel to the floor. If the ball hits above the line or if the player steps into the front court, another trial is allowed. Five strokes with each hand are made, and the total number of points is recorded as the score.

Reliability:

Not determined.

Validity:

For criterion scores, Cornish used the total number of points scored by a student in twenty-three games, minus the points scored by his opponents. With this criterion, a validity of .58 was obtained for the power test.

2. Thirty Second Volley (Cornish)

No special floor or wall markings are required for this test. The subject stands behind the service line and on

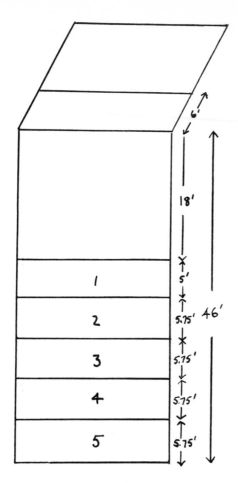

Figure 22. Court markings, Cornish power test in handball.

signal, drops the ball to the floor and strokes it continuously for thirty seconds. The ball must rebound far enough
from the wall to enable the contestant to remain behind the
service line. If the ball fails to return, the player may
step into the front court to strike the ball but must return for the succeeding stroke. If the contestant misses
the ball, another is handed to him and play continues. A
point is recorded each time the ball strikes the front wall,
and the total points at the end of thirty seconds constitutes the score.

Reliability:

        Not determined.

185

Validity:

.53, with criterion described for test 1.

Comments:

For additional tests, the reader is referred to the original source. Cornish obtained a multiple correlation of .694 for the combination of five tests. These tests appear to have value. The reliabilities should be determined; an increase in the number of trials might substantially improve their value.

SOCCER

Four tests selected from two studies of soccer skill tests will be included. The first study was made by Schaufele[46] and the tests reported included a repeated volleys test in which the ball is kicked successively against a wall; a passing and receiving test which involves dribbling the ball, passing it against a wall, controlling it on the rebound, and repeating; and a judgment in passing test which requires a dribble and kick for goal. The coefficients of validity with a criterion of subjective ratings of playing ability were .57, .50, and .34 respectively for the three tests, but were .77, .72, and .82 with a criterion of total test scores. When total test scores (scores of all tests in battery are T-scored and then added) are used as a criterion, the coefficient for each test should be higher because the test being studied is a part of the battery. The subjects in the Schaufele study were ninth- and tenth-grade girls. Bontz[27] developed a soccer test for use with fifth-and sixth-grade children which includes a straightaway dribble combined with a side pass to a wall and recovery, followed by a continued dribble and kick for goal. This test is highly reliable and produced a validity coefficient of .92 with a subjective rating criterion. It will be referred to in this study as Combination of Soccer Skills Test. For other usable soccer tests, see speedball test 3 in this chapter.

1. Volleying (Shaufele[46])

Equipment:

1. One soccer ball, fully inflated; one stop watch; one unobstructed wall space 15 feet long and 10 or more feet high.

2. Markings

(a) A target shall be outlined on the wall which is 15 feet wide, beginning 8 inches above the floor and continuing upward to at least 10 feet from the floor.

(b) A starting line 2 feet in length, shall be drawn on the floor parallel to the wall and 15 feet from the midpoint of the outlined wall target.

(c) An area shall be outlined on the floor which is 30 feet square, and it shall have as one side of the square the wall space upon which the target is marked, so that their midpoints coincide (See Figure 23).

Test:

The player places the ball on the starting line. At the signal, Ready, Go! he kicks the ball against the wall so that it hits within the outlined target; when the ball rebounds, he recovers it and kicks again. He continues this as rapidly as possible. The score is the number of times the ball strikes the wall within the target in one minute. The ball may be kicked, volleyed, or played with any technique which is legal in a regulation soccer game. After the first kick, the ball may be played from the point of recovery (provided that this point is within the 30-foot square on the floor) or the ball may be dribbled to a more advantageous position. If the ball bounds outside the 30-foot square, it will be stopped by one of the assistants and placed on the 30-foot square boundary line, where the player being tested may recover it and dribble or kick it again.

Note to test administrator: Station six assistants, two on each of the free sides of the 30-foot square as marked on the diagram by O's. These assistants are to stop any ball which is about to leave the square and place it with their hands on the boundary line at the point where it crossed the line.

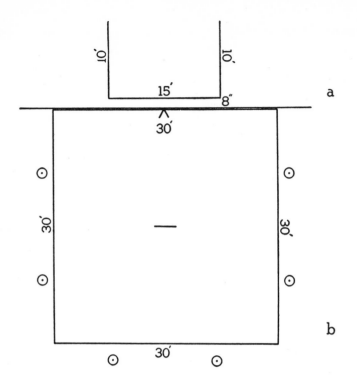

Figure 23. Wall and floor markings for soccer volleying test.

a = wall target.
b = floor diagram (should coincide with edge of wall).
∧ = center-of floor area and wall area (the two should coincide).
⊙ = assistants to recover balls going out of the area.

Practice: Allow each player one practice trial of one-half minute length.

Scoring:

Two trials are given each player, each on a separate day. Not more than a week should elapse between trials. The better of the two trials should count. One point is scored each time the ball strikes within the correct area. Balls hitting lines outlining the target are considered good.

Reliability:

The coefficient was .67 for first and second trials. The subjects were eighty-four ninth- and tenth-grade

girls, Fairview High School, Fairview Village, Ohio.   The
tests were given at the end of the season.

Validity:

The validity coefficient of this test was found to be
.57 when correlated with a criterion of subjective ratings.
When correlated with total test scores criterion, the coefficient of the volleying test was .77.

T-Scales:

See Table XIX below. One scale for the volleying
test was constructed from data on 253 ninth- and tenth-
grade girls in Ohio and Illinois,[46] the other on 141 college freshmen women.*

Table XIX.

T-Scales for Soccer Tests

T-SCORES	VOLLEYING*	VOLLEYING†	PASSING AND RECEIVING‡	JUDGMENT IN PASSING‡	T-SCORES
79	41				79
77	25	44			77
74	24				74
73		40			73
72	23				72
71	22	36		7	71
70	21		10		70
69	20	35			69
68		34			68
67	19			6	67
66	18	33			66
65		32			65
64		30			64
63	17	29	9		63
62		26		5	62
61	16	24			61
60		20			60

*Scott, Gladys: Unpublished studies.

189

Table XIX. (Cont.)

T-SCORES	VOLLEYING*	VOLLEYING†	PASSING AND RECEIVING‡	JUDGMENT IN PASSING‡	T-SCORES
59	15	19			59
58		18			58
57	14	17	8		57
56		16			56
55	13	15			55
54		14			54
53	12	13			53
52					52
51		12	7	4	51
50					50
49	11	11			49
48					48
47					47
46	10	10	6	3	46
45					45
44					44
43	9	9			43
42					42
41		8	5		41
40	8			2	40
39					39
38		7			38
37	7				37
36			4		36
35		6			35
34					34
33	6				33
32		5			32
31	5			1	31
30					30
29			3		29
28	4	4			28
25	3		2		25
23		3			23
21	2				21

*Scale constructed on data collected on 253 ninth- and tenth-grade girls, Fairview High School, Fairview Village, Ohio; and ninth grade girls in Blue Island Community High School, Blue Island, Ill.
†Scale constructed on data obtained on 141 University of Iowa students.
‡Scale constructed on data collected on 84 ninth- and tenth-grade girls, Fairview High School, Fairview Village, Ohio.

190

Comments:

The test appears to measure ability to control the
ball, judgment of speed and direction, and skill in maneuvering the ball, all of which are essential skills in the
game itself. An increase in the number of trials appears
to be indicated; four should be sufficient. A restraining
line might improve the test.

2. Passing and Receiving (Shaufele)

Equipment:

1. One soccer ball, fully inflated; one unobstructed
wall space 55 feet in length; one stop watch.

2. Markings

(a) A restraining line shall be drawn 8 feet from
the wall and parallel to it.
(b) Two boundary lines, perpendicular to the wall
and 12 feet in length, shall be drawn at the end of each
restraining line, extending out from the wall. These lines
shall be 55 feet apart (See Figure 24).

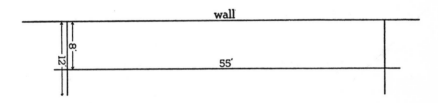

Figure 24. Floor markings for soccer passing and receiving test.

Test:

The ball is placed at the point where the restraining
line crosses the boundary line, with the wall on the player's left (indicated by A in the diagram). On the signal,
Go!, the player dribbles the ball forward a few feet and
then passes it with the side of the foot so that it strikes
the wall and rebounds. He runs forward to meet it as it
rebounds, and repeats, waiting for the ball to cross the
restraining line, as a pass may not be made from inside

191

the area. However, if the ball has not been sent with
enough force, it is permissible to go in to recover it and
dribble it outside the restraining line. The distance
must be covered in ten seconds, during which time three
passes are to be made against the wall, if possible. The
score will be the number of successful passes and recoveries made. The third pass and recovery will not count unless the ball has been touched beyond the finish line before the time limit. If the ball is recovered before
reaching the finish line, it may be dribbled up to the line
before time is up. The ball must be touched at least twice
between each recovery and the next pass.

Practices: Each player is given one practice trial before
the test begins.

Trials: The test consists of two trials from each end, the
first two from A with the wall to the left, and the next
two from B with the wall to the right.

Scoring:

The score shall be the sum of the number of successful
passes and recoveries made in the four trials. A successful pass and recovery shall be one in which the ball is
kicked against the wall from outside the restraining line
and first touched again with the foot outside the restraining line after the rebound.

Reliability:

r = .56 by the odd-even method; when corrected by the
Spearman-Brown formula, .72. The subjects were the same as
for Test 1.

Validity:

r = .50 with the subjective criterion, .68 with the
total test criterion.

T-Scales:

See Table XIX on page 189. The subjects were eighty-
four ninth- and tenth-grade girls in Ohio.

Comments:

This is a test involving difficult skills. Probably
the reliability and validity would both be higher for more

192

experienced players. Further experimentation needs to be done on distances, length of time, number of trials, and perhaps even on the amount of practice permitted. It is an excellent practice device.

3. Judgment in Passing (Schaufele)

Equipment:

1. One or more soccer balls, fully inflated; one stop watch; one bench 6 feet in length; one regulation soccer goal.

2. Markings

(a) Beginning from a point on the goal line and 4 feet inside the goal post, draw a line perpendicular to the goal line and 15 yards long. This is the restraining line.

(b) Extend the 12-yard line (regulation soccer marking) to a length equivalent to the length of the distance between the goal posts, and parallel to the goal line. This is the starting line.

(c) The 6-yard line on all regulation fields is also used in the test and is referred to as the 6-yard line.

(d) The bench is placed 4 feet from the goal, parallel to it, and in such a position that one end is exactly at the center of the goal and the other extends toward the right side as you face the goal from the starting line.

(e) For the second part of the test, the above directions shall be reversed, and the only additional line needed is a restraining line 4 feet inside the left-hand goal post and perpendicular to the goal line, 15 yards long. (See Figure 25 for test from the right-hand side.)

Test:

Place the ball on the 12-yard line, outside the restraining line. On the signal, Ready, Go!, dribble the ball forward, keeping to the right of the restraining line. After having passed the 6-yard line, the ball should be kicked for goal from the most advantageous position. Any type of kick is permissible but the ball must be kicked from outside the restraining line and it must enter the goal between the left end of the bench and the left goal post. Each trial must be completed in four seconds, from

193

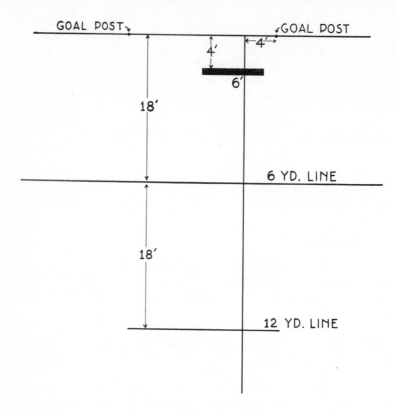

Figure 25. Field markings for soccer judgment in passing test. This illustrates the restraining line and position of the bench for a kick from the right. For the kick from the left, the bench would be moved to the left and a restraining line drawn 4 feet inside the left goal post.

the word <u>Go</u> until the ball is kicked. The trial will have to be repeated if any of the rules are violated, including exceeding the four-second time limit. Five trials are given from the right side, then five from the left.

Instructions to test administrator: For speed in administering the test, three or more balls should be made available. Have each player recover his own ball, carry it to the side of the field, and roll it to the person nearest the head of the line who does not have a ball. The entire test can be administered to as many as forty players in forty minutes. Only five or six players should be assigned to this test at one time.

Scoring:

One point is given for each goal scored in a legal trial. Five legal trials are given as described above, and then the bench is set up on the other side of the goal and the entire test is repeated on that side. The score is the total for the ten trials.

Reliability:

r = .69 when computed by the odd-even method. When the Spearman-Brown formula was applied, the reliability coefficient was raised to .82. The subjects were the same as for Test 1.

Validity:

r = .34 with the subjective criterion; .65 with the total test criterion.

T-Scales:

See Table XIX. The same subjects supplied the data for this test as for Test 2.

Comments:

This test is easily administered. The low validity figure is perhaps explained by the fact that judgment in placement and timing of passes is difficult to rate in an actual game situation.

4. Combination of Soccer Skills (Bontz[2])

Equipment:

1. Soccer balls, fully inflated; two goal posts or standards; one stop watch; playing surface 55 yards in length; and a wall space 12 feet long and 30 inches high. (Three locker room benches can be placed on their sides and stacked to present a smooth surface upon which the correct area can be painted with showcard paint. They should be braced and stacked in place in such a manner that there are no projections and there is little vibration.)

2. Field markings

(a) The soccer goal is 18 feet in width. Opposite the goal, mark a line 6 feet in length, parallel to the goal line and 55 yards from it. The center of this line should be directly opposite the center of the line between the goal posts. This is the starting line.

(b) Mark another line, to be used as a restraining line, extending from the left end of the starting line (as you face the goal) 25 yards toward the goal line.

(c) The "wall" is placed 12 feet to the left of this restraining line with the center of the marked target directly opposite the end of the 25-yard line.

(d) A 6-yard line, parallel to the end line, is also used.

(e) The description above is for testing with the right foot. When testing with the left foot, the markings differ as shown in Figure 26. If the wall is stationary, new markings with the goal line as the starting point and the starting point as the goal line should be made.

Test:

The ball is placed on the starting line. On the signal Ready, Go! the ball is dribbled and kept to the right of the restraining line until a point is reached where the ball can be kicked with the right foot diagonally forward to the wall, as though passing to another player. The player should run ahead to recover the ball as it rebounds and continue dribbling toward the goal until close enough to kick for goal. The ball must be kicked for goal before crossing the 6-yard line. The player must move as fast as possible without losing control of the ball. Four trials are given with the wall on the left, making the pass with the right foot; then four more trials are given with the wall on the right, passing with the left foot.

Note to test administrators: Allow two practice trials with each foot. Record actual trials in half seconds. Trials which include errors must be repeated.

Scoring:

The score is the total amount of time it takes to complete the eight trials; each one is timed separately.

Reliability:

r = .93 computed by the odd-even method, when corrected by the Spearman-Brown formula, .96. The subjects were 124 fifth- and sixth-grade children from public schools in Des Moines, Iowa, and in Webster Groves, Mo.

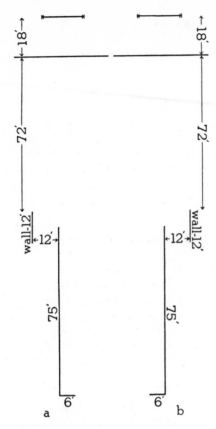

Figure 26.   Field markings for soccer combination of skills test.

a = markings for kick with right foot.
b = markings for kick with left foot.
||——|| = goal posts.

Validity:

For the ninety-two cases from Webster Groves, r = .92 with a subjective rating criterion. For the thirty-two cases from Des Moines, r = .53 with subjective ratings.

Scores:

The range for fifth grade was 95.5 to 226.5 seconds; median 139.2.

The range for sixth grade was 90.0 to 191.0 seconds; median 130.3.

The range for girls only was 102.5 to 226.5 seconds; median 143.4.

The range for boys only was 90.0 to 198.0 seconds; median 126.7.

Comments:

This test has proved interesting to players. If a stationary wall, such as a school building, is adjacent to the playing field, it can be used for practice outside of class time. Such an arrangement leaves the playing field free. It has been used with high school and college ages, but data are not available on the older groups.

BATTERY OF SOCCER TESTS

The one best test for high school girls appears to be volleying. A good two-item battery of tests is the combination of passing and receiving with volleying, which Schaufele found to give a coefficient of .85 with the total test criterion, or .63 with subjective ratings. The inter-correlation of these two tests is .46. Use the following equation in combining the two items:

2.0 passing and receiving + 1.0 volleying

An equally good two-item battery is the combination of judgment in passing with volleying, which gives a coefficient of .85 with the total test criterion (subjective estimate figures not given). The intercorrelation of these two tests is .41. The recommended weighting of scores is:

2.0 judgment in passing + 1.0 volleying

SOFTBALL

Two tests of throwing ability that are highly related are available and a choice is possible. The Repeated Throws Test is more economical of time but requires more balls and a large unobstructed wall surface. The Distance Throw test has yielded slightly higher validity coefficients.

THROWING

1. Repeated Throws

Equipment:

    1. A number of new 12-inch inseam balls; a flat, un-
obstructed wall surface about 15 feet or more high and 8
feet wide; a stop watch.

    2. Markings

        Draw a line on the wall 7 1/2 feet from the floor.
Draw a restraining line on the floor 15 feet from the wall
and parallel to it.

Test:

    The player being tested stands any place behind the
restraining line and facing the wall. On the signal,
Ready, Go! the player throws the ball against the wall so
that it hits above the 7 1/2-foot line, catches it, and repeats this as many times as he can in thirty seconds. One
ball is used throughout the test; if it gets out of control, it must be recovered by the player being tested.
(The loss of time is considered sufficient penalty.) Foot
faults (stepping on or over the line) are watched by the
scorer and the player is told to move back. Any throws
made while the player is on or over the line do not count.
A rest of two minutes is recommended between trials; this
can be easily administered if three or four girls take
throws at the same target. Six trials are given.

Scoring:

    One point is counted each time the ball hits on or
above the 7 1/2-foot line, provided the throw was made when
the player was behind the restraining line. The score for
the entire test is the total of six trials of thirty seconds
each.

Reliability:

    r = .89 by the odd-even method, .94 corrected by the
Spearman-Brown formula; subjects were sixty-six college
women. On another group of 210 University of Iowa students,

exactly the same results were obtained.* Underkofler[43] found slightly lower coefficients on a similar test for junior high school girls. The 14-inch ball was used, the line on the wall was 10 feet high, and the restraining line was 10 feet from the wall. In this case the r was .73 for first and second trials, stepped up to .84 because the sum of the two trials was used as the score.

Validity:

In the junior high school study cited above, the r with a subjective rating criterion was .64. In another study* this test was given to 173 college women in various institutions located in the central states. The coefficient was .51 with a subjective rating criterion. The comparatively low validity is doubtless partially explained by the fact that the same persons did not make all of the ratings; higher validities should be obtained from more experienced players.

T-Scales:

Three scales are presented. (See Table XX.) In the first scale, the score for the test was the sum of two trials and the data were collected on 118 seventh- and eighth-grade girls in Illinois. The second scale used the sum of six trials and was constructed from data obtained on 225 freshman and sophomore women at the University of Iowa.† The third was constructed on 159 freshmen major students at Illinois State Normal University.

Comments:

This test is highly reliable but does not differentiate clearly between students in the middle ability group. The better players will be able to throw the ball with sufficient force so that it rebounds to them without bouncing. To a certain extent it measures accuracy as well as power. It is easy to administer and can be given indoors. If there is sufficient wall space for ten targets, the entire test can be administered to a class of forty girls in fifteen minutes. The test is likely to result in muscle soreness if all six trials are given the same day; it is

---

*Research Committee, Central Association for Physical Education of College Women, Unpublished study.
†Department of Physical Education for Women, University of Iowa, Unpublished studies.

Table XX.

T-Scales for Softball Tests

T-SCORE	REPEATED THROWS*	REPEATED THROWS†	REPEATED THROWS‡	BATTING TEE&	DISTANCE THROW‖	FIELDING¶	T-SCORE
78		122					78
77						28	77
76	37	121			131		76
75		120	130		129		75
74		116		1120	127		74
73					126	27	73
72		115		945	124	24	72
71					123	23	71
70	36	114	126	920	121		70
69		113		845	120	22	69
68		109		820	118	21	68
67	35	108	122	795	117		67
66		106	118	720	115		66
65		103		695	114	20	65
64	34	102	114	670	112		64
63		98		645	110	19	63
62	33	94		620	109	18	62
61	32	93	110	595	107		61
60		92		570	106	17	60
59		90			104		59
58		89	106	545	103	16	58
57	31	86			101	15	57
56		85		520	100	14	56
55	30	84	102		98		55
54		82			96	13	54
53	29	81	98	495	95		53
52		78		470	93		52
51		77	94	445	92	12	51
50	28	76	90		90		50
49		75		420	87	11	49
48		73			85		48
47	27	72	86		82	10	47
46		71		395	80		46
45	26	70	82		78	9	45
44	25	69		370	75		44
43		68			73	8	43
42	23	67	78		70		42
41	22	66		345	68		41
40	21	65		320	65	7	40
39	19	64			63		39
38	18		74	295	60		38
37	16	63			58	6	37
36	14	62		270	55		36

201

Table XX. (Cont.)

T-SCORE	REPEATED THROWS*	REPEATED THROWS†	REPEATED THROWS‡	BATTING TEE&	DISTANCE THROW‖	FIELDING¶	T-SCORE
35	13	61		245	53	5	35
34	10	59		220	50		34
33		58	70	195	48	4	33
32	9			170	46		32
31	7	56		145	43		31
30		54	66		41	3	30
29		53			40		29
28	4		62	120			28
27						2	27
26		52					26
25			58			1	25
24	2						24
23							23
22		51					22
21							21

*Scale was constructed on data collected on 118 seventh- and eighth-grade girls in Riverside School, Riverside, Ill. Score is the sum of two trials.
†Scale was constructed on data collected on 225 University of Iowa women. The score is the sum of six trials.
‡Scale was constructed on data collected on 159 freshman majors at Illinois State Normal University. Score is the sum of six trials.
&Scale was constructed on data collected on 71 women majors at Illinois State Normal University. Score is the sum of 20 trials on Davis Test.
‖Scale was constructed on data obtained on college women.
¶Scale was constructed on data obtained on 151 freshman and sophomore women, University of Iowa.

recommended that the test be split with half of the trials given on each of two days. In an attempt to determine whether two trials might be enough, the first and second trials by 210 players were correlated and then the Spearman-Brown formula applied. The r in this case was only .78 in contrast to .94 for all six trials.

2. Distance Throw

Equipment:

A number of regulation softballs, and a field. (See Figure 59, page 474 for field markings.)

Test:

The player stands behind the line and throws the ball as far as possible with an overhand or sidearm motion. The player is limited to one step, which must be taken behind and not over the line. Three throws constitute one trial, and only the best throw of the three is measured and recorded. Three trials are permitted (nine throws in all).

Scoring:

The throw is measured as the distance in feet from the starting line to the spot where the ball first touches the ground. The best of the three recorded throws is used as the player's score.

Reliability:

r = .95, computed on successive trials. The subjects were 118 girls in the seventh and eighth grades in the Intermediate School, Riverside, Ill.

Broer[7] obtained an r of .94 for one group of 239 junior high girls and an identical reliability coefficient for another group of 141 junior high girls.

Validity:

r = .81 with ratings; subjects were 118 seventh- and eighth-grade girls, the same as for Test 1. r = .63 with ratings; subjects were college girls in various institutions, the same as for Test 1.

T-Scales:

One scale constructed on data from 173 college women is presented in Table XX. The subjects were from several colleges in the central states.

Comments:

Ability to throw the ball long distances is important in softball, and since there is a relationship between the distance that the ball can be thrown and the ability to throw the ball with speed, it seems all the more important that this skill be measured. This appears to be the best single test yet devised for measuring softball playing ability.

FIELDING

The fielding test* is a combination of throwing and footwork. Since the sequence of throwing is performed against time it is much more indicative of playing ability than the usual target throwing test.

Equipment:

1. Five or more regulation softballs. Stop watch.

2. Field markings

The test requires two wall surfaces at right angles to each other. On one is placed a target consisting of five concentric circles 3 inches, 12 inches, 21 inches, 30 inches, and 39 inches, respectively, in radius. The center of the target should be 48 inches from the floor. On the floor, directly in front of the center of the target, is a base one foot square and 45 feet from the target. The other wall should be situated on the player's left as she stands on the base facing the target. It may vary in distance from the base. It is recommended that it be at least 20 feet and not more than 40 feet (See Figure 27).

Test:

The player stands at base with any part of either foot touching the base, ball in hand. On signal Ready, Go! he throws the ball at the blank wall so that it will rebound. He fields it as quickly as possible, touches the base, and throws quickly at the target as though making a double play on bases. He takes another ball and repeats. A total of ten trials is allowed but it is suggested that there be a rest between the first five and the last five throws.

Scoring:

There are two aspects of the scoring. (1) The target throws are each scored for accuracy, 5 points for the center, 4, 3, 2, 1, respectively. The accuracy score is the sum made on the ten trials. (2) Time is taken on each trial from the release of the ball toward the first wall to the moment of contact on the target or on the wall near the

---

*Research Committee, Central Association for Physical Education for College Women, Unpublished study.

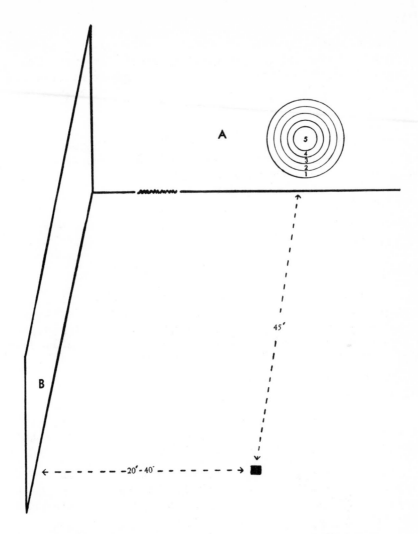

Figure 27. Wall and floor markings for softball fielding test.

A = target wall.
B = rebound wall.
■ = base.

target. The time score is the cumulative score on the ten trials. (It is preferable to use a stop watch which will continue rather than returning to zero each trial, thus avoiding necessity to add times later.) If the time is above a fixed minimum, one point should be subtracted from accuracy for each two seconds of time in excess. If below this fixed minimum, it is disregarded in scoring.

Reliability:

The reliability was .56 when computed by the odd-even method and corrected by the Spearman-Brown formula. The subjects were 151 freshmen and sophomore women at the University of Iowa.*

Validity:

The validity was .49 when correlated with judges' ratings of throwing form and footwork of 151 University of Iowa freshman and sophomore women.*

T-Scales:

Data for scales in Table XX were obtained from freshman and sophomore women at the University of Iowa.

Comments:

The fixed minimum of time can be determined only after experimentation or perhaps administration of the tests to the class. The time required is dependent upon the distance of the base from each wall and the nature of the wall surface, resulting in a slow or fast rebound.

Only balls in good condition should be used. An old ball which has become soft is slow on the rebound.

The test requires considerable space. However, if five balls are used and one or two students collect balls, the test can be given very quickly.

The scorer stands near the target where he can see the balls hit. The timer stands inside the angle formed by the two flights of the ball so that he can see the player and the target.

BATTING

Batting ability is difficult to measure since it depends partially upon the skill of the pitcher. Attempts have been made to standardize the pitching and thus equalize the opportunity for the batters. Having the same pitcher pitch to all the batters being tested does not work

---

*Department of Physical Education for Women, University of Iowa, Unpublished studies.

satisfactorily as the pitcher varies in his deliveries and
the balls of some pitchers are easier to hit than the balls
of other pitchers. Until inexpensive and dependable cata-
pults are manufactured, ratings of batting ability should
be used to supplement a measure of power. Batting averages
if obtained from enough games over a fairly long season
serve as an excellent measure of batting ability but frequently such averages are unavailable. Two tests using a
batting tee are available and a choice between them should
be made.

1. Batting Tee Test (Davis[13])

Equipment:

1. One adjustable softball batting tee, an assortment
of official softball bats, several twelve-inch softballs in
good condition, measuring tape, lime, score sheets, and
yardage markers approximately fifteen inches square with
numerals at least ten inches high.

2. Field Markings

(a) Construct 15 parallel lines 35 yards long and
5 yards apart across an unobstructed area with a minimum
size of 35 yards by 70 yards. (If a football field is used,
it is necessary to add only the lines between each of the
ten-yard lines.)

(b) Mark a spot exactly in the center of the first
parallel line. Place the tee on this spot. (See Figure
28.)

(c) Place yardage markers at the end of each parallel line on one side of the field in a position easily
visible across the field.

Test:

The player being tested assumes his natural batting
position at the batting tee, and attempts to hit the ball
off the tee as far as possible. Five practice trials pre-
cede the test, which consists of 20 trials. The contestant
may adjust the height of the tee or change bats at any time
during the test.

Scoring:

The point where the ball first lands is the yardage
which should be recorded as the score for the trial. This

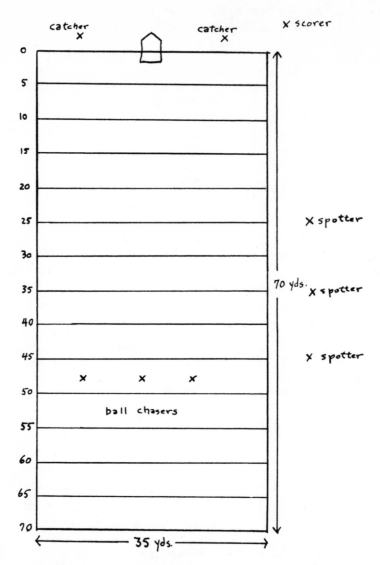

Figure 28. Field markings, Davis batting tee test.

is estimated to the nearest yard. If the batter swings and
misses the ball, or swings and hits the tee only, the score
is zero. The score for the test is the total yardage of
the twenty trials.

Directions for Administration

1. Ball Chasers: Stand near the 50-yard line to return balls to the catchers. Do not touch any ball until after it lands.

2. Catchers: Assume positions well away from the tee on each side of it to catch balls returned from the field and place them on the tee.

3. Spotters: Take positions opposite the 25, 35, and 45 yard markers along the side of the field, and call the yardage to the scorer. Move quickly along the side-line to get in a position directly opposite the ball as it descends.

There should be three spotters. If the spotters do not agree on the yardage for a trial, the decision should be made on the basis of the two in agreement, or if none agree, the median score shall be used.

4. Scorer: Stand at the extreme end of the 0-yard line on the same side of the field as the spotters, and record the scores on the score sheet.

Reliability:

.83 stepped up to .90 for 71 women major students, .71 stepped up to .83 for 27 women semi-professional softball players.

Validity:

Davis obtained the batting averages at the end of a playing season for the 36 players she tested and correlated their test scores against the batting averages. The resultant coefficient was .33. Davis concluded that her test was a highly reliable measure of ability to bat the ball off the tee but that it does not measure to a high degree the same ability as that determined by batting averages. She had no other measure of validity, but there can be little doubt that the test measures ability to hit the ball long distances.

2. Bat for Distance Test (Fox and Young[20])

Equipment:

An assortment of softball bats, a minimum of five good softballs, a standard batting tee (softball).

Field Markings:

A. A baseline on which the batting tee is placed.

B. Twenty lines three yards in length spaced ten feet apart and parallel to the baseline.

C. Twenty lines one yard in length midway between the three-yard lines and parallel to them.

D. The distance from the baseline is marked at the end of each of the three-yard lines.

Test:

Each player is given three warm-up hits at the ball which has been placed on the batting tee. The tee may be adjusted to any height during the practice hits. Five trials are then taken without pause.

Scoring:

The distance from the batting tee to the place where each ball first touched the ground is recorded. The score is the sum of the distance of each of the five trials. It counts as a trial and no score is given if the bat strikes the tee instead of the ball or if the ball is missed completely.

Reliability:

r = .87 when the Spearman-Brown Prophecy Formula was used to step up the split halves method of computation. The 62 subjects used were from the service program or were majors in physical education at the State University of Iowa.

Validity:

r = .64 when correlated with the sum of three judges' ratings. The number of subjects in the validity portion of the study was 58, from the above described group.

210

Comments:

It is necessary for players to have had some experience and practice in using the batting tee before the test is given.

BASE RUNNING

Tests of speed in base running have been developed but are not included here since base running speed seems to be relatively unimportant in a limited battery of tests. Higher validities are obtained when the test includes running from home plate to second base than in running to first base only or in running all four bases.

BATTERY OF SOFTBALL TESTS

There is no battery to recommend, if the term battery is used in a strict sense. The two throwing tests had an intercorrelation of .81 in one study which makes it seem unnecessary to give both. Studies of intercorrelation between the other tests have not been made.

SPEEDBALL

Since many of the skills used in soccer are also used in speedball, some of the same tests can be used. The test "Combination of Soccer Skills" is an example. See page 197. Three tests have been selected from an unpublished study by Smith,[50] two of which are specific to speedball. The third, Foot Pass to Wall, appears equally applicable to soccer. All of these tests can be given indoors.

1. Kick-up to Self

Equipment:

1. Stop watches, soccer balls.

2. Markings

Unobstructed wall space approximately 6 feet in width for each testing station; a restraining line drawn parallel to and 7 feet from the wall.

Test:

Player with soccer ball in hand stands behind the restraining line facing the wall. On signal, he throws the
ball against the wall at any height (2 to 3 feet above floor
level seems most satisfactory), and controls it on the rebound by executing a one- or two-foot kick-up to himself.
He continues throwing the ball and executing kick-ups for
a period of thirty seconds. Six trials are given with the
total of the six being used as the score. If the ball does
not rebound to or beyond the restraining line, the player
may cross the line and recover the ball with the hands, but
he must return beyond the restraining line before his next
throw. Three players to each testing station taking turns
assures a one-minute rest between trials.

Scoring:

The total number of successful legal kick-ups out of
six trials of thirty seconds each is the score, each legal
kick-up counting one point. (A legal kick-up is one which
goes directly off the player's foot or instep to the hands
and does not roll up the shin or touch any part of the body
other than the hands.)

Reliability:

The reliability, correlating odd and even trials, was
.81. When the Spearman-Brown Prophecy Formula was applied,
the reliability was .90. The subjects were sixty-three
freshman women majors at Illinois State Normal University.
The majority of the players had had no previous experience
in speedball before the season; the tests were given at the
end of eighteen forty-five minute periods of instruction,
extending over a period of nine weeks.

Validity:

The validity of this test for the above-described group
was found to be .54 with the criterion of subjective ratings
of playing ability in general, made by three teachers.[50]

2. Wall Pass

Equipment:

    1. Stop watches, soccer balls.

    2. Markings

       Unobstructed wall space approximately 6 feet in width for each testing station; a restraining line drawn parallel to and 7 feet from the wall.

Test:

       Player with ball in hands stands behind the restraining line facing the wall. On signal, the ball is thrown against the wall, caught on the rebound, thrown and caught again as quickly as possible. The throw may be of any type. Four trials of fifteen seconds each are given. Player may cross the restraining line to recover the ball but must be behind the line before the ball is thrown.

Scoring:

       Each throw from behind the line counts one point. The total for each trial is recorded and the score for the test is the sum of the four trials.

Reliability:

       By the odd-even method, the coefficient obtained was .75. When corrected by the Spearman-Brown Prophecy Formula, the reliability coefficient became .86. The subjects were the same as for Test 1.

Validity:

       The coefficient was .51 with the criterion of rating of general playing ability in speedball made by three judges; the subjects were the same as for Test 1.

3. Foot Pass to Wall

Equipment:

    1. Stop watches, soccer balls.

2. Markings

Unobstructed wall space of 12 to 18 feet for each testing station; a restraining line drawn on the floor 7 feet from and parallel to the wall. Two lines, each 4 feet in length, are drawn on the floor at right angles to the restraining line and 6 feet apart. The letters A and B are drawn to the left and right of these lines. (See Figure 29.)

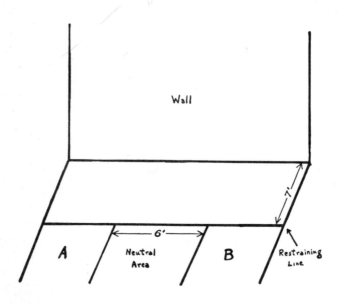

Figure 29.   Floor markings for foot pass to wall test.

Test:

The ball is placed on the floor at A. On signal, the player passes the ball with his foot diagonally to the wall so that it will rebound in a forward direction toward area B. He runs across the neutral area to B, where he receives the rebound and controls it with his feet and turns around, again passing to the wall, this time in such a manner that the ball will rebound to area A. The player continues this procedure, crossing the neutral area and passing alternately from areas A and B. Six trials of thirty seconds each are allowed. The player may cross the restraining line to recover the ball but must return to the proper area before making the next pass to the wall.

Scoring:

One point is scored each time the ball hits the wall on a pass started from behind the restraining line and outside the 6-foot neutral area. The sum of the scores made on the six trials is the score for the test.

Reliability:

By odd-even method, the coefficient was .46 for the sixty-three subjects in this study. This coefficient became .62 when the Spearman-Brown Prophecy Formula was applied. The subjects were the same as for Test 1.

Validity:

The coefficient was .30; criterion was subjective ratings; subjects were the same as for Test 1.

Comments:

This test should measure ability to control the ball while moving and should be as usable for soccer as for speedball. Examination of the scores indicates a definite trend for improvement as the trials progress, which could indicate the need for more practice trials or that the test would be a better test for players with more experience. It may prove to be more valuable as a practice device than as a test. It is included here because it represents an attempt to measure an important skill, and perhaps with further refinements it will prove useful. The distance from the wall or the width of the neutral territory may need to be adjusted.

The ratings for the Smith study were conducted as follows: Each team was watched approximately forty minutes by three experienced teachers who had served as raters in other similar studies. During the ratings, the six teams were rotated so that each ten minutes, two different teams played. Total playing time was 120 minutes. A five point scale was employed. In 8 per cent of the cases the disagreement between raters was two categories; they differed more than one category in twenty-two of the sixty-three cases. It is difficult to rate players adequately in that length of time in a team sport with twenty-two players on the field. Reliabilities, of course, are not affected by the criterion and they are adequate for the first two tests.

The third test needs further work but is included here because it represents an attempt to measure an important skill.

BATTERY OF SPEEDBALL TESTS

A combination of three tests yielded a multiple correlation of .63 with the criterion of combined subjective ratings of general playing ability in speedball. Some of the factors in the game situation that may have influenced the judges' ratings, such as speed in running, punting and drop kicking, are not measured in the tests. Tests 1 and 2 yielded an R of .53. The intercorrelations between the three tests were as follows: 1 and 2, .44; 1 and 3, .49; 2 and 3, .29.

SWIMMING

Swimming performance has been evaluated by various methods. The most common methods are subjective ratings (see Chapter 10), use of achievement charts for a tally of skills learned, and speed swimming measured as distance covered in a given time or time required for a given distance. Cureton[11],[12] has done considerable work in evaluating progress in swimming, with consideration of the speed aspect. Also, such standards as the Achievement Scales in Wartime Swimming[24] have proven useful in comparing speed scores.

The following test is based on the assumption that each stroke made should propel the swimmer through the water. It has proven objective in measuring that propulsion for side, back, crawl or breast stroke. Indirectly it would seem to reflect efficiency in the stroke and relaxation during the glide, without putting pressure on for speed of swimming. Since the majority of swimming classes do not aim primarily for speed, this would appear to be a better measure than a timed event.

Swimming Power Test (Fox)

Equipment:

A rope, 18 to 20 feet longer than the width of the pool, anchored firmly on one side of the pool one to two

216

feet from the end of the pool. A weight is attached to the
rope near the center of the pool. Markers (may be adhesive
or masking tape) at 5-foot intervals, starting with the rope
as zero, and continuing for 55 feet. If the markers at the
10-foot intervals are longer or a different color it facilitates scoring. (See Figure 30.)

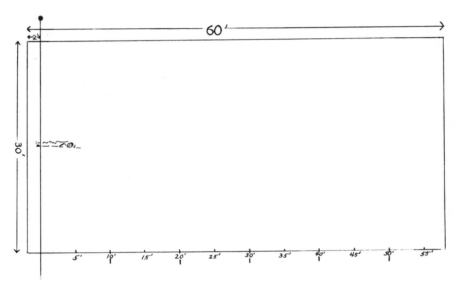

Figure 30. Pool markings for swimming power test.

Test:

The rope is pulled up to about 1 foot below water level
where weight is attached. The swimmer assumes the appropriate floating position for the stroke to be tested. Her
ankles rest on the rope. Care must be taken that the rope
is held so the swimmer does not drift from position and the
feet are not lifted above the water. The swimmer is instructed to swim six strokes after the starting signal, using a glide if she wishes on strokes normally permitting a
glide. On the signal "Go," the rope is dropped so the feet
are not supported. The swimmer starts from a motionless
float.

The distance is scored as follows:

For back, side or breast stroke: the distance the
ankles have moved from the starting line (judged to the

217

nearest foot) at the beginning of the recovery of the sixth stroke.

For back crawl or front crawl: Distance the ankles have moved from the starting line (judged to the nearest foot) at the moment the fingers enter the water for the beginning of the sixth stroke. Accuracy on stroke counting is improved if each arm stroke is counted. The distance is scored at the beginning of the 11th arm entry.

Comments:

Examiner should be parallel with the feet at the finish.

Swimmers should have two or three practice starts from the rope in one or more positions though it is not necessary for each stroke.

Scores will be recorded only on strokes performed with correct arm and leg action.

Any kick taken before starting arms or during a glide counts as a stroke.

Reliability:

Fifty swimmers took three trials each on the side stroke and front crawl. On the side stroke, trials 1 and 3 gave .96 and trials 2 and 3, .97. On the front crawl, the r's were .87 and .95 respectively.

Validity:

When correlated with form, the r on 57 cases was .83 for side stroke and .69 for crawl.

TABLE TENNIS

The only objective skill test in table tennis was developed by Mott and Lockhart[43] to measure the ability of players in rallying the ball against a perpendicular surface. The test has undergone scientific study and is recommended as a good test. When combined with tournament rankings, it should provide an adequate measure of skill.

1. Backboard Test

Equipment:

1. Stop watch, minimum of three table tennis balls in good condition, table tennis racket, an official table tennis table, hinged at the center, a kitchen match box approximately 5 inches by 2 3/4 inches, thumbtacked to the edge of the table and even with the end of the table (box should be placed on the right-hand side of the table as shown in the inset), score cards and pencils, wall space or post against which table may be propped in such a way that one-half of the table is horizontal, and one-half is perpendicular to the floor, as shown in the illustration (Figure 31).

Figure 31. Table as set up for table tennis backboard test. Insert shows box attached to edge of table.

2. Markings

A chalk line marked on the perpendicular half of the table at net height, 6 inches above the horizontal surface of the table.

Test:

The player being tested stands with a racket and one ball in hand behind the end of the horizontal table surface. Two or more extra balls are placed in the match box at the side of the table. At the signal Go, the player drops his ball to the table and then rallies it with the racket against the perpendicular table surface as many times as possible in thirty seconds. Any number of bounces shall be permitted on the horizontal surface. Whenever the player loses control of the ball, he may take another ball from the match box, drop it to the horizontal surface, and continue to play. An assistant replaces the balls in the match box as they are used. A hit to the perpendicular surface does not count if any of the following fouls are committed: the ball is volleyed (hit before being permitted to bounce); the player puts his free hand on the table during or immediately preceding a hit; the ball strikes the perpendicular table surface below the net line. An assistant stands near to count the number of successful hits made against the perpendicular surface.

Scoring:

The score for one trial is the number of times in thirty seconds that the ball is legally hit against the perpendicular surface of the table. Three trials are given. Rest must be permitted between the trials to avoid fatigue. The test score is the best score of the three trials.

Administrative Suggestions:

Before giving the table tennis test, it is recommended that the players be familiar with the technique of rallying the ball against a perpendicular surface. This may be accomplished by setting up tables in the manner required for the test, and permitting the players to rally the ball against the backboard as a practice device. If wall space is available, tables may be placed lengthwise against the wall. The ball is then rallied across the table width to the wall. More players may practice at one time with the latter arrangement, but the test should not be given in this way. If the class is organized into small squads, each squad may line up behind a table. A player scores for the player ahead of him in line, then takes the test and goes to the end of the line. This procedure is continued until all have had three trials. Only one timer is needed, since all tables may be started at the same time. With three tables, thirty players may be tested in a forty-minute period.

Reliability:

The reliability was .98 by the odd-even method, for seventy-nine players.

Validity:

Validity was .81 with subjective ratings of three judges. Each player was observed for three full games in a round-robin tournament.

T-Scales:

See Table XXI. The scale was constructed from data obtained on 162 college women at the University of Nebraska.

Comments:

This test is an excellent teaching and practice device as well as a good measuring instrument. It is economical of time.

TENNIS

Two tests have been selected for inclusion, one involving the use of a wallboard and the other a regulation court. These should be supplemented by subjective ratings of form (some suggestions for this appear in Chapter X) and by some measure of success in playing such as tournament rankings.

The wallboard test is a modification of the Dyer Wallboard Test,[14] a test which has been used extensively by both men and women teachers. The Forehand-Backhand Drive test is newer but appears promising. As stated by the test constructors,[6] "the results of this test are based on very small groups and can, therefore, only be taken as indications."

Table XXI.

T-Scales for Table Tennis Test*

T-SCORE	RAW SCORE	T-SCORE	RAW SCORE	T-SCORE	RAW SCORE
77	60	60	46	40	
76		59	45	39	28
75		58		38	27
74		57	44	37	26
73	58	56		36	
72					
71	55	55	43	35	25
		54	42	34	24
70		53	41	33	23
69	54	52	40	32	22
68	52	51		31	
67	51				
66	50	50	39	30	
		49	38	29	21
65	49	48	37	28	
64	48	47	36	27	
63		46	34	26	20
62	47				
61		45	33	25	
		44	32	24	16
		43	31		
		42	30		
		41	29		

*Journal of Health and Physical Education, 17: November 1946, p. 552. Quoted by permission of the publishers.

1. Wallboard Test (Modification of Dyer Test)

Equipment:

1. Backboard or wall, approximately 10 feet in height and allowing 15 to 20 feet in width per person taking the test at one time; stop watch; two balls and a racket per player. Balls should be in good condition and racket should be tightly strung. Box for extra balls, about 12 inches long, 9 inches wide, and 3 inches deep, placed on the floor where the re-straining line (described below) joins the side (at the left for right-handed players and right for left-handed players). A racket may be substituted for the box; the racket is placed

on the floor in the same position as that described for the box, and the balls are laid on the face of the racket.

2. Markings

A line 3 inches in width should be drawn on the wall to represent the net, so that the top is 3 feet from the floor. A restraining line, 27.5 feet from the base of the wall should be drawn on the floor, parallel to the wall.

Test:

On the word Go of the signal, Ready, Go! the player drops the ball and lets it hit the floor once and then starts rallying it against the wall. He continues rallying until the signal to stop. The ball may bounce any number of times or it may be volleyed. At the start of the test and whenever a new ball is put in play, it must be allowed to bounce before being hit. Any stroke may be used, but all strokes should be played from behind the restraining line. The player may cross the line to retrieve the ball but hits made from this position are not scored. If the ball gets out of control, the player may take another ball from the box.

Scoring:

Each time a ball strikes the wall on or above the net line, having been hit from behind the restraining line, one point is scored. Three trials are given, and the score is the sum of these trials: Subtract from total, the number of extra balls used from the box. The length of each trial is thirty seconds.

Reliability:

r = .58 on second and third trials during the eleventh two-hour lesson, stepped up to .80 by the Spearman-Brown formula. In contrast, r = .38 on the second and third trials for the second two-hour lesson, stepped up to .64; subjects were 165 freshman and sophomore women at the University of Iowa. The restraining line was 36 feet from the wall.

Validity:

On 468 University of Iowa students the correlation between test performance and the sum of ratings on stroke form and footwork by three judges was .61.*

*Department of Physical Education for Women, University of Iowa. Unpublished studies.

T-Scales:

See Table XXII for a scale on 583 University of Iowa women in beginning tennis classes. The test followed

Table XXII.

T-Scale for Tennis Backboard Test*

T-SCORE	BACKBOARD SCORE†
81	34
78	33
76	32
74	31
72	30
70	29
69	28
68	27
67	26
65	25
63	24
61	23
60	22
58	21
57	20
56	19
55	18
53	17
51	16
50	15
47	14
45	13
43	12
41	11
38	10
35	9
33	8
32	7
29	6
27	5
26	4
25	3
23	2
20	1

*Scale constructed from data obtained on 583 University of Iowa students.
†Score is the sum of three trials.

224

about thirteen two-hour lessons. The distance of the restraining line from the wall was 27.5 feet. The scores were
not corrected for extra balls.

Comments:

This test is satisfactory for a classification test. It
can be administered easily and is completely objective. When
the restraining line is placed at sufficient distance from the
wall, it serves to encourage better form. The line probably
should never be closer than 24 feet. A very "fast" wall might
give better results with the line 30 to 36 feet away. More
advanced players will profit by a more distant restraining
line, as they may then put their full power into the strokes.

McGee,[37] in her study of the relationship of general
motor ability to specific skill tests, correlated scores made
on the test with subjective ratings made by the instructor of
a group of thirty-eight freshman women majors at Illinois
State Normal University and secured a validity coefficient of
.78. She obtained a coefficient of correlation of .69 between
scores made on the Wallboard Test (using a 25-foot restraining
line) and the Scott General Motor Ability Test (Battery A).
This indicates a substantial relationship. However, in a
study of 468 subjects a coefficient of .35 was found between
the Wallboard Test (at 27.5 feet) and the Scott General Motor
Ability Test (Battery B).* This was a group with a wider
range of motor ability and probably represents more closely
the relationship for the total student population.

2. Forehand-Backhand Drive Test (Broer and Miller)

Equipment:

1. One regulation court and net, with a rope stretched
4 feet directly above the net and parallel to it, one racket,
15-20 good balls, and score cards for each player (See Figure 32) and pencils.

2. Court markings (See Figure 33)

Two chalk lines are drawn across the court parallel
to the service line, one 10 feet nearer the net than the service line and one 9 feet behind the service line. Two chalk

---

*Scott, Gladys: Unpublished studies.

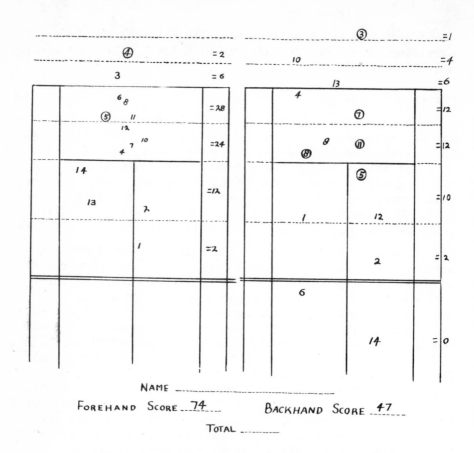

NAME _____

FOREHAND SCORE __74___   BACKHAND SCORE __47___

TOTAL _____

Figure 32. Computed score card for forehand-backhand drives.

lines are drawn across the court parallel to the baseline, one
nine feet nearer the net than the baseline and one ten feet
behind the baseline. Chalked numbers are placed near center
of each area to designate the scoring value. (See Figure 33.)

Test:

The player taking the test stands behind the baseline,
bounces the ball to himself, hits the ball and attempts to
place it in the back 9 feet of the opposite court. (This area
is shaded with diagonal lines in Figure 33.) Each player is
allowed fourteen trials on the forehand and fourteen trials
on the backhand. In order to score the values as shown in
Figure 33, balls must go between the top of the net and the
rope and land in the designated area or on lines bounding the

226

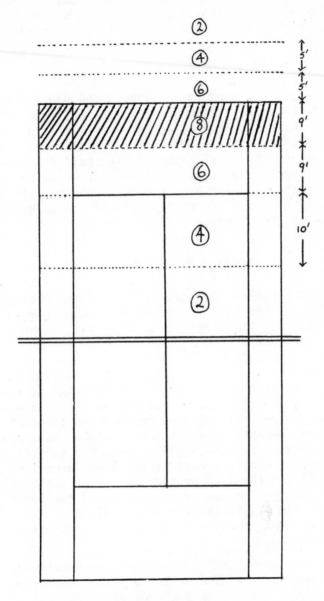

Figure 33. Special court markings for Broer-Miller
forehand-backhand drive test.

area. (Balls landing on a line receive the higher score for that area.) Balls which go over the rope score one-half the value of the area in which they land. If a player misses the ball in attempting to strike it, this is considered a trial. All let balls are taken over.

Scoring:

Score cards are used to facilitate the scoring and are replicas of the court, including the test markings. The number of each trial is recorded on the score card in the same relative position as the ball landing on the court. A circle is placed around the trial number if the ball went above the restraining rope. Such a hit is later scored as having half the value of the area in which the ball landed. The total score equals the sum of fourteen balls on the forehand and fourteen on the backhand.

VOLLEYBALL

All of the published studies[1,5,23] of the construction of volleyball skill tests and batteries have one test in common, repeated volleys. This test has several variations but in all forms the player is scored according to the number of times he can volley the ball to the wall above a line within a specified time limit. In the Brady test,[5] the subject is permitted to stand anywhere he wishes but the line on the wall is placed at a height of ten feet; in the Bassett, Glassow and Locke[1] test, no restraining line is used and the line on the wall is at net height, seven foot six inches for girls and women. In the French and Cooper[23] Test, the subject is required to remain behind a restraining line three feet distant from the wall and the line on the wall is at net height. The tests also vary in the number of trials and the length of each trial. For all of the various versions of the repeated volleys tests, acceptably high reliabilities and validities have been obtained.

Mohr and Haverstick[41,42] have presented evidence favoring moving the restraining line in the repeated volleys test still further from the wall, to a distance of seven feet.

A further complication is the recent change in girls' and women's volleyball rules which prohibits setting the ball up to oneself. If the test is changed to coincide with the rules, as seems desirable, it is not known how it will be affected.

Two tests of repeated volleys have been selected for inclusion: the Brady test because it is the only test for men that has been reported and the French-Cooper test, because it includes a restraining line and has had wide use. The Russell-Lange[45] test for Junior High School Girls is a modification of this test. They gave three trials of thirty seconds each and used the one best trial as the score, while in the French-Cooper test, ten trials of fifteen seconds each are given and the score is the sum of the five best trials. Broer[7] in a recent study used the Russell-Lange version.

1. Brady's Volleying Test, for College Men

Equipment:

    1. Stop watch, volley ball.

    2. Markings

        Horizontal chalk line 5 feet long is drawn parallel to the floor and 11 1/2 feet from the floor on a smooth wall. Vertical lines extend upward toward the ceiling from the horizontal line.

Test:

        The player stands facing the wall with a volley ball in his hands. On signal, he throws the ball against the wall. When the ball returns, the player must volley it against the wall and within the boundaries of the chalk lines described above. Only legal volleys are counted. If the ball is caught or "held" or gets out of control, it is started with a throw as at the beginning of the test. The player is timed for one minute.

Scoring:

        The number of successful legal volleys that hit within the chalk lines on the wall within one minute is the score. One trial is permitted.

Reliability:

        Reliability was .925. (For reliability study, the test was repeated after a suitable rest period. Data were collected from over 500 men.)

Validity:

Validity was .86 against a criterion of combined ratings of judges made during actual play.

Comments:

This test appears to be highly satisfactory. The test author states that it does not possess as much validity when used below the college level.

2. Repeated Volleys (French-Cooper)

Equipment:

1. Well-inflated balls, unobstructed wall space 10 feet long and 15 feet high (preferably several such areas), and a stop watch.

2. Markings

A line 10 feet long marked on the wall at net height, 7 1/2 feet from the floor.

A line on the floor, opposite the wall marking, 10 feet long and 3 feet from the wall.

Test:

The player being tested stands behind the 3-foot line, and tosses the ball to the wall with an underhand movement. When it returns, he volleys it repeatedly against the wall above the net line for fifteen seconds. The ball may be set up as many times as desired or necessary; it may be caught and restarted with a toss as at the beginning. If the ball gets out of control, it must be recovered by the subject and brought back to the 3-foot line to be started over again as at the beginning.

This procedure is repeated until ten trials have been given, each fifteen seconds in length.

Scoring:

The score for one trial is the number of times the ball is clearly batted (not tossed) from behind the 3-foot line on the floor to the wall above or on the net line. The score for the test is the sum of the five best trials out of ten.

Reliability:

r = .78, correlated by the odd-even method. It was not corrected by the Spearman-Brown Formula since only five of the trials are used in the final score. Reliability computed on the five best trials on successive days should yield an equally high, perhaps higher, coefficient. The subjects were forty-seven senior high school girls, University High School, Iowa City, Iowa. r = .82 computed by the odd-even method for the first four trials by 234 University of Iowa women. r = .92 computed by the odd-even method, stepped up to .96; subjects were 75 college women, University of Minnesota. Ten trials were used.

Validity:

r = .72 when correlated with a criterion of subjective ratings, made by four experienced teachers of volley ball.

T-Scales:

See Table XXIII. Four scales are available for the Repeated Volleys Test. The first scale was constructed from data on 349 high school girls in Illinois, using the sum of the five best trials out of ten as the score. The second scale was on data obtained from 120 high school girls in Iowa using the best single score out of three trials. The third scale was constructed on data from 136 college women, using the best single score out of three trials. The fourth was on 211 cases using the best three out of five trials. All the trials were fifteen seconds in length.

Comments:

This test measures the player's ability to control the ball and his judgment on position and playing the ball. It can be used for classification purposes early in the term and then again later to measure achievement. It can be administered economically with a large number of players taking the test at the same time, if wall space and balls permit. When the scores on this test for 106 freshman college women were correlated against the Scott General Motor Ability (Battery A) the coefficient was .38, which indicates that the tests are not measuring the same thing. A similar coefficient, .44, was obtained when the scores of 187 students were correlated with the Scott General Motor Ability (Battery B).

Table XXIII.

T-Scales for Volley Ball Tests

T-SCORE	REPEATED VOLLEYS*	REPEATED VOLLEYS†	REPEATED VOLLEYS‡	REPEATED VOLLEYS§	SERVE‖	SERVE¶	T-SCORE
80	130				48		80
79							79
78	126			106	47	44	78
77			40				77
76		25			46		76
75	124			104	45		75
74	122				44		74
73	120		38	102	43	40	73
72	118	24			42		72
71	116	23	37	98		35	71
70		22	35	96	41	34	70
69	114	21	34		40		69
68	110		33	92	39	33	68
67	108		32	88	38		67
66	106	20		86	37	32	66
65	104	19	31	84	36	31	65
64	102	18	30	82	34	30	64
63	100	17	29	80	33		63
62	98		27	78	32	29	62
61	96		26		30	28	61
60	94	16	24	76	28	27	60
59	92		22	74	27	26	59
58		15	21	72	26	25	58
57	90		20		25	24	57
56	88	14	19	70	24	23	56
55	86		18	68	23	22	55
54		13		66	22	21	54
53	84		17		21	20	53
52	82	12		64	20	19	52
51	78		16	62	19	18	51
50	76		15	60	17	14	50
49		11			16	13	49
48	74		14	58	15	12	48
47	72				14	11	47
46	70	10		56	13	10	46
45	68		13		12	9	45
44	64			54	10		44
43	62	9	12	52	9	8	43
42	58			50		7	42
41	56	8	11	48	8		41

232

Table XXIII. (Cont.)

T-SCORE	REPEATED VOLLEYS*	REPEATED VOLLEYS†	REPEATED VOLLEYS‡	REPEATED VOLLEYS§	SERVE‖	SERVE¶	T-SCORE
40	52		10		7		40
39	48			46	6	6	39
38	44	7	9		5	5	38
37	42			44			37
36	40			40	4	4	36
35	38			38	3		35
34	36	6	8			3	34
33	34			36	2		33
32	32		7		1		32
31	30	5		32		2	31
30	28						30
29	24	4					29
28				30			28
27	22		6				27
26	20						26
25	18						25
24	16	3		24			24
23							23
22				22			22
21	14						21

*Scale was constructed on data obtained on 349 girls in Blue Island Community High School, Blue Island, Ill., and in East Aurora High School, Aurora, Ill. The score is the sum of the best five out of ten trials.
†Scale was constructed on data obtained from 120 girls in Muscatine High School, Muscatine, Iowa; score is the best score out of three trials.
‡Scale was constructed on data obtained on 136 University of Iowa students. The score is the best of three trials.
§Scale was constructed on data obtained on 211 University of Iowa students. The score is the best three out of five trials.
‖Same group as in first column, repeated volleys*; score is total of ten trials.
¶Same group as in second column, repeated volleys; score is total of ten trials.

3. Serve

Equipment:

1. Regulation court and tightly strung net, well-inflated balls.

2. Markings

(a) A line across the court 5 feet inside and parallel to the end line.

(b) A line across the court parallel to the net and 12 1/2 feet from the center line which is directly under the net.

(c) Two lines, each 5 feet inside the court and parallel to the side lines, extending from the line under the net to the 5-foot line described in (a).

(d) The score values of each area should be marked on the floor as indicated in the diagram (Figure 34).

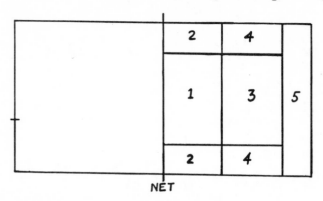

Figure 34. Floor markings for volleyball serve test.
1-5 = scores for respective areas.

Test:

The player being tested stands in the proper serving area on the court opposite the target and is given ten trials to serve the ball into the target in the court across the net. Any legal serve is permitted. Foot faults count as trials; "let" serves are re-served and do not count as trials. The scorer stands on a chair near one side line about 15 feet from the net.

Scoring:

The score values are indicated on the diagram.

A ball landing on a line separating the two spaces scores the higher value. A ball landing on an outside boundary line scores the value of the area the line bounds. Trials in which foot faults occur score zero. Ten trials should be allowed.

Reliability:

r = .68 by the odd-even method, stepped up to .81 by the Spearman-Brown formula. The subjects were the same as for Test 1. (University High School, Iowa City.)

234

Validity:

r = .63, with a criterion of ratings (same as Test 1).

T-Scales:

See Table XXIII. Two scales are available for the Serve Test, the first on 349 high school girls in Illinois and the second on 136 University of Iowa women students.

Comments:

This test is time-consuming, since it requires so many trials. When the target is painted on both sides of the court, two players can be tested at the same time on each court. The use of ball chasers to keep the servers supplied with balls facilitates the testing. It is an excellent teaching device for practice of placement in serving. A circular target with concentric circles might improve this test. Reducing the number of trials is not advisable since it has been shown that to do so substantially reduces the reliability of the test. Broer[7] used a simplified target, giving the highest score to the area within three feet of the baseline and giving credit for any ball landing within the side lines of the court. She states that twenty trials are essential for reliability on her test for junior high school girls.

BATTERY OF VOLLEYBALL TESTS

The best single test for girls and women is the Repeated Volleys Test. Repeated Volleys and the Serve Test together yielded a correlation coefficient with the criterion (rating of playing ability) of .81 in the study cited here. This combination can be administered at the same time, if floor space permits. The low intercorrelation of .39 between the two tests indicates that they measure different things. The formula for combining the two tests to insure giving proper weight to each, is as follows:

1.0 repeated volleys + 2.0 serve

SUMMARY

The skill tests selected for inclusion in this book do not include all of the tests that have value. Some of the tests that have been omitted have value for the research worker but are not recommended for the uses most commonly made of tests in teaching. Still others, particularly those involving more than one performer or being scored subjectively, have been omitted because they fail to meet several of the criteria for effective tests, listed in Chapter II. More tests need to be developed, particularly for boys and men and in those activities where the tests are obviously inadequate. Until objective tests that are valid, reliable, and easily administered are available, the present measures will have to be supplemented with ratings and other subjective estimates.

The selected reference list contains references to tests for some of the activities not included in this chapter, as well as for those that are included, and for tests which have limited use.

SELECTED REFERENCES

1. Bassett, Gladys, Ruth Glassow and Mabel Locke: Studies in Testing Volleyball Skills. Research Quarterly, 8: 60, 1937.

2. Bontz, Jean: An Experiment in the Construction of a Test for Measuring Ability in Some of the Fundamental Skills Used by Fifth and Sixth Grade Children in Soccer. Unpublished master's thesis, State University of Iowa, Iowa City, 1942.

3. Borleske, Stanley E.: A Study of the Achievement of College Men in Touch Football. Unpublished master's thesis, University of California, Berkeley, 1936. (Reported in part in an article by Cozens, Frederick W. Research Quarterly, 8: 73, 1937.

4. Brace, David K.: Validity of Football Achievement Tests as Measures of Motor Learning and as a Partial Basis for the Selection of Players. Research Quarterly, 14: 372, 1943.

5. Brady, George F.: Preliminary Investigations of Volleyball Playing Ability. Research Quarterly, 16: 14, 1945.

6. Broer, Marion R., and Donna Mae Miller: Achievement Tests for Beginning and Intermediate Tennis. Research Quarterly, 21: 303-321, 1950.

7. Broer, Marion R.: Skill Tests for Junior High Girls. Research Quarterly, 29: 139-145, 1958.

8. Colvin, Valerie, Ruth Glassow and Marguerite Schwarz: Studies in Measuring Basketball Playing Ability of College Women. Research Quarterly, 9: 60, 1938.

9. Cornish, Clayton: A Study of Measurement of Ability in Handball. Research Quarterly, 20: 215, 1949.

10. Critz, Mary Ella: An Objective Test for Beginning Canoeists. Unpublished master's thesis, State University of Iowa, Iowa City, 1948.

11. Cureton, Thomas K.: How to Teach Swimming and Diving, Vol. 1. New York, Association Press, 1934, Chapter 9.

12. Cureton, Thomas K.: A Test for Endurance in Speed Swimming. Research Quarterly, 6: 106, 1935.

13. Davis, Rosemary: The Development of an Objective Softball Batting Test for College Women. Unpublished master's thesis, Illinois State Normal University, Normal, 1951.

14. Dyer, Joanna Thayer: Revision of the Backboard Test of Tennis Ability. Research Quarterly, 9: 25, 1938.

15. Dyer, Joanna, Jennie Schurig, and Sara Apgar: A Basketball Motor Ability Test for College Women and Secondary School Girls. Research Quarterly, 10: 128, 1939.

16. Edgren, H. D.: An Experiment in the Testing of Ability and Progress in Basketball. Research Quarterly, 3: 159, 1932.

17. Edgren, H. D., and G. G. Robinson: Individual Skill Tests in Physical Activities. Chicago, The authors, 5315 Drexel Avenue, 1937.

18. Everett, Peter W.: The Prediction of Baseball Ability. Research Quarterly, 23: 15-19, 1952.

19. Fox, Katharine: A Study of the Validity of the Dyer Backboard Test and the Miller Forehand-Backhand Test for Beginning Tennis Players. Research Quarterly, 24: 1-7, 1953.

20. Fox, Margaret G., and Olive G. Young: A Test of Softball Batting Ability. Research Quarterly, 25: 26-27, 1954.

21. Fox, Margaret G.: Swimming Power Test. Research Quarterly, 28: p. 233, October 1957.

22. Friedel, Jean: The Development of a Field Hockey Skill Test for High School Girls. Master's thesis, Illinois State Normal University, Normal, 1956. Micro-cards, P.E. 289, University of Oregon, Eugene.

23. French, Esther, and Bernice Cooper: Achievement Tests in Volleyball for High School Girls. Research Quarterly, 8: 150, 1937.

24. Hewitt, Jack E.: Achievement Scale Scores for War Time Swimming. Research Quarterly, 14: 391, 1943.

25. Hyde, Edith I.: The Measurement of Achievement in Archery. Journal of Educational Research, 27: 673, 1934.

26. Hyde, Edith I.: An Achievement Scale in Archery. Research Quarterly, 8: 109, 1937.

27. Johnson, Joan: Tennis Serve of Advanced Women Players. Research Quarterly, 28: 123, May 1957.

28. Johnson, William L.: Objective Tests in Basketball for High School Boys. Unpublished master's thesis, State University of Iowa, Iowa City, 1934.

29. Jones, Edith: A Study of Knowledge and Playing Ability in Basketball for High School Girls. Unpublished master's thesis, State University of Iowa, Iowa City, 1941.

30. Kelson, Robert E.: Baseball Classification Plan for Boys. Research Quarterly, 24: 304-307, 1953.

31. Knox, Robert Dawson: An Experiment to Determine the Relationship between Performance in Skill Tests and Success in Playing Basketball. Unpublished master's thesis, University of Oregon, Eugene, 1937.

32. Lamp, Nancy A.: Volleyball Skills of Junior High School Students as a Function of Physical Size and Maturity. Research Quarterly, 25: 189-197, 1954.

33. Lehsten, Carlson: A Measure of Basketball Skills in High School Boys. The Physical Educator, 5: December, 1948.

34. Leilich, Avis: The Primary Components of Selected Basketball Tests for College Women. Doctoral

dissertation, Indiana University, Bloomington, 1952.
Microcards, P.E. 108, Health and Physical Education,
University of Oregon, Eugene.

35. Lockhart, Aileene, and Frances A. McPherson: Development of a Test of Badminton Playing Ability. Research
Quarterly, 20: 402, 1949.

36. McDonald, Lloyd G.: The Construction of a Kicking
Test as an Index of General Soccer Ability. Springfield College, Springfield, Massachusetts, unpublished
master's thesis, 1951.

37. McGee, Rosemary: The Relationship of General Motor
Ability to Specific Skill Tests. Unpublished master's
thesis, Illinois State Normal University, Normal, 1949.

38. McKee, Mary Ellen: A Test for the Full-Swinging Shot
in Golf. Research Quarterly, 21: 40-46, 1950.

39 Miller, Frances A.: A Badminton Wall Volley Test.
Research Quarterly, 22: 208-213, 1951.

40. Miller, Wilma K., Chairman: Achievement Levels in
Basketball Skills for Women Physical Education Majors.
Research Quarterly, 25: 450-455, 1954.

41. Mohr, Dorothy R., and Martha J. Haverstick: Repeated
Volleys Tests in Women's Volleyball. Research Quarterly, 26: 179-184, 1955.

42. Mohr, Dorothy R., and Martha J. Haverstick: Relationship Between Height, Jumping Ability and Agility to
Volleyball Skill. Research Quarterly, 27: 74-78, 1956.

43. Mott, Jane A., and Aileene Lockhart: Table Tennis
Backboard Test. Journal of Health and Physical Education, 17: 550, 1946.

44. Phillips, Marjorie and Dean Summers: Bowling Norms and
Learning Curves for College Women. Research Quarterly,
21: 377-385, 1950.

45. Russell, Naomi, and Elizabeth Lange: Achievement Tests
in Volleyball for Junior High School Girls. Research
Quarterly, 11: 33, 1940.

46. Schaufele, Evelyn F.: The Establishment of Objective
Tests for Girls of the Ninth and Tenth Grades to De-
termine Soccer Ability. Unpublished master's thesis,
State University of Iowa, Iowa City, 1940.

47. Schmithals, Margaret, and Esther French: Achievement Tests in Field Hockey for College Women. Research Quarterly, 11: 84, 1940.

48. Scott, M. Gladys, Chairman: Achievement Examinations in Badminton. Research Quarterly, 12: 242, 1941.

49. Scott, M. Gladys: Assessment of Motor Ability of College Women through Objective Tests. Research Quarterly, 10: 63, 1939.

50. Smith, Gwen: Speedball Skill Tests for College Women: Unpublished study, Illinois State Normal University, Normal, 1947.

51. Snell, Catherine: A Study of Rates of Learning in Selected Sports as Related to General Motor Ability. Unpublished doctoral dissertation, State University of Iowa, Iowa City, 1948.

52. Stalter, Evelyn, and Esther French: A Study of Skill Tests in Badminton for College Women. Research Quarterly, 20: 257, 1949.

53. Vanderhoof, Ellen R.: Beginning Golf Achievement Tests. Master's thesis, State University of Iowa, 1956. Micro-cards, P. E. 306, University of Oregon, Eugene.

54. Young, Genevieve, and Helen Moser: A Short Battery of Tests to Measure Playing Ability in Women's Basketball. Research Quarterly, 5: 3, 1934.

55. Watts, Harriet: Construction and Evaluation of a Target on Testing the Approach Shot in Golf. Unpublished master's thesis, University of Wisconsin, Madison, 1942.

Chapter VII

ANTHROPOMETRIC MEASURES AND WEIGHT PREDICTION

The earliest form of measurement in physical education was of body size. In that period more than a half century ago, not only the height and weight were measured regularly but also the dimensions of segments both on the long and transverse axes. Any changes found from time to time were attributed, for the college age at least, to be the result of physical activity. It does not seem essential that we discuss the place exercise has in growth and physical development, but in many school systems it is the physical education teacher who has the responsibility of measuring height and weight and keeping the growth records.

This growth record needs to be taken carefully, at regular intervals, by uniform techniques, and with some basis of interpretation. It is not sufficient to simply record a measure of height or weight without considering it in light of previous records, type of build of the individual, age, health history, and present health regime. These measurement techniques are not difficult but they need to be learned and all personnel working on this form of measurement in a school system must follow uniform techniques if the continuous records on the child are to be meaningful.

BODY TYPE

Everyone who has worked with children has observed that some children are built like a bean pole, grow tall and slender, look fragile and ill-padded while others have more the proportions of a brick, broad, thick, and solidly built. In between these two extremes are children with moderate characteristics of the pole or brick, or even such a nice blending that they seem to belong to neither type. These are sometimes referred to in a general way, with an aesthetic quality to the designation, as "well built."

There are different ways of referring to these variations in structure. Probably the simplest is a descriptive three-way grouping into slender, stocky, and average. The first two are sometimes called linear and lateral. The majority do not fall undebatably into a specific category, since a total population shows a continuous distribution over this entire range of structure. Sheldon[13] has a rather elaborate system of a seven point scale on each of three characteristics of build. This leads to a degree of classification that is probably not necessary for the average teacher. It could be very useful for research purposes. Wetzel[19] has a plan which classifies the child into one of seven channels as based on the proportions of longitudinal and cross section proportions. Meredith[9] working with Iowa Child Welfare data proposes a channel classification which has many of the same characteristics as Wetzel's but is a little simpler to use.

The designations of linearity or slenderness refer primarily to skeletal structure. The size of the bones can be observed best at articulations such as the elbow, wrist, knee or ankle. Also the proportion of width to length of hands and fingers, feet and toes or thorax can be a basis for subjective classification. On the slender streamlined frame there is usually a slender musculature. However, there may be any amount of fat padding. This often leads one to an error in observational judgment and therefore a gross error in assessing the weight status of the individual.

The broader or more massive skeletal system is usually equipped with a large, bulky system of muscles. If the person has used these muscles well they become very solid. Since both the bones and muscles in this child are very heavy he is inevitably going to weigh more than the slender one of the same age and sex. Judged observationally, particularly with clothing on, two children may appear to be about the same size. However, the stocky or brick type will weigh more than the more slender build, heavily padded with adipose tissue.

Subjective classification may be useful if using age-height-weight tables. Careful classification can lead to acceptance of some deviation up or down (5 or 10%) from the weight norm. It is a technique that the parent might use with instruction or the adult might use it as a means of

242

establishing an approximate norm modified from undifferen-
tiated age-weight tables.

In general, body type has not been found to be closely
related to success in motor activities. However, there are
some generalizations which can be made that apply to enough
individuals that it is worth the teacher's awareness of
them. The slender or linear type is particularly prone to
a fatigue slump kind of posture deviation. It may be in
the form of forward head, round shoulders, or an entire
slump. Their flexibility is apt to be good unless they are
excessively long in the lower extremity, out of proportion
to trunk. Frequently, they are above average in agility,
quick in reaction time and in general quite active and pro
ficient in those skills requiring agility, speed and flexibility.

On the other hand the stocky or lateral type have some
characteristics distinguishing most of them from the linear
ones. Postural defects are less often of the slumping type
Backs are usually fairly normal or even flatter than average. However, the lower extremity, with the greater angula-
tion of the femur sometimes suffers an exaggerated knock-
knee effect and flattening of the arches of the feet due to
the medial thrust. Flexibility is somewhat restricted, not
in the sense that it is for the obese person, but because of
the resistance of strong antagonistic muscles. With more
body mass to control, they frequently move in a more flat-
footed fashion and show less proficiency in change of direction situations, and starting and stopping. However, on the
tests of pure strength they are apt to have an advantage.

ANTHROPOMETRIC EQUIPMENT

The equipment for anthropometric measurement is not
elaborate. That which is needed is dependent upon the use
to be made of measures. Most of the weight prediction formulas have special forms of each measure which must be obtained in the exact fashion, using the precise landmarks.
The most common equipment is described here.

Scales.

The platform scale with the balance arm is usually the
more accurate. Most of them are calibrated in pounds and

quarters (or tenths) thereof. Some have pounds on one side of the balance arm and kilograms on the other side. The pounds are essential to insure a meaningful interpretation to the children. The kilograms might be helpful with some weight prediction formulas which compute weight in those units. Conversion is simple and there need be no real problem in using any calibration for any or all formula. The scale should be checked for proper balance before each session of weighing.

Stadiometer and Square

The stadiometer is used for measuring height in either standing, sitting or lying. The lying measure is seldom used for any except the infant. The type which is least accurate is the sliding rod with horizontal arm at the top which is frequently found on scales. The looseness of the rod, which is necessary to make it slide easily, permits inconsistency when bringing it down on the head of the subject for measurement.

The ideal stadiometer is a portable one built of a supporting base and a vertical backboard. It should be well enough braced that there is no sway even if it is not otherwise supported. The vertical backboard may be very carefully marked for increments above the base, through at least the range to be needed by the group of persons to be measured. In an elementary school this would require a very wide range. Yardsticks or rulers could be very carefully mounted on the backboard and the feet renumbered at the 4, 5 and 6 foot points. It is also possible to buy a paper scale* calibrated from 0 to 7 feet and in a parallel column the heights are calibrated in the metric units. It has parallel calibration in inches and centimeters. The paper should be carefully and permanently mounted with paper cement to the backboard and it will serve for several years. If a wall surface is used instead of the stadiometer, the quarter round, baseboard and all other projecting points must be removed.

---

*This may be purchased from the Iowa Child Welfare Research Station, Iowa City, Iowa.

The square is a small device for determining the level of the top of the head. It is built as a half box, or two sides at right angles to each other with a handle inside the angle. One side slides down the backboard of the stadiometer and the other must be long enough to touch the top of the head of the subject as he stands against the backboard.

Sliding Caliper

The sliding caliper has two arms projecting at right angles to the long calibrated arm of the caliper. The arm at the end of the caliper is solid, the other slides easily along the calibrated rod. The same problem is met here as was mentioned with respect to the stadiometer which slides up and down. The sliding arm should fit snugly and be so braced that pressure at the end of the arm does not cause it to deviate from 90 degrees with the long arm. In general the metal caliper is more satisfactory in this respect than wooden ones.

It is essential that one check the caliper to see which point on the sliding arm is at zero when the arms of the caliper are together. That same point must be used for reading the position of the open arms. On the wooden calipers the reading point is usually on the inside edge of the sliding arm. On the steel calipers it is usually a designated hairline somewhere in the case sliding along the calibration.

The steel caliper should be kept warm enough to be comfortable to the subject. This is particularly important if used for chest measurement. It is a means of saving time, as subjects usually withdraw from cold calipers.

The spreading caliper is sometimes used for the same purpose. However, accuracy of measurement is more difficult as the two converging points of the arms must be placed in exactly the right point.

Tape

The tape is used for all measures of circumference or girth. It may be obtained in either linen or steel. The linen is subject to shrinkage from perspiration picked up during measurement, and if used over long periods of time may eventually become worn and stretched. Either type of

change would destroy the accuracy of the measurement. The
steel tape avoids the problem of changing units but has the
disadvantage of feeling cold to the subject. This reaction
to the cold could easily affect chest measurement and might
even affect muscle girths. Care can be taken to see that
the tape is reasonably warm to touch and therefore the steel
tape would seem to be the better choice.

Fat Calipers

Some weight prediction formulas call for measurement of
the thickness of the subcutaneous fat pads. The fat caliper
is a small size adaptation of the spreading arm caliper but
with somewhat expanded, flattened points to the arms. It is
equipped with a spring which causes the points to be pulled
together at all times when not in use, and to fit snugly on
the skin fold when a measurement is being made. Calibration
is usually in millimeters.

MEASURING TECHNIQUES

All measurements must be taken with the utmost care,
and in uniform fashion at all times. The points to be observed by the examiner are:

1. choice of the piece of equipment
2. landmark to be used
3. instructions to the subject
4. operation of the equipment
5. fit of the equipment on the subject
6. readings to be taken
7. method of rechecking for accuracy.

Consistency and accuracy are much easier to obtain on some
measures than others. For example, the condylar width of
the elbow or knee is fairly easy, while the chest width,
depth or circumference are difficult because of the changing
state of expansion of the thorax and the necessity for cooperation from the subject to attempt uniformity. In a
measure such as iliac width there is little problem of the
exact landmark, but in shoulder width and trochanteric width
both landmarks are more difficult to locate and are more or
less movable.

Considerable practice is necessary for anyone who
wishes to use any of the anthropometric measures, even one

that may seem as simple as height. Practice should include
rechecking with instruction from the source of the formula
to be sure that technique has been correctly interpreted
and acquired.

The techniques given here are taken from the Iowa Child
Welfare manual.[7] Some of the following measures are used
in their prediction of normal weight. Others are added for
use in other formulas quoted later, or for further description of body build in research or other purpose. At no
time would all of these measures be given to an entire
class.

All measurements are taken on the left side for uniformity. They should be taken with a minimum of clothing on
the subject in order to have a true measure of size, to secure uniformity from time to time, and to facilitate locating landmarks.

Height

Subject removes shoes; stands with back against the
calibration on the stadiometer; heels, hips, shoulders and
head touching the backboard. The head should be erect with
the chin tucked in slightly. The Frankfort plane (line from
the outer, lower corner of the eye socket to the little
prominence at the front of the lower ear lobe) should be
horizontal. Subject should stand as tall as possible.

The square is placed against the calibration on the
backboard above the head of the subject. It is brought down
until it fits firmly against the top of the subject's head.
The square must fit both the backboard and the head and must
be horizontal, not tilted. The reading is taken at the
lower edge of the square. It may be helpful to ask the subject to bend knees and step away. Record to nearest 1/4
inch.

Weight

Subjects should always be weighed without shoes, coats,
sweaters, or other heavy garments. It is preferable to
weigh in the nude or only with minimum underclothing, but
children in school usually can not be weighed in that fashion. Uniformity in amount of clothing from time to time for
each person is the next best goal.

Estimate the weight of the subject and place the heavy weight on the balance arm of the scale in the groove for the first unit below the estimated weight. The subject stands in a steady position on the center of the platform and the small weight is moved until the balance arm is in a steady position. Be careful to read the weight at the proper edge of the weight or hairline designated for the reading. Record to nearest half pound.

The following measures are taken with the sliding caliper. In order to avoid fatigue if doing measures on a number of subjects and to facilitate measurement it is essential that the caliper be balanced on the hands. The fixed arm of the caliper should be taken in the nondominant hand. The hand is underneath and the caliper arm rests between the thumb and index finger as one would hold a pencil. The movable arm is taken in the dominant hand in the same fashion, like a pencil projecting between thumb and index finger for writing. The grip is far enough back on the arms so that the caliper balances on the hands without being grasped.

The movable arm is carried back and forth by its position in the V of the hand. The middle finger is immediately below the caliper arm and is used to locate the landmarks and then the caliper is slipped down to fit onto the landmark. This also avoids using the ends of the caliper arms for the contact and permits a very relaxed use of the hands during the measurement.

Chest Width

The measurement is taken facing the subject. The measure is taken at xiphoid level by placing the fixed arm against the side of the thorax so that it projects backward slightly beyond the contact areas. With the caliper in a horizontal position and passing in front of the xiphoid the movable arm is brought in lightly against the other side of the chest. The subject should be in mid-position in respiration.

Chest Depth

The measurement is taken from the left side of the subject. The fixed arm of the caliper is placed on the xiphoid

248

with the end projecting onto the far side of the thorax.
The subject should be in mid-position in respiration.

Shoulder Width

The measurement is taken behind the subject; the scapu-
lae should be flat and mildly adducted so that the arms
hang easily at the sides. The fixed arm of the caliper is
placed against the end of the acromion process of the left
shoulder, and the movable arm is brought in a corresponding
position firmly against the right acromion. The end of the
middle finger should be used to locate the landmark and then
the arm of the caliper is moved down into position. (Placing the caliper too high permits it to slip when pressure is
applied. Placing it too low increases the reading by getting it over the tuberosity of the humerus and the bulk of
the deltoid muscle.)

Iliac Hip Width

The measurement is taken facing the subject. The fixed
arm of the caliper is placed against the crest of the ilium,
with about a quarter inch of the caliper extending down the
side of the ilium. The end of the caliper arm should project backward beyond the area of contact. The movable arm
is brought in a similar position against the left ilium.
Pressure is applied. (Placing the caliper too high permits
it to slip when pressure is applied. Placing it too low increases the reading by getting it over the lateral gluteals
and the fat pad which frequently covers these muscles.)

Trochanteric Hip Width

The measurement is taken facing the subject. The subject stands with the feet parallel, not more than 2 inches
apart, weight distributed equally on both feet. The middle
finger of each hand is brought down the thighs until the
subcutaneous prominence of the trochanter is located on each
side. On an obese person this is hard to find; it may be
helpful to have the subject bend the knees slightly. The
trochanteric landmarks are at approximately the level of the
anterior angle made at the hip by the knee flexion. The
movable arm is brought into easy contact with the left trochanter; do not apply pressure.

249

Breadth of Left Knee

Have subject place the left foot on a stool 12 or 15 inches high in such a position that the knee is flexed to a right angle. Measurement is made facing the subject. Place the caliper arms against the sides of the knee with the ends of the arms projecting in to bisect the angle formed by the knee. Apply pressure.

The following measures are taken with the tape. It should be held in the dominant hand and pulled out with the other hand. One finger on the trigger which rolls the tape back in makes it possible to pull the tape in easily if too much is unrolled.

Chest Circumference

The measurement is taken facing the subject. The tape should circle the thorax snugly in a horizontal position at xiphoid level. Pull out about half enough to extend around the thorax of the subject. Place it across the back, with the free end extending around the left side, observing carefully to see that it is at proper level and horizontal. Pull gently on both ends of the tape; this will keep the tape from slipping and will unwind the tape. Bring the end of the tape and the reel together in front of the subject where it can be read. Cross the tape in front and while the thorax is in mid-position of respiration, read the circumference.

Post-adolescent girls and women sometimes have pendulous breasts which cover the thorax at xiphoid level. The tape can be placed at the proper level by leading with the hand as the two ends of the tape are brought forward around the thorax. The hands slip under the breasts and the tape fits the thorax smoothly. Care must be taken in this case to see that the end of the tape comes squarely over the xiphoid so that the crossing of the tape will be exposed for reading. If a steel tape is used for this measurement, it must be removed carefully so that the skin will not be scratched or cut.

Girth of Upper Arm

The left arm of subject should be hanging relaxed.
Place the tape around the upper arm at its largest circumference (over bulge of biceps and triceps) in a horizontal
position. Cross the tape to get the point for the reading.
The tape should be pulled just tight enough to make it fit
smoothly but not tight enough that it makes an indentation
in the contour of the arm.

Girth of Lower Arm

The left arm of subject should be hanging relaxed.
Place the tape around the largest circumference (just below elbow level) in a horizontal position. Cross the tape
to get the point for the reading. The tape should be
pulled just tight enough to make it fit smoothly but not
tight enough that it makes an indentation in the contour of
the arm.

Girth of Wrist

The left arm of subject should hang relaxed, hand open
and fingers extended in line with forearm. Place the tape
in the smallest circumference of the wrist (just below the
distal ends of the radius and ulna). Cross the tape to get
the point for the reading. Pull the tape tight. (This
technique is from Willoughby[21, p. 69] rather than from the
Iowa Child Welfare Research Station.)

Girth of Thigh

The subject stands with the feet about 4 to 6 inches
apart. Place the tape around the left thigh horizontally
in a position so that it will rest in the gluteal fold
(angle made by the curve of the gluteus maximus with the
near vertical line of the thigh). Cross the tape to get the
point for the reading. The tape should be pulled just tight
enough to make it fit smoothly but not tight enough that it
makes an indentation in the contour of the leg.

Girth of the Calf

Have the subject stand with feet slightly apart and weight equally distributed between the two feet. Place the tape around the lower leg at its largest circumference (over the bulge of the gastrocnemius) in a horizontal position. Cross the tape to get the point for the reading. The tape should be pulled just tight enough to keep it from slipping, but not tight enough that it makes an indentation in the contour of the leg.

Girth of the Ankle

Have the subject stand with weight equally on both feet, feet flat on floor. Place the tape around the ankle at the smallest circumference (just above the malleoli) and in a horizontal position. Cross the tape to get the point for the reading. Pull the tape tight enough to fit snugly but not tight enough that it makes an indentation in the contour of the leg.

The following measures are made with the fat caliper. It is held in the right hand with the thumb on the outside of the fixed arm and the middle finger on the outside of the movable arm. Pressure of the thumb and finger opens the caliper, and it can be supported in a horizontal position by the 4th or 5th finger.

With the left hand, pick up a fold of skin between the thumb and middle finger. Care must be taken to pick up only skin and subcutaneous fat rather than muscle. The fold should be sufficient that about a half inch will extend out beyond the finger and thumb. The expanded ends of the caliper arms are then placed outside the skin fold adjacent to the thumb and finger.

The thumb and finger press against the subject thus relieving the compression on the skin fold and at the same time keeping the skin from creeping and being pulled out of the caliper. Pressure of the right hand is removed thus permitting the caliper to close firmly on the skin fold, the caliper is supported on the fingers. After taking the reading, open the caliper and remove it before releasing the skin fold.

There is some fat deposited in almost all the subcutaneous fascia throughout the body. The back of the hands

252

and the eyelids are about the only exceptions. However,
some areas collect much more than others and may have it in
fairly localized pads. This varies somewhat with different
age levels. For example, the infant has rather heavy fat
pads on the plantar surface of the feet, but the middle-
aged and elderly have them on hips, abdomen, under the chin
or over the 7th cervical vertebra.

Chest Front Fat

The skin fold is taken over the front of the left
lateral thoracic wall. The point can be located by projecting an imaginary line out and downward from the suprasternal notch at 45 degree angle with the vertical through
the center of the sternum. The skin is usually fairly loose
here and the fold should be just enough to give space for
the caliper but not enough to make excess rolls of skin.
After the fold is lifted the pressure is against the ribs
to hold the fold in place until the reading is taken.

Chest Back Fat

The fold is taken over the back of the left thoracic
wall, a little downward and lateral to the inferior angle
of the scapula when the arms are hanging relaxed at the
sides. The skin is usually a little tighter than in front
and there is more possibility of picking up muscle with the
skin fold. Pressure is against the ribs to hold the skin
fold for measurement.

Side Fat

The skin fold is taken a little above and medial to the
left anterior spine of the ilium. It is on a line between
this anterior iliac point and the umbilicus. Having the
subject contract the abdominal muscles will help to minimize
the possibility of lifting muscle as well as skin and fas-
cial pads.

Abdominal Fat

The skin fold is taken to the left of the mid-line of
the abdomen and about half way up between umbilicus and

xiphoid. It should be over the left rectus abdominus muscle.

There are several other measures which are sometimes used for quick estimates of body proportions, or for research needs. These are listed briefly to show similarities to above.

Sitting Height

Place a stool (12 to 15 inches in height) in front of the calibration on the stadiometer. Have the subject sit on the stool with hips, back and head against the back. Knees should be flexed, slightly apart, feet should be on the floor board as for standing height. Use the square as for standing height. Subtract the height of the stool from level of top of head while sitting.

Another variation of this measures length of trunk only. A yardstick is stood upright on stool between subject's legs, zero end down. A horizontal pointer is placed in the suprasternal notch, extending horizontally to obtain reading on yardstick.

Arm Span

Mount a scale or set of rulers horizontally on a flat surface in the same fashion that the calibration is mounted vertically for the standing height measure. Have a corner or solid block at the zero end. If measuring children of various heights stools can be used for subject to stand on to bring the shoulders within range of the horizontal calibration. Or for older persons, the span can be measured in the sitting position described above for sitting height. Subject should turn the palms forward, extend the arms sideward horizontally. The fingers of one hand should be extended against the zero block, the square is placed against the longest finger tip of the opposite hand and the reading taken as for standing height.

Forearm Length

This is a measure of the forearm and hand. The sliding caliper may be used. Lay the caliper on the table. Flex the elbow to 90 degrees. The point of the elbow is placed against the fixed end of the caliper. The forearm is extended along the calibration, palm up, fingers extended. The movable arm is brought in to the longest finger tip.

Hand Width

This is a measure of the palm of the hand. Lay the sliding caliper on the table. Lay the palm on the caliper, thumb abducted so the palm fits against the fixed arm of the caliper. The fingers should be straight and adducted. Bring the movable arm in for easy contact with the lateral side of the hand.

Finger Span

Lay the caliper on the table. Abduct the thumb and fingers as far as possible. Lay the hand on the caliper, end of thumb on the fixed arm, the movable arm is brought in against the end of the fifth finger.

Leg Length

This measure may be taken from either a back lying or a standing position. The back lying is less reliable because the position of femoral head in the acetabulum may vary considerably. The superimposed weight in standing makes for firm juxtaposition of bones in the hip joint.

In the back lying position the legs should be allowed to relax and rotate outward. The measure is taken with a tape from the anterior superior spine of the ilium to the middle of the inner malleolus.

In the standing position the subject should stand barefoot with the toes turned out with about a 45 degree angle between them. The measure may be taken to the same two landmarks or from iliac spine to the floor.

GROWTH RECORDS

Anthropometric measures may be used in the schools in various ways. However, the purpose is usually to trace the growth and development physically of the children. The

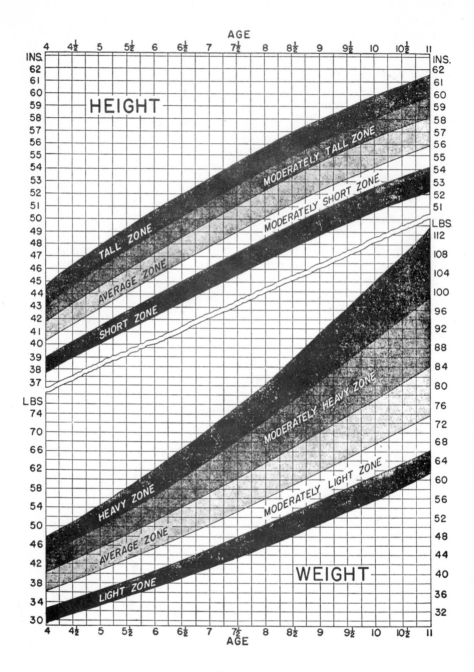

Boys

256

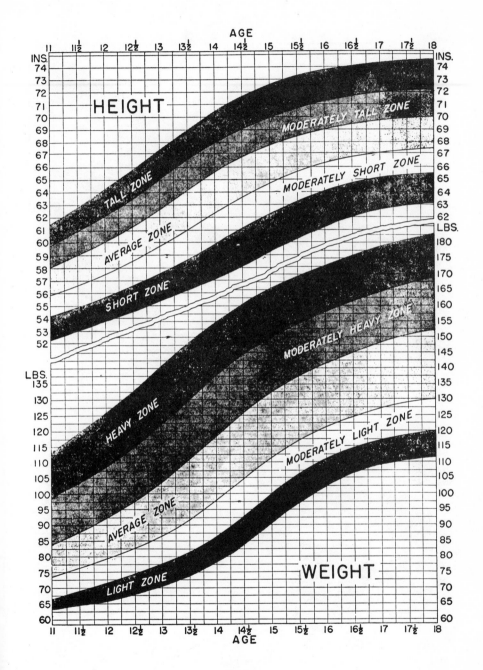

Boys

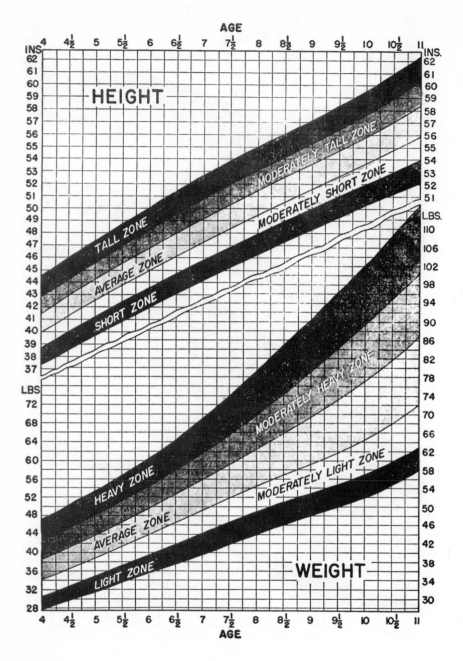

Girls

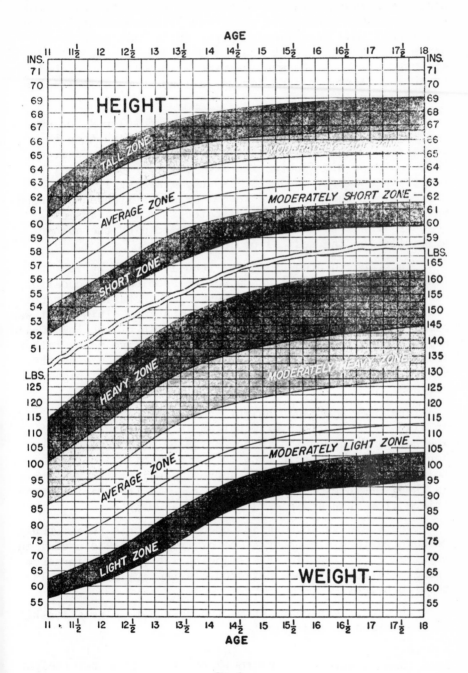

Girls

simple descriptive values represented by height and weight are not always indicative of growth or developmental needs. The traditional height-weight-age tables have been inadequate to evaluate growth and detect problems. When these are used they must be supplemented with estimates of body build and allowance made for deviations above or below the quoted norms.

More recently techniques have been developed for determining a type based on body proportions, and then by repetitive measures chart his growth curve. If repeated measures show him fluctuating from one type or channel of growth to another, the cause is sought medically. One of the first of these was the Wetzel Grid.[19] It has been used extensively, but is more complicated than the average teacher wishes to use. It was recommended by the author primarily for the medical profession.

In order to produce a tool readily usable by the teacher, a joint committee on Health Problems in Education of the N.E.A. and the A.M.A., developed a chart for graphically tracing the height and weight changes. This chart was based on growth data collected by Meredith of the Iowa Child Welfare Research Station. This chart has five zones rather than the seven channels of Wetzel's Grid. The age-height and the age-weight points can be quickly plotted (pages 256-259).

Whenever a child's height and weight points do not fall in like zones, further examination is made to determine whether it is accounted for by build or health conditions. Repeated records should show the normal child acquiring height and weight increments approximately at the same rate as those shown by the appropriate zone in the chart. Deviations from this again call for medical diagnosis.

There are various ratios used to indicate relationship between parts of the body. One of those which is useful in physical education, in understanding the motor performance and limitations of some children, is the arm span in relation to height.

The following chart shows the most common relationship between arm span and height:

Boys	Age	Girls
Less than height	Up to 10 years	Less than height
Equal to height	10-13 years	Equal to height
Greater than height	13 years up	Equal to height

Another ratio which sometimes proves useful is the Ponderal Index. This is

$$\sqrt[3]{\frac{\text{weight (kgm)}}{\text{height (cm)}}}.$$

If weight has been taken in pounds, it can be converted by dividing by 2.2. The height can be converted from inches to centimeters by multiplying by 2.54.

An understanding of the gradual growth of a child, as well as the individual variations can be obtained from study of Figures 35 and 36. The pattern on weight increments and height are similar.

ESTIMATION OF NORMAL WEIGHT

Experience has shown that overweight is to be preferred to underweight in the pre-adolescent child. In the post-adolescent overweight is to be avoided because of associated health hazards. Insurance company statistics show that the obese adult is a considerably poorer risk than those of more normal weight or even than those underweight. The adolescent girl or young woman is very conscious of weight and often is interested in dieting and weight loss when it is actually not desirable. She is sometimes led to believe that she is overweight by using the age-height-weight tables. If she belongs to the stockier build, she should weigh more than another of the same age and height who is of the slender type.

Tables such as the one on page 264 are based on insurance statistics and can be very helpful for the college girl or older. This is an example of the newer tables which recognize the differences in build, or as it is called here, frame. See Table XXIV.

Various systems have been devised for determining an ideal weight for each person in terms of bony structure or build. One of the earliest of these was Willoughby who attempted to establish optimal proportions for the male and female body. His goal of a theoretical optimum did recognize variations therefrom, or the practical optimum as an approximation of the former. This is apt to be of most use in inviting interest of the adolescent or young adult in

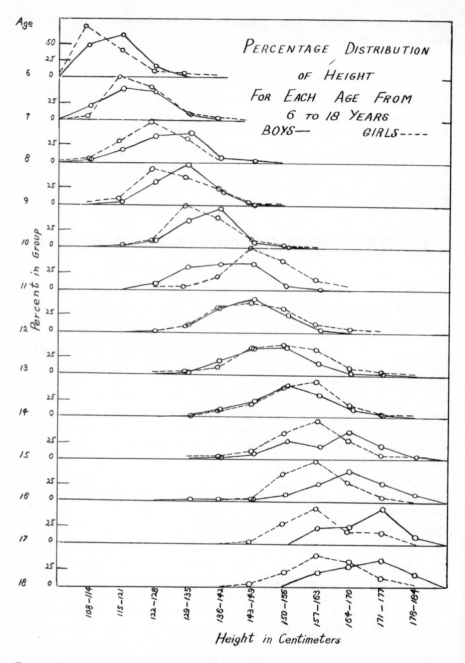

Figure 35. Percentage distribution of height for each age from 6-18 years, boys and girls. (Adapted from data presented by Bird T. Baldwin in Growth of Children from Birth to Maturity, Iowa Child Welfare Study.)

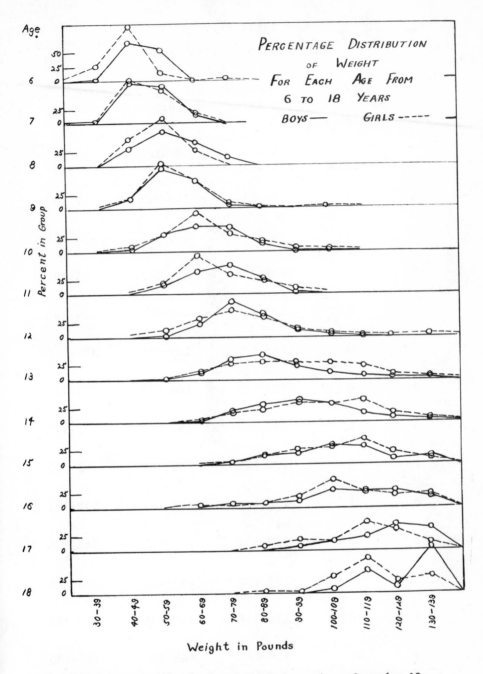

Figure 36. Percentage distribution of weight for each age from 6 to 18 years, boys and girls. (Adapted from data presented by Bird T. Baldwin Growth of Children from Birth to Maturity, Iowa Child Welfare Study.)

263

Table XXIV.

Desirable Weights for Women

Height (with shoes on - 2-inch heels)		Weight in Pounds According to Frame (as Ordinarily Dressed)		
Feet	Inches	Small Frame	Medium Frame	Large Frame
4	11	104-111	110-118	117-127
5	0	105-113	112-120	119-129
5	1	107-115	114-122	121-131
5	2	110-118	117-125	124-135
5	3	113-121	120-128	127-138
5	4	116-125	124-132	131-142
5	5	119-128	127-135	133-145
5	6	123-132	130-140	138-150
5	7	126-136	134-144	142-154
5	8	129-139	137-147	145-158
5	9	133-143	141-151	149-162
5	10	136-147	145-155	152-166
5	11	139-150	148-158	155-169

body proportions. Some of the ratios proposed by Willoughby[21] which should be helpful for that purpose are:

Dimensions	Sex	Ratio Presented Minimum	Maximum	Optimal
Girth of Hips	M	4.062	4.447	4.260
Girth of Ankle	F	4.267	4.421	4.537
Trochanteric Width	M	1.415	1.580	1.467
Girth of Ankle	F	1.397	1.712	1.511
Calf Girth	M	1.646	1.779	1.693
Ankle girth	F	1.579	1.712	1.647
Iliac width	M	1.128	1.362	1.268
Girth of Ankle	F	1.244	1.452	1.341
Chest Girth	M	4.337	5.180	4.695
Girth of Ankle	F	3.663	4.605	4.065
Forearm girth	M	1.706	1.833	1.745
Girth of wrist	F	1.492	1.644	1.578
Wrist Girth	M	.743	.857	.805
Ankle girth	F	.698	.787	.740
Both chest diameters	M	.463	.513	.490
Chest circumference	F	.516	.575	.540

Ludlum and Powell[6] made a useful suggestion for a quick estimate of normal weight for young women. Their suggestion is for use of chest dimension and height only. The formula is:

Weight (lbs.) = 2.65 height (in.) + 2.56 chest depth (cm.) + 2.59 chest width (cm.) - 154.3
or Weight (lbs.) = 2.6 × Σ all measures - 154.3

The chief disadvantage is that chest measures are not always highly correlated with other transverse dimensions of the body. For general use it is probably accurate enough to use the simpler formula.

Turner's[15] proposal was much more ambitious including different measures combined as follows:

Weight (lbs.) = .23 height (in.) + 6.29 chest width (in.) + 3.14 iliac width (in.) + 4.89 trochanteric width (in.) + 7.25 wrist girth (average of right and left) + 11.85 ankle girth (average of right and left) - 179.02

265

This is time consuming though tables are available for the computations. It probably will be used only for the occasional case where guidance is needed.

Another of the more elaborate systems of normal weight prediction is that of the Iowa Child Welfare Station: All measures used are in centimeters. The formula for college women is:

Weight (kilos) = .3165 height + .8041 chest circumference
+ .6508 iliac width + 3.608 knee - 105.23

In addition to taking these measures, four fat measures are taken and used to correct chest and iliac measures before computing the formula above.

The fat corrections are computed by means of Table XXV. To correct the chest circumference, add chest front and chest back fat measures. Compare with average sum for appropriate age. Correct chest circumference by adding or subtracting the obtained value according to deviation of fat from the average (See Table XXV). Use this corrected chest circumference in the formula.

To correct the iliac width, find the side fat reading in column marked caliper reading in Table XXVI. Take corresponding correction and add or subtract to the obtained iliac diameter. Use this corrected iliac width in the formula.

One of the advantages of this formula is that complete tables are available for this formula. Even though it is rather complex it can be computed very quickly. The actual measurement can be made in about the same time as those for the Turner formula.

If one is working with younger ages the formulas are similar. There is also the advantage of formula for both sexes. See list of formula. Tables are available for each of these in the Iowa Child Welfare bulletin.[7]

These formulas are too complex and time-consuming for routine testing of all children in a school. They may be used for those who seem to be over or underweight, or who fall in different zones in the height and weight segments of the growth chart. They could also be useful for guidance of the adolescent or adult who insists on dieting but needs guidance on whether he does or does not need to diet or engage in excessive reducing activities.

Table XXV

Fat Corrections for Chest and Hip Measures of Women

Chest Correction for Women and Girls				Hip correction for Women	
Age	Average Chest Front plus Chest Back	Corrections for Chest Girth (if actual is more than normal subtract from Chest Girth, if less, add)		Caliper Side	Correction
		Deviations	Correction		
29	49			15	+ 1.2
28	48			16	+ 1.1
27	48			17	+ 1.0
26	48	1	.16	18	+ .9
25	47	2	.31	19	+ .8
24	46	3	.47	20	+ .7
23	44	4	.63	21	+ .6
22	44	5	.79	22	+ .5
21	44	6	.94	23	+ .4
20	44	7	1.10	24	+ .3
19	44	8	1.26	25	+ .2
18	43	9	1.41	26	+ .2
17	41	10	1.57	27	+ .1
16	39	11	1.73	28	0
15	37	12	1.88	29	- .1
14	35	13	2.04	30	- .2
13	34	14	2.20	31	- .3
12	33	15	2.36	32	- .4
11	32	16	2.51	33	- .5
10	31	17	2.67	34	- .6
9	30	18	2.83	35	- .7
8	30	19	2.98	36	- .7
7	28	20	3.14	37	- .8
6	27	21	3.30	38	- .9
5	27	22	3.45	39	- 1.0
4	27	23	3.61	40	- 1.1
3	28	24	3.77	41	- 1.2
Pre-Sch	27			42	- 1.3
				43	- 1.4
				44	- 1.5
				45	- 1.6

Table XXVI.

Prediction of Weight (kgm) from Sum of Weighted Height, Iliac Width, Chest Circumference and Knee Width (cm.)

Boys

| Age | Weightings | | | | | R |
	Height	Iliac Width	Chest Circumference*	Knee Width	Constant	
5	.1128	.1961	.3951	1.6586	- 30.2065	.91
6	.1912	.3785	.5907	.7245	- 46.4538	.92
7	.1293	.6199	.4890	1.3739	- 42.9970	.90
8	.1607	.4028	.6789	2.1453	- 60.2709	.92
9	.1906	.5886	.5477	1.9372	- 58.4834	.92
10	.2183	.2743	.7577	2.1438	- 70.5147	.92
11	.2297	.1934	.5615	3.1072	- 66.1434	.90
12	.2230	.2457	.5204	5.7727	- 69.7569	.90
13	.2476	.0812	.8151	4.2135	- 93.4790	.97
14	.2712	.7361	.7935	3.1487	-101.9942	.96
15	.3008	.9060	.6489	4.3726	-111.8544	.95
16	.2808	.6960	.7840	5.0191	-119.3305	.92
17	.2897	.7082	.7270	5.0149	-115.2652	.92
18	.2359	1.1402	.9641	2.4796	-112.7968	.89

*Chest circumference corrected for fat.

Table XXVI. (Cont.)

Girls

	Weightings					
Age	Height	Iliac Width	Chest Circumference*	Knee Width	Constant	R
5	.1502	.3327	.4730	1.1673	- 36.9006	.94
6	.1053	.2633	.5137	1.6253	- 35.3942	.90
7	.1945	.3750	.6070	1.2585	- 50.9433	.93
8	.1798	.1687	.5505	2.1443	- 42.2626	.91
9	.1391	.3127	.7506	1.9510	- 56.6639	.95
10	.0966	.7730	.7034	2.4933	- 61.8757	.93
11	.1593	.8849	.5217	2.3366	- 60.2732	.94
12	.1234	1.0364	.6959	3.6990	- 78.0477	.93
13	.1337	1.4422	.4933	4.3232	- 83.9531	.93
14	.2170	.8422	.6187	3.7842	- 84.4909	.90
15	.1546	.7290	.5870	4.7586	- 77.6805	.85
16	.1347	1.0977	.5353	4.8507	- 82.2678	.87
17	.1233	1.0291	.4985	3.7574	- 64.6120	.87
18	.3165	.6508	.8041	3.6080	-105.2300	.93

*Chest circumference corrected for fat.

Table XXVII.

Chart of Anthropometric Measures

Measure	Equipment	Landmark	Special Cues	Pressure	Readings	Check
Standing Height	Stadiometer	Top of head	Head, shoulders, hips, heels touching wall.	Firm	1	Check position of subject
Sitting Height	Stadiometer and square	Top of head	Head, shoulders, hips touching wall. Legs crossed and relaxed.	Firm	1	Check position of subject
Knee width	Sliding caliper	Condyles of left knee	Knee at right angle. Bisect right angle.	Firm	2	Successive
Shoulder width	Sliding caliper	Acromion process	Scapula flat.	Firm	2	Successive
Iliac width	Sliding caliper	Iliac crests	Caliper arms protruding at rear, half the width in contact.	Firm	1	Check landmarks
Trochanteric width	Sliding caliper	Subcutaneous surface of trochanter	Feet parallel, weight equally distributed.	Light	2	Successive
Chest width	Sliding caliper	Xiphoid level, sides of thorax	Caliper horizontal mid-position in breathing.	Light	2	Successive

Table XXVII. (Cont.)

Measure	Equipment	Landmark	Special Cues	Pressure	Readings	Check
Chest depth	Sliding caliper	Xiphoid level	Caliper horizontal mid-position in breathing.	Light	2	Successive
Chest circumference	Steel tape	Xiphoid level	Encircling horizontally, mid-position in breathing.	Snug	2	Successive
Girth of upper arm	Steel tape	Largest Diameter	Arm hanging relaxed.	Light	1	Check position of tape
Girth of lower arm	Steel tape	Largest diameter	Arm hanging relaxed.	Light	1	Check position of tape
Girth of wrist	Steel tape	Smallest diameter	Hand hanging open, relaxed.	Light	1	Check position of tape
Girth of Thigh	Steel tape	Gluteal fold	Weight on both feet	Light	1	Check position of tape
Girth of Calf	Steel tape	Largest diameter	Weight on both feet	Light	1	Check position of tape

Table XXVII. (Cont.)

Measure	Equipment	Landmark	Special Cues	Pressure	Readings	Check
Girth of Ankle	Steel tape	Smallest Diameter	Weight on both feet.	Light	1	Check position of tape
Chest front fat	Fat caliper	Left front thoracic wall	Hold skin fold against thorax.	Tension of caliper	2	Successive
Chest back fat	Fat caliper	Left back thoracic wall	Hold skin fold against thorax.	Tension of caliper	2	Successive
Side fat	Fat caliper	Medial and superior to anterior superior iliac spine	Hold skin fold against abdominal wall.	Tension of caliper	2	Successive
Abdominal fat	Fat caliper	Over left rectus abdominus above umbilicus	Hold skin fold against abdominal wall.	Tension of caliper	2	Successive
Arm span	Horizontal stadiometer and square	Arms horizontal palms forward	Fingers extended.	Light	1	Check position of subject

Table XXVII. (Cont.)

Measure	Equipment	Landmark	Special Cues	Pressure	Readings	Check
Forearm length	Sliding caliper	Fingertips, elbow	Palm up, fingers straight.	Light	1	Check position of subject
Hand width	Sliding caliper	Palm	Palm down, just proximal to meta-carpal-phalangeal articulation.	Light	1	Check position of subject
Finger span	Sliding caliper	Thumb, 5th finger	Spread thumb and fingers.		1	Check position of subject

SELECTED REFERENCES

1. Baldwin, Bird T.: The Physical Growth of Children from Birth to Maturity. University of Iowa, Studies in Child Welfare, 1, p. 149-150, 1921.

2. Broer, Marion, and Naomi R. G. Galles: Importance of Relationship between Various Body Measurements in Performance of Toe-Touch Test. Research Quarterly, 29: p. 253, October 1958.

3. Clarke, H. Harrison: Relationships of Strength and Anthropometric Measures to Physical Performances Involving the Trunk and Legs. Research Quarterly, 28: p. 223, October 1957.

4. Clarke, H. Harrison: Relationship of Strength and Anthropometric Measures to Various Arm Strength Criteria. Research Quarterly, 25: p. 134, May 1954.

5. Hall, D. M.: Determining Healthy Growth for 4-H Club Members. Research Quarterly, 24: p. 284, October 1953.

6. Ludlum, F. E., and Elizabeth Powell: Chest-Height-Weight Tables for College Women. Research Quarterly, 11: p. 55, October 1940.

7. McCloy, C. H.: Appraising Physical Status: Methods and Norms. University of Iowa, Studies in Child Welfare, 15, 1938.

8. Meredith, Howard V.: Measuring the Growth Characteristics of School Children. Journal of School Health, Dec. 1955.

9. Meredith, Howard V.: A Physical Growth Record for Use in Elementary and High Schools. American Journal of Public Health, 39: p. 878, 1949.

10. Perbix, Joyce A.: Relationship between Somatotype and Motor Fitness in Women. Research Quarterly, 25: p. 84, March 1954.

11. Ratcliffe, J. D.: Wetzel Grid Tells How Children Grow. Science Illustrated, 2: p. 66, October 1947.

12. Rindeau, R. P., B. E. Welch, C. E. Crisp, L. V. Crowley, P. E. Griffin, and J. E. Brockett: Relationships of Body Fat to Motor Fitness Test Scores. Research Quarterly, 29: p. 200, May 1958.

13. Sheldon, W. H.: Atlas of Man. New York, Harper & Bros., 1954.

14. Slater-Hammel, A. T.: Performance of Selected Groups of Male College Students on the Reynolds' Balance Test. Research Quarterly, 27: p. 347, October 1956.

15. Turner, Abby H.: Body Weights Optimal for Young Adult Women. Research Quarterly, 14: p. 255, October 1943.

16. Tyrance, Herman J.: Relationships of Extreme Body Types to Ranges of Flexibility. Research Quarterly, 29: p. 349, October 1958.

17. United States Department of Health, Education and Welfare: Basic Body Measurements of School Age Children, A Handbook for School Officials, Architects and Design Engineers in Planning School Buildings, Furniture and Equipment. U. S. Government Printing Office, Superintendent of Documents, Washington, D. C., 1953.

18. Wetzel, Norman C.: Assessing the Physical Condition of Children, I, II, III. Journal of Pediatrics, 22: January, February, March, 1943.

19. Wetzel, Norman C.: The Simultaneous Screening and Assessment of School Children. Journal of Health, Physical Education and Recreation, 13: December, 1942.

20. Wetzel, Norman C.: Unhappy Children Fail to Grow, What's New. Abbott Laboratories, March 1949.

21. Willoughby, David P.: An Anthropometric Method for Arriving at the Optimal Proportions of the Body in Any Adult Individual. Research Quarterly, 3: p. 48, March 1932.

Chapter VIII

EVALUATION OF PHYSICAL FITNESS

Relationship of Physical Education and Fitness

Some objectives have been accepted by most physical educators throughout the years. Development of physical stamina, organic stimulation, over-all muscular efficiency, and efficient functioning of the entire body in motor performance are four long-term objectives almost universally accepted. The terminology has changed from one decade to another. The specific concept of efficiency has varied. The method of evaluation of pupil achievement has been altered; for example, the evaluative techniques have included anthropometric measurement of body parts, vital capacity, muscle girths, strength tests, cardiac functional tests, and coordination tests of various kinds.

It was during the war years of the early 1940's that the terms physical fitness and total fitness became generally used. These terms were applied to the various capacities which have been recognized for decades as part of the contributions of physical education. While the term fitness and its usage were relatively new, the concept and its meaning to physical education were not new. Programs were modified to give greater emphasis to the fitness objective, and in many cases evaluative techniques were used. The latter were usually selected on the basis of expediency and seldom with the usual attempt to validate in terms of a standard which was consistent with the definition of fitness which had been accepted.

The popular interest in fitness during those years made the use of the term fairly easy. The decline in general interest since that time has meant simply a change in popular attitude, not a change in the aims or responsibilities of the physical educators. The basic responsibility, that of helping to develop a sound functioning organism for whatever tasks the individual needs to participate in, is recognized as a persistent one irrespective of national

epochs. However, it was under the stimulus of the war
years and the more popular interest of the subsequent decade which has been developed by action of the federal government that research was undertaken to learn more about
measurement of fitness.

Fitness Defined

The critics of physical education, both within the profession and from outside, have accused physical educators
of not understanding fitness, and of doing nothing about it
in the programs for which they are responsible. In some
instances this is true. However, in many instances it
would appear to be partly a matter of semantics. Since the
concepts of fitness differ, the methods of achieving fitness
and of measuring it must differ.

Perhaps the term efficiency would be a better one to
use than fitness. Perhaps some entirely new term should be
created. Perhaps various adjectives should be used with
the term to describe the various components of total fitness, as for example, muscular fitness, organic fitness,
cardio-respiratory fitness, mental fitness, etc. While
terminology is actually relatively unimportant, it can be
the stumbling block resulting in poor selection of programs
and tests, rejection of certain activities and tests, and
the basis of needless argument and debate.

The basic concept of fitness is that of an effective
total response to work or activity of whatever intensity
may be required. It is immediately apparent that individual
needs or levels of fitness vary. That does not alter the
need for an efficient operation of the total organism, an
efficient motor mechanism, an efficient organic mechanism,
and an efficient mental functioning, all of which are
sparked by a sound emotional control. In short, the fit
person is one who is free of limiting and debilitating ail-
ments, who has the stamina and skill to do the day's work,
and who has sufficient reserve of energy not only to meet
emergencies but to provide a zest for leisure time living.
This broad concept provides a basis for understanding the
measurement techniques used for these capacities. It is
consistent with the official statement of the American Association for Health, Physical Education and Recreation.

The Need for Fitness Tests

Every objective held valid by the teacher requires some evaluation of results. The physical education teacher and the student have a partial estimate of fitness or lack of it in such things as symptoms of chronic fatigue, of degree of endurance in games, or in stunts or special feats which students are able to perform. However, such estimates are quite subjective and very general in nature.

One of the values of tests is that they tend to clarify for both student and teacher the objectives and capacities which are being developed. Most of our students have been brought up to expect a test score which is indicative of relative status. For example, the I.Q. or our corresponding motor quotient is used by the schools, and the wide-scale programs of testing student achievement give the student or school a percentile ranking. Even the popular magazines feature self-administering tests which provide the reader with a score which purports to indicate his status in some ability. The fact that there is a need for evaluating fitness and that students are conditioned to expect objective evidence on the capacities accepted as goals point to the teaching opportunity inherent in the wise use of fitness tests.

The evolvement of suitable measuring techniques has been slow. During the years of development there have been two types of tests for measurement of physical fitness. The first type was based on the physiological work principles and consisted principally of measures of cardiovascular or respiratory functioning. Most of them involved highly complex apparatus and required administration as an individual test although they showed such low reliability that they seemed better adapted to group than to individual interpretation. The second type purporting to measure fitness included strength tests as indicators of health, vigor, and fitness; most teachers considered these claims as exaggerated and considered them as another specific, a strength measure.

The answer on how to measure fitness was not available in the early 40's when the problem of testing fitness suddenly took on new importance. A common practice was to empirically select one, two or three tests to measure what appeared to be important aspects of fitness. Procedures

278

were almost as numerous as teachers. Into this situation came the efforts of many groups such as the United States Office of Education; the respective state departments of public instruction; committees of state and national physical education, professional organizations; the workshop held by the National Association for Physical Education of College Women; the various branches of our armed services; and many independent research workers. It was mainly the latter, the independent research worker, and to some extent the armed services, who persisted during the first eight or nine postwar years to try to find ways of measuring aspects of fitness. Each tended to go his own way with his definition of fitness.

The programs of fitness testing that were developed in the schools show certain characteristics and trends. Much more work has been done toward developing tests for the college level than for the high school level. Fitness tests have been used more at the college level than at the high school level. There probably are several reasons for this. It is partially a reflection of the fact that more suggestions on suitable tests have been made for the older group. The apparent immediacy for the college student of military or civilian work demanding a high level of fitness has resulted in greater emphasis on development of fitness in the college programs.

One of the outstanding points to be noted in studying testing programs is the great variation of test items. Some institutions give a very limited battery, others a very extensive battery, but brief or extensive, there is very little exact duplication from school to school. The similarity lies in testing for specific phases, usually of "motor fitness." A survey of tests used in the college women's program showed that the batteries used were as varied as the schools.

The college men's plans for testing fitness showed almost as much variation as those for women. There was perhaps a little more influence from testing programs in the armed services and for that reason more agreement on the basic items. An example of a men's battery in wide use is that developed in Indiana.[3] In general the men have attempted to evaluate the results of the program by means of tests more frequently than have the women. Examples of this work appear in the bibliography.

As the mid-fifties approached there was little additional evidence as judged either on the basis of quantity or on the basis of validation or general agreement and acceptance. This is understandable, since research is time-consuming. Perhaps more important is the American heritage of local automony in problems of education. Our teachers are traditionally selecting their own content for teaching and ways of teaching it which includes ways of testing outcomes. Popular and professional interest was shocked into being by accusations of Kraus concerning lack of fitness in American children as based on his proposed fitness test. The physical education profession, the federal government, and the American public responded, each in their own way. The federal government held a national conference and appointed a Council on Fitness for American Youth; the A.A.H.P.E.R. held a fitness conference,[2] has published research in this area as fast as it is available, and has started an evaluative program on a national scale;[14] the American public has become receptive to and concerned about fitness and ways of assessing it. Here is physical education's opportunity to act, to select the best of the tests now available and to improve on them as rapidly as possible for educational use, and to educate the public to the health issues involved.

SELECTION OF FITNESS TESTS

Each test should be selected for a specific purpose, to measure a particular capacity. A few or several tests may be chosen according to the elements of fitness considered essential, the time available for testing, and the merits of the various tests. The elements of fitness for which one is striving must be decided in each instance in light of student needs. The other two points, time available and the merits of the tests, will be discussed.

1. _Time_. Economy of time in test administration has been discussed in other chapters with respect to general testing programs. The possibilities for economizing in fitness testing are probably greater than in many other areas. The first advantage is that many tests can be given to large groups. Mass tests are usually limited only by the number who can be put into the testing area. Partners are instructed on the method of scoring and the test then requires just long enough to give it to two persons. Some tests have limited use because they require equipment or special areas

for their performance. For example, arm strength may be
measured by pull-ups or chinning in various forms, by push-
ups in several forms, or by push-pull tests with the dynamometer. The dynamometers are expensive and hence prohibi-
tive for many schools. Dynamometers and equipment for
hanging or pull-ups are usually limited and thus accommodate
very few students. The push-up test has no requirement
other than padding for the knees, and might appear to be the
best selection from the standpoint of time. However, it
must be administered very carefully, usually by one or two
very carefully trained test administrators. Outdoor equipment on the playground usually provides several places for
hanging or pull-ups. Scheduling of the tests so that outdoor equipment may be used, may be the answer to economy of
time in testing arm strength. In general, the use of special equipment usually slows the testing schedule because
only a few students can be tested at one time.

Time can be saved by avoiding use of two· or more tests
which measure the same thing, or which have extremely high
correlation with each other. Possible duplication can be
determined by a subjective analysis of what the tests involve, or preferably by statistical analysis if such is
available. For example, Wilson's study on strength tests
for college women indicated some significant relationships.[43] The Wilson study started with tests which were believed to measure similar capacity. Statistical evidence
bears out similarity in some, differences in others. See
Table XXVIII. Mohr's study started with tests which were

Table XXVIII

Intercorrelation of Strength Tests in the Wilson Study

RELATED TOO HIGHLY TO GIVE BOTH TESTS								NOT HIGHLY RELATED			
	1	2	3	4	5	6	7		1	2	3	4
1. Bent arm hang								1. Bent arm hang			
2. Push-up (from knees)	.43							2. Weight holding	.34		
3. Push-up (on bench)	.54	.76						3. Push-pull	.25	.21	
4. Pull-up	.56	.68	.63					4. Vertical pull	.23	.23	
5. Pull-up (knees bent)	.54	.48	.53	.58				5. Rope climb	.12	.27	.26
6. Rope climb (arms only)	.52	.61	.62	.62	.46			6. Push-up (bench)	.37	.10	.10
7. Push-pull								7. Pull-up	.27	.27	.35
8. Vertical pull							.61	8. Pull-up (knees bent)	.30		

believed to be different as judged subjectively.[25] The
statistical evidence corroborates that selection. See
Table XXIX.

Table XXIX.

Intercorrelation of Tests in the Mohr Study

	1	2	3	4	5
1. Sit-ups					
2. Chair stepping	.101				
3. Push-up	.494	.043			
4. Bouncing	.261	.218	.329		
5. Pull	.299	.101	.042	.207	
6. Obstacle race	.411	.077	.349	.341	.262

Likewise the Magnusson[21] study assumed the tests unrelated. This was confirmed as shown in Table XXX.

Table XXX.

Intercorrelations of the Muscular Fitness Tests
in the Magnusson Study

Test	Push-ups	Flexibility	Sit-ups
Bent arm hang	.12	.07	.01
	.11	-.31	-.08
Push-ups		.07	.04
		-.35*	.00
Flexibility			-.07
			-.20

*Difference from zero significant at the 5% level.
Upper coefficient is for girls, lower for boys.

The scoring method may affect the time required. Most
of these tests allow only one or two trials so there is no
problem of many repetitions. However, a test may be set up
with a specified time limit and scored on the number of repetitions performed in that interval, or it may be scored as
the time required to perform a specified number of movements. The uniform time is better, as it makes it possible
to administer a test to the whole group with a single timer

282

and stop watch, to know the exact amount of time needed, and to avoid having the faster ones wait while the slower ones perform. Whether uniformity in time or in repetitions is used for a test, if the duration of the test is comparatively short, the capacity measured is essentially the same; that for maintaining a maximum rate for a brief period of time.

Tests should develop directly out of regular instruction. In that case a minimum of specific instruction and special practice will be necessary when the testing is conducted. With careful organization of partners or assistants and a scoring and recording system, little time need be spent in testing. Building of fitness requires time; in most instances time is already too short to accomplish all that is desired. It is essential that the teacher avoid spending unnecessary amounts of time on testing.

Additional time will be saved if the tests are self-administering or can be given to each other. This means that the scoring must be simplified and the performance so obvious that no errors in scoring can be made after brief instructions. When each person must be judged by the teacher, or equipment must be adjusted for each person by assistants, too much time is spent in waiting for turns. Furthermore, the tests must be given to all in sequence rather than simultaneously.

Tests which require equipment of any type create a problem. Strength testing equipment is expensive and sometimes impossible to procure. Where spring balance scales can be obtained, they may be used for substitute tests very successfully. They have been found to be about as valid and reliable as the dynamometer tests.* If equipment seems necessary, it is advisable to use that which is already available in the gymnasium. Obstacle courses have been used quite extensively as a means of measuring endurance and general agility. Most of these require considerable space

---

*Marjorie Wilson[43] gives the following:
  Reliability -- grips, pull, push, .94, .89, .76 respectively; spring scale: thrust, horizontal pull, vertical pull, .91, .82, .91 respectively.
  Validity -- correlated with the Rogers short strength index, push and pull, .49; vertical pull, .59.
  Dorothy Mohr[25] gives the following:
  Reliability -- vertical pull, .93.

and are laborious to construct. Shorter courses may be arranged in the gymnasium with equipment which is there. If an obstacle course is used, instruction should be given on each part of it and practice permitted before it is done under pressure of time; this will do much to avoid injuries. The obstacle courses in schools have frequently been built for the boys and then used by the girls. This invites injuries because the distance to be jumped or the heights to be scaled are usually too great for the majority of the girls. The boys' obstacles are seldom padded sufficiently to give adequate protection for the girls. This problem may be solved partially by providing different obstacles along the same course for the girls.

2. Difficulty. Another requirement of good tests is that there be no zero scores, or no undue massing of scores at any point along the scale. This is sometimes very difficult to avoid in this type of testing because of the great range in ability and because the standards which are considered desirable are likely to be far above the ability of many of the group. One might argue that the tests should not be modified for the weaker group because it gives them a false impression of their status. However, one of the chief purposes of the whole testing procedure, motivation, is defeated if some adjustment is not made. If a student and all his friends in the class get a zero score he is much more impressed by that fact than he is that a few persons made a very high score. Tests may be modified to suit this large group of less capable ones and then increased in difficulty as the students improve. In other words, the tests should be adjusted so as to be a challenge, rather than a source of discouragement and criticism. If this procedure is followed, it will eliminate some forms of the push-up, of the sit-up, and of climbing for most girls' classes.

In order to obtain this progression in difficulty and to select tests wisely on the basis of abilities involved, a careful analysis of each test must be made. For example, a sit-up is much more difficult if the legs are not held down and much easier if the head and arms may be allowed to lead. Likewise, a running test may measure speed if set up to get maximum performance for a very short time, or it may measure endurance if planned for a longer period at maximum or submaximal speed. Another running test may measure leg strength, and, in slightly different form, agility. If tests are to be used in a series, this analysis of the test is essential also to determine proper sequence of tests in order to avoid fatigue and a resultant handicap on later tests.

3. Motivation. The tests should be presented in such a way that the students want to do well on them. If tests are to measure ability accurately, they must result in little or no muscular soreness afterward and a limited amount of discomfort while doing them. Motivation is the controlling factor here which will encourage effort in spite of consequences, but effort cannot be forced, especially against such odds. A college woman is more likely to consider such discomfort unnecessary and the person who works to that point a "sucker," than will the high school girl. Hence, this point is much more important in working with college women. The student may work to the limit the first time but she remembers her previous experience and will not really try the second time. There are certain tests which students associate with immediate or later discomfort and hence they develop a distinct dislike for the test, a dislike which is likely to spread throughout the group. Soreness can be avoided to a considerable extent by aiming the conditioning program directly toward the capacities represented by the tests. Motivation is usually easier with boys and men than with girls and women.

Tests may provide for a limited time interval in which the student seeks to achieve a maximum rate; or the tests may encourage what the student considers an optimum rate which he continues to exhaustion, or to the point where he thinks he can no longer continue. The former type usually elicits better effort from students. The physiological effects on a muscle worked to the limit cannot be totally avoided even in a trained muscle. Fatigue products accumulate and the muscle works under ever less favorable circumstances as the muscle approaches the contracture of fatigue. The protective reaction of the organism tends to make the person decrease effort when it becomes too painful; it therefore takes a superior type of motivation to get continued effort on endurance tests after discomfort sets in. Not only is submaximal effort obtained from practically all, but they quit at different points along the fatigue curve. Both of these factors make the measure unreliable.

4. Safety. Safety should be considered as carefully as any quality in selecting tests. As in any activity, there may be an occasional injury, but most of these can be

prevented by forethought. Certain tests, such as sit-ups or squat thrusts, are conducive to strains in the abdominal muscles or to various ill effects on viscera by increased abdominal pressure. These certainly should not be engaged in by anyone subject to conditions such as hernia, appendicitis, or severe dysmennorhea. Likewise, the squat thrusts, deep knee bends, and many forms of jumping are hard on knees, particularly if the knee is already weak or if the person is extremely overweight. Tests which require a quick turn immediately on landing from a jump or following any deep knee bend may result in knee injuries.

Some tests of endurance involve a run of 150 to 200 yards or more. Such runs should not be taken unless the individual has been trained for such strenuous activity. Standards of competition for women and girls have always contraindicated such events. Tests are actually competition; they are competition against standards, or the rest of the class, or one's previous record. It would seem that similar criteria concerning strenuousness should be applied to the so-called competitive events and to test events. The minimum requirement certainly should be adequate training for both boys and girls.

Adequate training to insure safety in the test prohibits the practice of giving certain tests very early in a season or semester. Of course, the best means of showing improvement is to test at the beginning and again at the end of the learning interval. However, care should be taken, particularly on endurance events, that they are not given without reasonable preconditioning. Attention should be given also to the warm-up immediately preceding testing. If students know that the lesson is to consist primarily of testing, many of them are prone to avoid their usual initial activity before the class begins on the false assumption that it is better to conserve energy. A warm-up should be planned carefully in terms of the type of testing and the intensity of the testing to follow.

If obstacle courses are to be used for junior and senior high school ages, provisions should be made for adjustable or alternate obstacles for the smaller students. Obstacles which are to be climbed or which must be scaled by dragging oneself over are not desirable for girls from the safety standpoint, and if used should be well padded.

5. Tests in Relation to Objectives. Before a teacher starts a program of testing for fitness it seems important

that certain questions be considered.   The program is
determined largely by the answers to:

(1) What aspects of fitness am I teaching?

(2) Is that kind of fitness measurable, and if so,
in what units?

(3) Shall I attempt to measure comprehensively
or just one or two aspects?

The answers to the above questions would doubtless
point toward the use of comparatively few tests of the
qualities of total fitness which are best achieved through
physical education experiences.   The questioning then continues.

(4) Shall I rely only upon highly refined measures or something which in spite of technical shortcomings
will motivate interest and effort?

(5) What measures are available which will have
the least technical shortcomings?

The decisions on these two questions may leave one only
a very limited choice or may give one opportunity for experimentation and ingenuity.   Both courses have advantages.
The final questions may be of this type:

(6) Is the time of training sufficient to produce
results which are measurable?

(7) Is the time which is available sufficient to
justify more than very brief testing?

There is similarity between the fitness tests in use
for the two sexes.   However, some variations are essential.
The tests suggested in this chapter are primarily for the
girls and women.   A few of the tests may be adapted for
boys, or other tests may be selected in keeping with the
considerations discussed above.   The following sources may
be used for additional information on testing for men.

In most of the classifications below, two or three
tests are suggested.   Seldom, if ever, would that many tests
for a given purpose be used for a single class.   Careful
selection should be made from these suggestions, or from
other tests, according to the ability of the class, the
equipment available, and the requirements for good testing
suggested above.   These tests have been found valuable but
others may be better adapted to certain situations.

In choosing a battery of tests some consideration should be given to their cumulative effect on the students, especially if they must be given in a single class period. When a series of extremely strenuous tests is given with the tests following each other in rapid succession, there may be fatigue to the point where the scores are reduced. Alternation of types of tests during administration will be helpful, but if a very extensive battery is to be given, it is usually preferable to give it in halves on successive days.

TESTS OF STRENGTH

A. Tests for Arm and Shoulder Girdle Strength.

Several tests are suggested. Select one or two if measuring different muscle groups.

1. Vertical Pull with Dynamometer

Use a dynamometer with push-pull attachment. The dynamometer is fastened to an adjustable cross bar and placed for each subject at such a height that when the subject grasps the lower handle the elbow is level with or slightly higher than the top of the shoulder. A special standard may be built or the horizontal ladder in the gymnasium usually permits such adjustment (see Figure 37). The doorway gym bar would also serve though not as readily adjustable. With any of these pieces of equipment it is desirable to line the class up by height so that there are relatively few adjustments to be made during the testing of the class.

Description:

Stand with the heels and back against the wall, shoulder lined up with the dynamometer (right shoulder for right-handed persons). Grasp the handle on the attachment with the palm turned toward the wall. Stretch tall, back firm against the wall and pull down (in chinning fashion) as hard as possible. There should be no movement of the body. The score is the number of pounds registered on the dynamometer (one hand only).

a   b

Figure 37. Pull test.

a = with dynamometer.
b = with spring scale.

Reliability:

The reliability was .90 for successive trials by fifty-
five college women.* Morris[26] computed reliability on
fifty-four children, grades one to three and obtained .88.

Validity:

See the following test for information concerning the
validity of this type of test. The change in equipment has
been made since validation of the test. For fifty women
taking the test on both pieces of equipment, the coefficient
on their two scores was .45. This was believed to be due to
the fact that in this form it was possible to eliminate
trunk twisting and other aids and thereby get more nearly

---

*Scott, Gladys: Unpublished studies.

arm and shoulder girdle strength only. This is borne out by a correlation coefficient of .86 between the sum of the push-pull scores and this test on performance of ninety-seven college women at the University of Iowa.* Wilson,[43] in attempting to establish the test as a measure of strength, obtained an r of .59 with the Rogers Short Index.

Suggestions:

Watch to see that student does not bend knees or trunk or twist the shoulder away from the wall.

Arrange the students according to height in order to avoid having to adjust the cross bar for every student. Give instructions to all rather than individually as each starts the tests. This test may be used for boys or men but the feet must be fastened down to prevent their lifting themselves from the floor. Girls do not have adequate strength to lift themselves with one arm. The correlation coefficient on performance of fifty college women with and without feet strapped down was .90. This is approximately the reliability of the test and indicates that time for applying straps is unnecessary. Also, observation of hundreds of college women taking the test has never revealed a single one whose single arm strength came even close to matching her total weight.

2. Vertical Pull With Spring Scale

This is the same test as above but with inexpensive equipment (see Figure 37). Use a good grade spring scale (may be purchased at any hardware store). The lower end of the scale is fastened to the floor. A rope, securely fastened to the upper end of the scale, is run through an overhead pulley so that the handle end can be reached from a standing position, with the arms slightly flexed. The length of the rope should be adjusted to the height of the shortest student. The rope may be shortened for taller persons by slipping a wooden peg through one or more loops of the rope.

Description:

Stand erect, in a comfortable stance and with shoulders fixed. Pull down as hard as possible without bending

---

*Scott, Gladys: Unpublished studies.

the knees or hips or twisting the body. The score is the number of pounds registered on the scale.

Reliability:

The coefficient was .95 on successive trials by 140 college women at the University of Iowa. Similarly, a coefficient of .91 was obtained for scores of fifty-two women.

Validity:

When correlated with the Rogers Short Index of strength in determining the validity of the pull test as a general measure of strength, an r of .59 was obtained. When correlated with scores showing work output on a bicycle ergometer in determining the validity of the pull test as a fitness measure, an r of .49 was obtained.

Suggestions:

The examiner must have his eyes on the level of the scale in order to read it accurately. The scale does not hold the reading as does the dynamometer.

Watch to see that the subject does not bend knees or trunk, then quickly read the scale while she continues pulling.

Take the girls in order of height to save time in adjusting the rope. Give instructions to all rather than individually.

This test may be used for boys or men but would require a much stronger scale.

The correlation between the two forms of the test given above was .45 on fifty subjects. The relatively low relationship doubtless represents the variations in the spring scale technique due to different body positions. This test is considered less satisfactory than the previous one using the dynamometer.

3. Push and Pull

Use the hand dynamometer with the push-pull attachment.

Description:

Hold the apparatus in front of the chest, one hand on each handle; elbows bent and arms in a horizontal plane. Pull as hard as possible. This pull is similar to that exercise in which one tries to touch the elbows behind the shoulders. (Assistant records score and resets dynamometer.) In same position push in on apparatus as hard as possible; the heel of the hand may be used. Do not brace the apparatus against the chest in either trial.

Reliability:

The reliability was .91 for successive trials by sixty-two college women at the University of Iowa.* Wilson,[43] in computing the two parts of the test separately, obtained reliability r's of .89 and .76, respectively, for the pull and push.

Validity:

Validity coefficients have been established in various studies and always run fairly high, as would be expected from the nature of the test itself. However, in the Wilson study, when it was correlated with the Rogers Short Strength Index for fifty-two subjects, it yielded a coefficient of only .49.

T-Scales:

A scale for college freshmen and sophomores appears in Table XXXI.

Suggestions:

If the handles have sharp edges, they should be covered or padded with adhesive tape or something that will not slip. This test may be used in this form for boys and men.

4. Push-Up on Knees

The knees should be protected by placing performers on mats, or, if the floor is not too slippery, by folding a sweat shirt or towel under the knees.

---

*Scott, Gladys: Unpublished studies.

Table XXXI.

T-Scales for Push-Pull Test

T-SCORE	PUSH-PULL*	T-SCORE	PUSH-PULL*
81	166	45	88
76	152	44	86
74	150	43	84
72	148	42	82
71	146	41	80
70	144	40	78
69	140	39	76
68	136	38	74
67	132	37	72
66	130	36	
65	128	35	70
64	126	34	68
63	124	33	66
62	122	32	64
61	120	31	62
60	118	30	60
59	116	29	58
58	112	28	52
57	110	27	
56	108	26	
55	106	25	50
54	104	24	
53	102	23	
52		22	
51	100	21	48
50	98	20	
49	96	19	
48	94	18	
47	92	17	38
46	90	16	

*Scale was constructed on 892 freshman and sophomore women at the University of Iowa. Score is the sum of the push and the pull scores.

293

Description:

Lie in the prone position with hands under the point of the shoulders, elbows spread slightly (a in Figure 38). Feet may be raised from the floor, or knees may be left relaxed if preferred. Keep body straight and extend arms

Figure 38. Push-up from knees.

a = top view
b = side view

fully; weight will be resting on hands and knees (see b). Bend arms so that chest again touches the floor. Repeat promptly and continue as long as possible or for a stated number of times. Score is the number which can be done before stopping or before position is changed.

Reliability:

Reliability was .93 on trials on successive days by 140 college women at the University of Iowa. This high a reliability could not be obtained unless the same person administers the tests to all subjects. Magnusson[21] obtained an r of .52 on first graders but .83 on sixth graders. Buxton's r was .83 on a sample from grades one to nine.[5]

Validity:

Wilson[43] obtained a coefficient of .72 with the Rogers Short Index.

Suggestions:

If the hips and lower back are allowed to sag at all, the weight is transferred progressively up the thigh, hips, and trunk during body lowering, and in reverse order in the lift. It is necessary to keep the back straight and to hold the hips in very slight flexion (not exceeding 5°) in order to keep the weight on the arms.

If the performer continues regular breathing, he will be more comfortable and this tends to give greater endurance.

Students must be taught the proper form and how to judge form and errors when observing others. After they have learned the proper form, it is possible to give the test to one-half the class with partners scoring. This is a time-saving technique but may reduce reliability of scores.

This test may be used for boys who have little strength. Later, after improving strength and for older and stronger boys, it is better to give the push-ups in a full prone position with knees straight and weight supported on hands and toes.

5. Pull-up on Horizontal Bar

Adjust the bar to the level of the xiphoid (angle between the ribs at the base of the sternum) when the subject stands erect.

Description:

Grasp the bar with the hands about shoulder width apart and palms toward the face. Move the feet far enough beyond the bar that when the weight rests on the heels, with knees, hips, and back straight, the line of the body forms a right angle with the line of the straight arms.

(See Figure 39.) Keep the body straight and bend the arms until the neck or upper chest touches the bar. Extend arms again. Repeat again without pausing and continue as long as possible or for a stated number of times. Score is the number which can be done before stopping or before the body begins to sag or sway.

Figure 39. Pull-up on horizontal bar.

Validity:

The validity was .80 when correlated with the Rogers Short Index.

Suggestions:

The sides of parallel bars may be used if a horizontal bar is not available. This does not permit quite as exact an adjustment for height. Flying rings may also be used but give less uniform results because they swing. Equipment is usually very limited so only a few need be trained to administer the test.

A similar form may be done with a partner who holds a wand and stands astride the performer. Performer starts lying on her back, shoulders under the wand. The performer grasps the wand and pulls up until the chest touches the

bar, lowers to full arm length, and repeats. The top
person must stand straight and firm, and with feet far
enough apart to permit the performer to reach the wand.
Since the top person may tire before the one who is taking
the test, it is better to have two persons hold the wand,
one at each end. One of the advantages of having the wand
held is that there is no need for adjustment of the bar.
If wands are not available, small-sized softball bats may
be used. Another form of this test puts the performer's
feet flat on the floor, knees bent at right angles, trunk
and thighs horizontal, and arms vertical. When the chinning is done, the movement is at the knees, not at the
ankles. A little practice is necessary on the test in
order to standardize form.

This test may be used for boys who have little
strength. For most boys and men, the test should be given
on a horizontal bar adjusted high enough that it may be
grasped in a free hanging position and the entire weight
lifted.

6. Hanging

Adjust the bar to the approximate level of the top of
the head, or if it is higher have a small bench on which
the subject can mount to grasp the bar.

Description:

Grasp the bar with the hand about shoulder width apart
and palms toward the face. Spring upward so that the arms
are flexed firmly against the body, the chin is well above
the bar and the body hangs straight and unsupported except
for the hands. (See Figure 40.) Hold this position as
long as possible; if the arms start to extend, go down as
slowly as possible.

Reliability:

Magnusson[21] computed reliabilities on 55 first graders
and a similar number of sixth grades, obtaining r's of .83
and .90 respectively. Morris[26] obtained .67 on 54 children
grades one to three.

Figure 40. Hanging.

Suggestions:

This may be done on a horizontal bar, a doorway gym bar, the side of a parallel bar, the top round of stall bars, side of a horizontal ladder, round on jungle gym or other similar equipment.

The most objective means of scoring the test is to time it to the moment when the chin is lowered to the level of the top of the bar. This is also a faster method of administering the test and one which students can learn to score for each other very well. The other version is to time to full extension of the arms. This requires that the bar be high enough that the feet will not touch even with fully extended arms. In this case there will be need for a means of climbing into the hanging position.

The test may be given to all levels of strength, though the strongest may continue for a very long period of time. It is also adaptable to younger age levels who may not understand tests of pull-up or push-up or even the dynamometer tests. Also, it is usually more interesting to younger age groups than some of the other tests.

B. Test of Abdominal Strength

Several tests, and variations thereof, are suggested. Choose one.

1. Sit-up

It is preferable to give this test on mats or on the turf.

Description:

Assume a hook sitting position with feet flat on the floor, back straight. Place hands on the shoulders with elbows reaching forward to rest on top of the knees. When feet are properly placed a partner will hold them in position. Lie on back while waiting for the starting signal, keeping the hands on the shoulders. On signal, Ready, Go! lift trunk far enough to touch the point of the elbows to the knees and return to back lying (back, but not head touching). You may stop, rest, and restart if you wish. The score is the total number of correct movements (up and down) performed in one minute.

Reliability:

Reliability was .94 for trials on successive days by 140 college women. Magnusson's[21] reliability r's were .68 on first grade and .77 on 6th grade. Buxton[5] obtained .94 on a random sample from first to ninth grade.

Validity:

The coefficients, when the sit-up scores were correlated with work output on the ergometer, were .48 and .52 in the two successive studies.

Suggestions:

Trunk flexion should be encouraged throughout the test. The marked flexion of the hip joint resulting from the placement of the feet reduces to a very minimum amount the effectiveness of the hip flexors. The work of lifting the trunk must be done by the abdominals and trunk flexion facilitates abdominal muscle action. It is permissible to lead with the head, and this makes it unnecessary to judge for fouls.

The hands must be kept on the shoulders throughout. This minimizes momentum which may be gained by swinging the arms, and encourages trunk flexion. The arm position also standardizes the height to which the trunk is lifted.

Partners should hold the feet firmly. The partner's hands should be on the instep, arms straight and shoulders over the hands.

The partner's knees may be placed on the performer's toes, if necessary, to keep the feet down.

This test may be used for boys and men, but the time allotment should be increased to match the ability of the students.

Variations:

The disadvantages of alternative forms follow:

1. Hands behind neck, elbows kept back -- encourages forward head and permits excessive arm pull.

2. Hands on the opposite shoulder, elbows against the ribs -- reduces arm momentum but it is difficult to keep arms firm on the chest. An advantage is gained from arm movement and the test is difficult to judge; in fact it is almost impossible to get uniformity by using student partners as judges.

3. Arms extended along sides and hands kept on the floor -- avoids a high arm lead, but may permit a push-off with the hands or elbows from the floor.

4. Arms extended, hands sliding along on top of thighs -- difficult to prevent the subject from pulling up by grasping the thighs or clothing.

5. Hands on shoulders, legs straight, bend forward far enough to touch the elbow to the opposite knee, alternating right and left -- uses oblique abdominal muscles more in latter stage of the sit-up, encourages pronounced spinal flexion.

6. Head, neck, and back held straight throughout -- constitutes one of the most difficult variations of the sit-up exercise and is not suited to most groups. It also puts greater demand on hip flexors than on abdominal muscles and therefore would not usually be selected as a fitness test. Furthermore, it is difficult to obtain uniformity in the judging and scoring of performance.

300

7. No support on feet -- makes the test difficult, may result in many zero or low scores for girls.

8. Legs straight, heels on floor -- there is a tendency to hollow the lower spine excessively, the hip flexors do more of the work than when the knees are bent.

2. Rocker

A mat or turf is preferable to bare gymnasium floor.

Description:

Start in back lying position, hands on the shoulders with elbows extended straight sideward. Raise the feet and trunk off the floor a few inches so only the hips are in contact with the floor. Rock gently from side to side while holding this flexed position. Sideward movement is checked by contact of the elbow on the floor; a push-off with the elbow is permitted. The score is the number of seconds the position and action are maintained.

Suggestions:

Continue regular breathing for greater comfort. Keep the trunk flexed very slightly. No studies are known dealing with validation of the test but it should be a good practice test at least.

Variations:

1. V position held with no rocking movement, arms extended just off the floor. Rocking gives the advantage of momentarily moderately relaxing the muscles on alternate sides of the abdominal wall; therefore, it slightly prolongs the time and gives better distribution of scores. In the V position, it is difficult to keep the extended arms off the floor or thighs.

2. V position, held with hands holding the thighs. The position is fixed and the abdominal muscles are almost entirely relieved of action. This is primarily a balance test.

C. Test of Foot Strength

1. Bounce

Description:

Take a full squat sitting position with the back as
straight and erect as possible. Place the arms down the
outside of the legs, hands grasping instep or ankle. Hold
the elbows firmly extended to immobilize the knees. Extend
ankle (as in a jump) so that you rise to the end of the
toes or slightly off the floor. Repeat as long as possible
in rhythm established by the timer who counts aloud. If
you lose your balance and can restart within three counts,
you may continue. Score is the total number of bounces
you can perform (count on which you quit minus the counts
lost during stops).

Reliability:

The coefficient was .79 for trials on successive days
by 140 college women.

Validity:

The coefficient was .45 in each of the two studies
comparing scores with work output on the ergometer.

Suggestions:

Timing is two counts per second; counting should be
loud enough that all scorers can hear. If large numbers
are working, the use of a drum may help to make the rhythm
audible. Scorers can score from one to four students depending upon their experience in administering the test.
When scoring several persons, tallies are made for each
person who may fall over and restart, and the final count
for each is recorded. After all have finished the deduc-
tions are made at the rate of three counts for each time
the performer stopped.

Check technique each student uses before starting the
test. Emphasize elbows firm and hands low on ankle. This
form improves score by minimizing knee action. The force
should come from the ankles and feet. Emphasize head up
and back straight, and a low, rhythmic bounce. This improves balance and prevents moving around and bumping into
others.

Timer stands near a blackboard, counts aloud to 10;
records 1 on board, repeats count to 10 and records 2; and
continues by tens until all performers have stopped. This
avoids errors in counting and by watching a stop watch
constantly it is possible to keep proper rate and a perfectly even rhythm. The score is ten times the last number on the board plus the count on which the student stops.
For example, the last score on the board is 18, count is 4
on next round, broken rhythm 2. Score = $(10 \times 18) + 4 - 6$
= 178. Scorers should be stationed facing the timer and
the blackboard. The performers face the scorer, backs
turned to timer. This discourages their concentrating on
the score while performing and deciding to quit when they
reach a convenient count. Partners may do the scoring.

TESTS OF ENDURANCE

Endurance is the most difficult aspect of fitness to
measure. Endurance is primarily the result of a physiological capacity of the organism to continue functioning
satisfactorily. Endurance may be measured by either the
ability to maintain action at maximum speed for a short
period of time, or the ability to maintain action at a
slower rate for an indefinite period of time. The former
type of endurance is the easier on which to set up tests,
but it does assume that the subject will put forth the effort to work at a maximum rate.

The tests listed here are considered the most satisfactory of those now in use when the criteria presented in
the first of this chapter are applied. Select one.

1. Chair Stepping

Use chairs of a standard type. Arm chairs from a
classroom are suitable. The only requirement is that all
are of the same height for any groups to be compared; most
chairs are 18 inches in height and that is the maximum
which should be used for this test. The number of chairs
required is one-third that of the students to be tested, if
the test is scored by students.

Work in groups of threes. One performs, two holds
the chair and holds the right hand of performer. Three
also holds the chair, counts aloud the number of times one

mounts the chair, and records the score on an individual score card.

Description:

The starting position is beside the chair with one foot on the chair and the right hand in partner's hand. Maintain this hand position throughout the test. On the signal, Ready, Go!, rise to an erect position on the chair; the supporting knee must be straight, the other foot may be off the chair. Immediately step down to the floor with the same foot that started on the floor. Continue as rapidly as possible until the final whistle. Disregard the whistle which blows immediately after starting. Avoid fatigue in the legs by changing feet occasionally, making the shift while both feet are on the chair. The score is the total number of correct movements (up and down) performed in one minute.

The timing is done centrally by one timekeeper who has a stop watch and whistle. The timer gives the starting signal; at the end of two seconds she blows a whistle. The final whistle blows sixty seconds later (or sixty-two seconds after the starting signal). The scorer starts counting on the first whistle (at two seconds) and stops on the final whistle, a total period of one minute.

Reliability:

The coefficient was .95 for trials on successive days by 140 college women.

Validity:

The coefficients comparing this test and work output on the ergometer were .37 and .58, respectively, on the two studies.

Suggestions:

The two assistants should each place a foot on a chair round to prevent the chair from slipping. The partner behind the chair should grasp the performer's hand and hold until after he finishes the test. This is a safety measure to prevent loss of balance or unsteadiness when he becomes fatigued.

Encourage the performer to alternate feet on the chair frequently. Give a demonstration of technique for changing while upon the chair. If the knee extensors are thoroughly fatigued, they do not have time to recover within the minute. Frequent alternation of leading leg prevents such muscular fatigue.

Encourage maximum effort throughout, although it is permissible to stop and rest, if necessary, and then re-start. The score on the first two seconds is not counted because performers respond to the starting signal at very different rates. All should be in motion in two seconds. A loss of two seconds in getting started gives an undue penalty to slow reaction time.

It is best to emphasize maximum effort throughout and not to stress the endurance element or to imply that the performers may become tired from maximum effort. Since this is a test of maintaining maximum effort over a short period of time, the students must be motivated to give that effort or the test is useless. Complete cooperation is essential on all endurance tests and it is difficult to obtain from some individuals.

All performers should wear shoes for the protection of the feet. All chairs should be firm and stable as a safety precaution.

If the test is used for boys and men, it needs to be given for a longer time interval, probably two to four minutes, depending upon the training and condition of the class.

2. Triple Lap

Lay out a course, either circular or shuttle, which is a total of 25 or 30 yards. The shorter distance is preferred for young performers and for those with little real training for endurance. Trained groups may use a course up to 50 yards. This course may be out-of-doors, or in the gymnasium if it is long enough. Most gymnasiums are large enough for a shuttle course diagonally across the floor, if not lengthwise. If a shuttle course is used, more uniformity will be obtained if a post or standard is set up at the far end and the runner required to go around it, rather than running to a line and then turning.

Description:

Run one lap at top speed. The score is the number of seconds (to the nearest tenth of second) required to run the lap. Immediately turn and run a second time, the score being the number of seconds required. Immediately run a third lap again (s   ə is the time required). The endurance score is the ⸺cio of total time to that of the best lap, or $\dfrac{\text{total time}}{\text{shortest time for one lap}}$.

Reliability:

Mohr[25] failed to obtain a satisfactory reliability (.29) on this test. Good motivation should be provided and several trials used with the best being considered as the endurance score. It is probably best as a training device and a means of increasing interest.

Suggestions:

Best results will be secured if a timer calls the time to a scorer who stands beside him. The watch is started when the runner crosses the starting line, and stopped when he returns across it. The runner should be instructed to finish the lap at top speed. That means overrunning it a few steps. By the time he returns to the starting line the timer has read the time for the scorer and is ready to start the watch again for the next lap.

Maximum effort should be encouraged on each lap.

This type of test may be used on a course in the water to measure endurance in swimming. Again in this case it is doubtless of more value as a motivational device to develop endurance than as an actual measure of that endurance.

Other tests of endurance are principally one of two types, namely, measures of cardiorespiratory function or tests for performance over longer periods of time. The cardiorespiratory tests are not practical for most school situations and are too variable in results to be usable for individual records. This variability is due largely to the unreliability of the heart rate. Evidence on undesirability of such tests may be found in various sources.[25,36] Tests of performance over longer periods of time are impractical to administer.

FITNESS BATTERY

A battery of tests for college women has been developed which serves to differentiate satisfactorily between levels of general endurance, which serves as an incentive for work, and which represents varied ability, demanding effort toward abilities often neglected. The development of the tests has occurred in successive stages reported in several articles. The selection of a battery should be made from the following batteries. The correlation between the combined tests and the measure of work output are stated.

	R
Chair stepping, sit-ups	.634
Push-pull, chair stepping, sit-ups	.688
Vertical pull, chair stepping, sit-ups	.666
Vertical pull, obstacle race, sit-ups	.650
Push-pull, sit-ups, bounce, chair stepping	.687
Vertical pull, sit-ups, bounce, chair stepping	.669
Vertical pull, obstacle race, sit-ups, bounce	.651
Vertical pull, obstacle race, sit-ups, bounce, chair stepping	.689
Push-pull, obstacle race, sit-ups, bounce, chair stepping	.686

The T-scales for several of these tests appear in Table XXXII. Most teachers prefer to use several tests but to give the student a single composite score in addition to comparative scores on the separate tests. Each of the various tests may be T-scored from Table XXXII or on T-scales established on students in one's own school. The test scores may then be compared with each other. The T-scores may be added together. The average score is 50 times the number of tests used, since 50 is the mid T-score in each scale.

Table XXXII.

Fitness Scales for College Women
(Arranged for Construction of Student Profile)

T-SCORE	BOUNCE	SIT-UP	CHAIR STEPPING	OBSTACLE RACE	DYNAMO-METER PULL	SPRING SCALE PULL	T-SCORE
84	325				120		84
83	300	100			115		83
82	280		165	17.0-17.4	112	92	82
81	260	96	162		110	91	81
80	250		160	17.5-17.9	107	89	80
79	245	95	157		103	87	79
78	240		154		100	84	78
77	235	94	153		96	81	77
76	230		151		94	80	76
75	225	93	150	18.0-18.4	93	79	75
74	220		149		92	78	74
73	215	92	148		91	77	73
72	210	91	146	18.5-18.9		76	72
71	205	90	142		90	75	71
70	200	88	141		89		70
69	195	87	139	19.0-19.4	88	74	69
68	190	86	138			73	68
67	185	85	137		87	72	67
66	180	84	136		86	71	66
65	175	82	134	19.5-19.9	85	70	65
64	170	80	132		84	69	64
63	165	79	130		83	68	63
62	160	77	128	20.0-20.4	82	67	62
61	155	75	127		81	66	61
60	150	74	126		80	65	60

Table XXXII. (Cont.)

T-SCORE	BOUNCE	SIT-UP	CHAIR STEPPING	OBSTACLE RACE	DYNAMO-METER PULL	SPRING SCALE PULL	T-SCORE
59	145	73	124	20.5-20.9	79	64	59
58	140	72	122		78	63	58
57	135	71	121		77		57
56	132	70	120	21.0-21.4		62	56
55	128	69	118		76		55
54	124	68	117	21.5-21.9		61	54
53	120	66	116		75	60	53
52	116	65	114		74	59	52
51	113	64	112	22.0-22.4	73	58	51
50	110	63	110		72	57	50
49	108	62	108		71	56	49
48	106	61	106	22.5-22.9	70	55	48
47	104	59	105		69		47
46	102	58	104		68	54	46
45	100	57	102	23.0-23.4		53	45
44	98	56	100		67		44
43	96	54	98	23.5-23.9		52	43
42	94	53	96		66		42
41	92	52	94	24.0-24.4	65	51	41
40	90	50	92		64	50	40
39	87	49	90			49	39
38	84	48	88	24.5-24.9	63		38
37	81	47	86		62	48	37
36	78	46	84			47	36
35	72	45	82	25.0-25.4	61		35
34	70	43	80	25.5-25.9		46	34
33	68	42	78		60		33
32	65	40	74	26.0-26.4		45	32
31	62	39	72	26.5-26.9	59		31
30	60	37	70			44	30
29	58	36	69	27.0-27.4	58		29
28	55	35	68	27.5-27.9		43	28
27	52	34	67		57		27
26	50	33	66		56	42	26
25	47	31	65	28.0-28.4	55	41	25

Table XXXII. (Cont.)

T-SCORE	BOUNCE	SIT-UP	CHAIR STEPPING	OBSTACLE RACE	DYNAMO-METER PULL	SPRING SCALE PULL	T-SCORE
24	43	30	63		54	40	24
23	40	29	62	28.5-28.9	53	39	23
22	37		60		52		22
21	33	28	58			38	21
20	30	27	54	29.0-29.4	51		20
19	28		52		50	39	19
18	27		50		49		18
17	26	26	48	29.5-29.9	48	36	17
16		25	45	30.0-30.5			16

TESTS OF AGILITY

1. Obstacle Race

The race which is described in Chapter IX, p. 344, may be used as an agility test, particularly after practice has been allowed on the race as a whole, or on situations similar to the component parts of the test. If the test is given at the beginning of the year as a motor ability test, a single administration may serve the purpose in both batteries. However, after practice on the skills involved in the tests, marked improvement can be expected, and the variability of the group may decrease.

2. Shuttle Race

This race is described in Chapter IX, p. 359. If used as an agility test it should be shortened to less than the 25 foot area described in this test. A 15 foot area without dividing zones might well be used. This would be the same as the shuttle on the end of the obstacle race, and should be timed for 4 or 5 round trips, or trips counted for a 20 or 30 second interval. In the latter form it is a little more economical of time than the obstacle race since it can be given to several at the same time; it is a little less reliable than the obstacle course.

3. Figure Eight

Two Indian clubs or other small objects are placed on the floor 10 feet apart. A starting line projects to the right of one club.

Description:

Stand with toes on or behind the starting line. On the signal, Ready, Go!, run past the first club to the right, then to the left of the second, and around it and back to the right of the first. Continue around the clubs alternating right and left sides in a figure-eight pattern.

TESTS OF FLEXIBILITY

Flexibility must be considered in terms of a given joint or of adjacent joints, just as strength is considered with reference to specific muscle groups. Flexibility is desirable only as it contributes toward some other ability or to freer movement. Determine the type or types of flexibility desired and choose one test for each type selected.

Tests of Hip and Back Flexion

1. Standing, Bending Reach

Arrange a scale marked in half-inch intervals on the front of a chair, stool, or platform, with the inches marked above and below the level of the chair surface. The scale should be not more than three inches wide, and the chair must be steady. (Figure 41.)

Description:

Stand with the toes even with the front edge of the chair and against the sides of the scale. Let the arms, trunk, and neck relax and hang forward, fingers in front of the scale. Reach down slowly as far as possible, the finger tips of both hands moving along parallel and equally down the scale. The knees must be kept straight. The score is the lowest point reached by the finger tips in the downward stretch.

Figure 41. Standing, bending, reach test.

Reliability:

Poley[30] obtained a coefficient of .93 on performance of sixty-three college students. Magnusson[21] obtained r's of .70 and .84 respectively on first and sixth grade children. Buxton[5] found .95 on a sample from grades one to nine.

Suggestions:

A 20-inch scale has been found necessary to provide for the variability found in a group of children. The scale may be marked with the chair level at zero and deviations progressing upward and downward from that point. The score is then minus if the reach is short of the stool level, or plus if it is beyond that level. If the accepted standard is the ability to reach the surface on which one stands, this is a very descriptive form of scoring and is preferable.

An alternate scale is one of similar length, attached to the chair so that zero is up and 10 represents the level of the top of the chair. This is the better arrangement if the suggested standard of performance is for some point above or below the chair level. Recent studies seem to indicate that the distance expected in the reach should vary with different age groups.

The test may be scored as the point to which the subject can reach in a series of quick bobbing movements. This will increase the scores slightly but makes it more difficult to score and reduces objectivity and reliability.

The emphasis with the subject should be on relaxation of the back as he bends forward. It is preferable to teach relaxation in the forward position before giving the test.

It is preferable to give two or three practice trials or warm-ups before measuring the reach. This may be after mounting the chair, or it may be done while waiting, immediately before taking the test. Again this should be done in a relaxed fashion, permitting easy bobbing and a stretch into a standing position between each trial. These warm-up attempts will raise the scores and increase the reliability.

In order to score accurately, the person giving the test must have the eyes down on a level with the reach. A student assistant is helpful; she should watch the bent knees and also be ready to give support if the performer loses her balance.

2. Sitting, Bending Reach

Description:

Sit on the floor with the legs straight and extended at right angles to the line of the boards in the floor. Place the heels on a crack between the boards with feet about 5 or 6 inches apart (just wide enough to get the hands between the heels). A partner stands with her feet against those of the performer to prevent the latter from slipping. The performer bends forward, reaching as far forward as possible on the floor. The knees must be kept straight. The score is the farthest point reached by the finger tips.

Suggestions:

This may be given as a mass test. Since its main advantage over Standing Reach is for quickness of administration, it would seem advisable not to use special floor markings. If sufficient rulers are available, they may be held in place by one foot of the standing partner. Then the zero point is the heel line represented by the mid-point on the ruler. The score is plus if the finger tips reach beyond the heels or minus if they do not go as far as the heels.

313

The quickest and most satisfactory procedure is to use the boards of the floor as units of measurement. Most gymnasium floors are laid with 2 1/4 inch boards. The score is measured to the nearest half of the board (in other words, to the nearest inch). For example, if the reach is almost to the middle of the second board beyond the heel, the score is +1 1/2. If the reach is almost to the second crack beyond the heel the score is +2. If narrower boards are used, count to the nearest crack.

A variation of these tests which is sometimes used is done in a sitting position with the legs straight and together. The performer bends forward to touch the forehead to the knees. If the head touches, he spreads the legs just enough to get the head between the legs and bends forward to touch the forehead to the floor. This method has the advantage of eliminating all direct measurements and of reducing the influence of arm length. It also includes neck flexion, which is omitted in the other forms. However, it leaves most of the class in one of two categories, those touching the knees and those not touching. There will be a third group, a comparatively small number who reach the floor. This may be adequate differentiation and it is faster, each one scoring his own performance.

These tests all measure almost identical forms of flexibility. However, the standing scores will always run a little higher because of the more effective use of gravity and because the hips are shifted back of the heels when standing, thus shortening the distance to the feet. These tests measure not only back and hip joint flexibility but also elasticity and relaxation of the hamstring (posterior thigh) muscles. This is doubtless of more importance as a basis for success in certain activities such as dance or tumbling rather than in everyday activities. It also seems to be related to ease and economy of muscular effort in many movements.

Evidence on the reliability of these flexibility tests is limited. The Standing Reach was studied by Buxton[5] who obtained an r of .95, and Magnusson[21] who obtained an r of .70 on first graders and .84 on sixth graders.

Range of motion is known to vary considerably with such factors as effort, warm-up before starting the test, amount of muscle soreness and the individual's tolerance for it, ability of the individual to relax, room temperature, and other environmental factors. Also in the case of the standing test the degree of confidence of protection against loss of balance may affect results. Consideration must be given to obtaining optimum conditions for administration of the test and in maintaining uniformity of conditions in so far as possible.

Students who take flexibility tests sometimes comment on the disadvantage which they have because of the shortness of arms or trunk. Teachers who are considering the use of the tests are also prone to think of body build as a determining factor in the scores obtained. With this in mind, anthropometric measures were taken on a hundred college women acting as subjects in a flexibility study.* There is no evidence from these data to indicate that variations of body build as found in a cross section of college age women would affect flexibility scores unduly. The correlations with Standing Reach Test and the measures which might have appeared to affect flexibility follow:

Height . . . . +.157

Trunk length . . . . +.148

Arm length . . . . +.294

Trunk and arm length . . . . +.297

Ankle flexion . . . . +.178

Spinal extension . . . . +.262

The correlations between spinal extension (described in the following test) and various measures are equally low.

Shoulder flexibility . . . . +.262

Trunk length . . . . +.180

Pull strength . . . . +.138

However, studies of the elementary and secondary school age consistently show changing degrees of this type of flexibility. The decrease in flexibility in the "pre-adolescent growth spurt" would seem to indicate some factor in disproportion of body segments or in inelasticity of muscles being stretched by lengthening bones.

---

*Wilson, Marjorie, and Scott, M. Gladys: A Study of Flexibility in Relation to Physical Education Activities, Unpublished study.

Tests of Extension in Upper Back

1. Spinal Extension

Description:

Lie in a straight prone position on the floor or a
table. Clasp hands together above the hips. Raise the head
and shoulders from the floor by arching the upper back; pull
with the arms keeping the lower corner of the ribs on the
floor. Score is the vertical distance from the suprasternal
notch (top of the sternum) to the floor.

Reliability:

Poley[30] obtained a coefficient of .87 on 63 college
students.

Suggestions:

Fixation of the ribs on the floor is best assured by an
assistant who places a finger on the lower points of the rib
cage where contact is to be maintained. The assistant can
ask for adjustment of position if the performer arches so
much in the lower back that the ribs leave the floor.

Measurement can be made most easily by placing one end
of a string on the suprasternal notch when she starts to
lift. The string is pulled taut and straight to the floor
(vertically) while she is at the top of her extension.
Measurement of the string from finger tip to finger tip is
then made on a ruler. The score is read to a scorer.

Measurement is most rapid if students lie down side by
side always with one or two ready ahead of the one being
measured. When each girl is measured she may go on to the
next test or to practice.

2. Wing Lifts

Description:

Lie in a straight prone position on the floor. Grasp
hands together behind the neck. Raise the head and arms
from the floor by arching the upper back, keeping the lower
corner of the ribs on the floor, and the feet on the floor.
Lower head and arms toward the floor but do not allow them

316

to touch; reverse direction and continue rhythmically
raising and lowering.

Suggestions:

An observer can check to see that form is maintained.
The foot contact is designed to limit the action to thoracic
spine and it is important that this be watched to insure
uniformity.

The score is the number that can be performed in one
minute. Stopping to rest with arms or chin on floor termi-
nates the trial. The scorer must decide when inadequate
range of motion has been reached and terminate the scoring.

This type of flexibility facilitates many movements.
A reasonable degree is also important in maintenance of good
posture. The Wing Lift is to some extent a measure of
strength of spinal extensors.

Range in trunk twisting is also desirable in many activities but measurement techniques are highly unreliable.
Measurement should be in a sitting position if movement is
to be limited to the spine, standing position if hip rotation is to be included. Variations in shoulder girdle action also add to the unreliability and variability from one
individual to another.

Tests of Shoulder Joint Range

Shoulder joint and shoulder girdle movement are invariably associated. Therefore, discussion relative to shoulder
will be assumed to involve both rather than be delimiting.
Use of a goniometer of some form, preferably the gravity
type, makes it possible to measure shoulder range in any direction. However, this is more suited to research purposes
than to routine class testing. The following tests have
been used and demonstrated feasible. Comparison from one
individual to another is probably not very meaningful, except to contrast the extremes. However, repeated testing of
individuals for study of changes in the individual himself
could be very helpful.

317

1. Opposite Arms Across Back

Description:

Subject is standing with nose, sternum, and abdomen against a projecting corner or a vertical pole. Raise right arm, bend elbow and reach down across the back. At the same time extend left arm behind back, bend left elbow up the back and try to cross the fingers of one hand over those of the other.

Reliability:

Nicoloff[28] found an r of .94 on the right arm up and .96 on left arm on 87 college men. Buxton[5] obtained an r of .94 with the right arm up and .95 with the left, on a sample of children grades one to nine.

Suggestions:

By using a ruler the score can be obtained to the nearest half inch. If the fingers overlap the score is a plus; if they fail to meet, the score is negative; zero, if the ends of the fingers just touch.

It is almost invariably found that the range is greater with one arm up than with the other.

For the following tests the prominence of the seventh cervical vertebra should be marked with a skin pencil or other small marker. A ruler is used to measure deviation from this point. These measures have been found to be unrelated to width of shoulders and also to length of arms, with the possible exception of the reach across the chest.

2. Reach Down the Back

Description:

Stand with nose, chest and abdomen against a projecting corner or a vertical pole. Left hand is on the hip. Raise the right arm over the shoulder and reach down along the spine as far as possible. Hold it until the reach is measured.

Do the same with the left arm.

Reliability:

Nicoloff[28] found a reliability of .81 on each arm on 87 college men.

Suggestions:

The shoulders must be kept level and the reach a steady one with no jerky movements. A ruler may be used to measure from the landmark established at the seventh cervical vertebra to the end of the finger tip furthest down the back.

Ability involved here is very similar to that in Opposite Arms Across the Back; do not use both tests.

3. Reach Across the Chest and Down

Description:

Reach with the right arm over the left shoulder and down the back as far as possible. Hold it until the reach is measured.

Do the same with the left arm over the right shoulder.

Reliability:

Nicoloff[28] obtained a reliability of .88 on the right arm and .83 on the left arm on 87 college men.

Suggestions:

A ruler may be used to measure.

TESTS OF BALANCE

The ability to balance easily in a static position or in motion is a function of the mechanism in the semicircular canals, the kinesthetic sensations in the joints and muscles, visual perception of motion, and the degree of coordination in response to these three sources of stimuli. Individuals doubtless vary in the quality of this total neuromuscular organization. Further variations appear because some have been trained to use kinesthetic awareness as a basis for balance and weight control; others have never had such training, nor have they developed such awareness through their own efforts. From the skill standpoint and from the safety standpoint, good balance seems important.

Experience has shown that excessive fatigue, particularly long-term chronic fatigue, reduces balance control. Balance tests appear to be useful in somewhat of a diagnostic or interpretive way. For example, poor balance may explain erratic performance on certain skills, tension in trying to perform static activities, poor performance on activities such as skating, skiing, diving, dancing, trampolining, or others where dynamic balance is important. Also, a marked drop in ability to balance may be associated with fatigue.

Various tests have been used to measure balance. Balance beam activities are primarily balance. Many of the activities in stunts and tumbling are predominantly balance. Stunts have held a prominent place in tests of motor educability. Few of the stunts or apparatus events are objective enough to be really satisfactory as a testing tool.

Research and experience with the following tests indicate considerable merit in them.

1. Sideward Leap

Prepare the floor by marking three 1-inch square spots in a straight line 18 inches apart. Place additional marks on the floor in a line at right angles to the previous line. These marks should be 3 inches apart and range in distance from A (see Figure 42) from 24 to 40 inches according to the age and height of the class. In most classes three or four marks properly placed will cover the range in height found within the group. Place a small cork or other light object on spot B. (The cork may be cut off the bottom of an old badminton bird.)

Measure the length of the student's leg from hip joint to the floor. Select the spot on the floor which corresponds in distance from A most closely to leg length. Explain and demonstrate the test.

Description:

Place left foot on mark X; leap sideward and land on A with right foot; immediately lean forward and push the cork off spot B; hold a balanced position for five seconds (it may be either forward or erect). It is a failure if you (1) fail to cover A on the leap, (2) move the foot after landing on A, (3) fail to lean forward and to move the cork

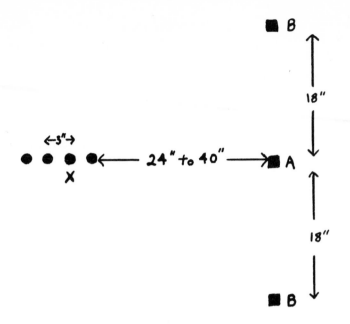

Figure 42. Floor markings for sideward leap balance test.

X = starting point.
A = point of landing on sideward leap.
B = point for finger contact, upper B for leap to right, lower B
for leap to left.

from B immediately, (4) rest the hand on the floor at any
time, (5) fail to hold the balance five seconds, (6) fall
down. You will have three trials to the right, three to the
left, and then repeat three to the right and three to the
left. The score is one point for each successful trial.

Reliability:

The coefficient was .88 when computed on alternate
trials of a series of ten and stepped up by the Spearman-
Brown formula. Subjects were 116 college students.*
Riley[32] found slightly lower coefficients for elementary
school children. These reliabilities were by grades,:
1, .77; 2, .68; 3, .77; 4, .80; 5, .73; 6, .70. These were
obtained by correlating the odd and even trials of a series
of 12, and stepped up with the Spearman-Brown formula.

---

*Scott, M. Gladys: Unpublished studies.

The persons giving the test should be trained in judging performance and timing.

If careful timing is done on the time that the balance is held after touching the floor, it is possible to score according to the number of seconds the position is held. This makes possible a score of 5 for each trial, or a possible total of 60 instead of 12. By giving credit for balance held three or four seconds, differentiation is secured from those who cannot hold the position at all. This makes for a better distribution of scores for the class.

2. Balance on Stick

A stick which is 1 inch square and 12 inches long should be laid on one side and securely fastened to the floor. Stripping with adhesive tape is adequate. Have a blindfold ready to put on the student after one practice trial.

Description:

Place your right foot lengthwise on the stick. As soon as you have your foot securely placed, lift your other foot and hold it off the floor as long as possible. You will be timed from the moment you lift your foot until you touch the floor again with any part of your body. There will be three trials with the right foot, three with the left, and then a repetition of three right and three left. The final score is the total time you are in balance on the twelve trials.

Reliability:

Coefficient obtained on 116 college women was .72.* Roloff[33] subsequently measured a comparable group and obtained an r of .86. Riley[32] computed for each of the six elementary grades: 1, .69; 2, .73; 3, .72; 4, .80; 5, .73; 6, .78.

Suggestions:

Any position is possible as long as the foot is completely on the stick and not braced on the floor and the

*Scott, M. Gladys, Cordelia Lundquist, Ruth Russell, Mary Lou Keener: Unpublished studies on balance.

free leg is kept off the floor. Hands, of course, must be kept off the floor.

It is advisable to have a helper nearby to prevent actual falls.

The same type of test may be given with only the ball of the foot touching the stick and the foot crosswise of the stick. If this form is used, it should be given in addition to the lengthwise, but not in substitution for it.

Balance Battery

The choice of balance tests should be made in terms of the type of balance needed. There is considerable evidence in unpublished studies that the sideward leap is primarily a measure of dynamic or moving balance, while the balance on the stick is primarily static balance:* If it is desirable to have full knowledge of the balancing ability of the individual, both tests should be given. They should be combined as follows:

1.3 sideward leap + 1.0 balance on stick

FITNESS BATTERIES FOR CHILDREN

The exact tests chosen for a fitness battery will depend upon the definition of fitness which is adopted. The basic minimum accepted by most physical educators is that of muscular or motor fitness. For that purpose the following battery is recommended and can be used for all the twelve years the child is in the public schools. However, difficulty may be experienced with testing of first graders. It may be desirable to do little or no testing at that age.

Buxton and Magnusson worked on similar batteries for muscular fitness. That developed by Magnusson is brief enough to be practical and samples strength of arm flexors, arm extensors, abdominals, and flexibility or elasticity of back and hamstring muscle as measured by Standing Reaching. She established T-scales for girls and for boys. She found need to differentiate between sexes, but found no need to differentiate for age. The use of a single scale for all elementary ages makes it possible to show increments or

---

*Scott, M. Gladys, Cordelia Lundquist, Ruth Russell, Mary Lou Keener: Unpublished studies on balance.

changes continuously for any part or all of the elementary
school years. The Magnusson T-scales appear in Tables
XXXIII to XL.

Table XXXIII.

T-Scale for Bent Arm Hang

Girls

Seconds of Hanging	T-Score	Seconds of Hanging	T-Score
86.0-87.5	80	19.0-19.5	58
78.0-85.5	78	18.0-18.5	57
74.0-77.5	77	17.0-17.5	56
72.0-73.5	76	16.0-16.5	55
66.0-71.5	75	15.0-15.5	54
64.0-65.5	74	14.0-14.5	53
62.0-63.5	73	13.0-13.5	52
52.0-61.5	71	12.0-12.5	51
50.0-51.5	70	11.0-11.5	50
44.0-49.5	69	10.0-10.5	48
40.0-43.5	68	9.0-9.5	47
38.0-39.5	67	8.0-8.5	46
36.0-37.5	66	7.0-7.5	44
34.0-35.5	65	6.0-6.5	42
30.0-33.5	64	5.0-5.5	41
28.0-29.5	63	4.0-4.5	39
26.0-27.5	62	3.0-3.5	37
24.0-25.5	61	2.0-2.5	35
22.0-23.5	60	1.0-1.5	33
20.0-21.5	59	0.0-0.5	28

Table XXXIV.

T-Scale for Bent Arm Hang

Boys

Seconds of Hanging	T-Score	Seconds of Hanging	T-Score
114.0-115.5*	83	21.0-22.5	55
94.0-95.5	80	19.0-20.5	54
92.0-93.5	78	18.0-18.5	53
90.0-91.5	77	16.0-17.5	52
86.0-89.5	76	15.0-15.5	51
84.0-85.5	75	14.0-14.5	50
80.0-83.5	74	13.0-13.5	49
76.0-79.5	73	12.0-12.5	48
74.0-75.5	72	11.0-11.5	46
72.0-73.5	71	10.0-10.5	45
70.0-71.5	70	9.0-9.5	44
68.0-69.5	69	8.0-8.5	43
64.0-67.5	68	7.0-7.5	41
58.0-63.5	67	6.0-6.5	39
54.0-57.5	66	5.0-5.5	37
50.0-53.5	65	4.0-4.5	35
46.0-49.5	64	3.0-3.5	34
42.0-45.5	63	2.0-2.5	33
37.0-41.5	62	1.0-1.5	31
35.0-36.5	61	0.0-0.5	27
32.0-34.5	60		
30.0-31.5	59		
28.0-29.5	58		
25.0-27.5	57		
23.0-24.5	56		

*One boy scored in this interval; no one scored between this and 95.5.

Table XXXV.

T-Scale for Push-ups

Girls

Number of Push-ups	T-Score	Number of Push-ups	T-Score
75	78	35	61
74	75	34	60
73	75	33	60
72	75	32	60
71	75	31	59
70	75	30	58
69	75	29	57
68	74	28	57
67	73	27	56
66	73	26	56
65	73	25	55
64	73	24	54
63	73	23	54
62	73	22	53
61	72	21	52
60	72	20	51
59	71	19	51
58	71	18	50
57	71	17	49
56	71	16	48
55	71	15	47
54	70	14	46
53	70	13	45
52	69	12	45
51	69	11	44
50	69	10	42
49	69	9	41
48	68	8	40
47	67	7	38
46	67	6	37

Table XXXV. (Cont.)

Number of Push-ups	T-Score	Number of Push-ups	T-Score
45	66	5	35
44	65	4	34
43	65	3	33
42	65	2	31
41	64	1	28
40	63	0	24
39	63		
38	62		
37	62		
36	61		

Table XXXVI.

T-Scale for Push-ups

Boys

Number of Push-ups	T-Score	Number of Push-ups	T-Score
75	72	35	55
74	69	34	54
73	69	33	54
72	69	32	54
71	69	31	53
70	68	30	52
69	68	29	52
68	68	28	51
67	67	27	51
66	67	26	50
65	66	25	50
64	66	24	49
63	66	23	48
62	66	22	48
61	65	21	47

Table XXXVI. (Cont.)

Number of Push-ups	T-Score	Number of Push-ups	T-Score
60	65	20	46
59	64	19	45
58	64	18	45
57	64	17	44
56	63	16	43
55	63	15	42
54	63	14	42
53	62	13	41
52	62	12	40
51	62	11	39
50	61	10	38
49	60	9	37
48	60	8	36
47	60	7	35
46	59	6	33
45	59	5	32
44	59	4	30
43	58	3	29
42	58	2	28
41	58	1	26
40	57	0	24
39	57		
38	56		
37	56		
36	55		

Table XXXVII.

T-Scale for Flexibility

Girls

Flexibility Reach in Inches	T-T-Score	Flexibility Reach in Inches	T-Score
8.0	80	0.5	44
7.5	77	0.0	41
7.0	74	-0.5	39
6.5	72	-1.0	38
6.0	70	-1.5	36

Table XXXVII. (Cont.)

Flexibility Reach in Inches	T-Score	Flexibility Reach in Inches	T-Score
5.5	68	-2.0	34
5.0	66	-2.5	32
4.5	64	-3.0	30
4.0	61	-3.5	28
3.5	59	-4.0	26
3.0	57	-4.5	24
2.5	54	-5.0	22
2.0	52	-5.5	21
1.5	49	-6.0	17
1.0	46		

Table XXXVIII

T-Scale for Flexibility

Boys

Flexibility Reach in Inches	T-Score	Flexibility Reach in Inches	T-Score
9.0	83	-1.0	43
8.5	81	-1.5	41
8.0	81	-2.0	40
7.5	81	-2.5	38
7.0	80	-3.0	36
6.5	76	-3.5	34
6.0	73	-4.0	32
5.5	72	-4.5	31
5.0	70	-5.0	30
4.5	68	-5.5	28
4.0	65	-6.0	26
3.5	63	-6.5	24
3.0	61	-7.0	24
2.5	59	-7.5	22
2.0	56	-8.0	20
1.5	54	-8.5	19
1.0	52	-9.0	17
0.5	49		
0.0	47		
-0.5	45		

Table XXXIX.

T-Scale for Sit-ups

Girls

Number of Sit-ups	T-Score	Number of Sit-ups	T-Score
49	80	24	50
48	78	23	48
47	77	22	47
46	76	21	46
45	76	20	44
44	75	19	43
43	75	18	42
42	73	17	41
41	72	16	39
40	71	15	38
39	69	14	36
38	68	13	35
37	67	12	34
36	65	11	33
35	64	10	31
34	63	9	29
33	62	8	29
32	61	7	29
31	59	6	28
30	58	5	28
29	56	4	27
28	55	3	26
27	54	2	26
26	52	1	25
25	51	0	21

Table XL.

T-Scale for Sit-ups

Boys

Number of Sit-ups	T-Score	Number of Sit-ups	T-Score
49	80	24	48
48	76	23	46
47	74	22	45
46	73	21	44
45	72	20	43
44	70	19	42
43	69	18	41
42	68	17	40
41	67	16	39
40	65	15	38
39	64	14	37
38	62	13	36
37	61	12	35
36	60	11	34
35	58	10	33
34	57	9	32
33	57	8	32
32	56	7	31
31	55	6	29
30	54	5	28
29	53	4	27
28	52	3	26
27	51	2	25
26	50	1	24
25	49	0	21

Buxton[5] was endeavoring to obtain data on boys and
girls in Iowa on the Kraus-Weber test, and to improve on
that battery in measurement of muscular fitness. Tables
XLI to XLVII show the maximum scores made and the quartile
points for the group described as eastern Iowa. These data
come from large and small schools, public and parochial
schools, schools with and without a physical education program. It will be observed that the back strength tests of
the Kraus-Weber battery are nondifferentiating, that is,
they give massed scores. The bent arm hang and the vertical
jump would appear to improve this battery for diagnosing the
level of muscular strength.

Table XLI.

Forward Bending Reach

(Buxton -- Eastern Iowa Data)

Girls | | | | | | Age | | | | |
|---|---|---|---|---|---|---|---|---|---|

	6	7	8	9	10	11	12	13	14	15
Max.	6.25	5.00	4.00	6.50	6.25	6.25	6.25	6.25	6.25	6.25
Q3	+1.00	+1.25	+1.75	+.75	+.75	+1.00	+.25	+2.25	+2.50	+1.00
Q2	0	.25	0	-.50	-.50	-.50	-1.75	0	-.25	0
Q1	-1.75	-1.50	-3.25	-3.00	-3.00	-2.75	-4.50	-2.75	-3.75	-3.00

Boys | | | | | | Age | | | | |
|---|---|---|---|---|---|---|---|---|---|

	6	7	8	9	10	11	12	13	14	15
Max.	+6.00	+3.00	6.25	5.00	3.50	3.50	1.00	5.00	6.25	6.25
Q3	+.75	+1.00	+.50	+.50	+.25	-1.25	-2.00	+.75	+.25	+2.00
Q2	-1.00	-1.00	-.75	0	-1.50	-3.00	-3.25	-1.75	-2.25	0
Q1	-3.00	-3.00	-2.75	-4.00	-3.25	-4.50	-5.00	-5.00	-4.25	-3.50

Buxton also demonstrated that lack of understanding and experience prevent many children from maximum reach in the first trial. Two or three practice trials before being measured in the Forward, Bending, Reach improved the performance of many. This may possibly be explained by better feeling of their own abilities, better motivation, or warm-up. In any case it seems best to give a group previous experience in this test, perhaps instruction in relaxing and letting the head drop while reaching. The child should be up on a platform or stool so the test administrator can be down at foot level to see the extent of the reach and so the child does not raise the head to see what the administrator is doing. The suggestion to the subject to look back between his legs will help to get his head down and facilitate the bend.

Table XLII.

Number of Seconds Lower Back Extension

Buxton -- Eastern Iowa Data

Girls	Age									
	6	7	8	9	10	11	12	13	14	15
Max.	180	180	180	180	180	180	180	180	180	180*
Q3	180	180	180	180	180	180	180	180	180	180*
Q2	180	180	180	180	180	140	165	180	140	180*
Q1	100	145	110	100	75	80	70	85	70	90

Boys	Age									
	6	7	8	9	10	11	12	13	14	15
Max.	180	180	180	180	180	180	180	180	180	180*
Q3	180	180	180	180	180	180	180	180	180	180*
Q2	180	180	180	180	180	180	180	125	180	120*
Q1	100	130	100	110	100	120	105	75	85	80

*Subjects stopped at 180 seconds.

Table XLIII.

Number of Seconds of Upper Back Extension
Buxton -- Eastern Iowa Data

Girls				Age					
	6	7	8	9	10	11	12	13	14	15
Max.	180	180	180	180	180	180	180	180	180	180*
Q3	180	175	180	180	180	180	180	180	180	180*
Q2	120	120	120	140	145	155	140	180	180	180*
Q1	65	75	85	90	95	85	80	135	125	120

Boys				Age					
	6	7	8	9	10	11	12	13	14	15
Max.	180	180	180	180	180	180	180	180	180	180*
Q3	120	165	155	180	180	180	180	180	180	180*
Q2	85	120	95	110	125	150	135	180	155	150
Q1	55	80	65	70	75	105	90	100	120	100

*Subjects stopped at 180 seconds.

Table XLIV.

Number of Sit-ups Knees Flexed
Buxton -- Eastern Iowa Data

Girls				Age					
	6	7	8	9	10	11	12	13	14	15
Max.	66	44	80	58	60	48	54	84	50	75
Q3	12	14	20	16	20	18	21	24	24	24
Q2	4	6	6	6	12	12	15	18	16	18
Q1	0	0	0	0	8	6	6	12	10	9

Boys				Age					
	6	7	8	9	10	11	12	13	14	15
Max.	34	50	60	96	123	70	100	130	108	108
Q3	12	16	20	24	21	15	30	30	45	48
Q2	7	8	12	15	18	10	15	20	33	33
Q1	0	0	4	6	9	5	10	10	18	24

Table XLV.

Number of Sit-ups, Knees Straight
Buxton -- Eastern Iowa Data

Girls					Age					
	6	7	8	9	10	11	12	13	14	15
Max.	175	175	126	195	98	105	70	119	56	98
Q3	70	70	49	63	56	35	35	35	28	35
Q2	49	35	28	28	21	21	14	14	14	21
Q1	28	14	14	14	14	7	7	7	7	7

Boys					Age					
	6	7	8	9	10	11	12	13	14	15
Max.	195	155	150	150	150	115	180	130	120	140
Q3	80	70	55	60	45	55	45	45	55	45
Q2	45	35	25	45	25	25	25	20	35	30
Q1	20	20	10	20	10	10	10	10	15	10

Table XLVI.

Height in Inches of Vertical Jump Without Arm Action
Buxton -- Eastern Iowa Data

Girls					Age					
	6	7	8	9	10	11	12	13	14	15
Max.	11	14	13	14	14	15	14	16	16	16
Q3	8	10	10	10	11	12	12	13	13	14
Q2	7	8	8	9	10	11	11	12	12	13
Q1	7	8	8	8	9	10	10	10	10	11

Boys					Age					
	6	7	8	9	10	11	12	13	14	15
Max.	11	12	14	14	14	16	16	19	21	21
Q3	9	10	10	10	12	12	13	15	16	17
Q2	8	8	9	10	11	11	11	13	15	16
Q1	7	7	8	8	10	10	10	11	13	14

Table XLVII.

Seconds Held on Bent Arm Hang
Buxton -- Eastern Iowa Data

Girls				Age					
	6	7	8	9	10	11	12	13	14	15
Max.	39	24	33	51	33	45	48	51	45	51
Q3	9	6	3	15	15	12	12	15	9	12
Q2	3	3	3	6	6	3	3	6	3	6
Q1	0	0	0	0	0	0	0	0	0	3

Boys				Age					
	6	7	8	9	10	11	12	13	14	15
Max.	35	35	135	65	60	100	75	125	100	100
Q3	10	10	25	25	25	30	35	55	60	60
Q2	5	10	10	15	20	15	20	30	40	40
Q1	0	5	0	5	5	5	10	10	25	30

Children may also be encouraged to use other activities as a measure of fitness. For example, many children have a bicycle and may be encouraged to ride for increasing distances and increasing rates. If this is to be done it would be helpful if special riding courses could be set up for greater safety but also for a familiar area on which the self-testing can be done with a minimum of supervision. Likewise, endurance swimming can be developed as a measure of fitness for either low or high intensity work depending upon the kind of swimming which is done.

An example of this type can be found in the George Williams College manual, "How To Keep Fit and Like It." This is a manual for adults so their youngest age group is 18 - 25. They suggest a test of endurance (38, p. 69) as bicycling 15 miles in 1 hour, or swimming a half mile without stopping, or run and walk one mile in 9 minutes. These standards could be adjusted to the age, skill and physical condition of the child.

FITNESS BATTERY FOR ADULTS

The battery desirable for adults who are very active would not vary much from that for college women. It might well consist of push-pull, chair stepping, sit-ups which gave a validity R of .69 for college students when compared with their all-out work capacity on the bicycle ergometer.

If the chair stepping is too strenuous, the adult might work with the Run in Place. This simply consists of running in place, feet close to the floor, as fast as possible for 10 seconds; follow by a 10-second rest; repeat as many times as reasonable for the individual, attempting to keep the rate on successive innings of running up to the initial rate.

The adult may also use other activities, such as swimming, for testing of endurance. Walking at a brisk pace, or bicycling, may be used in the same way. Note the George Williams College standards quoted above for the 18 - 25 year olds. The bicycling distance in their recommendation decreases to 13 miles for the age group 26 - 35, to 12 for the 36 - 45, and 10 for 46 or older. Likewise the walk goes up in time for the mile, from 9 minutes to 12 minutes.

Since increasing years may bring loss of both strength and flexibility it would seem desirable to choose from tests of both types to train for and try at regular intervals. Careful conditioning is recommended before starting in on these tests, however.

SELECTED REFERENCES

1. American Association for Health, Physical Education and Recreation, Exercise and Fitness: Journal of Health, Physical Education and Recreation, 29: September, 1958.

2. American Association for Health, Physical Education and Recreation: Conference on Fitness, Fitness for Youth. Journal of Health, Physical Education and Recreation, 27: p. 10, November 1956.

3. Bookwalter, Karl W.: Test Manual for Indiana University Motor Fitness Indices for High School and College Men. Research Quarterly, 14: p. 356, December 1943.

4. Brouha, Lucien: The Step Test, A Simple Method of Measuring Physical Fitness for Muscular Work in Young Men. Research Quarterly, 14: p. 31, March 1943.

5. Buxton, Doris: Extension of the Kraus-Weber Test. Research Quarterly, 28: p. 210, October 1957.

6. Cousins, George F.: A Factor Analysis of Selected Wartime Fitness Tests. Research Quarterly, 26: p. 277, October 1955.

7. Espenschade, Anna: Report of the Test Committee of the Western Society of Departments of Physical Education for Women in Colleges and Universities. Research Quarterly, 14: p. 397, December 1943.

8. Espenschade, Anna: Fitness of Fourth Grade Children. Research Quarterly, 29: p. 274, October 1958.

9. Espenschade, Anna, Robert R. Dable, and Robert Schoendube: Dynamic Balance in Adolescent Boys. Research Quarterly, 24: p. 270, October 1953.

10. Hall, D. M., and J. R. Wittenborn: Motor Fitness Tests for Farm Boys. Research Quarterly, 13: p. 432, December 1942.

11. Hall, D. M.: Selection and Standardization of Strength Tests for 4-H Club Members. Research Quarterly, 27: p. 285, October 1956.

12. Hall, D. M.: Standardization of Flexibility Tests for 4-H Club Members. Research Quarterly, 27: p. 296, October 1956.

13. Havlicek, Frank J.: Speed Sit-Ups. Research Quarterly, 15: p. 75, March 1944.

14. Hunsicker, Paul: AAHPER Physical Fitness Battery. Journal of Health, Physical Education and Recreation, 29: p. 24, September 1958.

15. Karpovich, Peter V., Raymond A. Weiss, and Edwin R. Elbel: Relation between Leg-Lift and Sit-up. Research Quarterly, 17: p. 21, March 1946.

16. Kistler, Joy: A Study of the Results of Eight Weeks of Participation in a University Physical Fitness Program for Men. Research Quarterly, 15: p. 23, March 1944.

17. Knapp, Clyde: Achievement Scales in Six Physical Education Activities for Secondary School Boys. Research Quarterly, 18: p. 187, October 1947.

18. Leighton, Jack R.: A Simple Objective and Reliable Measure of Flexibility. Research Quarterly, 13: p. 205, May 1942.

19. McCloy, C.H.: A Factor Analysis of Tests of Endurance. Research Quarterly, 27: p. 213, May 1956.

20. McCue, Betty Foster: Flexibility Measurements of College Women. Research Quarterly, 24: p. 316, October 1953.

21. Magnusson, Lucille I.: The Effect of a Specific Activity Program on Children with Low Muscular Fitness. Ph. D. dissertation, State University of Iowa, 1957.

22. Mathews, Donald K.: Comparison of Testers and Subjects in Administering Physical Fitness Index Tests. Research Quarterly, 24: p. 442, December 1953.

23. Mathews, Donald K., Virginia Shaw, and Melra Bohnen: Hip Flexibility of College Women as Related to Length of Body Segments. Research Quarterly, 28: p. 352, December 1957.

24. Miller, Ben W., Karl W. Bookwalter, and George E. Schlafer: Physical Fitness for Boys. New York, A. S. Barnes & Company, 1943, Chapter X.

25. Mohr, Dorothy: Measured Effects of Physical Education Activities on Certain Aspects of the Physical Fitness of College Women. Research Quarterly, 15: p. 340, December 1944.

26. Morris, Margaret: Measured Effects on Children in the Primary Grades from Use of Selected Playground Equipment. Ph. D. dissertation, State University of Iowa, 1955.

27. National Association of Physical Education for College Women: Proceedings of Victory Through Fitness Workshop, 1943, p. 43.

28. Nicoloff, Christine: Effects of Clothing on Range of Motion in the Arm and Shoulder Girdle. M. A. thesis, State University of Iowa, 1955.

29. Phillips, Marjorie, Carolyn Bookwalter, Charlotte Denman, Janet McAuley, Hilda Sherwin, Dean Summers, and Helen Yeakel: Analysis of Results from the Kraus-Weber Test of Minimum Muscular Fitness in Children. Research Quarterly, 26: p. 314, October 1955.

30. Poley, Margaret: Postural Characteristics of College Women as Related to Build. Ph. D. Dissertation, State University of Iowa, 1948.

31. Rarick, Lawrence, Katherine Gross, and Mona J. Mohns: Comparison of Two Methods of Measuring Strength of Selected Muscle Groups in Children. Research Quarterly, 26: p. 74, March 1955.

32. Riley, Marie: The Measurement of Balance in the Elementary Grades. M. A. Thesis, State University of Iowa, 1952.

33. Roloff, Louise: Kinesthesis in Relation to the Learning of Selected Motor Skills. Research Quarterly, 24: p. 210, May 1953.

34. Scott, M. Gladys, and Helen Mathews: Fatigue Effects Induced by an Efficiency Test for College Women. Research Quarterly, 20: p. 134, May 1949.

35. Scott, M. Gladys, Margaret Mordy, and Marjorie Wilson: Validation of a Mass-Type Physical Fitness Test with Tests of Work Capacity. Research Quarterly, 16: p. 128, May 1945.

36. Scott, M. Gladys, and Marjorie Wilson: Physical Efficiency Tests for College Women. Research Quarterly, 19: p. 62, May 1948.

37. Seashore, Harold G.: The Development of a Beam Walking Test and Its Use in Measuring Development of Balance in Children. Research Quarterly, 18: p. 246, December, 1947.

38. Steinhaus, Arthur H: How To Keep Fit and Like It, 2nd edition. Chicago, The Dartnell Corporation, 1957.

39. United States Office of Education: Physical Fitness for Students in Colleges and Universities. Washington, D. C., Superintendent of Documents, U. S. Government Printing Office, 1943.

40. United States Office of Education: Scales for Tests for High School Boys of Strength of the Abdomen and Back. Education for Victory, 3: p. 4, August 21, 1944.

41. United States War Department: WAC Field Manual, 35-20, Physical Training. Washington, D. C., Superintendent of Documents, U. S. Government Printing Office, 1943.

42. Wilbur, Ernest A.: A Comparative Study of Physical Fitness Indices as Measured by Two Programs of Physical Education; The Sports Method and the Apparatus Method. Research Quarterly, 14: p. 326, October 1943.

43. Wilson, Marjorie: Study of Arm and Shoulder Girdle Strength of College Women in Selected Tests. Research Quarterly, 15: p. 258, October 1944.

Chapter IX

MEASUREMENT OF MOTOR ABILITY

MOTOR ABILITY DEFINED

Every experienced teacher knows that some students learn much more rapidly and with less apparent effort than others. Some children are awkward and clumsy in even the simplest coordinations while others imitate promptly and successfully motor performance of a complex type. It is well-known also that after an interval of instruction and practice, some students have a greater variety of skills and greater proficiency than the rest of the class. This is both a problem and a challenge to the thoughtful teacher.

This type of individual difference has usually been referred to as a variation in motor ability. Writings by various authors have led to the use of several similar terms with different connotations. This has sometimes been confusing; therefore, discussion of these terms follows.

Motor educability is the inherent aptitude (motor and mental) for learning new skills quickly and effectively. Tests devised to measure this characteristic involve motor problems new to the subject; they are presented through the usual media of instruction, verbal description, and demonstration; they prohibit preliminary practice and allow very few trials; they are of a success or failure type. Most of the tests which are proposed for measuring educability are of a stunt type and usually include several stunts in order to secure satisfactory reliability. Some difficulty is encountered in devising motor problems which are new to the performer.

Motor capacity is very similar to educability but is really a little broader. Such batteries may contain an educability test plus general agility items such as obstacle or dodge runs, shuttle type races, or squat-thrust test.

Physical capacity implies a fitness or capability for performing motor activity. Since that capability is

342

dependent upon several things the tests vary from physiological functioning of circulatory and respiratory systems
to strength or reaction time. Such tests will not be considered here as they are partially taken care of by proper
medical examination and partially in fitness testing.

The term motor ability is sometimes used to mean
achievement in basic motor skills, or it may be interpreted
as a more general term combining the concepts of motor educability and achievement. How successfully achievement and
educability can be separated is still an unsolved question.
Motor ability measurement is usually concerned with some
form of running, throwing, and jumping; tests are repeated
from time to time, and sometimes brief practice on them is
permitted. The level of ability recorded may be due to
capacity for neuromuscular coordination, to practice, to
strength, or to other less evident factors.

It seems that the information needed by the teacher
concerning the student, at least from junior high school
age up, is aptitude for learning, ability in the fundamental skills, and ability in the various sports or activities.
The first two points are of a general nature and can be interpreted in relation to any activity. Further ability is
specific for each activity. In every case it is necessary
to abbreviate testing as much as possible and to relate
tests whenever possible.

REQUIREMENTS FOR A MOTOR ABILITY TEST

Since it is very difficult to separate the measurement
of aptitude and of achievement, and for the sake of abbrevi-
ation of the testing procedures, it would seem advisable to
follow the second interpretation of motor ability, that of
a general term combining the concepts of motor educability
and achievement. Motor educability and achievement are
considered thus as dual and interdependent aspects of general motor ability. There are certain requirements for this
type of test battery that are not true of all other types
of tests.

1. It is necessary to have unusual situations or motor
acts relatively new to the subjects.

2. Students should not practice on the test as such.

3. It is essential that students be given a clear idea of the problem presented by the test. However, the explanation should not include specific coaching or instruction on techniques to be used.

4. Principal activities in the physical education program should be analyzed for the skills that they have in common. For example, balance and weight control, eye-hand coordination, strength, agility, and speed are more or less essential to all activities. The tests should be set up to include as many of these as possible.

5. Tests combining more than one element in a significant way should be used when possible.

6. Part of the test should give opportunity to demonstrate skill developed by those who have worked hard previously.

7. The tests should not put undue emphasis on endurance, strength, or any other one factor.

8. The battery should have some variety in the skills represented so that the results are at least partially indicative of the strengths and weaknesses of the students.

A MOTOR ABILITY BATTERY

The motor ability test battery presented here has been successfully used both with college women and high school girls. Let us consider this battery in light of the above criteria which are peculiar to this type of test and supplement those criteria discussed in Chapter 2.

The minimum battery recommended is the obstacle race, basketball throw, and standing broad jump. The four-second dash and wall pass may be added or substituted for the obstacle race.

1. Obstacle Race

The space needed is 55 feet by 12 feet; equipment needed, three jump standards and a cross bar at least 6 feet long; lines on the floor (see Figure 43).

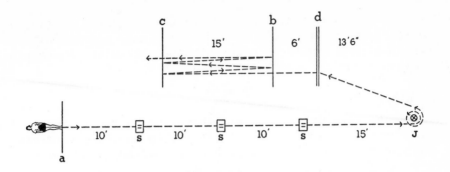

Figure 43. Floor markings for obstacle race.

a = starting line.
b = line for shuttle.
c = finish line.
d = cross-bar (18 inches high).
J = jump standard.
S = spot on floor (12 x 18 inches).
----- = path of runner.
       Distance from end of cross-bar to line of inner sides of
       spots, 4 feet 4 inches.

Description:

Start in a back-lying position on the floor with the
heels at line a. On the signal, Ready, Go! get up and start
running toward J. As you come to each square on the floor,
step on it with both feet. Run twice around J, turn back
to d, go under the cross bar, get up on the other side, run
to line c and continue running between line b and c until
you come to c for the third time. The score is the number
of seconds (to the nearest .1 second) that is required to
run the course.

Reliability:

A coefficient of .91 was obtained on University of Iowa
students taking the test on two successive days.[26]

Validity:

The coefficient between this form of the test and a
longer but similar test was .94 for 200 students. The
longer obstacle race with which it was compared was validated against several criteria. When correlated with the
McCloy total points score (running, throwing, and jumping),
the coefficient obtained for 155 subjects was .65. When
correlated with a composite criterion combining the total

345

points, additional sports items, and a subjective rating of ability, the coefficient was .58. It would appear that either of the two forms might be used, but ease of administration makes the short form preferable.

Suggestions:

Give instructions to all the class so repetition is not necessary when individuals are ready to run. Demonstrate what is meant by stepping with both feet on each square.

Each successive runner should lie down as soon as the girl ahead is up. This avoids delay in starting new runners.

If two timers and watches are available, the next girl starts as soon as the one ahead finishes circling the standard. Approximately twice the number can be scored on the same course with this arrangement.

Do not call the runner back if the toe or heel extends outside of the square. Some feet are too large to fit inside the square if the heel is lowered. Judge performance on whether the stride is adjusted to contact the square and whether there is a transfer of weight from one foot to the other while in the square.

2. Basketball Throw for Distance

Space needed is about 80 feet long and 20 feet wide, a throwing line marked about 8 feet from one end of the course and parallel lines every 5 feet beginning 15 feet in front of the throwing line.

Description:

Start anywhere you wish behind the throwing line, but do not step on or across the line when throwing. Throw in any way you wish, three consecutive times. The score is the distance from the throwing line to the spot where the ball touches the floor. Only the longest throw counts.

Reliability:

An r of .89 was obtained on successive trials by 200 women at the University of Iowa.

Validity:

Using the same two criteria as described for the obstacle race, the coefficients were .79 and .78 respectively, for the 155 subjects.

Suggestions:

Explain carefully but do not demonstrate. Answer questions about the test, except those on throwing technique. If asked whether the throw should be overhand or underhand, whether from a stationary position or with a step or run, simply reply that the throw may be of any type providing the feet are kept behind the line; the purpose is to throw the ball as far as possible. This may not be good teaching procedure, but it is essential for this form of testing if you wish to know how the student is likely to meet similar problems of throwing in a game.

It is true that some will profit more than others from seeing other students perform, but they are also the ones who learn quickly from class instruction. The ones who do not profit from errors or success of classmates doubtless will be slow to profit from class instruction.

If the gymnasium is too short and the test cannot be given outside, a diagonal course across the gymnasium may be used. This insures sufficient distance in practically any gymnasium but leaves little space in which to carry on other class activities during the test.

3. Standing Broad Jump

If the test is given outside, it is necessary to have a jumping pit with sunken take-off board within 30 inches of the edge of the pit. If given indoors, the test requires mats at least 7 1/2 feet long and a solid board at least 2 feet long (beat boards used with apparatus are excellent) placed against the wall to prevent slipping. If the mat is marked in 2-inch intervals, it eliminates the need to measure each jump with a tape.

Description:

Stand on the take-off board with feet parallel, toes may be curled over the edge of the board. Take-off from both feet simultaneously; jump as far forward as possible.

The score is the distance from the edge of the take-off board to the nearest heel (or to the nearest part of the body if the balance is lost). The best of three trials will be counted.

Reliability:

Successive trials yielded .79 for 252 women at the University of Iowa, .92 for 144 high school girls.

Validity:

Using the same two criteria as described for the obstacle race, coefficients were .79 and .78 respectively for the same 155 subjects.

Suggestions:

Preliminary swinging of arms and flexing of knees are permissible providing the feet are kept in place on the board until the actual take-off.

Be sure the performer understands what is to be done. The two-footed take-off is the point most frequently not comprehended from the description.

When the use of a take-off board is not feasible, jumping may be done from the mat if the mat is heavy enough that it will not slip.

The following two tests may be added if time permits the administration of the additional items. The obstacle race need not be given if these are added.

4. Wall Pass

A flat wall space is necessary at least 8 feet square. A line is drawn on the floor parallel to the wall and 9 feet from it. Several such spaces are desirable in order to test several persons at one time. A basketball is needed for each testing area. Timing for all areas may be done by a single timer.

Description:

Stand facing the wall, behind the line. Throw the ball against the wall, catch it when it comes back and repeat again as quickly as possible. Stay behind the line all the time. The throw may be of any type and the score is the number of hits on the wall in the time allowed. (15 seconds.)

Reliability:

The r was .62 on successive trials by 188 women at the University of Iowa, .75 on successive trials by 185 high school girls.

Validity:

Using the same two criteria as described for the obstacle race, the coefficients were .47 and .54 respectively for the same 155 subjects.

Suggestions:

The test may be administered very quickly if several testing areas are available and about four players start at each area. The first one is tested while the second counts the hits and watches the foul line. Then the first reports the score while the second is tested and the third counts. This is repeated until all are finished. A player who steps across the line slightly should be called back by the player scoring the trials. If the feet are in the proper position for the next throw, the error is not considered. If fouls are continuous, the entire trial must be repeated.

Allow each person time for three or four practice throws before taking the test.

If a ball drops between the wall and the line, it may be necessary for the player to cross the line to recover the ball. However, the next throw must be made from behind the line.

One trial is usually sufficient on this test. Second trials should be given, however, in case of interference of any type or if the ball gets entirely out of control. The test should not be repeated simply because of fumbling. If time and facilities permit administration of two or three trials for all, the higher score should be used.

5. Dash (4 seconds)

It is desirable to have a straight course at least 85 to 90 feet long and 4 feet wide. It may be laid out diagonally across the gymnasium if space is too short otherwise. The starting line should be at least 3 feet in front of the wall. The course is marked in one-yard zones beginning at 10 yards from the starting line to about 27 yards from the starting line. The additional distance allows the runner space in which to stop.

Description:

Start in any position you wish with the toes behind the starting line. On the signal, Ready, Go!, start running as fast as possible and keep going as fast as possible until the whistle blows. You may run as far as you wish after the whistle sounds (at the end of four seconds). The score is the distance you have run between the starting signal and the whistle.

Reliability:

The coefficient was .62 on successive trials by 88 women at the University of Iowa.

Validity:

Using the same two criteria as described for the obstacle race, the coefficients were .71 and .62 respectively, for the same 155 subjects.

Suggestions:

One trial is sufficient unless there is outside interference. The judge on this test should be carefully trained. It is best to use two persons, a timer and a judge. The timer starts the runner and blows the whistle. The judge determines the zone into which the foremost part of the body extends when the whistle blows. One person may assume both responsibilities after training. In this case, the watch is extended forward so the watch and the runner are in a straight line of vision at the end of the four seconds.

The judge should attempt to be parallel with the runner at the final signal. With very little experience the judge will learn by looking at the runner during the start and the first few strides whether the finish will be short, around 13 to 15 yards, or long, around 23 to 25 yards, or somewhere between.

If space permits more than one lane, additional lanes
should be used, providing sufficient judges can be obtained.

SCORING THE BATTERY

Two batteries, one of three tests and the other of four
tests, are recommended for use. The longer of the batteries, consisting of dash, basketball throw, broad jump, and
passes, yielded a multiple correlation coefficient of .91.
The second of the batteries consists of obstacle race, broad
jump, and basketball throw. The multiple coefficient in
this case was .87. The latter would be preferred in most
instances. It is easier to administer, and has relatively
little difference in validity. Years of experience with it
for college women have shown it to be very effective in
screening off the poorer students who need special help. It
also predicts very closely the rate at which students will
be able to achieve in physical education classes and qualify
for satisfactory achievement levels.

T-scales for each of the tests and for either battery
are shown in Tables XLVIII to L. The scores for high school
girls may be read from Table XLVIII, those for college
women from Table XLIX. Table L is for professional students (majors) in physical education.

Table XLVIII.

T-Scales for Motor Ability Tests for High School Girls

T-SCORE	WALL PASS (410)*	BASKETBALL THROW (FT.) (310)*	BROAD JUMP (IN.) (287)*	4 SEC. DASH (YD.) (398)*	OBSTACLE RACE (SEC.) (374)*	JUNIOR HIGH G.M.A.‡ (161)*	JUNIOR HIGH G.M.A.§ (161)*	SENIOR HIGH G.M.A.‡ (169)*	SENIOR HIGH G.M.A.§ (169)*	T-SCORE
80	16	71								80
79			96							79
78								150	226	78
77	15	68	94	27		148	205			77
76		66			18.5-18.9		201			76
75		65					196			75
74		64	92			146	194	148		74
73	14	63				140				73
72		61				134	192		222	72
71		59	90	26			190	146	218	71
70		55	88		19.0-19.4	132		142	214	70
69	13	54					188	140	208	69
68		52	86	25		130		138	204	68
67		51			19.5-19.9		186	136	198	67
66		50				128	180	134	194	66
65		49					178	132	192	65

Table XLVIII. (Cont.)

T-SCORE	WALL PASS (410)*	BASKETBALL THROW (FT.) (310)*	BROAD JUMP (IN.) (287)*	4 SEC. DASH (YD.) (398)*	OBSTACLE RACE (SEC.) (374)*	JUNIOR HIGH G.M.A.‡ (161)*	JUNIOR HIGH G.M.A.§ (161)*	SENIOR HIGH G.M.A.‡ (169)*	SENIOR HIGH G.M.A.§ (169)*	T-SCORE
64		48	84	24	20.0-20.4	126	176	130	190	64
63	12	47				124	174	128	188	63
62		46	82		20.5-20.9	122	172		182	62
61			80				168	126	178	61
60		45		23		120	166		172	60
59		44	78		21.0-21.4		162	124	170	59
58	11	43				118	160	122	168	58
57		42	76		21.5-21.9		158		166	57
56		41				116	156	120	164	56
55		40	74	22		114	154	118	162	55
54					22.0-22.4		152		160	54
53		39					150	116	158	53
52	10		72			112	148		154	52
51		37			22.5-22.9		146	114	150	51
50		36		21		110	144		148	50
49		35	70				142	112	144	49
48			68		23.0-23.4	108	138	110	142	48
47		34	66				136		138	47
46	9	33			23.5-23.9	106	134	108	136	46
45		32	64	20		104	132	106	134	45
44		31			24.0-24.4		130		132	44
43			62			102	126	104	128	43
42		30			24.5-24.9		124		126	42
41	8	29	60	19		100	122	102	124	41
40		28					120		120	40
39			58		25.0-25.4	98	118		118	39
38		27	56				114	100	116	38
37	7		54		25.5-25.9	96	112		114	37
36		26			26.0-26.4	94	110	98	110	36
35			52	18	26.5-26.9	92	108		108	35
34		25	50		27.0-27.4		106		106	34
33									102	33
32		24	47		27.5-27.9	90	104	96		32
31	6	23				88	102		100	31
30			44		28.0-28.4		100		96	30
29		22		17	28.5-28.9	86	96		92	29
28					29.0-29.4	84	94	94	90	28
27		21			29.5-29.9					27
26			40		30.0-30.4	82			88	26
25	5	20					92	92	84	25
24				16	30.5-31.4					24
23		19	36		31.5-32.4	80			78	23
22				15	32.5-34.9					22
21		16								21
20	4			14	35.0-36.0					20

*Indicates the number of subjects on which the scale is based.
†Junior high, seventh, eighth, and ninth grades.
Senior high, tenth, eleventh, and twelfth grades.
Subjects were from junior and senior high schools in Beaver Dam, Wis., University High School, Iowa City, Iowa; Muscatine, Iowa; and Vinton, Iowa.
‡.7 basketball throw + 2.0 dash + 1.0 passes + .5 broad jump.
§2.0 basketball throw + 1.4 broad jump - 1.0 obstacle race.

Table XLIX.

T-Scales for Motor Ability Tests for College Women

T-SCORE	BASKETBALL THROW	PASSES	BROAD JUMP	OBSTACLE RACE	G.M.A.*	T-SCORE
85	75	18	86	17.5-17.9	234-235	85
84						84
83	71	17		18.0-18.4	232-233	83
82					230-231	82
81		16	85		226-229	81
80	70	15			222-225	80
79	69			18.5-18.9	220-221	79
78	68	14	84			78
77	67		83		218-219	77
76	66				214-217	76
75	65		82	19.0-19.4	212-213	75
74	64		81		210-211	74
73	62		80		208-209	73
72	61	13	79	19.5-19.9	204-207	72
71	59				200-203	71
70	58		78	20.0-20.4	194-199	70
69	57		77		192-193	69
68	56		76		188-191	68
67	55		75	20.5-20.9	186-187	67
66	54	12	74		182-185	66 ·
65	52				178-181	65
64	51		73	21.0-21.4	176-177	64
63	50		72		172-175	63
62	48		71	21.5-21.9	168-171	62
61	47				164-167	61
60	46		70		162-163	60
59	45	11	69	22.0-22.4	158-161	59
58	44		68		156-157	58
57	43		67	22.5-22.9	152-155	57
56	42				150-151	56
55	41		66	23.0-23.4	146-149	55
54	40		65		144-145	54
53	39		64	23.5-23.9	142-143	53
52	38	10	63		138-141	52
51	37			24.0-24.4	136-137	51
50	36		62		132-135	50
49	35		61	24.5-24.9	130-131	49
48			60		128-129	48
47	34		59	25.0-25.5	126-127	47
46	33		58		122-125	46

Table XLIX. (Cont.)

T-SCORE	BASKETBALL THROW	PASSES	BROAD JUMP	OBSTACLE RACE	G.M.A.*	T-SCORE
45	32	9	57	25.5-25.9	120-121	45
44	31				118-119	44
43			56	26.0-26.5	116-117	43
42	30		55		114-115	42
41			54	26.5-26.9	110-113	41
40	29		53	27.0-27.4	108-109	40
39	28	8	52		106-107	39
38				27.5-27.9	104-105	38
37	27		51	28.0-28.4	102-103	37
36	26		50		100-101	36
35			49	28.5-28.9	98-99	35
34	25		48	29.0-29.4	94-97	34
33			47	29.5-29.9	90-93	33
32		7	46	30.0-30.4	88-89	32
31			45	30.5-30.9	86-87	31
30	24		44	31.0-31.4	84-85	30
29			43	31.5-31.9	80-83	29
28	23		42	32.0-32.4		28
27	21		41	32.5-32.9	78-79	27
26		6	40	33.0-33.4	76-77	26
25	20		39	33.5-33.9	74-75	25
24			38	34.0-34.4	72-73	24
23		5	37	34.5-34.9	68-71	23
22			36		66-67	22
21	19			35.0-35.4	64-65	21
20					60-63	20
19			35	35.5-35.9		19
18					38-59	18
17	18	4				17
16						16
15						15
14				43.5-43.9		14
13			30	45.5-45.9	34-37	13

*2.0 basketball throw + 1.4 broad jump - 1.0 obstacle race.
These scales were all constructed on data obtained from 2,500 students at the University of Iowa.

354

Table L.

T-Scales for Motor Ability Batteries
for Physical Education Major Students

T-SCORE	G.M.A.(1)*	G.M.A.(2)†	T-SCORE	T-SCORE	G.M.A.(1)*	G.M.A.(2)†	T-SCORE
80		228	80	50	124	160	50
79	166		79	49	122	156	49
78		226	78	48		154	48
77			77	47	120	152	47
76			76	46	118	150	46
75	156		75	45	116	146	45
74		224	74	44		142	44
73	154	222	73	43	114	140	43
72	152	220	72	42	112	138	42
71	152	218	71	41		136	41
70	150	216	70	40	110	134	40
69	148	214	69	39	108	132	39
68			68	38		128	38
67		212	67	37	106	126	37
66	146	210	66	36		122	36
65		206	65	35	104	120	35
64	144	202	64	34		116	34
63	142	200	63	33		114	33
62		198	62	32	102	112	32
61	140	194	61	31	100		31
60	138	192	60	30		110	30
59	136	188	59	29	98		29
58	134	186	58	28		108	28
57		184	57	27	96	104	27
56	132	180	56	26	92		26
55	130	176	55	25	90		25
54		172	54	24		96	24
53	128	170	53	23	86		23
52	126	166	52	22			22
51		162	51	21	84	92	21

*.7 basketball throw + 2.0 dash + 1.0 passes + .5 broad jump. This scale was constructed on data obtained from 263 University of Iowa students.

2.0 basketball throw + 1.4 broad jump - 1.0 obstacle race. This scale was constructed on data obtained from 295 University of Iowa students.

The composite on these batteries may be computed in either of two ways. The simplest and quickest is to take the average of the T-scores earned on the three or four tests given. For example, if a student's T-scores are obstacle, 58; basketball throw, 62; broad jump, 60; then the composite score representing the level of motor ability is the average of the three T-scores, or 60.

The second method uses the simplified regression equation derived from the multiple correlation. For the three tests the equation is:

2.0 basketball throw + 1.4 broad jump - obstacle race.

If the four tests are used without the obstacle race the equation reads:

.7 basketball throw + 2.0 dash + 1.0 passes
+ .5 broad jump.

The actual score may be multiplied by the proper weighting and these products added. It will be faster, however, to use Table LI, page 357. For example,

basketball throw . . . . 35 feet

dash . . . . 20 yards

passes 10

broad jump . . . . 61 inches

Look at Table LI and find the value of .7 of the basketball throw (24.5 for 35 feet) rather than to multiply it out for each case. Doubling the dash score or taking half of the broad jump can be done mentally; with little time and effort the total score can be added. Table LI also provides a multiplication table of 1.4 broad jump.

It would seem to make very little difference which method is used, that is, the average of the T-scores or the weighting of raw scores, since they yield composites which correlate very highly.

EVALUATING THE BATTERY

Let us now analyze these tests and the method of administration which has been outlined. As measures of innate capacity and educability, the following points seem significant:

1. The obstacle race presents skills relatively new as a speed event, yet within the range of experience, so that there is no question as to the problem presented.

2. The obstacle race presents a sequence of movements which is a test of the person's ability to remember directions and to adjust for the next movement while still performing a preceding one.

Table LI.

Multiplication Tables for Motor Ability Test Batteries

3-Item Battery	4-Item Battery
2.0 Basketball throw (feet)	.7 Basketball throw (feet)
+ 1.4 Broad jump (inches)	+ 2.0 Dash (yards)
- 1.0 Obstacle race (seconds)	+ 1.0 Ball pass (times)
	+ .5 Broad jump (inches)

BROAD JUMP ×1.4				BASKETBALL THROW ×.7			
RAW SCORE	×1.4	RAW SCORE	×1.4	RAW SCORE	×.7	RAW SCORE	×.7
32	44.8	57	79.8	20	14.0	45	31.5
33	46.2	58	81.2	21	14.7	46	32.2
34	47.6	59	82.6	22	15.4	47	32.9
				23	16.1	48	33.6
35	49.0	60	84.0	24	16.8	49	34.3
36	50.4	61	85.4				
37	51.8	62	86.8	25	17.5	50	35.0
38	53.2	63	88.2	26	18.2	51	35.7
39	54.6	64	89.6	27	18.9	52	36.4
				28	19.6	53	37.1
40	56.0	65	91.0	29	20.3	54	37.8
41	57.4	66	92.4				
42	58.8	67	93.8	30	21.0	55	38.5
43	60.2	68	95.2	31	21.7	56	39.2
44	61.6	69	96.6	32	22.4	57	39.9
				33	23.1	58	40.6
45	63.0	70	98.0	34	23.8	59	41.3
46	64.4	71	99.4				
47	65.8	72	100.8	35	24.5	60	42.0
48	67.2	73	102.2	36	25.2	61	42.7
49	68.6	74	103.6	37	25.9	62	43.4
				38	26.6	63	44.1
50	70.0	75	105.0	39	27.3	64	44.8
51	71.4	76	106.4				
52	72.8	77	107.8	40	28.0	65	45.5
53	74.2	78	109.2	41	28.7	66	46.2
54	75.6	79	110.6	42	29.4	67	46.9
				43	30.1	68	47.6
55	77.0	80	112.0	44	30.8	69	48.3
56	78.4	81	113.4				

3. The obstacle race puts a premium on weight control, balance, total body coordination, and agility.

4. By avoiding specific instructions on how to throw the balls or make the jump, the tests measure more adequately than would otherwise be possible the performer's knowledge and ability or powers of observation acquired through previous training or experience.

As measures of achievement and general ability to perform, the following points should be noted:

1. The broad jump is related to leg strength, coordination of arms and legs, and an understanding of the use of effort and balance with respect to one's own body movement.

2. The basketball throw involves strength, coordination of body and arms, ball handling, and an understanding of the use of effort with respect to some other object.

3. The wall pass is primarily ball handling, including eye-hand coordination, speed of reaction, and an understanding of the reaction of balls at different angles and speeds.

4. The dash is considerably more than a pure speed event. Because of its brevity, the start is a very important element. The person who makes a good start and gets up speed quickly covers more distance. The person who gets a slow start does not have time to make up for that slowness. This is a matter of weight control and force as well as reaction time and is very similar to the situations presented in most sports where there are many quick starts.

5. The parallel lines used for the basketball throw for distance give an advantage to those who can control the ball sufficiently to deliver it at right angles to the throwing line.

Since we have defined general motor ability as inclusive of both aptitude and achievement, the two being impractical and undesirable to separate, this battery would seem to be especially suited to measurement of that general ability. Tests of this type when used for girls do not need to take into consideration a specific weighting for age or size. However, such a weighting is essential in considering scores for boys. The age, height, weight factors need to be computed by some procedure. That of McCloy is illustrative.

There are a few disadvantages in the tests but these can be overcome almost completely by proper administration.

1. The tests must all be administered individually except the wall pass. They may all be given simultaneously if there is sufficient help, or one each on successive days and the rest of the space used for regular class activity. Most of the mass tests which are sometimes used require one or two class periods to give and are, therefore, no more economical. If there is sufficient assistance, the tests may be given as a part of the physical examination though the students usually do not get sufficient warm-up under these circumstances.

2. Students may learn about the tests and practice on them. This can be prevented by giving them to successive classes without leaving intervening class periods with opportunities for practice.

SUBSTITUTIONS IN THE BATTERY

Other measures may be substituted for the above tests if facilities prohibit, or if for any other reason these seem inadvisable. Suggestions for substitutions are as follows:

1. Shuttle Race

Form 1. Parallel lines 15 feet apart. Score is the number of times the performer can cross between the lines in 15 seconds.

Form 2. Parallel lines 25 feet apart marked in 5-foot zones. (See Figure 44.) Work in partners.

Description:

Start at line X, run to line Y, change direction and return to X. Repeat this as many times as possible in thirty seconds. Record the number of times your partner runs each length of the course and note the letter of the area the runner reaches at the end of the thirty seconds. (Example, 10 B.)

Suggestions:

It is important that the runner wait until the whistle blows, and that lines X and Y be touched each

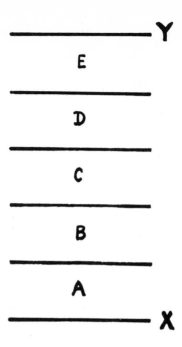

Figure 44. Floor markings for shuttle race.

A, B, C, D, E = zones in the shuttle area
X, Y = lines on which to reverse direction
X = starting line

time, and that the scorer record the area that the runner is in at the second whistle.

The shuttle race may be substituted for the obstacle race or the dash.

The reliability of the first form was .46 on successive trials of 33 college women, and .83 on 100 girls in high school. It would appear to be useful, though in terms of both reliability and validity it is somewhat lower than either the obstacle race or the dash.

2. Jump and Reach

Description:

Stand facing the wall, toes touching with both hands raised overhead. Reach evenly with both hands and mark the height of the reach. Then turn sideward to the wall, jump and reach with one hand touching as far up the wall as possible. The score is the difference between the reach while standing and while jumping.

Suggestions:

If the wall is such that water will show on it and not leave the wall disfigured, the easiest method is simply to dip the fingers in water when starting the test and then measure promptly. If this is not feasible, short pieces of chalk must be used.

With college women the original reach may be measured more accurately if they stand with backs to the wall. The assistant marks the reach.

This test may be substituted for the broad jump if mats or pits are not available for jumping.

3. Sandbag Throw

Use sandbags 4 inches square weighing one pound each, and with string tied tightly around the middle of each bag to prevent it from "sailing" through the air when thrown. The administration of the test is identical with the basketball throw for distance in all other respects.

This test may be substituted for the basketball throw for distance where balls are lacking or the space is short. It was found to be only a little below the basketball throw in both reliability and validity.

USING THE MOTOR ABILITY SCORES

The motor ability score is used to assign students to classes if ability sectioning is possible, to determine the level of achievement expected in future work and the amount of individual help which will be needed to achieve satisfactory results. For that reason the tests should be given at the beginning of certain phases of the student's physical education experience. This does not mean that they need to be given every year. It is probably best to give this battery at the beginning of the junior high school years, at the beginning of the senior high school course, and when entering college. The results will be used then for a two- or three-year period. Improvement doubtless occurs during this length interval but the relative standing of students will not change appreciably during that interval, unless some students practice specifically on these test items while others do not.

One specific example of the value of general ability tests lies in the economy of time for later testing. Placement by the general test can be used in connection with every activity, and therefore permits a very much shortened battery at the beginning of each activity season for classification in that activity. For example, if motor ability scores are known on a class starting basketball, it is usually sufficient to give a single test such as the 30-second basket shooting. With those two types of information individual status can be determined and teams or squads equated. Lacking the motor ability score, it would be necessary to give an additional test or two involving weight control and ball handling other than that included in the basket shooting.

The general battery gives a fairly good estimate of the level of ability to be expected of a person who is just starting to learn a new activity. If later achievement in that activity shows markedly superior status from that predicted, it can almost always be attributed to extra practice, exceptional motivation, or unusual interest and effort. Likewise, distinctly lower status than that predicted can usually be found to be due to lack of effort and practice.

Another use of the motor ability measures is in selecting the groups at both ends of the scale for special consideration. For example, the lowest 15 to 25 per cent in ability too frequently are simply spotted as dubs and left to shift for themselves as best they can in the class. The result is discouragement, dislike for the activity, and eventually lack of cooperation, not to mention the fact that they usually remain poor in skills. If those individuals can be given special help, preferably in classes by themselves for a time, most of them profit considerably. They may improve on specific skills by special help, they may learn to analyze skills more carefully, to compensate for some of their shortcomings in capacity or aptitude, and above all they have the opportunity to practice skills in a sympathetic group where they do not feel unnecessarily self-conscious.

The upper 15 to 25 per cent in ability can profit by special consideration, also. When all levels of ability are taught in the same class, by the same procedure, at the same rate, the most capable ones are not challenged by the material presented and often are discouraged because they work and play constantly with others possessing poor skills. Those with high general ability may be selected for leaders' classes, given additional skills or projects on which to work, placed in advanced classes, or placed in special classes with others of like ability. The latter procedure is very frequently followed in college courses, and these groups make phenomenal progress in most activities.

In short, the students of low ability can be taught to work hard, to achieve modest results and to work objectively on shortcomings, and to understand that if certain skills are to be passed or standards met, they must spend more time and effort than others. For example, beginning swimmers who are afraid of the water would be perfectly willing to concede that more effort is necessary for them to learn to swim than for those who are not afraid. Likewise, the persons who have little apparent aptitude for complex motor skills are just as aware of their difficulty as the frightened swimmer. If they are motivated to achieve some degree of skill, they will recognize the need for practice and be willing to exert the necessary effort.

In a similar manner, the student of high ability can be inspired by the variety of skills which may be acquired or the high level of skill which may be achieved. In both cases the students are aided in setting up their own goals; their effort is directed always toward improvement, not just in surpassing someone else.

Motor ability tests should be given more extensively about the fourth or fifth year of the elementary school and used diagnostically for identifying student weaknesses. If careful, analytical follow-up instruction is given during the remaining elementary school years, it is possible to prevent most of the cases of individuals with poor coordination who are self-conscious and unhappy in the high school and college activity class. Basic motor skills and attitudes toward activity are established primarily during the elementary school years. Instruction during those years should be of a most careful and thorough type.

GENERAL MOTOR ABILITY
FOR THE ELEMENTARY SCHOOL CHILD

The motor educability of the elementary child can be tested with the stunt-type of test such as the Brace test or the Iowa revision of the Brace test. The latter is half as long as the original Brace test. However, if the children have had a stunts and tumbling program and learned these or similar tests, the Brace tests are not useable. Therefore, for most groups, some other type of measure must be found.

Again it seems more practical to accept the concept of achievement as interrelated with innate capacity at least in the process of measurement. Any battery used should include at least one sample task from the running, throwing, jumping skills. There are several sources for such tests. This representation of running, throwing, jumping skills is found in tests for all age levels. Examples at the college age are in Highmore[10] and Barrow[1] batteries, examples at the elementary age follow.

Wilson[31] studied the jumping skills only, but included standing broad jump, running broad jump and vertical jump for an age range of 4 through 12 years. Her study shows increments in each of the three types of jumps with each successive age. There is superiority of boys over girls, becoming more marked with increasing age. The difference was least in the vertical jump. The angle of take-off on the broad jump appeared to be the most important single element in the success of a jump, suggesting the importance of coordination.

Latchaw[14] found similar increments with selected running, throwing and jumping events. These increments seemed to parallel grade levels much more closely than the age, height and weight factors. It would appear from studies such as Wilson's and Latchaw's and others that these fundamental activities might give an indication of "motor maturation" as much as achievement. The Latchaw battery follows:

1. Basketball Wall Pass (Latchaw)

This test measures the ability of the subject to throw a basketball successively into a given target area from a specified distance.

Equipment:

1. Regulation basketball, stop watch.

2. Markings

On a flat wall space, mark a target area eight feet wide and four feet high, at a distance of three feet from the floor. A restraining line eight feet long is drawn on the floor four feet from the wall and parallel to the wall target.

Test:

The subject stands at any place he chooses back of the restraining line. On the signal "Go" he throws the ball against the wall into the target area in any manner that he chooses, and continues successive throws until the signal "Stop" is given. If the ball gets out of control at any time, he must recover it himself without assistance. A successful throw is one that goes into the target area and is made from behind the restraining line. Line balls are not fair hits. The ball may be caught on a bounce if the subject so chooses. However, the ball need not be caught to constitute a successful throw.

A ten second practice trial is given while the test administrator scores verbally, encouraging the subject to retrieve lost balls rapidly, and to throw the ball as fast as he can successfully manipulate it. This score is not recorded.

Scoring:

One point is given for each successful throw. Two fifteen-second trials are given, after the practice trial. The total number of points is recorded for each trial. The better of the two trials is the final score for the test.

Suggestions:

One administrator can time and score approximately 50 subjects in one hour. If several testing areas and additional scorers are available, the tests may be given very quickly. It is possible that the children could score each other if they were given an opportunity to practice with the teacher beforehand.

It is important that the administrator demonstrate the test while he is explaining it to the subjects.

2. Volleyball Wall Volley

This test measures the ability of the subject to strike a volleyball with the hands repeatedly against the wall within a given target area and from a specified distance on the floor.

Equipment:

1. Regulation volleyball, stop watch.

2. Markings

On a flat wall space, mark a target area eight feet wide and at least four feet high, at a distance of three feet from the floor. A restraining line eight feet long is drawn on the floor four feet from the wall and parallel to the wall target.

Test:

The subject stands at any position he chooses in back of the restraining line. On the signal "Go" he tosses or throws the ball against the wall into the target area, and as it rebounds he continues to bat it repeatedly against the wall. The ball may be tossed against the wall when it is necessary to start it again. If the ball gets out of control, the subject retrieves it himself, brings it back to the restraining line and starts it again. A successful hit is one that, upon rebounding from the wall, is clearly batted into the target area from behind the restraining line on the floor. If the ball is thrown or pushed against the wall, it does not constitute a successful hit. Line balls are not fair hits.

The subject is given a ten-second practice trial. The test administrator scores verbally during this trial, calling the attention of the subject to balls that are not legal hits if he pushes the ball at any time. This score is not recorded.

Scoring:

One point is given for each successful hit. Four fifteen-second trials are given, after the practice trial. The total number of points is recorded for each trial. The best of the four trials is the final score for the test.

366

Suggestions:

One administrator can time and score approximately
30 subjects in one hour, if the subjects have had previous
experiences in volleyball. Inexperienced subjects need
more instruction in batting and are frequently unsuccessful
during the practice trial. When this is the case, the administrator should demonstrate proper hitting before each
of the test trials, or until the subject is able to execute
a correct hit. If the subject is unable to execute a correct hit throughout his four trials, his score for each
trial will be zero, and his score for the test will be zero.
This test is too difficult for children to score, unless
they have had considerable experience in judging a clearly
batted ball.

It is important that the administrator first demonstrate this test for the subjects being tested, being careful to distinguish clearly between a batted ball, a thrown
ball, and a pushed ball.

3. Vertical Jump

This test measures the ability of the subject to jump
vertically and reach as high as possible from a stationary
position on the floor.

Equipment:

One-inch cloth strips suspended from a horizontal bar,
and spaced at one-inch intervals from each other. The
longest strip is five feet from the floor and the shortest
strip is eight feet, eleven inches from the floor. Each
strip is weighted with a penny at the end nearest the floor
to insure even hanging.

Test:

The subject stands with both heels on the floor under
the suspended strips, and reaching with one hand, touches
the highest strip that he can. This is recorded under
"reaching height." The subject jumps from a stationary position under the bar, and reaches the highest strip that he
can. He may start from a crouch if he wishes, but he may
not take any steps or preliminary bounces. Any number of
trials is allowed, but it is advisable to estimate the approximate place along the scale where the subject's best

jump will be, in order to avoid fatigue from too many
trials.

Scoring:

The score is the difference in inches between the
height of the reach and the height of the best jump.

Suggestions:

When reaching height is taken, the subject is encouraged to stretch as far as he can, being sure that both heels
are on the floor. If the subject is reaching at his maximum height, the reaching shoulder will be higher than the
other shoulder.

Portable equipment was devised for this study to facilitate use in a number of schools. Two 9-foot uprights,
2 1/2 inches by 1 1/8 inches were hinged to a 9-foot cross-
bar of the same dimensions. The crossbar was itself hinged
in the center. The hubs of the hinges were countersunk and
reversed. The brad was removed from the regular hinge and
a bolt with a wing nut was used to give stability, and still
allow the hinge to fold. Each upright and half of the
crossbar could be folded compactly into four 1/2 foot
lengths.

For the base, two 2 × 4 pieces 2 feet in length, were
set on edge. A space 1 7/8 inches by 1 inch was left in
which to insert the uprights. Sixteen inch 2 × 4 crossbars
were laid flat to give additional strength to the base.

The cloth strips were tacked to the horizontal bar in
the manner previously described.

One administrator can test approximately 40 subjects in
one hour. As the administrator becomes experienced in estimating the approximate height the subject will jump, the
number of trials per subject may be cut down considerably,
which in turn decreases the testing time.

4. Standing Broad Jump

This test measures the ability of the subject to jump
horizontally from a standing position.

Equipment:

    1. Tumbling mat, at least nine feet long.

    2. Measuring tape, unless mat is calibrated permanently.

Test:

    The subject stands with both toes touching the restraining line that marks the take-off area, and from this standing position jumps as far forward as he can. Any preliminary movement that is made must be executed with some part of both feet in contact with the take-off area. The subject is given three successive trials and measurement is taken to the last inch. For example, if the subject jumps five feet, two and one-half inches, the jump is recorded as five feet, two inches. This distance is measured from the restraining line of the take-off area to the nearest contact made on landing. (This is usually to the first heel mark made on landing, but if the subject loses balance, falls backward and catches himself with his hand or body, the mark nearest the restraining line is used in measuring the distance of the jump.

Scoring:

    The best of three trials, in feet and inches, is the score for the test.

Suggestions:

    It is important to check the position of the feet of each subject, making sure that the toes are not over the restraining line. If any preliminary bounce or spring is taken in which one or both feet leave the surface of the take-off area, the jump is not legal and a score of zero is recorded. It is advisable to encourage the subject to throw his weight forward if he feels himself losing balance upon landing -- if he falls backward, the distance of his jump is considerably shortened.

    If a mat is used, the restraining line should be marked on the mat, rather than on the floor, and far enough from the end of the mat to allow the entire surface of both feet to rest comfortably on the mat. If an outdoor jumping pit is used, a stable surface for the take-off area must be provided. All subjects in this particular study were measured on a mat.

If a mat is used in giving this test, it may be calibrated by using India ink, or a cloth measuring tape may be fastened to one side of the mat with pins or scotch tape. This will facilitate speed and accuracy in measuring. If these methods are used, one administrator can test between 40 and 50 subjects in one hour.

5. Shuttle Run

This test measures the ability of the subject to run rapidly between two given marks, necessitating quick stops and changes of direction.

Equipment:

    1. Stop watch, calibrated in one-tenth seconds.

    2. Markings

    Two 12-inch lines are marked on the floor, parallel to each other and at a distance of 20 feet apart. The line that is indicated to be the starting line should have an area in back of it free from obstruction that is at least 20 feet long, to give the runner an opportunity to check his speed <u>after</u> passing this line upon completing his run.

Test:

    The subject stands with the toe of his forward foot on the starting line. On the signal "Go" he runs to the opposite line, touches it (or beyond it) with one or both feet. This constitutes one complete trip. The subject does not stop, but continues running to the opposite line until he has completed three trips, or a total of 120 feet. If the subject fails to touch, or step over, a line at any time during the run, he is stopped at once and no score is recorded for the trial. After a brief resting period, he is given one opportunity to repeat this performance, and if he fails again to execute the test correctly, a score of zero is recorded for the trial.

    The time in one-tenth seconds is taken from the signal "Go" to the crossing of the starting line upon completing the three trips (120 feet).

    Two trials are given in this test. Subjects are tested in pairs, with one of the pair resting while the other is performing, thus alternating with each other on the trials.

370

Scoring:

The score for this test is the better of the two trials, recorded in seconds to the nearest tenth.

Suggestions:

This test should be demonstrated and explained carefully, thus avoiding the necessity of a practice trial on the part of the subject, as his best score is frequently made on his initial performance.

The subject should be encouraged to run across the starting line (which is also the finish line) at full speed upon the completion of his third trip, in order that he may make the best possible score. Gymnasium shoes are necessary for executing this test; street shoes or stockings present too many difficulties for the quick turns that are necessary in this test.

If a number of subjects are to be tested, chalk is not practical for the floor markings because it rubs off too easily; white tempera paint (washable) is recommended.

One administrator can test between 40 and 50 subjects in one hour.

6. Soccer Wall Volley

This test measures the ability of the subject to kick a soccer ball repeatedly against the wall within a given target area and from a specified distance on the floor.

Equipment:

1. Regulation soccer ball, stop watch.

2. Markings

On a flat wall space, mark a target area four feet wide and two and one-half feet from the floor. A similar area is marked on the floor, four feet wide and two and one-half feet from the wall target, parallel to the wall target. The four-foot line on the floor, farthest from the wall target, is extended one foot on either side, and constitutes the restraining line (six feet long).

<u>Test</u>:

The ball is placed back of the restraining lines at
any position desired by the subject (usually toward the
center of the line). On the signal "Go" the subject kicks
the ball against the wall into the target area, and as it
rebounds he continues to kick it repeatedly against the
wall. If the ball gets out of control, the subject retrieves it himself, brings it back to the restraining line
and starts it again. The subject may not touch the ball
with his hands while it is in the rectangular floor area between the restraining line and the target. If the ball
stops within this area, he must remove it by using his foot.
At any time that the ball is outside of this rectangular
floor area, the subject may use his hands in retrieving or
moving the ball.

A successful hit is one that is kicked with the foot
into the target area on the wall from <u>behind</u> the restraining
line on the floor. Line balls are not <u>fair</u> hits. To constitute a fair hit, the ball must be kicked from in back of
the restraining line (not <u>on</u> it), and must land between the
lines that bound the wall target.

The subject is given a fifteen-second practice trial.
The test administrator scores verbally during this trial,
calling attention to balls that are not legal hits. This
score is not recorded.

<u>Scoring</u>:

One point is given for each successful hit. Each time
that the ball is touched with the hands when it is inside
the rectangular floor area, one point is subtracted from
the score. Four fifteen-second trials are given, after the
practice trial. The total number of points is recorded for
<u>each</u> trial. The best of the four trials is the final score
for the test.

<u>Suggestions</u>:

One administrator can time and score between 25 and 30
subjects in one hour, if the group has had no previous experience in kicking a soccer ball. Inexperienced subjects
need more instruction in kicking the ball without raising
it above the target and are frequently unsuccessful during
the practice trial, necessitating further demonstration and
explanation by the administrator.

As for all floor markings, when a number of subjects are being used, white tempera paint is recommended in place of chalk.

7. Softball Repeated Throws

This test measures the ability of the subject to throw a softball, using an overhand throw, into a given target area from a specified distance.

Equipment:

1. Regulation twelve inch inseam softball, stop watch.

2. Markings

On a flat wall space, mark a target area five and one-half feet wide and at least ten feet high, at a distance of one-half foot from the floor. A throwing area, five and one-half feet square is marked on the floor at a distance of nine feet from the target and parallel to it. A backstop, twelve feet long and two and one-half feet high (at least) is placed fifteen feet in back of the throwing area.

Test:

The subject stands at any place he chooses inside of the throwing area. On the signal "Go" he throws the ball against the wall into the target area, using an overhand throw, and continues successive throws until the signal "Stop" is given. The balls may be received from the target either on the bounce or on the fly. If the ball gets out of control at any time, the subject must recover it himself without assistance. Most of these balls will be stopped by the backstop, but if this is not the case, the subject must chase the balls himself. A successful throw is one that is an overhand throw that goes into the target area and is made from inside the throwing area. Line balls are not fair hits.

The subject is given a ten-second practice trial. The test administrator scores verbally during this trial. This score is not recorded.

Scoring:

One point is given for each successful throw. Two fifteen-second trials are given, after the practice trial.

The total number of points is recorded for <u>each</u> trial. The better of the two trials is the final score for the test.

Suggestions:

One administrator can time and score approximately 50 subjects in one hour. If other testing areas and scorers are available, the test may be given very quickly.

A backstop may be readily devised by using an ordinary table and turning it on its side, with the table surface facing the target.

If a number of subjects are to be tested, white tempera paint is recommended for all markings.

The performance scales presented here are based on 100 to 150 boys and a similar number of girls in each of the three grades. They were enrolled in 21 Iowa and 3 Illinois schools in 18 different towns. The scale is presented in percentiles and in T-scores. Either may be used.

Table LII.

Achievement Scales for Boys and Girls:
Vertical Jump
(Inches)

	Girls			Boys			
T-Score	Grade IV	Grade V	Grade VI	Grade IV	Grade V	Grade VI	Percentile
76		16			17	19	99
73						18	98
72	14		16	15		17	98
71					16		98
70		15					97
68			15				96
67	13					16	95
66		14		14	15		94
64			14				92
63		13				15	90

374

Table LII. (Cont.)

T-Score	Girls Grade IV	Girls Grade V	Girls Grade VI	Boys Grade IV	Boys Grade V	Boys Grade VI	Percentile
62	12				14		88
60				13			84
59		12				14	81
58			13				78
57	11				13		75
56				12		13	72
53		11					61
52			12	11	12		57
51	10					12	53
50							50
48				10			42
47		10	11		11		38
46						11	34
45	9						30
43				9			24
42		9	10		10		21
40	8					10	15
39			9				13
38				8			11
37		8			9		9
35	7					9	6
34			8		8		5
33				7			4
32		7					3
30						8	2
29					7		2
28	6			6			2
27			7				1
24		6		5		7	1

375

Table LIII.

Achievement Scales for Boys and Girls:
Standing Broad Jump
(feet)

| T-Score | Girls | | | Boys | | | Percentile |
	Grade IV	Grade V	Grade VI	Grade IV	Grade V	Grade VI	
76	5-6			6-2	6-3	6-5	99
75							99
74	5-5	5-8		6-1			99
73	5-4		5-7	6-0	6-2		98
72	5-3			5-11	6-1	6-4	98
71	5-1			5-10			98
70	5-0			5-8	6-0		97
69		5-7		5-7		6-3	97
68		5-6		5-6			96
67					5-11	6-2	95
66	4-11	5-5	5-5	5-5	5-9	6-1	94
65		5-4		5-4	5-8	6-0	93
64		5-2	5-4		5-7	5-11	92
63	4-10	5-1	5-3	5-3	5-6	5-10	90
62	4-9	5-0	5-2	5-2	5-5	5-9	88
61	4-8	4-11	5-1	5-1	5-4	5-8	86
60		4-10			5-3	5-7	84
59	4-7	4-9	5-0	5-0		5-6	81
58		4-8	4-11	4-11	5-2	5-5	78
57	4-6	4-7	4-10		5-1	5-4	75
56	4-5	4-6	4-9	4-10		5-3	72
55	4-4	4-5	4-8	4-9	5-0	5-2	69
54	4-3	4-4		4-8			65
53	4-2	4-3	4-7		4-11	5-1	61
52	4-1		4-6	4-7	4-10	5-0	57
51		4-2	4-5	4-6			53

Table LIII. (Cont.)

	Girls			Boys			
T-Score	Grade IV	Grade V	Grade VI	Grade IV	Grade V	Grade VI	Percentile
50	4-0	4-1	4-4		4-9	4-11	50
49	3-11	4-0		4-5	4-8	4-10	46
48	3-10		4-3		4-7	4-9	42
47		3-11	4-2	4-4	4-6	4-8	38
46	3-9		4-1			4-7	34
45		3-10		4-3	4-5		30
44			4-0	4-2	4-4		27
43	3-8	3-9	3-11		4-3	4-6	24
42				4-1	4-2		21
41		3-8	3-10	4-0	4-1	4-5	18
40	3-7			3-11	4-0		15
39		3-7	3-9	3-10	3-11	4-4	13
38		3-6				4-3	11
37	3-6	3-5	3-8	3-9	3-10	4-2	9
36		3-4	3-7	3-8		4-1	8
35		3-3	3-6	3-5	3-9		6
34	3-5			3-3		4-0	5
33	3-4	3-2					4
32	3-3	3-1	3-5	3-2		3-11	3
31	3-2	3-0	3-4	3-1	3-8	3-10	3
30	3-1	2-11	3-3			3-9	2
29		2-10	3-2			3-7	2
28	3-0	2-9	3-0			3-6	2
27	2-11	2-8	2-11			3-5	1
26	2-10			3-0		3-4	1
25							1
24	2-9		2-10		3-7	3-3	0

Table LIV.

Achievement Scales for Boys and Girls:
Shuttle Run

T-Score	Girls Grade IV	Grade V	Grade VI	Boys Grade IV	Grade V	Grade VI	Percentile
77			11.2				99
76		11.6		11.0	11.2	10.0	99
75						10.2	99
74	12.0		11.3	11.1		10.3	99
73			11.4		11.3	10.4	98
72		11.7		11.3	11.4	10.5	98
71	12.1			11.4		10.6	98
70	12.2	11.8	11.5	11.6		10.7	97
69	12.3	11.9		11.7	11.5	10.8	97
68	12.4			11.8		10.9	96
67		12.0	11.6		11.6	11.0	95
66		12.1	11.7	11.9	11.7		94
65	12.5	12.2	11.8	12.0	11.8	11.1	93
64	12.7	12.3	11.9	12.2	11.9	11.2	92
63	12.9	12.4	12.1	12.3	12.0	11.3	90
62			12.2	12.4		11.4	88
61	13.0		12.3		12.1		86
60	13.1	12.5		12.5	12.2		84
59	13.2	12.6	12.4		12.3	11.5	81
58		12.7		12.6	12.4		78
57	13.3	12.8	12.5	12.7		11.6	75
56	13.4	12.9		12.8		11.7	72
55		13.0	12.6	12.9	12.5	11.8	69
54	13.5	13.1		13.0		11.9	65
53	13.6	13.2	12.7	13.1	12.6		61
52	13.8	13.3	12.8	13.2		12.0	57
51	13.9	13.4	12.9	13.3	12.7		53

378

Table LIV. (Cont.)

	Girls				Boys		
T-Score	Grade IV	Grade V	Grade VI	Grade IV	Grade V	Grade VI	Percentile
50	14.0			13.4	12.8	12.1	50
49	14.1	13.5	13.0		12.9	12.2	46
48	14.2		13.1	13.5	13.0	12.3	42
47	14.3	13.6	13.2		13.1	12.4	38
46	14.4		13.3	13.6	13.2	12.5	34
45	14.5	13.7	13.4	13.7	13.3	12.6	30
44	14.6	13.8		13.8	13.4	12.7	27
43	14.8	13.9	13.5	13.9	13.5	12.9	24
42	14.9		13.6	14.1		13.0	21
41	15.0	14.0	13.7	14.2	13.6	13.1	18
40	15.1		13.8	14.3	13.7	13.2	15
39	15.2	14.1	13.9	14.4		13.4	13
38	15.3	14.2	14.0	14.5	13.8	13.5	11
37	15.4	14.3	14.2		13.9	13.5	9
36	15.5	14.4	14.4	14.6		13.7	8
35	15.6		14.6	14.7	14.0	13.9	6
34	15.8		14.7	14.8	14.1	14.0	5
33	16.0	14.5	14.9	14.9	14.3	14.3	4
32	16.1	14.7	15.0		14.4	14.5	3
31	16.3	14.9	15.1	15.0	14.6	14.6	3
30	16.5	15.1			14.8	14.7	2
29		15.4	15.2		14.9	14.8	2
28	16.6	15.6	15.3		15.0	14.9	2
27	16.7	15.8	15.4		15.1	15.0	1
26	16.8	15.9	15.5			15.1	1
25						15.3	1
24	16.9	16.0		15.1	15.9	15.4	1
23			15.6			15.5	0

Table LV.

Achievement Scales for Boys and Girls:
Softball Repeated Throws

	Girls			Boys			
T-Score	Grade IV	Grade V	Grade VI	Grade IV	Grade V	Grade VI	Percentile
78	9	10					99
76				12			99
74			12			15	99
73				11	14		98
72	8	9					98
68					13	14	96
66		11					94
65				10			93
64					12		92
63	7					13	90
61			10				86
60					11		84
58				9		12	78
55		8	9		10		69
54						11	65
51				8	9		53
49			8			10	46
48		7					42
47	6						38
46					8		34
45			7	7			30
44						9	27
41	5						18
40		6			7		15
39				6		8	13
38			6				11
35	4						6
33				5		7	4
32		5			6		3
29			5				2
28	3	4				6	2
27				4			1
24		3	4		5	5	1

Table LVI.

Achievement Scales for Boys and Girls:
Basketball Wall Pass

| T-Score | Girls | | | Boys | | | Percentile |
	Grade IV	Grade V	Grade VI	Grade IV	Grade V	Grade VI	
77				24	27		99
76	19						99
75			22	23	26	30	99
74					25		99
73		20		22	24		98
72	18				23	29	98
71				21	22	28	98
70						27	97
69						26	97
68	17		21		21	25	96
67		19				24	95
66				20			94
65						23	93
64		18	20				92
63	16	17		19	20		90
62						22	88
61				18			86
60	15		19		19		84
59		16		17			81
58						21	78
57			18		18		75
56	14	15		16			72
55							69
54			17			20	65
53					17		61
52	13	14					57
51			16			19	53

Table LVI. (Cont.)

T-Score	Girls Grade IV	Grade V	Grade VI	Boys Grade IV	Grade V	Grade VI	Percentile
50	12				16		50
49						18	46
48			15	14			42
47	11	13			15		38
46						17	34
45	10		14				30
44		12		13	14		27
43	9						24
42			13			16	21
41		11		12	13		18
40	8						15
39		10			12	15	13
38			12				11
37				11	11		9
36	7	9				14	8
35			11				6
34		8		10	10		5
33			10				4
32	6	7				13	3
31				9	9		3
30			9				2
29					8		2
28		6			7		2
27				8			1
26	5						1
25			8		6	12	1

Table LVII.

Achievement Scales for Boys and Girls:
Soccer Wall Volley

T-Score	Girls			Boys			Percentile
	Grade IV	Grade V	Grade VI	Grade IV	Grade V	Grade VI	
76		15		14	16		99
74	13					18	99
73		14			15		98
71				13		17	98
70		13	13				97
69	12					16	97
68					14		96
67						15	95
66	11	12	12				94
65				12			93
64		11			13	14	92
63	10						90
61			11		12		86
60		10		11		13	84
59	9						81
57			10		11		75
56		9		10		12	72
54	8						65
53			9	9	10	11	61
52		8					57
49	7					10	46
48			8	8	9		42
46		7					34
44	6					9	27
43			7	7	8		24
40		6				8	15
39					7		13
38			6	6			11
37	5						9
35						7	6
34		5					5
32			5				3
29	4					6	2
27		4		4			1
26			4				1
24			3	3	5	5	0

Table LVIII.

Achievement Scales for Boys and Girls:
Volleyball Wall Volley

	Girls			Boys			
T-Score	Grade IV	Grade V	Grade VI	Grade IV	Grade V	Grade VI	Percentile
77			21			29	99
76		18					99
75						28	99
74	13	17				27	99
73		15	20	20		26	98
72	12	14			20		98
71	11	13	19	18		25	98
70				16		24	97
69	10		18	15			97
68		12		14	19		96
67			17	13		23	95
66	9			12	18	22	94
65		11		11	17	21	93
64			16		16		92
63	8	10	15		15	20	90
62			14	10		19	88
61		9			14	18	86
60			13				84
59	7		9			17	81
58		8	12		13		78
57			11		12	16	75
56	6	7		8	11		72
55			10				69
54					10	15	65
53	5		9	7			61
52		6			9	14	57
51							53

Table LVIII. (Cont.)

T-Score	Girls Grade IV	Girls Grade V	Girls Grade VI	Boys Grade IV	Boys Grade V	Boys Grade VI	Percentile
50	4		8	6	8	13	50
49							46
48		5			7	12	42
47						11	38
46	3		7	5			34
45						10	30
44					6		27
43		4				9	24
42			6	4		8	21
41					5		18
40	2						15
39		3				7	13
38				3			11
37			5		4	6	9
36							8
35						5	6
34		2		2			5
33							4
32	1				3	4	3
31							3
30			3			3	2
29		1					2
28							2
27						2	1
26				1			1
25							1
24					2	1	1
23			2				0

Magnusson[18] devised some modifications of certain tests
of achievement to supplement a battery of muscular fitness
tests. These comprised ball handling, jumping, running, and
balance. They are as follows:

1. Ball handling (using a rubber volleyball)

Purpose: To test ability to keep control of a ball.

1st, 2nd grades:

Equipment:

Circle on floor 3 feet in radius, 1 ball, 1 stop watch.

Directions:

See how many times you can bounce the ball staying in
this circle. Both you and the ball must stay within the
circle. I will count each bounce you make in 30 seconds.
If you lose control of the ball, hurry to get it and bring
it back to the circle and start bouncing right away.

Scoring:

Count the number of times the ball is bounced within
the circle while child is also within the circle. (2 trials, using the best of the 2.)

3rd, 4th, 5th, 6th grades:

Equipment:

Line on floor, 6 feet from wall, 1 volleyball.

Directions:

Stand behind this line. Throw the ball at the wall,
and keep it going as fast as you can. The score will be
the number of times the ball hits the wall between the time
I say, "Go," and "Stop." It may be volleyed or caught and
thrown. If you lose control of the ball, get it as quickly
as possible and come back to line and start the ball again.

Scoring:

One point for each time the ball hits the wall (except
when it is rolling on the floor) during 15-second interval.
Give three trials with rest of at least one minute between
trials.

2. Broad jump

Purpose: To test coordination and leg strength and power.

Equipment:

Tumbling mat, at least 9 feet long. Mat should be marked every inch from 2 feet on. There should be a restraining area of one and a half feet at the end of the mat.

Directions:

Stand with your toes touching the restraining line that marks the take-off area and from this standing position jump as far forward as possible. Keep both feet in contact with the mat before jumping and land with both feet at the same time. Throw your weight forward when you land so that you do not lose your balance backward. You will get three trials, one right after the other.

Scoring:

Measure the distance from the restraining line of the take-off area to the nearest contact made on landing (this is normally the first heel mark made on landing but if the jumper loses his balance, falls backward and catches himself with his hands or body, the mark nearest the restraining line is used in measuring). Record all three jumps to nearest inch.

3. Obstacle race

Purpose: To test agility and speed.

Equipment:

Area marked on floor. (An Indian club or small post, a cross bar between jump standards 18 inches high, or a rope stretched tight between the standards at 18 inches height.) (See Figure 45.)

Directions:

Start flat on your back with heels at this line (a). On the signal, "Ready, Go," get up and start running as quickly as possible toward the Indian club (b). Run behind

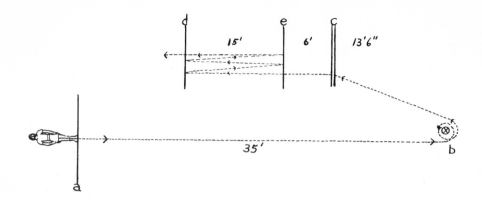

Figure 45.   Obstacle course for elementary school children.

the club twice and continue on, going under the rope (c).
Get up on the other side and run to this line (d) and continue running between these two lines (d and e) until you
come here (d) for the third time.   I will tell you when to
stop.

Scoring:

The score is the number of seconds to the nearest .1
that is required to run the course.   If the child does not
follow directions, stop him as soon as possible and after a
short rest and further explanation give the test again.

4. Throw for distance

Purpose: To test coordination and arm strength and power.

Equipment:

Have area marked off in 5-foot intervals from starting
line.   Two volleyballs.

Directions:

Stand behind this line.   Throw the ball any way you
wish trying to make it go as far as possible.   It counts
where it first touches the floor.   You will have 3 trials.

Scoring:

Note length of throw to the nearest foot.   Use the
longest throw.

5. Stork Stand

Purpose: To test static balance.

Equipment:

1 stop watch.

Directions:

Stand on one foot, place the other foot on the side of your knee. Close your eyes and stand as long as possible. Keep your foot in the same spot.

Scoring:

Seconds between time eyes were closed and balance is lost or foot moved about.

Many cities and some states have set up plans for wide scale testing of elementary children in order to better understand the total development of the child. The Greensboro, North Carolina, public schools undertook a study to select objective measures of motor performance to motivate student accomplishment and to help emphasize the importance of motor development. The preface, written by the Greensboro Superintendent of Schools, opens with the statement: "Motor performance is an important aspect of individual personality. The measurement of motor performance is a device useful in motivation for capacity performance and improvement commensurate with the growth and development limitation of the individual."

The tests selected were ball bounce, jump rope, jump for height, wall ball, throw for accuracy, side stepping, distance throw, duck and run, climbing, and chinning.

The results are presented as scores on the decile points and show performance of white, negro and mixed populations, for grades 3 through 6. The brochure on results is available from the Greensboro school system.

Programs such as this can constitute the whole program if poorly administered and poorly interpreted. They can be a real challenge and basis of expanded curricular experience for the children if properly handled.

The choice of items from various sources would seem to be dependent upon definition of objectives, space and assistance for testing.

KINESTHESIS TESTING

Kinesthesis is defined here as that sense which enables the person to perceive the position and movement of the total body and of its parts. It is the basis for balance, both dynamic and static, for knowing the gradations of effort put into a movement, and for duplicating movements previously performed. Kinesthesis operates much as vision, in that the individual takes it for granted, is not really aware of the process or able to analyze what is happening. But like vision and the other senses there are individual variations in acuity of the sense and the way in which the individual becomes conscious of what he is seeing, feeling and the like.

Acuity of kinesthesis is closely related to this general motor ability as we have defined it. The person who perceives his own efforts, positions and motor adaptations and has developed empathy for observing movement of others will learn quickly and perceive motor problems readily. With any opportunity for practice he will demonstrate greater accomplishment than a person without that acuity.

It has been shown that kinesthesis, like flexibility, is highly specific to the respective areas of the body. On must decide what component of kinesthesis one needs to meas ure or to select tests which will supplement, not duplicate each other. Russell[24] and Witte[32] studied kinesthesis batteries by means of factor analysis. Each arrived at essentially the same conclusions, specificity and diversity of component factors. Scott[25] studying the problem from simple patterns of intercorrelation of items in an extensi battery arrived at essentially the same conclusions. The following grouping of tests is built on these findings.

Some of the following tests are practical for classroom, or testing of a total group. They will be so designated. Others listed here will be of value primarily for the occasional diagnostic work with a student or for research purposes.

Arm Positioning

1. Arm Raising Sideward 90°

Equipment:

A stick figure drawing with one arm in horizontal position. A goniometer, either a gravity or caliper type.

Instructions:

Stand, look at this figure. Close your eyes and raise your right arm out sideward to a position matching that of the figure, with palm facing down.

Scoring:

Degrees of deviation from the horizontal. (Arm is lowered and then raised again and measured. Then the left arm is raised twice in the same fashion.) Score is the sum of deviations for the four trials.

2. Pronation-Supination

Equipment:

A knob, 3 inches in diameter, mounted in front of a protractor. A pointer is attached to the knob at the 90° position. Resistance can be provided by suspending a 1000 gram weight from the knob. Knob is mounted on edge of table.

Instructions:

Sit here in front of the equipment so that you reach forward enough to clear your elbow from your side when you grasp the knob. While looking at the pointer, turn the knob so the pointer is at 140°. Concentrate on the feeling of the amount of movement necessary to reach 140°. Release. Now I will block your view of the dial, turn the knob again and say "now" when you think you have it at 140°. You will have three more trials.

You will now repeat turning the pointer in the other direction to 40°. Practice once while you concentrate on the feeling. You will have four trials.

Scoring:

Sum of the deviations from the designated position for the eight trials.

Leg Positioning

1. Leg Raising

Equipment:

A stick figure drawing of a man lying on his side with the upper leg raised 20°. A gravity goniometer.

Instructions:

Lie on your side and look at this figure. Close your eyes and raise your leg until you think it is in the same position as in the drawing.

Scoring:

Deviation from the 20°. (The subject repeats the second time with the same leg, then turns over and tries twice with the other leg.) Score is the sum of deviations on the four trials.

Suggestions:

Another version of this test is to have the subject raise the leg to the desired position while concentrating on feeling. She then repeats according to feeling of the movement. The goniometer should be attached to the ankle.

2. Lower leg raising

Equipment:

A gravitv or caliper-type goniometer.

Instructions:

Stand here with your hand on the edge of the table for support. Bend your right knee so that the lower leg is in a horizontal position.

Scoring:

Deviation from 90°. The subject tries twice with each leg. Score is the sum of the deviations for the four trials.

Effort Matching in Upper Extremity

1. Grip to designated amount.

Equipment:

Grip dynamometer.

Instructions:

Watch the dial on the dynamometer while you grip it to exactly 20 lbs. Concentrate on the feeling of the effort. Now with eyes closed, bring it to the same point again.

Scoring:

Deviation from 20 lbs. The subject tries three times with each hand. Score is the sum of the deviations on the six trials.

Suggestions:

The number of pounds used should be determined by the age and strength of the group being tested. The grip used should be less than the maximum grip for any subject.

2. Push-pull to designated amount

Equipment:

Hand dynamometer with push-pull attachment. (See Chapter VIII for push-pull test.)

Suggestions:

This test may be done as either the push or the pull or both. It is similar to tne Grip to Designated Amount in setting a submaximal point which subjects attempt to repeat after a trial to the precise amount.

Balance

1. Sideward leap (See Chap. VIII)

2. Balance on Stick (See Chap. VIII)

3. Weight shifting sideward

Equipment:

A bathroom scale and a block of wood 6 inches by 12 inches and of a thickness exactly matching the height of the scale.

Instructions:

Stand with one foot on the block of wood, place the other foot on the scale. Now shift your weight on to the scales just enough to bring the pointer to ____ lbs. You may have two practices to run the scale up to ____ lbs., concentrate on the feeling of the shift. Then while your view of the dial is blocked you will shift again. Say "now" when you think it is the right amount. You will have two trials.

Scoring:

Deviations from the designated amount. (The block is moved to the other side of the scale and the practice trials and the two scored trials are done on the opposite foot.) Score is the sum of the deviations on the four trials.

Suggestions:

The subject should be weighed a few minutes ahead of taking this test in such a manner as not to associate it with this test. The scale reading requested in the test is one-half her weight.

Orientation in Space

1. Walking a triangle

Equipment:

A large smooth area where there will be no distractions. Three points located so as to form the points of a right angle triangle. Blindfold.

Instructions:

Stand here and put on the blindfold. I will place my hands on your hips to guide you while we walk. When I remove my hands and leave you, you are to return to this point. Stop and hold the position when you think you have arrived.

Scoring:

Distance (to the nearest inch) from the starting point to the nearest toe.

Suggestions:

The two sides of the triangle should be of different lengths, such as 12 and 20 feet. None of the three sides of the triangle should be near a wall or other obstruction. If space and testing time permit a small triangle and a large triangle would be desirable, providing two trials.

The subject is started at one point facing toward the right angle corner. She is walked to the corner, turned toward the other corner and left facing out from the triangle.

There should be no noise in the vicinity of the testing area and the examiner should not talk after starting the subject until the finish point is marked.

2. Walking a straight line with turns

Equipment:

A large smooth area with no obstructions. Near the center of area a line, 1 inch wide, about 18 feet long. Blindfold.

Instructions:

Start here at this end of the line. After your blindfold is on, you will start walking down the line. Take two steps forward, then bring your rear foot forward parallel to your other foot but not touching it. Do a complete turn in place keeping your feet apart. Then take two more steps forward and repeat your turn. Continue until you have made four turns. Hold the position until it is marked.

Scoring:

Number of inches from the line to the nearest toe, measuring at right angles to the line.

Suggestions:

There should be no noise in the room and the examiner should not talk after the subject starts.

3. Broad Jump Specified

Equipment:

Two lines on the floor, 1 inch wide, 24 inches between nearest edges.

Instructions:

Stand with your toes just behind this line. Jump across the second line so that your heels just clear. You may have two trials and try to concentrate on the feeling of the effort. Now with your eyes closed, repeat the jump and hold the position until it is measured.

Scoring:

Zero point would be with the heels exactly at the far edge of the second line. Score is the deviation to nearest half inch in either direction from the zero point, and total score is the sum of the deviations on the two trials.

The tests which are most feasible to use in the classroom situation are the Arm Raising Sideward, Balance Leap, Balance on Stick, Grip to Designated Amount, and Broad Jump Specified. These are each measuring different aspects of kinesthetic function. They might be selected as they appear to serve diagnostic purposes or to point up the need for awareness of bodily sensations in movement.

SELECTED REFERENCES

1. Barrow, Harold M.: Test of Motor Ability for College Men. Research Quarterly, 25: p. 253, October 1954.

2. Bennett, Colleen L.: Relative Contributions of Modern Dance, Folk Dance, Basketball and Swimming to Motor Abilities of College Women. Research Quarterly, 27: p. 253, October 1956.

3. Broer, Marion R.: Reliability of Certain Skill Tests for Junior High School Girls. Research Quarterly, 29: p. 139, May 1958.

4. Clark, Helen: The Relation of Kinesthesis to Certain Measures of Hand Function. Ph. D. Dissertation, State University of Iowa, 1957.

5. Cooper, Bernice: The Establishment of General Motor Capacity Tests for High School Girls. Ph. D. Dissertation, State University of Iowa, 1945.

6. Cumbee, Frances Z., Margaret Meyer, and Gerald Peterson: Factorial Analysis of Motor Coordination Variables for Third and Fourth Grade Girls. Research Quarterly, 28: p. 100, May 1957.

7. Estep, Dorothy P.: Relationship of Static Equilibrium to Ability in Motor Activities. Research Quarterly, 28: p. 5, March 1957.

8. Greensboro Public Schools: Experimental Testing Project in Physical Education in the Elementary Schools. Greensboro, N. C., 1958.

9. Hatlestad, Lucille: Motor Educability Tests for Women College Students. Research Quarterly, 13: p. 10, March 1942.

10. Highmore, George: A Factorial Analysis of Athletic Ability. Research Quarterly, 27: p. 1, March 1956.

11. Johnson, Granville: Physical Skill Tests for Sectioning Classes into Homogeneous Units. Research Quarterly, 3: p. 128, March 1932.

12. Kammeyer, Shirley J.: Reliability and Validity of a Motor Ability Test for High School Girls. Research Quarterly, 27: p. 310, October 1956.

13. Kistler, J. W.: The Homogeneous Grouping of Junior and Senior High School Boys for Physical Education Class Activities. Research Quarterly, 8: p. 11, December 1937.

14. Latchaw, Marjorie: Measuring Selected Motor Skills in Fourth, Fifth, and Sixth Grades. Research Quarterly, 25: p. 439, December 1954.

15. Lafuze, Marian: A Study of the Learning of Fundamental Skills by Freshmen Women of Low Motor Ability. M. A. thesis, State University of Iowa, 1950.

16. McCloy, C. H.: The Measurement of General Motor Capacity and General Motor Ability. Research Quarterly, 5: p. 46, Supplement March 1934.

17. McCloy, C. H.: An Analytical Study of the Stunt Type Test as a Measure of Motor Educability. Research Quarterly, 8: p. 46, October 1937.

18. Magnusson, Lucille: The Effect of a Specific Activity Program on Children with Low Muscular Fitness. Ph. D. Dissertation, State University of Iowa, 1957.

19. Metheny, Eleanor: Studies of the Johnson Test as a Test of Motor Educability. Research Quarterly, 9: p. 105, December 1938.

20. Phillips, Marjorie: A Study of a Series of Physical Education Tests by Factor Analysis. Research Quarterly, 20: p. 60, March 1949.

21. Phillips, Marjorie, and Dean Summers: Relation of Kinesthetic Perception to Motor Learning. Research Quarterly, 25: p. 456, December 1954.

22. Riley, Marie: The Measurement of Balance in the Elementary Grades. M. A. thesis, State University of Iowa, 1953.

23. Roloff, Louise L.: Kinesthesis in Relation to the Learning of Selected Motor Skills, Research Quarterly, 24: p. 210, May 1953.

24. Russell, Ruth I.: A Factor Analysis of the Components of Kinesthesis. Ph. D. Dissertation, State University of Iowa, 1954.

25. Scott, M. Gladys: Measurement of Kinesthesis. Research Quarterly, 26: p. 324, October 1955.

26. Scott, M. Gladys: The Assessment of Motor Ability of College Women. Research Quarterly, 10: p. 63, October 1939.

27. Scott, M. Gladys: Motor Ability Tests for College Women. Research Quarterly, 14: p. 402, December 1943.

28. Smith, Jean A.: Relation of Certain Physical Traits and Abilities to Motor Learning in Elementary School Children. Research Quarterly, 27: p. 220, May 1956.

29. Way, Eunice E.: Relationship of Lateral Dominance to Scores of Motor Ability and Selected Skill Tests. Research Quarterly, 29: p. 360, October 1958.

30. Wiebe, Vernon R.: A Study of Tests of Kinesthesis. Research Quarterly, 25: p. 222, May 1954.

31. Wilson, Marjorie: Development of Jumping Skill in Children. Ph. D. Dissertation, State University of Iowa, 1945.

32. Witte, Faye: A Factorial Analysis of Measures of Kinesthesis. Doctoral Dissertation, Indiana University, 1953.

33. Worchel, Philip: The Role of the Vestibular Organs in Space Orientation. Journal of Experimental Psychology, 44, 1952.

Chapter X

RATINGS AND EVALUATION FORMS

A variety of methods should be used for evaluating performance in activities. Some activities lend themselves less readily to objective measures than others; in some activities objective measures are lacking. Complete reliance on objective measures in any physical education activity is questionable and probably inadvisable at present.

Subjective but systematic ratings of performance are used frequently in the area of dance. Teachers recognize that a measure of the relative status of individuals in dance activities is just as desirable as in sports. The need for a measure of improvement to motivate effort presents itself in all activities. Sometimes ratings may substitute for objective tests when the latter are unavailable.

In many activities objective measures should be supplemented with ratings or charts on which are recorded details of performance. For example, in basketball there are tests of skill in shooting, of speed in passing, and of ability to jump, but as yet there are no tests to measure ability to intercept passes, to block shots, or to secure rebounds. A chart on which a tally is kept of the number of times a player is successful in executing some of these skills can be used. Subjective ratings, or evaluation of performance with respect to some standard, can be very useful if made while the players are engaged in game play.

Swimming, stunts and tumbling, archery, golf, and bowling are examples of activities that are self-testing in nature. A progression scale of the separate units or skills which have been taught can be made. It usually has some qualitative rating of the degree of success that each student has had. Such combined progression charts and rating scales can be used not only as a measure of progress in learning but also serve the teacher to determine the desirable sequence and rate of presenting material.

For some activities such as diving, form is the quality being judged, and one would probably rely entirely upon a rating scale involving subjective judgment. For beginners in diving the rating scale will be very different than the one used in judging divers in competition.

The players who make high scores in skill tests and knowledge tests are not always the players who are the best performers in a game. This same situation is common to all education; tests, after all, are but samples of performance. In physical education, a measure is needed of the use that a player makes of his skills and knowledge in a game situation. A record of wins and losses in an individual sport may yield desirable information concerning the player's rank in the round-robin tournament in which each player has had an opportunity to play every other player a specified number of times under standardized tournament regulations. This kind of record in the team games is of little value in evaluating the contribution of each player. It follows that, particularly in the team sports, ratings may be needed to evaluate each individual's performance in actual game situations.

In addition to providing a measure of the student's achievement, ratings yield other desirable results. The teacher who rates his students must discerningly observe them as individuals. He must think through the activity and analyze the various parts or units of the activity and determine their relative values when constructing his rating scale. By rating player performance regularly he should grow in his ability to quickly identify movement patterns and to evaluate them. The teacher who wishes to use ratings to evaluate some of the less tangible objectives, such as attitudes toward activity, habits of good sportsmanship, and positive social behavior, finds that the use of the rating scale gives the student better understanding of the total objectives of physical education.

While ratings and achievement progressions have certain elements in common, they will be discussed separately in this and the following chapter. Samples are provided to familiarize the reader with several types. However, rating scales must always be adapted to the group and the type of instruction given. These samples may prove useful as they are, they may be only guides to construction of new ones for a special purpose.

401

RATINGS

All teachers use ratings whether they realize it or not. Whenever a teacher expresses an opinion concerning an ability or trait, he is making an estimate or a rating. There are certain things that can be done to increase the accuracy of such estimations to eliminate unrelated factors, such as the halo effect or the influence of physical appearance and personality characteristics. The use of the devices that will be described insures greater uniformity than would be secured by a single expression of opinion or a snap judgment.

The rater is limited in the accuracy of his ratings by his experience, by the opportunity he has had to observe the subject, by his knowledge of the activity or trait being rated, by the degree to which he can be objective in making judgments, and by his ability to concentrate on the task at hand. The reliability of ratings can be increased by combining the several ratings of the same pupil made by different judges. The amount of agreement between well-qualified raters who observe performance simultaneously is high if the conditions under which they work are satisfactory.

Preliminary Preparations

Certain preliminary preparation must be made to make the ratings valid:

1. The nature of the content of the activity or trait to be rated must be determined.

Usually the ratings should include only those phases of an activity that cannot be measured satisfactorily by objective means. An exception would be in the event of an experimental study to compare new objective measures with subjective ratings.

Generally it is better to divide large units of playing ability into smaller units and rate each separately. For example, in tennis each player is rated on one stroke, the serve for instance, and then in turn on other strokes.

Phases of performance that can be rated only in the game situation, such as strategic returns and ability to cover court, should be broken into units and rated. This method is preferable to watching players only in the game and then assigning a single score, since it directs the rater's attention to more aspects of the game and tends to prevent giving an undue amount of credit, out of proportion to real ability, to a player who makes one spectacular and perhaps lucky play. This procedure enables the summarizer of the ratings to weight the more important items.

2. The number of categories to be used must be determined.

Usually better results are obtained when five or more categories are used. The number of categories is related to the degree of discrimination desired. If discrimination between small differences is wished, more categories are needed than when the players will merely be classified as above average, average and below average. The use of more than seven categories requires a high degree of discrimination and becomes too time-consuming. There is a relationship between the number of categories and the use to be made of the ratings.

3. Each category or point on the scale must be clearly defined.

The definition should be in terms of the particular activity and should describe the various levels of ability known to be present in the group to be rated. For example, in rating a swimming stroke for a class in intermediate swimming, the following definition of categories might be used.

3 -- good: Position correct, coordination and timing accurate, power present in drive, minimum resistance, relaxed stroke.

2 -- fair: Position reasonably good, coordination correct but lacking proper rhythm and force.

1 -- poor: Recognizable stroke, poor or inconsistent position, too much effort with little result, ease and relaxation lacking, poor coordination.

0 -- fail: Inability to swim across the pool maintaining proper floating position and stroke coordinations.

If more categories are desired, the analysis of coordination and timing can be carried further. Too much detail should be avoided in defining each category as the swimmer no longer fits completely into any one description.

4. The opportunity for ratings must be carefully planned.

Ratings should not be made from memory nor from general impressions; they should be made while observing the performer in action. The rating periods should be planned to come at the time that best fits the purpose of the ratings and the use to be made of them. If the objective is to divide the group into ability groupings to facilitate individualization of instruction, the time for ratings would be earlier in the unit of instruction than if the ratings are to be used to measure relative standing or amount of improvement.

One of the most important factors in planning ratings is the amount of time involved to make the ratings; all too often insufficient time is allotted. The time required varies somewhat with the nature of the activity; in general, individual sports require less time than team sports. Among the team sports, volleyball is perhaps the easiest to rate, provided the rotation style of play is being used. Field hockey is one of the sports requiring a great amount of time if the players are to be rated in the game situation. All players must be provided with a number of opportunities to demonstrate their abilities in the various phases of the game. Some types of dance require less time to rate than others. Square dancing, for example, requires more time than social dance, since not all dancers are in action continuously.

Another factor in planning ratings is equalization of opposition. A player of average ability may look good when matched with a poor opponent, but would seem poor against a superior player. Obviously, some control must be made of this factor and a plan evolved for rotating the players so that the opposition is equalized. Consideration of this factor must be made in all ratings involving group action, but it is easier to arrange in individual sports than in team sports.

If four teams are to be rated, the judges observing the players of two teams while the other two teams practice on an adjacent field or court, the following plan can be used:

404

Playing Period	Being Rated	Practicing
First	A vs. D	B vs. C
Second	B vs. C	A vs. D
Third	A vs. C	B vs. D
Fourth	B vs. D	A vs. C
Fifth	A vs. B	C vs. D
Sixth	C vs. D	A vs. B

The number of playing periods needed in order that each team play every other team can be determined by the formula:

$$\frac{n\ (n-1)}{2}$$

$$n = \text{number of teams}$$

Ten playing periods would be required if each of five teams were to play every other team. The length of the playing period should be determined in advance; in making the plans, ample time should be allowed for teams to change fields and get ready to play. Time should be allotted at the start of the class period for the warm-up time and all necessary routines such as attendance check and announcements.

5. The rating forms or score sheets should be prepared in advance.

Advance preparation of forms provides for accuracy and convenience in recording and directs the attention of the rater to the more important aspects of the abilities to be rated.

Unless names of all players are well-known to all of the raters, a means of identifying them must be worked out in advance. If the placement of players is to remain the same throughout the ratings, the identification can be made in relation to playing area, as for example, in table tennis, players can be identified by table number and side of net. Players may be identified by wearing numbered suits, pinnies, or temporary large number tags.

Various samples of rating forms are shown in the materials appearing later in the chapter. The sample rating sheet for softball batting form (page 422) is an example of an individual form (one form for each player being rated) while the sample chart for tennis ratings (page 425) is an example of a group form (all players rated on the same sheet). Regardless of the form used, the code for marking or the definition of categories should appear on each sheet.

405

6. The raters must be selected and trained.

In situations where only one teacher was available, students have been used with good results. Some of the desired qualities for raters have been mentioned previously. Being unbiased and approaching ratings with an objective frame of mind is more difficult for some persons than for others. All raters should realize the need for being impartial, for forgetting previous impressions, and for ignoring personality traits when they are rating skill in activities. They need to be aware of the common pitfalls of overrating and underrating. A rater finds it easy to overrate the student who is helpful in class, who gives evidence of thoroughly enjoying the game, who is obviously popular with his classmates, who is polite, who has a pleasing appearance, or who appears to have some handicap such as lack of height. The same rater must guard against underrating the student who lacks the above traits or who has an irritating or annoying personality.

Following a discussion of the need for objectivity, the skills to be rated should be demonstrated by persons exhibiting various degrees or levels of attainment while the raters have an opportunity to practice rating under direct supervision. Comparisons can then be made of the different scores, followed by more discussion and more practice, if the need for it is indicated. Any rater who differs radically from the others should be given additional guidance and practice. The rating scale may need to be revised after this preliminary tryout; the number of categories or the definitions of some of the categories may need to be changed. The raters should practice with a different group of players from those to be rated.

If the raters fail to use all of the categories, it may help to indicate the approximate number of cases that should fall within each category. If the group has approximately a normal distribution and the number of categories is five, then the raters can be told how many students would constitute the 7 per cent to receive "5," the 24 per cent to receive "4," the 38 per cent to receive "3," the 24 per cent to receive "2," and the 7 per cent to receive "1." This device has proved helpful in guaranteeing the use of all categories.

Some persons using ratings prefer that the raters use a scale with an even number of categories. This prevents a middle category in which players may be placed if the rater can't quite make up her mind; she is forced to decide above or below average for each. As a more extreme means of securing differentiation in the ratings, a scale with an odd number of categories has been used with the middle one not being assigned. For example, in a seven category scale, the middle one would not be used, the three on each end would be. This is rather hard on the raters as it is frequently difficult to say that players are that much different when in the approximately average range of ability.

A player-to-player comparison has been used[20] to aid the raters in gaining a picture of the various levels of skill. Players are observed who have been selected by the instructor as fitting the described categories.

If the ratings are to be used to help students, the students should see the ratings after they have been completed. Each student should be helped not only to interpret the final score but also to make use of the rating in planning his future development. If possible, all students should be given an opportunity to make a self-rating and to rate a few other students in order to obtain maximum value from the rating process.

Descriptions follow of ratings in several activities (diving, posture, dance, softball batting form, and tennis form). The scales presented should be considered as samples; they should not be used in their exact form but should be adapted to fit specific situations.

RATINGS IN DANCE

Ratings represent almost the only approach to measurement in dance, and are used for evaluating ability in the various skills and types of dance. A student may be rated on response to various rhythms; performance of fundamental movements (skip, leap, swinging movement); performance of traditional dance steps (waltz, schottische, polka, fox trot); or the execution of an entire dance (folk dance, square dance). It is easier to rate a small group, but to alleviate embarrassment, several persons may dance while only a few are being judged.

The rating scale on a dance skill might read as follows:

5 -- <u>excellent</u>: Dancer is accurate in rhythm and is skillful in steps involved; knows formations, positions, floor pattern, and sequence of steps; shows a feeling of assurance and of enjoyment, and expresses the spirit of the dance.

4 -- <u>good</u>: Dancer executes the steps correctly in form, rhythm, and sequence, but lacks something in ease, naturalness, or expression.

3 -- <u>average</u>: Dancer performs the dance correctly with only minor errors which he corrects himself or by cues from other dancers, and apparently knows it well enough to enjoy it.

2 -- <u>fair</u>: Dancer can execute the basic steps involved and can perform the dance reasonably well by the lead of partner or other dancers; rhythmically he makes an occasional error and is unable to readjust readily; he may or may not enjoy the dance, depending upon whether he is disturbed by his own errors.

1 -- <u>poor</u>: Dancer performs dance steps poorly; he is almost entirely dependent upon others for cues for sequence; rhythmically he is inaccurate and apparently unaware of it.

Subjective ratings of rhythmic accuracy and dance technique can be valuable and sufficiently economical of time to be feasible if carefully planned. The best type of accompaniment is a recording; this permits identical testing stimuli and time for each student. Since no one commercial recording carries enough variety of music or is so arranged as to be practical, a recording should be made for testing purposes. Music should be selected with care to give opportunity for the performance desired in testing. Experimentation will show the number of measures of each excerpt that is necessary for students to pick up the rhythm, start action, and for the judges to see the movement of each student. In most cases it will be sixteen to thirty-two measures. If you are testing for rhythmic ability rather than learned dances, the music should be different from that with which they have practiced, but of similar quality.

408

Simple but explicit instructions should be given by means of the recording. A brief time interval, at least seven seconds, should be left on the record between musical excerpts.

Items which have proved useful in determining general rhythmic ability as associated with dance experience are the following: fundamentals -- running, walking, skipping; derived dance steps -- fast and slow waltz, polka, and schottische.

Students should be judged in small groups of two to four without other students present. This facilitates the work of the judges, prevents too many opportunities for the students to pick up clues from others, but is adequate to prevent self-conscious, tense performance which might result if they were asked to perform alone. Judges need to be given instructions, not only in the skills they are observing and the scale they are to apply but on observation technique. Unless both feet are kept flat on the floor the free leg is likely to swing in time with the music and so set up a cue for the observant student. The same type of error may occur with a pencil as the judge unconsciously taps the rhythm while watching the performers and making the evaluation of the movement. The judge's attitude should be one of friendly interest but with no verbal comments on the music or the student's performance. If the student is uncertain whether to begin or to continue to listen, the prompting for action should be given off beat so that the student must show her own ability to correct her performance if aware of the error.

Students may rate each other, particularly in the dance forms in which they are dancing with partners. Figure 46 provides an illustration of a rating form to be used in social dance.

RATING OF DIVING

Diving is judged subjectively, whether in competitive meets, in trying for swimming and diving awards, or in regular class instruction and rating. This subjective rating is made reasonably accurate by setting up the important elements of the dive and a scale which determines the proper classification for a performance with various combinations of these elements. The following discussion illustrates

RATING SCALE	NAME OF PARTNER	RATING
5 Is among the best in the class	1. _____	_____
4 Is better than average	2. _____	_____
3 Is average	3. _____	_____
2 Is below average	4. _____	_____
1 Is among the poorest in the class	5. _____	_____
	6. _____	_____

LEADER: Is his lead timed well?
Does he hold you properly?
Does he have variety?

Do you trust the evaluation made of you by your classmates?_____

FOLLOWER: Does she keep her balance?
Are her feet in the way?
Can you move her at will?

Your name_____

Figure 46. Student evaluation of partners in social dance.

the general procedure for rating diving. In some cases of special dives additional points may be added.

Elements of good form in diving:

1. The position of readiness is erect and well-balanced.

2. The approach is legal (at least three steps in case of a running dive).

3. The approach is smooth, easy, and in good posture.

4. The hurdle and take off are timed with the board.

5. The body is straight, with effective arm and leg action at the take-off.

6. The height of the flight is sufficient to permit the necessary movements or position.

7. Body position during flight conforms to specifications of the dive (tuck, pike, layout, twist, or number of revolutions).

8. All body movements during flight are smooth, easy, and limited to those which are essential.

9. The entry into the water is with body straight, close to the line of the take-off.

For regular class use a scale of five points is recommended. It should be arranged as follows:

5 -- <u>Excellent</u>: Dive meets all specifications for good form with no apparent errors.

4 -- <u>Good</u>: Dive gives a general impression of good form but minor variations exist, the correction of which would improve the dive.

3 -- <u>Average</u>: Dive meets the basic specifications but lacks smoothness and ease or lacks control in some one respect which affects the dive as a whole. (For example, too much forward lean on the take off decreases height and moves the point of entry farther from the take off.)

2 -- <u>Fair</u>: Dive is inadequate and full of errors, but indicates some control or merit.

1 -- <u>Poor</u>: Dive is recognizable but fails to meet the standard in practically every element involved.

Competitive diving rules usually require that dives be judged on a ten-point scale. This scale differentiates within each of the five categories above and gives corresponding points as follows:

5 -- 8 1/2, 9, 9 1/2, or 10

4 -- 6 1/2, 7, 7 1/2, or 8

3 -- 5 or 6

2 -- 3 or 4

1 -- 1 or 2

However, in judging competitive diving the dive is automatically scored as zero if it is not the particular variation of the dive which is entered or announced. Competitive diving further varies the points awarded according to the difficulty of the dive. This has nothing to do with the judging. The dive is usually given the average of the ratings of three judges who work independently. To illustrate, a competitor receives an average rating of 8 from the three judges on each of three different dives. The rules specify that one dive is classed as 1 in difficulty, another is more difficult and classed as 2, the third is still more difficult and classed as 3. The number of points the competitor earns by these three dives is the judges' rating, 8, multiplied by the difficulty value 1, 2 or 3. Therefore, the dives win points 8, 16, and 24, respectively. This procedure is usually not followed in class work where students are likely to be working on dives similar in difficulty.

The judges will have the most complete view of the dive if one stands at the side approximately in line with the end of the board, a second on the opposite side a little beyond the end of the board, and the third back near the rear end of the board.

It is understood that diving judges in competitive swimming must be highly qualified, that the same judges rate all divers, and that they each follow the exact specifications and scale prescribed for the dives. Under these circumstances, the ratings by the various judges will be to a high degree consistent and will serve as a satisfactory means of evaluating the performance.

RATING OF GOLF

For beginning golfers the playing of games is too time-consuming a method of evaluating their degree of skill. Likewise they are erratic in their performance; therefore, it is better to watch several strokes under similar circumstances than to judge by playing a few holes.

In doing the ratings it is usually best to have some semblance of a game situation. For example, the drive should be from a teeing ground toward a green where the flag is in sight, or an approach shot should be made onto a green with bunker or sand trap, or up-hill or down-hill lie as one may wish to judge the players adjustment. If the regular course cannot be used for such purposes, then the following devices can be used. For the drives or longer iron shots, set up a flag at the other end of the practice area or use a small tree or post which may be visible as a point of aim. Some three to five players may be driving at the same time but all are aiming at the same flag. Therefore, if they are properly aligned for the shot they will assume their stance at slightly different angles rather than all parallel. For an approach shot, again a flag or post should be used for the point of aim. A rope may be stretched between players and flag, or a bench, chairs or other handy obstacle may be set up to create the situation of a bunker. With the shorter shots it will be even more apparent whether each player is aligned toward the flag or is imitating a neighboring player.

In judging putting, it is practically essential that a green be used for this purpose. Otherwise one cannot tell whether the player is able to adjust to the relatively short shots and fast action of the ball on a good green. The indoor use of a carpet is about the only substitute that is in any way adequate.

The ratings on the various strokes with the different clubs should be done independently and combined if a composite rating is needed. The minimum shots for a beginner is a drive with one of the wood clubs, a short approach shot with a five or seven iron, and a putt. For more advanced players one may add a distance shot with the midiron, and a chip shot with a seven or eight iron, or special lies which are designed to test the players adaptability and steadiness of play.

The elements to be decided on a golf stroke are the following:

1. Stance -- is it appropriate to the type of shot to be made?

2. Grip -- will it permit effective use of the hands and wrists and give proper direction to the ball?

3. Coordination of body and arms -- are the various parts used appropriately for the type of shot to be made?

4. Timing and rhythm -- is the action smooth, continuous and forceful?

5. Path of club head -- is it moving from behind, under and through the ball?

6. Fixation of the head -- is it kept in position serving as a pivotal point around which the action takes place?

Note from the above that the flight of the ball is not the important thing. The flight can be highly erratic and create real problems in trying to arrive at a decision. However, if the rater concentrates on what the player does, she can learn the potential merit of the shot much sooner.

RATING OF POSTURE

Evaluation and rating of posture has never been thoroughly satisfactory. One method used is to ask the person to stand in either a good or a habitual position and have one or more persons rate that position. This procedure is made slightly more objective by the use of plumb lines or vertical lines in the background and by indication of certain landmarks. A valid objection to this procedure is that one is moving much more of the time than standing, and that ability to stand well does not always insure ability to move well.

Another alternative for the same type of posture rating is to take a posture picture or silhouette and make a rating of the picture. This plan has certain advantages, namely: (1) the record is permanent and better comparison of similar figures and more uniformity of rating will be obtained, (2) the picture can be taken at successive times and direct comparisons made, (3) the picture provides the student with an opportunity to see how he looks. The disadvantages of the posture picture are: (1) the stationary pose, (2) the lack of an objective criterion or measure to be employed, and (3) the expense and impracticality in some cases.

The main objection to these two methods is partially overcome by asking the person to perform specific movements, and a rating is made of that performance. Ratings may be made in succession in a class or may be done informally by watching the person in the daily activities of walking, sitting, going up or down stairs or carrying books and other loads. The latter method has the advantage of seeing the person in natural activities and emphasizes the need for good posture at all times; it has the disadvantages of being time-consuming for the rater and difficult to see all students in a sufficient number of situations.

A solution to the majority of the drawbacks is suggested in the plan for class testing discussed below. This plan provides for the organization of the class and selection of activities in which posture is to be rated. Whether standing position only is to be rated, or simple and complex movements are to be included, the outline of elements in posture must be available for the rater.

Elements in good standing posture

1. Back and Head

a. The three curves of the spine should be moderate.

b. The head should appear well balanced on top of the spine with the line of vision and the chin horizontal.

c. The trunk should appear easily erect without being stiff.

d. The outline of the sternum and ribs should be more or less straight in front, with a long vertical axis, rather than sunken, collapsed, and with a concave axis.

e. The spine should appear straight when viewed from the rear.

2. Abdomen and Pelvis

a. The line of the abdomen should be straight or very mildly convex. An exception must be made in the case of a small child up to about 6 years of age; the abdominal line is usually convex.

b. The abdominal wall should be mildly firm; not relaxed and sagging, not stretched nor containing excessive fat deposits.

c. The lower line of the abdominal wall should be behind the lower end of the sternum.

d. The pelvis should be held squarely beneath the trunk, not with the lower back and abdominal wall projecting forward at a pronounced angle.*

---

*The pelvis may be considered as a box, even though it is distinctly irregular in shape. (See Figure 47.) That box should be kept squarely aligned as though resting on a level surface and not tipped up on edge. Tilting the pelvis invariably causes the buttocks to project backward more prominently and causes increased concavity of the lumbar spine. However, care must be taken to judge pelvic alignment by the position of the pelvis itself and not the spine and abdomen above it. The contour of buttocks is not an accurate means of judging alignment since there is great variation in the muscular development and the outline of the hip. Figure 47 illustrates the same girl with the pelvis in the correct and incorrect positions.

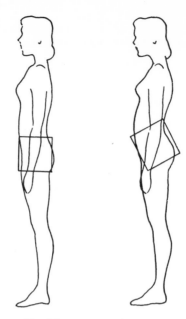

Figure 47. Illustration of pelvic alignment.

3. Shoulder Girdle and Arms

a. The shoulder blades should not deviate appreciably from the contour of the spine and thorax. When viewed from the side, as in a posture picture, they should not markedly exaggerate the convex line of the upper back.

b. The shoulder girdle should be carried far enough back so that the arms hang easily at the sides.

c. The shoulder girdle should be retracted without giving the appearance of stiffness and without thrusting the ribs and sternum forward unduly.

d. The shoulders should be low, not shrugged or tense.

4. Feet and Legs

a. The feet should be parallel.

b. The inner line of the feet should be straight from heel to toe rather than convex.

c. The heel cord in the rear should be straight, not turned in at ankle level.

d. The upper surface of the feet should appear straight. or convex, not sunken and spread just back of the toes.

e. The knees should be straight without rigidity, not flexed.

5. General Alignment and Weight Control

a. The following landmarks should be situated one above the other when the person is viewed from the side; lobe of the ear, point of the shoulder, hip joint, rear of the patella.

b. The line through these four points should be vertical and extend downward through the feet midway of the base (heel to ball of foot), bringing it a little in front of the ankle joint.

c. General appearance is of relaxation and control rather than rigidity.

When the rating is made during movement, the majority of the same points still apply and the following are added.

Walking:

1. The contact for each step should be made first with the heel.

2. The push-off at each step should come from the toes, principally the great toe. Failure to get a drive from the toe gives an appearance of rocking over the foot and then simply lifting it without noticeable ankle and foot action.

3. The leg action should be free, without tenseness and without conspicuous swaying of the hips in either a lateral or vertical direction.

4. The arms and shoulders should be relaxed but controlled within a relatively small arc.

5. The balance should be maintained over the base without stiffness or flexion at the hips or hyperextension in the lower back.

6. There should be no jar to the body at the moment of heel contact.

Running:

1. The contact should be made first with the ball of the foot.

2. The push-off from the toes should be strong.

3. Vertical bobbing should be minimized by knee action.

4. Excessive forward reach by the legs should be eliminated by bringing the leg downward and backward for the step rather than stretching it out for a long stride.

5. Body lean should be greater with increased speed, but should result from the body inclining forward as a whole, not from trunk or hip flexion.

Miscellaneous Activities:

1. The body, even when lifting or carrying weights, should always be in optimum position of balance, resulting in conservation of muscular effort and reduction of strain.

2. Excessive range of movements and superfluous movements are always undesirable.

3. Relaxation should be as complete as is possible for good body mechanics in the task involved.

A very practical and useful diagnostic test might be organized as in the chart on the following page, which would take care of a squad of ten girls, the number that can be scored conveniently at one time.

A three-point scale could be used; 3, good; 2, fair; 1, poor. Standing and walking posture would doubtless be included. Use of the feet in walking is more easily rated separately from the general rating of walking. The additional items to be included in the test would probably be chosen from activities such as running, stair climbing, sitting, stooping, reaching overhead, carrying a load, pushing, or pulling.

In preparing for the test ten chairs are placed in line, one in front of the other, with a little space between. There should be some open floor space beside them. Names of squad members are entered on the score sheet; when the test is given, students are seated in the same order as on the list and they remain in the same order throughout the test. Adequate rating can be given only if the students are dressed in swimming suits or dance leotards, and are barefooted.

| Name | Foot Mechanics | | | Standing | Walking | Running | Sitting | | Stairs | Total Score |
	Lack of pronation	Feet parallel	Heel to toe contact	Alignment and re-laxation	Alignment and ease	Alignment and coor-dination	Alignment seated	Rising and sitting	Up Down	

Figure 48. Sample of body mechanics test score sheet.

419

The examiner stands to one side of the row of chairs.*
See Figure 49.

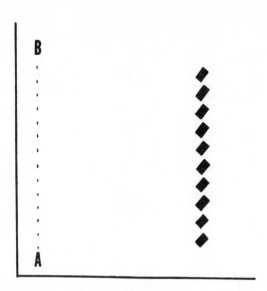

Figure 49. Arrangement of class for body mechanics test.

A - B = area in which examiner moves while observing each student.
The space between the dotted line and the chairs is for
students' use in performing activities for the rating.

Procedure in Rating Posture

1. Each student in turn walks a few steps toward the
examiner, turns and walks away again. This gives opportunity for judging the foot alignment and pronation.

2. Each student in turn walks a few steps forward (with
side to the examiner). This gives opportunity to examine
for heel contact, weight transfer, and toe drive.

3. Each student stands in line while the examiner moves
down the line rating standing posture.

4. The students walk two or three at a time back and
forth beside the line of chairs. During this the examiner
rates the walking posture. Having more than one walk at a
time helps to avoid self-consciousness and unnatural gait.

---

*The test and chart represent modifications of a test developed by the Staff
of the Department of Physical Education for Women, University of Iowa.

5. Students sit in the chair in a natural sitting position for rating. Each rises and then sits again to be judged on balance and movements.

6. Movement on stairs should be both up and down. The test may be given on real stairs, preferably wide ones for a better view and to accommodate two persons at a time; or it may be given on stairs constructed for this use in the gymnasium.

Other items in the test can be set up in a similar manner, preferably with some properties or a setting to make the movements seem natural.

Ratings of Riding

Riding is an activity that is judged according to form and no objective measure has been devised. The Riding Committee of DGWS has prepared standards and rating instructions for judges of intermediate and beginning levels of riding ability. Ratings are given to applicants on the basis of scores on a knowledge test and rating on riding ability and control of the horse.

Rating of Softball Batting Form

The construction of objective skill tests in batting has been made difficult by the lack of a mechanical device which would deliver the ball in the same manner to all batters. Some robots are now available but they are too expensive for the average school. The ability of the pitcher is known to affect the ability of the batter. Since batting comprises the major part of the offensive action in a game, it is important that it be measured in as nearly an objective manner as possible. Having the same pitcher deliver the ball to all batters being tested has been tried; usually the number of balls that must be delivered is too great for the pitcher's endurance. Batting is a skill in which the element of chance operates, and therefore a large number of pitches must be made to each batter. Batting tests are time consuming and take considerable space. The use of a rating form during actual playing times seems to be a useful substitute for more time-consuming tests. See Figure 50.

The rating forms can be mimeographed with one cumulative form for each player. For use in instruction, these

Directions to Raters:

Player: _____

1. This is a cumulative chart. Arrange papers according to batting order. Fill in date and your name on each.

Captain: _____

Class Hr., Days: _____

2. Rate the player each time at bat. Place tally mark in the space which precedes the best description in each of the six categories. Rate as good, fair, or poor.

Date	Rater
_____	_____
_____	_____
_____	_____
_____	_____

3. Indicate your observation of errors on the right-hand side of the page. Write in any additional errors and add comments at bottom of the page. Please be critical.

RATING   ANALYSIS OF ERRORS

1. Grip

1. _____ Hands too far apart.
_____ Good _____ Wrong hand on top.
_____ Fair _____ Hands too far from end of bat.
_____ Poor

2. Preliminary Stance

2. _____ Too near the plate. _____ Too far from plate.
_____ Good _____ Too far forward toward pitcher.
_____ Fair _____ Too far backward toward catcher.
_____ Poor _____ Rear foot closer to plate than forward foot.
      _____ Bat resting on shoulders.
      _____ Shoulders not horizontal

3. Stride or Footwork

3. _____ Fails to step forward.
_____ Good _____ Fails to transfer weight.
_____ Fair _____ Lifts back foot from ground.
_____ Poor

4. Pivot or Body Twist

4. _____ Fails to twist body.
_____ Good _____ Fails to "wind up."
_____ Fair _____ Has less than ninety degrees of pivot.
_____ Poor

5. Arm Movement or Swing

5. _____ Arms held too close to body.
_____ Good _____ Rear elbow elevated.
_____ Fair _____ Bat not held so that head is higher than wrists.
_____ Poor _____ Batter fails to use enough wrist action.
      _____ Wrists are not uncocked forcefully.

6. General

(Eyes on ball, judgment of pitches, general impression)

6. _____ Movements are jerky.
      _____ Tries too hard; "presses."
_____ Good _____ Fails to look at exact center of ball.
_____ Fair _____ Poor judgment of pitches.
_____ Poor _____ Appears to lack confidence.
      _____ Poor selection of bat.

Additional Comments:

Figure 50. Sample of rating sheet for softball batting form.

forms should be ready for use in the early part of the season. They can be handed to the player after each turn at bat. The same form can be used in a few tournament games at the end of the season with the tally marks being recorded in a different color on successive ratings so that improvement can be noted. The ratings will be fairly reliable if each batter is rated in three games at the start of the season and two or three at the end. Student leaders can be taught to do the rating; it is important that they understand the fundamentals of good batting form.

The rater should stand behind the plate umpire and slightly toward first base, in foul territory. The use of several raters is preferable.

The detailed form presented in Figure 50 does not include the result of each batter's turn at bat. That record can be obtained from the score book or seasonal batting averages, and should not unduly influence the rating of form. If time is limited, the checking of errors can be omitted. Their inclusion is mainly to facilitate using the blank as a teaching device.

Ratings in Tennis

Accuracy of placement of the serve and ability to keep a ball in play can be tested objectively. Form must be rated subjectively; this can be done while the players are playing regular games, using the scale below as a guide. It is presumed that the students are divided into two ability groupings for instructional purposes and that the rater will have had contact with the group over a period of time.

For Beginners:

5 -- Good: Player executes all strokes in good form; has learned rapidly; profits by all suggestions.

4 -- Above average: Player plays the game sufficiently well to avoid being conspicuous on the courts for poor playing; has shown definite improvement and is anxious to learn.

3 -- Average: Player shows fair but somewhat inconsistent form; knows the essentials of game procedure.

423

2 -- Near dub: Player can stroke in fair form but is careless; has improved some but has little knowledge of the game.

1 -- Dub: Player has poor strokes and has made little progress; makes little effort to improve.

For Intermediates:

5 -- Expert: Player has good form and plays consistently well; is fast, knows the game and uses excellent strategy and can play either singles or doubles reasonably well.

4 -- Near expert: Player usually has good form and plays strategic tennis; perhaps plays singles better than doubles, or vice versa; is somewhat erratic but knows the game.

3 -- Average: Player usually plays a good game and tries out new tactics; is analytical concerning own game; needs practice.

2 -- Fair: Player is weak on some techniques but has ability to improve; understands weaknesses and has knowledge of game procedure.

1 -- Poor: Player has not overcome poor habits of technique; has little knowledge of the game or analytical ability.

The above scale is general in nature and can be used by various raters even though they disagree about certain points on form. Another method of rating which is more specific but is limited to the ability to execute strokes is described later. Its chief advantage is that it is more economical of time than the first method, which measures the ability of the player to use his skills and knowledge in a game situation.

For rating the serve, the players are divided into small groups and supplied with several balls. They are lined up along the base lines, all on the same side of the net. For indoor rating, the base line is placed at official distance from the net or backboard, allowing about 5 to 10 feet between players. As many as ten can be judged at the same time. Names should be listed on the score sheet in the same order as the line-up of players. The number of repetitions necessary before the raters make final judgment will depend largely on the experience of the judges. The entire process, rating the three basic strokes, should not take more than sixty activity minutes for a class of forty players.

For the forehand and backhand, other players are needed for putting the ball in play. The class can be divided into three groups, with the throwers stationed near the net, the strokers behind the baseline on the opposite side of the net from the throwers, and the ball chasers behind the throwers. When the rating is conducted indoors, precautions must be taken to protect the ball throwers from possible injury. The ball chasers can be eliminated and the number of strokers may need to be reduced. The ball throwers can be asked to kneel on the floor behind the net. Since the ability of the ball throwers affects the ratings, a rotation plan should be used to insure that no one player be handicapped throughout the test by having to work with a poor thrower.

When the game is subdivided, with each stroke being rated separately, a chart similar to that in Figure 51 can be used. It can be extended to include the volley and lob. Rate on a three- or five-point scale.

Name	Fore-hand	Back-hand	Serve		

Figure 51. Sample chart for tennis ratings.

SELECTED REFERENCES

1. Ashton, Dudley: A Gross Motor Rhythm Test. Research Quarterly, 24: p. 253, October 1953.

2. Bennett, LaVerne Means: A Test of Diving for Use in Beginning Classes. Research Quarterly, 13: p. 109, March 1942.

3. Bovard, John F., Frederick W. Cozens, and Patricia E. Hagman: Tests and Measurements in Physical Education. Philadelphia, W. B. Saunders Company, 1949, Chapter 12.

4. Buhl, Olga Anderson, and Warren P. Morrill: The Measurement of Postures. Research Quarterly, 12: p. 581, October 1941.

5. Harrison, Clarke H.: The Application of Measurement to Health and Physical Education, New York, Prentice-Hall, Inc., 1945, Chapters 10 and 11.

6. Coppock, Doris E.: Relationship of Tightness of Pectoral Muscles to Round Shoulders in College Women. Research Quarterly, 29: p. 146, May 1958.

7. Crabtree, Helen Kitner: A Test for Riding. Journal of Health and Physical Education, 14: p. 419, October 1943.

8. Davies, Evelyn A.: Relationship between Selected Postural Divergencies and Motor Ability. Research Quarterly, 28: p. 1, March 1957.

9. Elbel, E. R., and Forrest C. Allen: Evaluating Team and Individual Performance in Basketball. Research Quarterly, 12: p. 538, October 1941.

10. Fox, Margaret G., and Olive G. Young: Placement of the Gravital Line in Anterio-Posterior Standing Posture. Research Quarterly, 25: p. 277, October 1954.

11. French, Esther: Player Performance Analysis. Sports Bulletin for Girls and Women, 2: p. 9, December 1947.

12. Frost, Loraine: Posture and Body Mechanics. University of Iowa Extension Bulletin, No. 479, 1940.

13. Hyde, Edith I.: An Achievement Scale in Archery. Research Quarterly, 8: p. 109, May 1937.

14. Judd, Mary: A Study of the Distribution of Weight on Foot Walking with and without Shoes. M. A. thesis, State University of Iowa, 1943.

15. Kelly, Ellen Davis: Teaching Posture and Body Mechanics. New York, A. S. Barnes & Company, 1949, Chapter 6.

16. McCloy, C. H., and Norma Young: Tests and Measurements in Health and Physical Education. New York, Century-Appleton-Crofts Company, 1954.

17. Mathews, Donald K.: Measurement in Physical Education. Philadelphia, W. B. Saunders Company, 1958, Chapter 10.

18. Poley, Margaret: Postural Characteristics of College Women as Related to Build. Ph. D. Dissertation, State University of Iowa, 1948.

19. Snell, Catherine: A Study in Rates of Learning in Selected Sports as Related to General Motor Ability. Ph. D. Dissertation, State University of Iowa, 1948.

20. Stalter, Evelyn, and Esther French: A Study of Skill Tests in Badminton for College Women. Research Quarterly, 20: p. 257, October 1949.

21. Storts, Saralea: A Study of the Relationship between Three Measures of Volley Ball for High School Girls. Master's thesis, Illinois State Normal University, 1948.

22. Trumbull, Katherine: Form Diagnosis. Journal of Health and Physical Education, 15: p. 149, March 1944.

23. Voltmer, E. F., and Ted Watts: A Rating Scale of Player Performance in Basketball. Journal of Health and Physical Education, 11: p. 91, February 1940.

24. Wickens, J. Stuart, and Oscar W. Kiphuth: Common Postural Defects of College Freshmen. Research Quarterly, 13: p. 102, March 1942.

Chapter XI

PERFORMANCE CHARTS AND ACHIEVEMENT PROGRESSIONS

Performance charts and achievement progressions are used to supplement information obtained through objective tests and subjective ratings. They are used not only to evaluate and analyze performance but to indicate the next steps to be taken and thus give direction to the efforts of the teacher and the student.

PERFORMANCE CHARTS

A performance chart is a form for recording specified incidents or occurrences. Upon it is recorded the number of times that a specified action occurred, sometimes the location of such action, and in some types of charts, as for example, in a chart of basketball shots, there is an indication as to the success of the action. In its pure form, the user of the performance chart is not required to make a judgment concerning the quality of the movement or action, as is the user of a rating form. The scorebook is an example of a player performance chart but it is quite limited in the information that it yields.

Player performance charts of one type or another are devised and used by many coaches to supplement the information that they glean from observation of the play generally, from game movies, and from scorebooks. They rely on such information to aid them in making decisions such as the specific skills each player needs to work on, which players need to be encouraged to be more aggressive, which players work together best, and which players are contributing the most to the team, perhaps defensively. Overuses of certain skills or tactics may be revealed. It would be impossible to list all of the possible uses.

Certainly players need to know if they are improving and there are many factors in an activity which are not measurable by the present existing objective tests. Players also need to know where further improvement is needed.

428

Attitudes toward working during practice periods improve when evidence is presented concerning certain deficiencies or weaknesses. For example, if a record is kept in basketball of the number of rebounds secured by each player and this information is made known to all of the players, players become more conscious of this phase of the game and more willing to listen to instructions. In soccer or speedball, a player performance chart can be used to give credit to the less spectacular but all important general position play. The player who roams, plays independently, or crowds his teammates can be detected. As with tests, player performance charts are devised with a particular purpose in mind and no one chart, like no one test, will serve all purposes. In field hockey, for example, if the teacher or coach has observed that the forwards are not rushing in to follow up their shots at goal and are permitting the goal keeper to have time to clear the ball out between them, someone can be assigned the task of counting the number of goals scored by each team in several games on follow-up tactics as compared to the number of goals scored from shots made from the edge of the striking circle. Such information is more convincing than any amount of talking on the part of the teacher-coach.

The physical education teacher's task in analyzing performance is complicated by the large number of players to be taught and the wide range in skill. While they are not called upon to make some of the decisions that coaches must make, such as selecting teams, starting line-ups, etc., they have other needs for the information revealed by performance charts. If such devices served no other purpose than to motivate students toward greater improvement, they would be worth using. Individualization of instruction is a problem for both coaches and teachers. The degree of success with which the teacher meets this problem is not shown in a win-loss record or by displays before the thousands of spectators but it is evidenced in the interest and enthusiasm for learning displayed by the students in classes and in intramurals.

Archery

One of the greatest aids toward diagnostic analysis in archery is the use of a score sheet which consists of a miniature replica of a target face rather than the usual score card. Each arrow is plotted by number on the scoring target in a corresponding position to which it hits or passes the side of the target. Three or four ends may be plotted on the same target. It is then possible to tell whether the player's shots are highly erratic or whether they tend to fall in a definite grouping with respect to the gold. This is similar to the score sheets used in rifle markmanship.

Badminton

A diagrammatic chart can be prepared similar to that suggested for archery, but a replica of the court. It can then be used in a number of ways, such as (1) recording the number of times that an opponent is forced to move into the rear one-third of the court, (2) the variety of strokes used and their placement, using a code such as "C" for clear, "D" for drive, etc., and (3) the pattern of the player's footwork between returns. The choice depends on the need observed by the teacher. If the player is consistently having to run several steps in order to reach a return, then an area would be drawn on both the floor and the diagram, representing "home plate" (the place to which players should return between strokes, usually near the center of the court). Then, a tally mark can be used to indicate where he has moved and from which position he must start.

Obviously, teachers cannot be involved in doing this chart work. This can be done by players awaiting their turns to play and some learning accrues to both the player being charted and the student doing the recording. Care should be taken to avoid overusing these devices.

Similar charts can be used in other activities such as tennis.

Basketball

The basketball chart presented in Figure 52 is representative of a type used when selected actions of an entire team are being recorded on one chart. Because the action is so fast in basketball and the ball changes hands frequently, it is necessary to have a judge and a recorder for each team. Players can learn to do these jobs, taking turns doing them when not playing. Coaches usually assign these tasks to team managers. The running chatter of the judge

430

GIRLS' BASKETBALL CHART

Team:_____ Judge:_____ Recorder:_____

Forwards

Number and Name	Shots		Rebounds	Passes		Errors			
	Field Goals	Free Throws	Secured	Inter-cepted	Excel-lent	Bad Pass	Fum-ble	Foul	Viola-tion

Guards

Number and Name	Shots			Rebounds	Passes		Errors			
	Rushed, Spoiled	Blocked, Prevented	Scored On	Secured	Inter-cepted	Excel-lent	Bad Pass	Fum-ble	Foul	Viola-tion

DIRECTIONS: Watch only one team. The chart is arranged in two sections, one for forwards and one for guards. The first column is concerned with scoring or defense against scoring. When a forward makes a field goal, record a "2" after her name in the column headed field goals; when she attempts a field goal and misses, record a "0" after her name in the Field Goals column. If she makes a free throw, record a "1" after her name in the Free Throws column; when she attempts a free throw and misses, record a "0" after her name in the Free Throws column. Under Passes -- Intercepted, credit the player who makes the interception if she is on the team you are charting by use of a tally mark. If one of your players makes a pass that is intercepted, record it as a Bad Pass or as a Fumble.

If a guard on the team whose performance you are charting rushes a forward who is in the act of shooting and by so doing causes the shot to be missed, credit it in the Rushed-Spoiled column. If she deflects the ball after it has been shot or intercepts the ball during its flight to the basket, record it in the Rushed-Spoiled column. If she prevents the forward from shooting by covering the ball, record it in the Blocked-Prevented column. When in doubt as to the classification, enter it with a question mark in both columns and connect the two question marks with a line.

Figure 52. Sample of basketball performance chart.

431

resembles that of a sports broadcaster, except that his calls are confined to one team. The running account may sound somewhat like this: "Credit 6 with an excellent pass -- 7 shot but missed -- 6 rebounded but fumbled. (Quiet, while the other team has possession of the ball.) -- 13 intercepted -- 7 violation (Quiet) -- 14 rebound -- 14 excellent pass -- 6 violation. (Quiet) -- 13 blocked shot -- opponents scored on 14." After some preliminary practice, the recorder will have little difficulty in locating spaces on the chart. There will be minor difficulties, such as those involved in making borderline decisions as to whether or not the fumble was the result of a poor pass or the fault of the receiver, and frequently, in determining upon whom the shot was scored.

At the same time that this type of record is being made, others can be in use, as for example, a record of shots attempted and shots made, with the location on the floor being recorded on a corresponding position on a court diagram.

Regardless of the difficulties encountered, the use of these and similar charts have proved to be of great value in analyzing performance and in improving player attitudes. The use made of the information affects the value. If the students see that it is for their benefit, much more learning results than otherwise.

Volleyball

Another use of an analysis chart is in comparing the number of times each skill is used. For example, in volleyball, are the skills that are most frequently used receiving the amount of practice time that they deserve? Are there valuable skills which are not being used in the game situation? A simple tabulation form can be used to provide such information. If it is desirable to learn which player is using what skills, then a form similar to that shown in Figure 52 will be helpful, with suitable headings.

If volleyball players are informed that they will be playing against teams which make frequent use of the spike, for example, then they will be interested in practicing a defense against it and in learning to execute various forms of the block. Unless opportunity is provided in a game situation to use skills, players see little point in learning them.

432

Skills and Tactics Common to Team Sports

A list follows of some of the skills and tactics which can be analyzed by means of charts, in addition to those already mentioned.

1. Ball Handling

Timing of release of passes.

Passing sufficiently hard (note: the ability to pass forcefully can be measured by means of an objective test but the ability to pass with just the right degree of forcefulness, varying with the demands of the situation, may have to be determined subjectively).

Directing passes into open spaces or directly to teammates, as opposed to haphazardly returning ball in same direction from which it came.

Fielding (trapping, catching) reliably.

Using variety of passes, as opposed to overuse or incorrect choice of passes.

2. General Position Play

Playing in proper territory, being where he belongs as opposed to wandering.

Aggressively taking advantage of openings.

Shifting from offense to defense quickly, and vice versa.

3. Offensive and Defensive Play

Advancing quickly to force passes, to set up interceptions for teammates, as opposed to waiting or backing up as opponents advance.

Backing up of teammates, both on offense and defense.

Fitting into the general pattern of defensive or offensive play.

Timing of defensive and offensive maneuvers.

SUMMARY

As stated previously, player performance charts are used to supplement the information obtainable from the use of objective tests and subjective ratings. They help give the teacher or coach a clearer picture of the use each player makes of his skills and knowledge. They tell the player what he is doing well and wherein he needs to make further improvements. They serve to give direction to the teacher's planning of instruction and to the students' use of free practice time. Thus, they are both teaching and evaluation devices.

ACHIEVEMENT PROGRESSIONS

Some activities build naturally from one skill or ability to another, as for example, swimming and tumbling. Classes in these activities can be organized in such a manner that students progress individually and are not required to keep repeating a skill until all in the class have mastered it. Items are listed on a chart and are checked off as they are accomplished; the student has only to consult the chart to know what progress he has made and upon wha he needs to work. Extensive and profitable use has been made of this type of organization in many of the individual activities, among them archery, bowling, golf, tennis, stunts and tumbling, and swimming.

The charts should be used in such a way that the student knows immediately the results of his effort. Opportunity should be given him to study the chart in order that he may determine what to do next and may set his own goals and rate of work. The goals should be individualized; they should be in relation to the student's ability and within the realm of possibility. The steps between skills, as represented by items on the chart, should be gradual, and some choice should be permitted. For example, see the sample achievement chart for stunts and tumbling, Figure 54. The stunt, Through the Stick, is relatively easy for those individuals having a high degree of flexibility and long arms, while others may find it physically impossible. Such students would be discouraged and their progress stalled if required to work on that stunt until they have passed it or the term ends.

A progression chart should reflect the teaching plans, the level of skill expected, and the steps by which the skills are to be achieved; it should, however, be used as a map with detours permitted and there should be flexibility in points of destination.

Charts of the type illustrated here can be used by class members rating each other if the standards which constitute success are well defined and well demonstrated. If more discrimination is desired, depending upon the use to be made of the records, leaders can be trained and performance in the various units can be rated in more categories. The examples from swimming, stunts and tumbling, bowling and archery which follow are included to illustrate the points already discussed. Like all of the other charts included in this chapter, they are intended only as illustrations.

Swimming

The achievement chart for elementary swimming is for a series of eighteen to twenty-four lessons for a beginning class which is being taught swimming as a safety and recreational skill. Some members of the class may not finish the last three or four items. Items of that difficulty are essential if those who learn more rapidly are to be stimulated to real effort. If members of the class start with some ability, then obviously each should accomplish the items which are starred, since these represent merely progressive steps into something else.

The standards for passing each item might be similar to those listed below the chart and are simple enough to be judged by class members. This is a fairly detailed chart; if time is limited and the class is progressing rapidly, some of the optional items might be omitted so that class members can be encouraged to start on those items usually included on a chart for intermediate swimmers. See Figure 53.

Stunts and Tumbling

The tumbling stunts are divided into groups according to the principal skills involved. The progression chart includes stunts of increasing difficulty within each group. The various groups are usually carried along simultaneously, with some students making more rapid progress in one group

Class: / Squad: / Names:	*Jelly-fish float	Face float and recovery	Back float and recovery	Rhythmic breathing	Elem. back stroke -- 60 ft.	*Flutter kick -- 20 ft.	Seal dive from side	Surface dive -- shallow water	*Kneeling dive from side	*Side stroke -- 20 ft.	Vertical float -- deep water	Treading water -- 30 seconds	*Elementary crawl -- 20 ft.	Five-minute swim	Standing dive -- deep water	Side Stroke -- 60 ft.	Deep water shuttle	Treading -- 2 minutes	Crawl -- 60 ft.	Fifteen minute swim		

*Optional items.

Jelly-fish float. Swimmer assumes tuck position and holds while partner counts 10, recovers standing position without help.

Face float. Swimmer assumes straight prone position and holds while partner counts 20, recovers standing position without help.

Rhythmic breathing. Swimmer stands with trunk bent forward, face in water, arms moving for crawl stroke (or windmill fashion). Exhales under water, turns head and breathes in; turns face under water and exhales. Repeats rhythmically at least 10 times. (This should be taught with the same timing between arm action and breathing as used later in the crawl.)

Elementary back stroke. Swimmer continues regular stroke full length of pool. (Swimmers are not sent full length of the pool until the instructor passes the stroke for deep water swimming.)

Flutter kick. Swimmer assumes face float with push-off from the side, uses rhythmical and symmetrical flutter kick until he reaches the other side.

Five-minute swim. Swimmer uses any stroke. The start is in the water and swimming or floating continues without touching sides or bottom of pool. One timer can time all, starting and stopping the interval with a whistle.

Deep water shuttle. Swimmer jumps in feet first, levels off and swims any stroke 15 feet, stands, submerges until the head is entirely under water, comes up and levels off, swims back 15 feet with another stroke, does a swimming turn (turns while stroking in horizontal position), swims by means of a third stroke 15 feet, stands and treads water for at least three kicks, levels off and swims back to starting position. (Note that this requires the use of all three strokes learned but they may be used in any order.)

Fifteen-minute swim. Swimmer dives in head first, swims or treads continuously for the first 7 1/2 minutes; floats, swims, or treads for the last 7 1/2 minutes.

Figure 53. Sample achievement chart for elementary swimming.

of stunts than in others. This chart is simply illustrative
of method and is not meant to indicate the exact events to
be taught. See Figure 54.

Bowling

The bowling score in itself is indicative of relative
ability of players. However, it does not analyze strong
and weak points in one's game. To be of greatest value in
teaching, a record should be kept of some of the setups
which occur frequently in the game. The number to be included in the chart will depend upon the time allotment.

When practice is exclusively on regular games, the only
setup which students face with any consistency is the full
ten-pin arrangement. The percentage of strikes or spares
can be kept on total frames rolled. A chart of the type included here gives the score on special setups for the second
ball or spare attempt.

An individual score sheet with a continuous record is
preferable. That is the form indicated here. This score
sheet makes an excellent teaching device and gives a diagnostic record for both teacher and student. See Figure 55.

Archery

Archery is a self-testing activity and is scored so
that every arrow shot is rated for its relative accuracy.
Scoring permits a partial analysis of performance, that is,
whether the shooting is consistent or variable, whether one
distance is more difficult than a shorter or longer one.
The officially recognized rounds provide exactly the same
kind of a score as that obtained from tests in other sports.
The scores on a given round may be used as a measure of performance, or scores on the same round may be compared at
intervals to measure improvement. For the college student
Hyde[5] presents standards of performance on the first and
last Columbia Rounds, and therefore suggests the amount of
improvement which may be expected from students.

Snell,[7] while studying learning of high and low motor
ability groups, found a close relationship between learning
rate in archery and level of motor ability. She suggests
reducing the number of lengths at which shooting is done
during any one season of instruction for all players; this

Flexibility	Balance	Agility	Strength	Coordination
Wicket walk	Dwarf walk	Bear dance	Walrus walk	Knee stand to standing
Crab walk	Head stand	Top	Single squat	Heel jump
Worm walk	Hand stand	Forward roll	Horse and rider	Fish flop
Through the stick	Forearm stand	Backward roll	Dead man's lift	Cart wheel
Jack knife	Chest balance	Wind the clock	Elbow dip	Hand spring
Stork stand	Standing mount	Jump the stick		Snap up

Class:

Squad:

Names:

Figure 54. Sample achievement chart for stunts and tumbling.

438

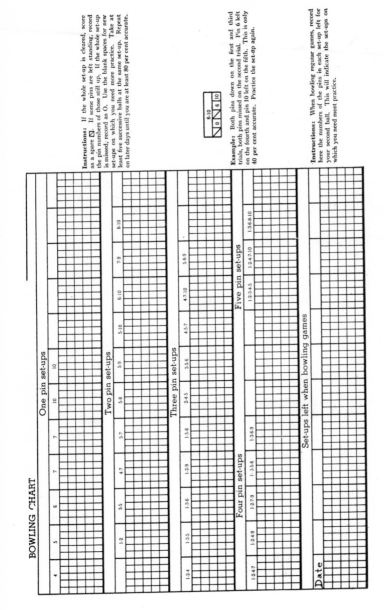

Figure 55. Sample achievement chart for bowling practice.

439

is especially important for those toward the low end of the motor ability range. Thus progress may be obtained at the one or two lengths practiced, otherwise improvement may not be shown by many students.

SUMMARY

Achievement progressions are usually planned after the level of skill has been determined, unless students are classified before being admitted to class. The teacher and student should cooperatively determine the objectives. Usually only a portion of the class time is devoted to the chart items since most teachers will want to include some group experiences, perhaps of a recreational nature, as simple water games in swimming and some couple or group activities in stunts and tumbling. It is not intended that such charts should serve as the only basis for grades but they could be used as a partial basis. The main purpose of achievement progression charts is to provide a means for individuals to progress without having to wait for the slowest student in the class.

SELECTED REFERENCES

1. Alexander, John: A Motivating Individual Record. Journal of Health and Physical Education, 10: 582, 1939.

2. Cureton, Thomas K.: How to Teach Swimming and Diving. New York, Association Press, 1934.

3. Elbel, E. R., and Allen, Forrest C.: Evaluating Team and Individual Performance in Basketball. Research Quarterly, 12: 538, 1941.

4. French, Esther: Player Performance Analysis. Sports Bulletin for Girls and Women, 2: 0, 1947.

5. Hyde, Edith I.: An Achievement Scale in Archery. Research Quarterly, 8: 109, 1937.

6. Rehling, Conrad H.: Analysis of Techniques of the Golf Drive. Research Quarterly, 26: 80-81, 1955.

7. Snell, Catherine: A Study of Rates of Learning in Selected Sports as Related to General Motor Ability. Unpublished Ph. D. dissertation, State University of Iowa, 1948.

8. Streit, W. R.: A Stunt Meet for Elementary School Boys, Journal of Health and Physical Education, 10: 584, 1939.

Chapter XII

ATTITUDE SCALES

Physical education teachers are concerned with the development of positive mental attitudes and they accept this as one of their responsibilities. This concern is revealed in many ways, including the time given to orientation, the various methods used to motivate students to put forth their best efforts, and the use made of pupil-teacher cooperative planning. Usually the list of objectives includes a statement concerning the development of desirable attitudes. If we are to measure the extent to which all of the objectives of the program are being achieved, then obviously the measurement of attitudes should be a part of the over-all measurement plan.

For many years, attitudes have been classified with the so-called intangibles and quite generally their measurement has been ignored. It is known that attitudes are important and that they play a major role in determining the amount of learning that takes place.

Progress has been made in measuring what an individual is able to do. While the measures are not perfect, we at least rely upon some of them to tell us the mental abilities and general motor abilities of our students. Measures are used to indicate what the individual can do in skills, how much knowledge he has acquired, and his present level of physical fitness. There is no doubt about the fact that attitudes are difficult to measure and that it may be easier to measure what a person can do than it is to measure what he wants to do. Actually, what a person wants to do and what he can do are interrelated but the causal relationship is not clear. Certainly what a student wants to do will affect the amount of learning that takes place. The use he makes of the activities included in the school program will surely be largely determined by his attitudes toward these activities and by the amount of satisfaction that he derived from participation.

One of the criticisms of the usual type of attitude questionnaires or inventories is that they are not valid measures of true attitudes; that there is a difference between written responses to printed statements and the attitudes generally held. The same thing can be said of health inventories which use the same method. Nevertheless, there are advantages to be gained from the use of such instruments if care is taken in interpreting them. A physician makes use of various measures in making a diagnosis but he does not rely solely upon the data obtained. A farmer makes use of soil analysis but supplements this information with his knowledge of other factors, such as the length of the growing season and the average amount of rainfall, in determining what he will plant. The teacher using an attitude measuring device must use the results for what they are, a summary of the opinions of the persons in the sample. It would seem that it is the abuse rather than the use that should be eliminated. One of the worst abuses is drawing conclusions from a meager and inadequate sample.

In this chapter, a variety of uses for attitude measures will be discussed and illustrated by references to studies. The procedures recommended for use in preparing attitude measuring instruments will be outlined and suggestions will be made concerning their administration.

VARIETY OF USES

The attitudes expressed by students and by alumni are frequently used as a partial basis for curriculum and course revision. While few teachers would want to limit their programs to activities that the students say they like, for example, it is helpful to have such information. Good programs are built on the basis of meeting student needs and students are not always in the best position to judge needs. However, there are times when a choice is possible and student preferences might well be heeded.

Student opinion concerning the relative value to them of certain experiences provided within a course should be solicited. In addition to furnishing information that will be helpful to the teacher in improving the course, solicitation of student opinion may lead to better attitudes on the part of the students. If they are asked to list good as well as poor points, they may discover there were many good things included in the course or unit. Most important

of all, they will be learning to evaluate in terms of the
objectives and to do critical thinking.

Attitude tests can be used to identify the factors
least liked by students. If teachers and administrators can
discover what it is that tends to discourage the desire to
participate, they will have information of value to them in
curriculum revision. The term curriculum is being used in
a broad sense, including conduct as well as content of the
program. Several studies have been conducted to ascertain
attitudes of students concerning the required program in
colleges[4,8,14,18] and in high schools[10,22]. Some of the
items ranking high on the dislike list are beyond the control or jurisdiction of the physical education department,
as for example, no academic credit being given[4,18]. Others,
however, are within the control of the department and could
be remedied if it seemed advisable to change procedures.
For example, having to wear an all-white uniform[18] or having to wear a specified style (tunic instead of shorts and
blouse)[14], and the scheduling problems caused by double
periods being reserved for physical education[4,18] Still
other objections which could be remedied within the con-
fines of the department are the basis for grades (objection
was to being graded on ability alone with no consideration
being given to effort), the lack of objectivity in grading,
and students being placed in classes without regard to
skill abilities and previous experience in an activity.

The relationship of attitude to success in physical
education activities was studied by Carr[10] and by Plummer[32],
and the relationship between personality adjustment and
achievement in physical education activities was studied by
Sperling[35]. These studies represent another use of attitude surveys. The findings of such studies reinforce the
quite generally held belief that the students who do well
in physical education are the ones whose attitudes are good
but they do not answer the question as to whether their attitudes are favorable because they are successful in their
achievements or the success results from the good attitudes. Very few attempts have been made to study the
causal relationships. Hunter[18], however, used a free response type of questionnaire to supplement the attitude inventory, and concluded that learning skills early and having interested parents who included their children in their
sports and recreational activities were factors that pro-
moted a lasting favorable attitude toward these activities.

443

Another use of attitude surveys is to provide information concerning the attitudes of an entire group, rather than the attitudes of a vociferous or troublemaking few. Such information could be helpful in giving a principal, an attendance officer, or a school nurse a better picture of typical attitudes. Some of these persons and some parents hear more complaints than favorable reactions, and may judge on too limited a sample. Kelly[21] has commented upon this use and states that it is particularly encouraging in the field of physical education because our satisfied though silent pupils are so much more numerous than is often supposed.

Measurement of attitudes on health practices has been more frequent than in physical education. Mayshark[26] presents a critical summary of those efforts.

The studies cited previously are all measures of student attitude toward the general program and the situation in which physical education instruction is carried out. Attitude is sometimes determined for a selected group or relative to a particular thing. The measuring device on these studies also varies.

McGee[28] studied attitudes towards intensive competition for high school girls. Her subjects were teachers, administrators and parents. They were given a scale composed of 70 items to each of which they made a reaction on a five-point scale ranging from strongly disagree to strongly agree. The scale may be found in her report in the Research Quarterly. Scott[33] devised a scale relative to competition at the elementary level.

Bowman[6] used a similar scale in which parents of 5th grade children were asked to state how they felt about activity for their 5th grade son or daughter. The 43 items of the original inventory appear in Bowman's report. Also the 20 most discriminating items are presented as a measure of the parents favorable or unfavorable attitude toward the child's participation.

Jaeger[20] worked only with freshmen and senior majors in physical education. She studied their attitudes toward leadership experiences, and particularly those of the physical education teacher. She used the free response type of projective test. Instructions for the test were:

"The purpose of this test is to find out how you go about understanding various people and situations that arise in physical education. You have been given a set of pictures. Look at each picture and imagine that you are the teacher appearing in each one. Then write a story about the teacher and the students pictured on the cards. Use your imagination as much as you want to. It may help you if you:

1. think of what is happening in the situation;

2. how the teacher feels about what is happening;

3. how the story ends.

Be brief. Each story should take no more than one page. Plan to spend about five to seven minutes per story."

The pictures were black and white sketches of gymnasium situations, dressing room scenes, playgrounds, committee work, home visitation and other common experiences of the teacher. Figure 56 shows two pictures from her series.

Sheffield[34] studied the group of swimmers previously identified as fear cases in swimming. She too used sketches as cues for subject response but had multiple choice options for their response. These had been prepared from free responses given previously by a similar fear group. This form is slower to prepare, faster to score, but perhaps less revealing at least for those who have been trained for interpretation of the free response. Examples of her pictures appear in Figure 57.

Safety is another area in which attitude is considered a fundamental basis for action. Myers[31] has presented a safety attitude scale for 7th grade students.

A more recent approach toward attitudes is not too different in meaning from the projective tests just discussed. This is the TST or Twenty Statements Test on attitudes toward self. This was first developed by Kuhn and McPortland[23] and has been used in several physical education situations. Bowman[6] used it with 5th grade children as a means of finding out how the children thought of themselves with respect to active games and sports. Isenberger[19] used it with physical education major students to determine their orientation to the profession.

The instructions for this test simply ask the student to write as quickly as possible twenty answers to the question, "Who am I." The scoring is usually on two things, i.e., social anchorage and salience. Social anchorage is

445

Figure 56. Sample of Jaeger's sketches for professional attitudes.

Figure 57. Sample of Sheffield's sketches for fear reaction.

the total responses of the twenty which "refer to groups and classes whose limits and conditions of membership are matters of common knowledge." For example: I am a girl, I am a pupil at Lincoln School. Salience is the number of items referring to the particular area in question. For example: I am a tennis player, I like sports. These would have salience value in either of the studies cited above. Salience is sometimes defined as the rank of the first item listed which is salient.

Success with either the projective test or the TST is dependent upon a spontaneous response of the student, avoidance of cues on what might be answered, assurance that there is no correct answer expected of all but rather only the idea which he has himself as he starts to write. It is also important that the student not be briefed ahead of time concerning the purpose and significance of the test as this is a form of cue.

Sociometric procedures may also be considered as a form of attitude measurement within a given group. The test is designed to locate those who are at the two ends of the scale on acquaintanceship, recognition of merit and leadership. The questions asked are geared to the interests of the groups. Examples for successive age levels might be: Name three you would like to invite if you were having a birthday party. Name five you would like to have on your team. Name five you would like to go with on a camping trip. Name six you would like to have at your dining table in the dormitory. Name five you would like to have on a WRA committee you are working on. A corresponding question is usually asked also; for example, Who would you not like to ....?

The analysis of such a response is made by drawing a sociogram. This permits identification of leaders, those most accepted within their groups, those who are social isolates, and cliques which exist within the group. Breck's[7] study is an example of this type of test applied in physical education and Hale[17] proposes a method of analysis.

Any of the attitude scales or tests may be repeated later and thus determine changes in outlook or status of individuals or a group. It is possible, however, that successive administrations do not secure as spontaneous and revelatory response as the initial one.

RECOMMENDED PROCEDURES

There are relatively few standardized attitude scales or inventories available in published form. For many of the purposes and for most situations, it is necessary to construct one's own forms. In doing this, there are usually several decisions to make. For example, are you concerned with the factors which have caused these attitudes? If so, you may need to request some supplementary information such as "Do your parents participate in sports activities?"

"What opportunities do you have to participate outside and away from the school environment?" "What experiences have you had that have affected your present attitudes?" Another decision involves the type of statement and the provision for the reply. In some instances, it is preferable to use open end (free responses) questions while in others, to make statements to which the respondents react by selecting a category. The following categories are commonly used: "Agree, undecided, disagree"; "Yes, mixed opinion, no"; "Does not apply, I do not recall"; and "I am very sure, I think so, I don't know, I doubt it, I disagree strongly."

It is essential to secure the cooperation of the respondents and to state the question or statement in such a way that no particular response is elicited. Students need to be assured that their responses will in no way affect their grades. See Chapter XIII, p. 463. McCue's study[27] provides valuable suggestions for persons constructing attitude statements.

Suitability of vocabulary should be considered. Kneer[22] used the Forbes-Cottle readability formula to determine the grade level reading ability of Wear's inventory and found it to be of 12th grade level. In adapting his inventory for use with high school girls (grades 9 to 12), she modified some of the wording and added statements pertinent to girls' physical education.

Plummer[32] likewise utilized this technique in her scale for college women. Her scale is similar to the Wear scale but has the distinct advantage of being much shorter.

PLUMMER'S ATTITUDE SCALE FOR WOMEN'S PHYSICAL EDUCATION

DIRECTIONS: This scale is not designed to measure your ability, only your attitudes in order that we may so construct your physical education program to better serve you. It will in no way affect your grade. Please express your honest opinions. Choose one of the code letters to fit your reaction to the statement, and indicate your choice in the proper column on the answer sheet.

STRONGLY AGREE	AGREE	UNDECIDED	DISAGREE	STRONGLY DISAGREE
a	b	c	d	e

1. Physical education is enjoyable and worthwhile.

2. Physical education should not be required.

3. There are many things I prefer to physical education.

4. My time could be spent more profitably than participating in physical education.

5. Physical education is a chore.

6. I enjoy wearing a gym suit.

7. Physical education helps me develop poise.

8. Physical education has helped me develop new and broader interests.

9. Some physical education activities are enjoyable, but not the type I am required to take.

10. Physical education activities give me a feeling of satisfaction.

11. Gym suits, tennis rackets, and similar equipment are too expensive for what I get out of physical education.

12. The gym and locker rooms are uncomfortable and unattractive.

13. When I take physical education I feel better.

14. Physical education has helped my personal appearance.

15. Physical education is of much more value to the curriculum than many other subjects.

16. I intend to participate in sports after college.

17. I would take more physical education if more credit were given for it.

18. Physical education makes an excellent contribution to any student.

19. Street clothes are more comfortable than gym suits.

20. Everyone may profit from physical education.

SUMMARY

To understand a student group, it is necessary to supplement knowledge of what they are <u>able</u> to do with the knowledge of what they <u>want</u>, since what they want plays such a major role in determining what they will do. The development of desirable attitudes is one of the objectives of physical education and it is distinctly worthwhile to measure attitudes if one wishes to know the extent to which this objective is being met. Information concerning attitudes toward a good program can be used to defend that program and to prevent it from being condemned on the basis of the criticism of a small group of dissatisfied persons. Care always needs to be taken in interpreting data. Improvement in techniques and better instruments will result in increased validity.

SELECTED REFERENCES

1. Baker, Mary C.: Factors which May Influence the Participation in Physical Education of Girls and Women 15 to 25 Years of Age. <u>Research Quarterly</u>, 11: p. 126, 1940.

2. Bateman, R. M., and H. H. Remmers: The Relationship of Pupil Attitudes Toward Social Topics before and after Studying the Subjects, <u>Studies in Higher Education</u>. Purdue University, 31, 1936.

3. Bean, C. H.: Psychology of Adherence to the Old or Acceptance of the New. <u>Journal of Social Psychology</u>, 6, August 1933.

4. Bell, Margaret, Etta Walters, and Staff: Attitudes of Women at the University of Michigan toward Physical Education. <u>Research Quarterly</u>, 24: p. 379, 1953.

5. Blanchard, Everard S.: A Comparative Analysis of Secondary Boys' and Girls' Character and Personality Traits in Physical Education Classes. <u>Research Quarterly</u>, 17: p. 33, 1945.

6. Bowman, Mary O.: The Relationship between Student and Parent Attitudes and Skills of Fifth Grade Children. Ph. D. dissertation, State University of Iowa, 1958.

7. Breck, Sabina June: A Sociometric Measurement of Status in Physical Education Classes. <u>Research Quarterly</u>, 21: p. 75, 1950.

8. Broer, Marion B., and Dolly A. J. Holland: Physical Education Interests and Needs of University of Washington Women in Service Classes. Research Quarterly, 25: p. 387, 1954.

9. Bullock, Marguerite and Florence D. Alden: Some of the Factors Determining the Attitude of Freshman Women at the University of Oregon toward Required Physical Education. Research Quarterly, 4: p. 60, 1933.

10. Carr, Martha G.: Relation between Success in Physical Education and Selected Attitudes Expressed by High School Freshmen Girls. Research Quarterly, 15: p. 176, 1945.

11. Collins, Patricia J.: The Development of a Scoring Key on the Strong Vocational Interest Inventory for Women Teachers in Physical Education. Research Quarterly, 13: p. 156, 1942.

12. Cowell, Charles C.: An Abstract of a Study of Differentials in Junior High School Boys Based on the Observation of Physical Education Activities. Research Quarterly, 6: p. 129, 1935.

13. Cowell, Charles C.: Validating an Index of Social Adjustment for High School Use. Research Quarterly, 29: p. 7, 1958.

14. Dunlap, Marjorie L.: Attitudes of Prospective Women Teachers toward Required Physical Education. Unpublished Master's Thesis, Illinois State Normal University, 1957.

15. Ferguson, Leonard W.: The Requirements of Adequate Attitude Goals. Psychological Bulletin, 36: p. 665, 1939.

16. Foehrenbach, Lenore M.: Why Girls Choose After-School Sports. Journal of Health, Physical Education and Recreation, 24: p. 34, 1953.

17. Hale, Patricia Whitaker: Proposed Method of Analyzing Sociometric Data. Research Quarterly, 27: p. 152, 1956.

18. Hunter, Sammie R.: Attitudes of Women Students Toward College Physical Education. Doctoral Study, University of Florida, 1956, Microcard, PSY 61.*

*Microcards listed are available from University of Oregon, Eugene. Card identity numbers are given.

19. Isenberger, Wilma: Self Attitudes of Women Physical Education Majors as Related to Measures of Interest and Success. Research Quarterly, 30: p. 167, 1959.

20. Jaeger, Eloise: An Investigation of a Projective Test in Determining Attitudes of Prospective Teachers of Physical Education. Ph. D. Dissertation, State University of Iowa, 1952.

21. Kelly, Ellen: Attitudes Are Important. The Physical Educator, October 1955.

22. Kneer, Marian: The Adaptation of Wear's Physical Education Attitude Inventory for Use with High School Girls. Master's thesis, Illinois State Normal University, 1956, Microcard PSY 64.

23. Kuhn, Manford H., and Thomas McPartland: An Empirical Investigation of Self Attitudes. American Sociological Review, 19: p. 68, 1954.

24. Likert, Rensis: A Technique for the Measurement of Attitudes. Archives of Psychology, 22: p. 5, 1939.

25. Longstreet, R. J.: An Experiment with the Thurston Attitude Scale. School Review, 43: 1935.

26. Mayshark, Cyrus: Critical Analysis of Attitude Measurement in Health Education, 1927-1957. Research Quarterly, 29: p. 309, 1958.

27. McCue, Betty F.: Constructing an Instrument for Evaluating Attitudes toward Intensive Competition in Team Games. Research Quarterly, 24: p. 205, 1953.

28. McGee, Rosemary: Comparison of Attitudes toward Intensive Competition for High School Girls. Research Quarterly, 27: p. 60, 1956.

29. McNemar, Quinn: Opinion Attitude Methodology. Psychological Bulletin, 63: p. 289, 1946.

30. Moore, Beverly Y.: The Attitude of College Women toward Physical Activity as a Means of Recreation. Research Quarterly, 12: p. 720, 1941.

31. Myers, Frank H.: A Safety Attitude Scale for Seventh Grade. Research Quarterly, 29: p. 320, 1958.

32. Plummer, Tomi: Factors Influencing the Attitudes and Interests of College Women in Physical Education. Ph. D. Dissertation, State University of Iowa, 1952, Microcard PE 128.

33. Scott, Phebe M.: Comparative Study of Attitudes toward Athletic Competition in the Elementary Schools. Ph. D. Dissertation, State University of Iowa, 1952, Microcard PE 131.

34. Sheffield, Dorothy L.: Construction of a Projective Test for Analyzing Individual Swimming Fears. M. A. thesis, State University of Iowa, 1955.

35. Sperling, Abraham P.: The Relationship between Personality Adjustment and Achievement in Physical Education Activities. Doctoral Study, New York University, 1941, Microcard PE 32.

36. Thorndyke, Robert L.: Personnel Selection. New York, John Wiley and Sons, Inc., p. 345-346, 1949.

37. Thurston, L. L.: Theory of Attitude Measurement. Psychological Review, 36: p. 222, 1929.

38. Thurston, L. L., and E. Chave: The Measurement of Attitudes. Chicago, The University of Chicago Press, 1929.

39. Toogood, Ruth: A Survey of Recreational Interests and Pursuits of College Women. Research Quarterly, 10: p. 90, 1939.

40. Wang, Charles K.: Suggested Criteria for Writing Attitude Statements. Journal of Social Psychology, 3, 1932.

41. Wear, Carlos L.: The Evaluation of Attitudes toward Physical Education as an Activity Course. Research Quarterly, 22: p. 114, 1951.

42. Wear, Carlos L.: The Construction of Equivalent Forms of an Attitude Scale. Research Quarterly, 26: p. 113, 1955, and Microcard, PE 59.

Chapter XIII

EVALUATION OF TOTAL PROGRAM

The measurement of student accomplishment and learnings is in a sense a measure of the effectiveness of an instructor, of a program, and perhaps even of a total department. Every test given should be studied by the instructor from the standpoint of "Where have I done my best teaching?" "Where have I failed?" "How can I improve?"

However, such self-analysis is not sufficient. Every department and every school should from time to time consider very carefully (1) its aims, objectives, and philosophy, (2) its means of carrying out these purposes, i.e., its staff, its curriculum, its facilities and equipment, (3) its results, i.e., student learnings; student's use of information and abilities; alumnae success, interests and activities. For the first two of these points, tools have been developed.

Appraisals of this type need to be done on a cooperative basis. Careful, objective discussion of factual evidence is essential. It needs to be carried on over a period of time because frequently points will arise on which facts must be obtained. As a staff works along on the routine tasks of teaching and conducting a program, general impressions are apt to be formed and observation of detail become modified by these general impressions. Factual data are an essential part of determining whether these general impressions are accurate, and essential to making decisions relative to the departmental operations. A second essential is a set of criteria which are applied to the issue in question. These have been developed recently for several phases of the program or for comprehensive evaluation of the total.

National Evaluation Schedules

A 1954 conference, sponsored jointly by the American Association for Health, Physical Education and Recreation, the College Physical Education Association, and the National Association for Physical Education of College Women, produced an appraisal form. This is the set of criteria which are to be applied locally in evaluating the instructional college program. Samples from this schedule follow. The entire form appears in the Washington Conference Report and may be purchased from the American Association for Health, Physical Education and Recreation.[6]

EXCERPTS FROM THE CRITERIA FOR APPRAISAL OF INSTRUCTIONAL PROGRAMS OF PHYSICAL EDUCATION IN COLLEGES AND UNIVERSITIES [6]

The checklist.....is designed as a convenient tool for program appraisal to be used by administrative and faculty personnel in departments of physical education in appropriate institutions of higher education. In using this instrument, each item should be discussed fully and consensus reached concerning the extent to which the principle is operative within the departmental structure of policies and practices. No objective standards have been established for determining an over-all categorical rating for any department. The values accruing from the use of the checklist come from the subjective evaluation of departmental policies and practices as they relate to the instructional program.

To what extent are the following general principles operative with the departmental structure of policies and practices as they relate to the instructional program of physical education?

    5 -- Completely
    4 -- To a great degree
    3 -- To a moderate degree
    2 -- Very little
    1 -- Not at all.

Philosophy and Objectives

1. The educational philosophy of the department has been formulated in writing and is subscribed to wholeheartedly by the instructional staff.

Administration

10. The department promotes continuous in-service education to stimulate professional growth and improved service to students.

12. The source of financial support for the physical education program is the same as that for all other instructional areas of the institution.

19. Facilities and equipment are adequate with respect to quality and quantity.

Program

25. The program provides instruction in activities for every student.

36. The physical education instruction program introduces students, and encourages their participation in the various recreational activities of the campus and community.

Evaluation

41. Selection and use of evaluation techniques are cooperatively planned within the department.

46. Evaluative measures are employed only if the results are to be used in some way.

In 1955, the same organizations sponsored a conference on intramurals.[5] Likewise, an appraisal form was developed for these recreational programs. In both instances they serve to measure the adequacy of programs in effect, and also to point the way to desirable procedures where inadequacies are uncovered.

The National Council for Accreditation of Teacher Education has worked on similar schedules for evaluation of the total teacher education programs in an institution. Evaluation schedules [2,3,4] have been developed by the American Association for Health, Physical Education and Recreation to supplement these. Attention is given to such factors as preparation of faculty, teaching load, curriculum-instructional patterns, library materials and services, facilities and equipment.

The La Porte score card is an older device designed to do much the same type of assessment.[9] It is concerned a little more with facilities than are the other schedules. It has been used extensively on surveys both of a local type and on a broad geographic scale.

With all of these schedules at least the initial work is done by the local staff. Greatest efficiency will result probably from an organization of subcommittees to gather information and prepare a tentative report on the respective standards proposed. Total staff discussions usually follow. Then the final recommendations may be made by the local staff, or an outside team of raters may be brought in to study the data assembled and to make recommendations. Either procedure is acceptable.

The purpose of such evaluations is not to produce a rating or a specific value designating over-all effectiveness. Instead the purpose is to do a diagnostic analysis of strengths and weaknesses, identifying those items that can be readily corrected and those which will need a more concerted attack. The evaluation schedules are simply devices to motivate discussion and action, and to provide the yardstick which enables a staff to get a clearer perspective of the total program.

State Evaluation Schedules

Illinois has developed an inventory for use in the public schools in much the same way as the college schedules are used. It is proposed that students, teachers and parents answer the inventory.[8] Their stated purposes are:

1. To come to an agreement on what faculty, pupils, parents, and other lay persons think your school should be doing in its physical education program.

2. To come to an agreement on what faculty, pupils, parents and other lay persons think your school is and is not doing in its physical education program.

3. To work out your own plan for doing a better job in your school in what seems to you to be the areas in need of improvement in your physical education program.

The inventory is organized around objectives such as:

1. Help students develop strength and endurance sufficient for every day living.

2. Help pupils become skillful enough to enjoy a variety of physical education activities.

3. Develop good sportsmanship.

4. Provide students with progressively advanced activities at each successive level.

5. Provide a variety of interscholastic athletic activities for boys.

The questions relative to each objective are as follows:

1. Should the objective be held?

2. How important is it?

3. To what extent is our school now doing it?

4. Should we attempt to plan for doing it in our school?

The answers are opinions on these questions, with multiple choice foils so that tallies can be run easily. There is more or less of a vote on each question. The summary and inventory are then used as a basis for discussion and tentative action.

A second inventory of similar type can be used as the basis for evaluating changes effected from discussion. A third has more detailed standards or suggestions for alterations of programs. These should be helpful in gaining public understanding and support. Copies may be obtained from the office of the Superintendent of Public Instruction, Springfield, Illinois.[8]

Curricular Evaluation

Probably the best known method of judging the results of a program is the application of a diagnostic battery of tests for a student body. One of these on a large scale basis is the Iowa Every Pupil Testing Program in which every pupil in the state is tested annually in all subject matter areas. Some schools have done a similar thing with achievement tests in the motor skills taught in physical education. Their merit rests entirely in the careful analysis of strengths and weaknesses revealed.

Another approach is through "consumer reports," involving the students' estimate of comparative worth and value for time spent. The interview, the check list, the diary, and the job analysis are all devices for obtaining this information. These procedures and the processes of curricular revision, and "action research" which may well be applied to curricular study, may be found in textbooks such as that of the American Association for Health Physical Education and Recreation.[1]

Students have very definite reactions concerning the worth of a class and the "climate" within the class. The best time to get this reaction is at the conclusion of a term when they can be frank and have full perspective of the entire course. The following example is a class evaluation prepared specifically for physical education classes and is designed to elicit statements which will promote thoughtful retrospection and also be helpful in a diagnostic way for the teacher.*

CLASS EVALUATION

The purpose of this evaluation is to help your instructor become a better instructor. The results will give the instructor information about your opinions concerning the class and procedures used. Please answer the questions frankly. DO NOT PUT YOUR NAME ON THIS PAPER.

Encircle the letter which most accurately describes your reaction.

a -- always   b -- nearly always   c -- sometimes

d -- seldom or never

Instructor

a b c d   Inspires confidence in knowledge of subject

a b c d   Presents subject skillfully

a b c d   Shows enthusiasm for subject

a b c d   Displays poise and self-confidence

a b c d   Has a sense of humor

a b c d   Speaks distinctly with pleasing voice

---

*This evaluation form was developed by the Staff of the Department of Physical Education for Women, State University of Iowa, Iowa City.

a b c d Maintains good posture

a b c d Presents an attractive appearance

Mannerisms which detract from effective teaching
(Please list)

Evaluation Procedures

a b c d Written tests representative of subject
matter

a b c d Skill tests representative of subject matter

a b c d Tests administered fairly

a b c d Basis for grading adequately explained

Student Reaction to Class

a b c d Could you ask questions and were they
answered satisfactorily

a b c d Could you accomplish as much as possible
during class time

a b c d Were you given help when you needed it

Preparation and Presentation of Material

a b c d Clear, brief explanations

a b c d Interesting, enjoyable lessons

a b c d Challenge to your abilities

a b c d Meaningful demonstrations

Theory Classes

a b c d Variety of teaching procedures utilized

a b c d Meaningful assignments

ACTIVITY CLASSES

1. Please check the following items which describe values
   obtained from this course.

   _____a. Improved mechanics and understanding of move-
   ment

   _____b. Improved performance in the activity

461

_____c. Acquired a better understanding of the activity

_____d. Acquired skills for recreational pursuits

_____e. Improved poise

_____f. Improved posture and appearance

_____g. Improved physical condition

_____h. Attained a feeling of well-being

_____i. Made new friends

_____j. Had fun and relaxation

2. Please check the statement below which most appropriately describes your reaction to this course.

_____a. Very worthwhile

_____b. Worthwhile

_____c. Adequate

_____d. Not worthwhile

3. Please explain briefly the reasons for your selection in Question 2.

4. Please write any additional comments concerning this course.

Class time should be given for its completion. Care should be taken to let students know it is anonymous, that it will not be used in relation to grading and will be seen only by the instructor. This may be accomplished by giving it to the class on one of the final days. The papers should be collected by a student leader who puts them in an envelope and seals them. He then keeps the papers until after grades are in, and returns them to the instructor.

The alert instructor obtains indirect information about the students' general appreciation of the program by careful analysis of the behavior of students. An abrupt increase in number of requests for permanent excuses from physical education probably reflects attitude more than health, and attitudes grounded in nonfruitful or unpleasant experience in class. A high absence rate with no unusual or obvious cause from epidemics and campus pressures may also reflect students' estimates of worth. The campus or community is apt to gain its knowledge of the department activities through the report of the student. These are all part of the interaction between student and teacher, between the learner and the classroom situation. This information looked at analytically and combined with other information may help in the overall evaluative process.

In summary, the educative process aims at the most learning for the most students. The barometer of success in this respect is constant attention to the many sources of information about individual developments.

SELECTED REFERENCES

1. American Association for Health, Physical Education and Recreation: Introduction to Research in Health, Physical Education and Recreation. Washington, D. C., 1959.

2. American Association for Health, Physical Education and Recreation: Evaluation Schedules in Physical Education. Washington, D. C.

3. American Association for Health, Physical Education and Recreation: Evaluation Schedules in Health Education. Washington, D. C.

4. American Association for Health, Physical Education and Recreation: Evaluation Schedules in Recreation. Washington, D. C.

5. American Association for Health, Physical Education and Recreation: <u>Intramural Activities in Colleges and Universities: Washington Conference Report</u>. Washington, D. C., 1955.

6. American Association for Health, Physical Education and Recreation: <u>Physical Education for College Men and Women</u>: Washington Conference Report. Washington, D. C., 1954, p. 36.

7. Erickson, Ed. K.: Questions from a Superintendent. <u>Journal of Health, Physical Education and Recreation</u>, 29: p. 36, September 1958.

8. Illinois Curriculum Program: <u>Consensus Study No. 12, Inventories A, B and C</u>. Office of the Superintendent of Public Instruction, Springfield, Illinois.

9. La Porte, William R.: <u>The Physical Education Curriculum</u> (A National Program). Los Angeles, The University of Southern California Press, p. 98, 1942.

10. Resick, Matthew C.: Methods of Evaluating Student Teaching in Physical Education. <u>Research Quarterly</u>, 24: p. 345, October 1953.

Chapter XIV

ADMINISTRATION OF TESTS

The administration of tests must be carefully planned if time is to be used to the best advantage and if the scores are to have the maximum degree of accuracy. Tests involving performance in physical activities present more difficulties in administration than do written tests of knowledge in that they involve the movement of students from one group or locality to another and frequently necessitate the handling of equipment.

The amount of time used in testing warrants particular attention in physical education since the time allotted to physical education is frequently less than that given to other subjects. From each activity period, time must be deducted for changing clothes and taking showers. The careful selection of tests to avoid duplication is but one of many ways in which the time to be devoted to testing can be reduced. Other methods for conserving time and for securing accurate scores will be described. The conditions vary so much from one teaching situation to another that only those principles fundamental to all testing will be included here. Suggestions for administering specific tests are included in the chapters describing those tests, Chapters VI to XII. The administration of knowledge tests is discussed in Chapter V. A few of the conditions which vary from one situation to another and affect the plan for administration of tests are the number of persons to be tested, the allotment of time, the amount of floor, field, and wall space, the amount of equipment, the number of teachers, and the use to be made of the test scores.

CLASS ORGANIZATION

The class organization varies with the type of test to be given. Some tests can be given to all the students in the class at the same time. In other instances, by working in partners, one-half of the class takes the test while the partner scores for the person being tested. Then, one repetition of the test has the entire class measured. In some tests only a few students can be tested at one time. When it is possible the testing station for such a test should be set up adjacent to the playing area in order that the teacher may be available to both those being tested and those participating in the regular activity. If the groups rotate to the testing area, a squad type of organization is helpful. Frequently the squad or team grouping used for class instruction can be the unit for testing.

For some testing, particularly for sports involving a number of separate skill tests, all the students may be engaged in testing activities at the same time but they are taking different tests at various stations. Time can be saved by explaining and demonstrating all of the tests at the beginning of the class period to the entire group before assigning squads to testing stations. The rotation of squads from one test to another is facilitated if the length of time required at each station is the same. If some tests require more time than others, students should be permitted to move to a new station as soon as they have finished a test. When this possibility is anticipated, individual score cards should be prepared which the student carries with him from station to station.

Some tests, such as strength tests, require that the elements of the test be given in a certain order; for these tests, the group follows a definite order in moving from one station to another. The testing may take a portion of several class periods, or it may require one or more entire class periods. If more than one day is required, it is better to complete one or more tests on the first day, and a different test or tests the second day. No one plan of organization is best for all situations and for all tests.

USE OF SPACE

A careful study should be made of all available space and plans made for its efficient use. Whenever several persons can be tested at once, the amount of time necessary for conducting the tests is reduced. For example, instead of having just one target in a test for accuracy in softball throwing, as many targets should be arranged as space and balls permit, care being taken to allow sufficient distance between targets for the scorers to stand without danger of being hit.

466

Another way to expedite the procedure is to arrange areas for practice trials at one side when limited space is available for the actual administration of the test. An example of this is the Badminton Serve Test described in the chapter on sports skill tests. Strings can be tied to posts or standards placed off the courts, one string at net height and another 20 inches above. Lines indicating the floor plan can be chalked or painted on the floor. Oilcloth targets, placed on the floor are convenient to use since they can be moved at will. This arrangement permits practice before going on the court for the actual trials. A similar arrangement can be constructed for practicing the Badminton Clear Test, Thirty-second Basket Shooting, Softball Repeated Throws, Volleyball Repeated Volleys, and many others. For some tests the amount of practice prior to testing should be equalized for all players. This can be done by student leaders.

All dimensions given by the test author should be carefully followed if comparable results are to be secured. If the teacher is only interested in making comparisons within his own group, then alterations in the tests can be made, but they should be the same for each person tested. Time intervals, amount of practice, and the number of trials should be held constant. Sometimes the wall space is interrupted so much by windows, stall bars, overhanging balconies, doors, and other fixtures that dimensions can be approximated only. When this is the case, there can be no assurance that the test results will be either as reliable or as valid as when administered under more ideal conditions.

TYPES OF SCORE CARDS

Score cards should be carefully planned to record the scores for all the trials in all tests to be given in the battery. Score cards should be prepared in advance showing the student's name, the date, and the number of trials to be taken on each test. When scores are to be converted into some other form, a space should be provided for the converted score adjacent to the total raw score.

If scores are to be used from one quarter or semester to another then the individual score card which can be turned over to the next instructor, or re-alphabetized in the new grouping, is preferable. A sample of such a card is shown in Figure 58.

```
┌─────────────────────────────────────────────────────────────┐
│                                                             │
│  NAME _____ CLASSIFICATION _____   │
│         Last     First    Middle                            │
│                                                             │
│                   FITNESS TEST SCORES                       │
│                                                             │
│  ┌──────┬────────────────┬────────┬───────────┬──────────┬─────┐ │
│  │ Date │ Class Activity │ Sit-up │ Push-Pull │ Chinning │ Run │ │
│  ├──────┼────────────────┼────────┼───────────┼──────────┼─────┤ │
│  │      │                │        │           │          │     │ │
│  ├──────┼────────────────┼────────┼───────────┼──────────┼─────┤ │
│  │      │                │        │           │          │     │ │
│  ├──────┼────────────────┼────────┼───────────┼──────────┼─────┤ │
│  │      │                │        │           │          │     │ │
│  ├──────┼────────────────┼────────┼───────────┼──────────┼─────┤ │
│  │      │                │        │           │          │     │ │
│  └──────┴────────────────┴────────┴───────────┴──────────┴─────┘ │
│                                                             │
│  Ht.___ Wt.___ Age___ Health Rating____ Posture Rating____  │
│                                                             │
└─────────────────────────────────────────────────────────────┘
```

Figure 58. Sample of individual score card.

Various types of score cards have been used and each
has its merits. It is important that one choose the type
best suited to a particular situation. The individual score
card gives greater flexibility in the administration of the
tests, and in most instances will save time because of this
freedom of the student to go to tests where he can be most
readily accommodated. It also gives him a certain experience in assuming responsibility for finishing, and he can
immediately see his test results and know how well he
achieved. The latter is particularly true if it is an individual score card used over and over, so he can compare
successive attempts. A system of individual cards has the
disadvantage of having one lost occasionally. This is particularly serious if several repetitions are recorded on
one card and then lost at a later time when learning rates
are to be studied. Students frequently fold or otherwise
mutilate the card so that it is very inconvenient to handle
it in the files. These points can be met by having one
card carried by the student for testing sessions, the final
score of each test is then recorded on a permanent record
for the student. This requires extra clerical help or

time, but if total cumulative records are desired it is practically essential.

Squad cards are convenient and economical when the testing is done with the squad as a unit. Sometimes the card used for taking roll will have sufficient spaces for recording test scores. When the number of trials is five or more, the addition of scores will be facilitated if the card is arranged so that the scores can be recorded in a vertical column rather than a horizontal row. Squad cards tend to put the responsibility on the squad leader rather than the individual, and make it more difficult for the student to know immediately how well he did on the test.

Score sheets for the total class are used if all the testing is to be done by one or two persons. The names are in alphabetical order on the sheet; the students may take the tests in any order or squad by squad. A casual study of class performance is easy from such a score sheet. Likewise, if achievement scales or other computations are to be made on the scores, it is probably faster than turning cards for the scores of each student. The same disadvantages are found with class records as with the squad cards.

If performance levels are available for the test, compiled from scores made by groups similar to the group being tested, it is helpful to have them placed on the individual score card. This makes it possible for a student to convert his raw score on an event into a point score. The student is thereby enabled to evaluate his own performances and is provided with a measuring stick against which to evaluate his own improvement. If it is not possible to have printed score cards, a conversion table can be posted for students' reference.

Whenever possible, achievement scales for all tests within one battery should be placed on the same individual score card. The student may then encircle all of his scores and connect the circles with lines, thus constructing a profile. The profile is diagnostic in that it compares the abilities as measured by the tests. Table XXXII is presented as a sample of an individual score card arranged for construction of the student's profile. This profile reveals that the student is above average in all items except sit-ups and bounce, and that the best performance was in the obstacle race. A composite score for all the tests in the battery may be included on the card. The reverse side of the card may be used for other test scores or for recording any pertinent information about the student.

If it is impossible to prepare score cards in advance, the students can make their own following a sample that has been placed on a blackboard. They should be supplied with cards; if only one side of the card is to be used, a supply of cards which have been used on one side and are no longer needed will suffice. Three-by-five filing cards are adequate in size for most purposes. A box of pencils should be placed in a convenient spot.

TRAINING THE ASSISTANTS

Whenever students are to assist in administering and recording, at least one organizational meeting should be held. The purpose of this meeting is to give everyone a complete understanding of the entire process. The instructions should be explicit and everyone should be impressed with the necessity of following uniform procedure. Definite typed or mimeographed instructions should be prepared and given to each assistant to be reviewed just prior to the actual administration of tests. Even on objective tests it has been found that scorers sometimes give different scores to the same performance. This may be explained partly by carelessness on the part of the scorer, partly in a real difference in what they see. It should be emphasized with them that test administration is a demanding task calling for constant alertness.

Scorers often need special training. This is particularly true when they have to make a split-second decision as to where an object landed. The scorers should experiment during the training period until they find the spot where visibility is best. Standing to one side and about 10 feet from the target is satisfactory for tests that involve wall targets. The object should be seen in flight and the scorer should shift his gaze directly to the target before the contact. Sometimes it is advisable to have both a spotter and a recorder, with the recorder repeating the score aloud before recording, as a further check on accuracy.

The training of assistants is especially important in events where form is to be judged or fouls called. It is desirable to have the assistants go through the tests themselves, emphasizing the correct and the wrong points, and then practice judging each other until the person in charge of testing is certain that they are judging with a high degree of uniformity.

Positive suggestions should be given to the assistants in order that they may motivate the students to their best efforts. The manner in which the tests are presented is extremely important and will be discussed later. Giving words of encouragement, having a sincere interest in the individual's score, and showing pleasure at extreme effort are but a few of the ways in which assistants can motivate students. Care must be taken not to embarrass the poorly skilled persons or to make the actual score seem the all-important thing. On the other hand, unless the students are motivated to their very best efforts, the scores are meaningless and the time spent in testing might better have been spent otherwise.

When the test directions call for stop watches, assistants should be given instructions concerning their use and how to read them. If there is any discrepancy between stop watches or doubt as to their accuracy, they should be checked by a jeweler immediately before the tests are conducted. It is advisable to have most assistants go through a similated performance and gain experience in actually running the stop watch. The same type of instruction and experience is desirable in preparing to use any other type of equipment, or targets, or to perform any responsibility where there is any opportunity to vary action or decisions in any way.

DEVICES FOR FACILITATING MEASUREMENT AND SAVING TIME

Targets are used in many tests. They may be painted on walls or floors with a quick-drying, washable paint. Showcard or poster paint, which can be purchased in a wide variety of colors, works satisfactorily. It lasts indefinitely on wall surfaces or on floors until they are scrubbed; or it can be removed with a damp cloth. Some colors may leave stains if applied to a porous surface and should be pretested. Masking tape can be used in constructing targets involving straight lines. It does not damage most surfaces even though left on for some time. It adheres well and does not scuff up on floors unless it is given excessive wear. Adhesive tape may be more readily available in the gymnasium. It can be torn in proper widths and used in constructing either wall or floor lines or targets. Although quick and handy, it is more expensive than the painted lines. Unlike the masking tape it is sometimes difficult to remove and often ruins the finish on wood surfaces.

When making targets of concentric circles, a string tied to a piece of chalk can be used to outline the pattern. Knots can be tied in the string, corresponding to the various radii. Care should be taken to select string that does not stretch easily. The directions for tests usually indicate the width of lines; a paint brush of the same width is convenient. When painting circles, the inside or outside edge of the line should be chalked in by the string technique just described. When painting straight lines, either chalk in one edge or use the crack between boards as a guide for one edge of the brush.

The use of different colors facilitates scoring. Another aid is painting the score value for each space on the target. Various devices have been tried in an effort to secure greater accuracy in scoring. Brophy[1] made an accuracy target with four concentric circles, alternating tin with wall space to secure different sound effects. Schmithals[10] placed a wooden board between the goal posts to assist in determining the exact second that the ball reached the goal line.

A large circular target has been used for tests such as a volleyball serve, or golf approach shots. Such a target is spread on the ground or floor much as the target for clout shooting in archery. Some special devices are cumbersome to move and require time and materials for construction. If the target is to be moved from place to place, it can be made of some light weight material, such as oilcloth. Crayons or colored chalk can be used on the rough side of oilcloth; the smooth side can be painted or outlined with India Ink. This type of target can be used on dirt or grass surfaces, can be placed on the floor, or attached to a wall.

Poles, ropes, or strings are used in some tests to indicate certain heights or distances. Two bamboo poles placed across jumping standards can be used to form a square or rectangular target. Javelins are a little firmer than the bamboo and may give a more exact line to the horizontal sides of the target. Either the poles or the javelins should be lashed to the standards to keep them from being displaced. A clothesline, in the Badminton Clear Test, is placed across the court 14 feet from the net and parallel to it, at a height of 8 feet from the floor. The rope can be attached to high standards, such as those used in the pole vault or for tetherball, provided that their bases are heavy enough to prevent the weight of the rope from tipping them slightly thus allowing the rope to sag. Sagging of the rope can be prevented by hanging weights on the ends of the rope, thus pulling it tight over the projections on the jump standards or through a pulley attached to the uprights. Screw rings can sometimes be placed in the walls; in brick walls, the screw can be inserted in the mortar between bricks. The strings used in tests such as the Badminton Serve Test, where the string goes directly above the net, can be tied to the same standards which support the net. If these standards are not high enough, they can easily be extended by taping light weight sticks, yardsticks, or wands to the standards. Sandbags can be placed on the bases of standards, if necessary, to hold them erect.

In tests involving throws, kicks, or hits for distance, time will be saved if the field is laid out so that the contestants can start from either end. Lines parallel to the starting line can be marked, thus permitting several persons to be tested at once, providing the field is wide enough and the supply of balls is ample. Markers can be placed along both sidelines, to indicate the value of the zones, progressing from the zero at the starting line to the highest score. These markers should be placed along the right-hand sideline (Figure 59). The lines across the field can be made with lime, using regular field liners. String or linen tape may be used if it is pulled taut and tied to sharp objects thrust into the ground. If the number of subjects or trials is small, these lines are not essential. Small objects such as sticks or stones, can be used to mark the landing spot. If each contestant is to have three trials, with only the best effort being measured, a pointed stick can be inserted at the spot. Tongue depressors are convenient for this purpose as the contestant's number or initials can be written on them. Measurements can then be made when all trials have been completed.

In some track and field events, such as in the discus throw and the shot put for boys, the regulations call for measuring directly from the starting point to the spot where the object first touched. There is no desire to penalize for lack of accuracy in direction. When zones are indicated

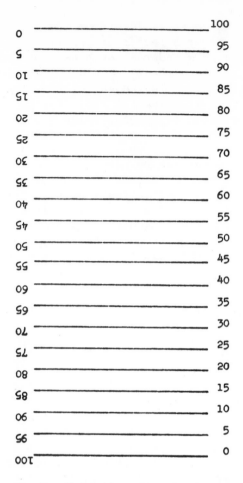

Figure 59. Parallel field markings for distance events.

by marking lines parallel to the starting line, there is a penalty for gross inaccuracies. To avoid this for events where power is the factor being measured, arcs may be drawn at convenient intervals (see Figure 60). Using the center of the contestant's throwing circle as the starting point, concentric arcs may be marked in front of the circle at specified intervals. The size of the interval between the arcs will depend on the event; for the shot put, one foot would be appropriate, while for the discus throw or basketball throw the arcs might be as far apart as 5 feet. In a test of ability to hit a softball long distances, the arc style of marking should be used. If accuracy of placement is desired as well as the ability to hit a long distance,

474

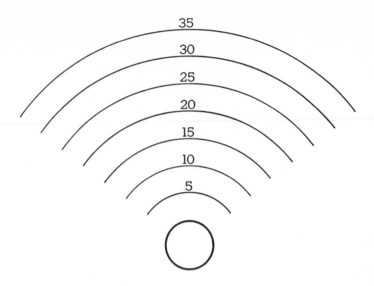

Figure 60. Concentric field markings for distance events.

then the parallel lines system should be used. Women's
track and field rules require measuring javelin, discus,
and shot put from a line; the men's rules provide for measuring the javelin from a line, the shot put and discus from
a circle.

Zones can be used in mass testing of speed in running.
Instead of timing each individual on the 50-yard dash, for
example, it saves time to have all individuals run a certain
number of seconds and to give each a score corresponding to
the zone reached with the forward foot when the signal
sounds marking the expiration of time. Thus, one stop watch
can be used for the entire group being tested. A spotter
assigned to each runner should be opposite the contestant at
the end of the time interval. With proper training in observing running skill, the spotter will be able to make adjustments in position for judging the various speeds. Markers which can be read easily should be placed along both
sidelines, so the spotter can score the finish by looking
across the lanes (see Figure 61). If this event is tested
indoors, the zone markings can be placed on the wall at eye
level.

Another method for timing several individuals with only
one stop watch and when the performance must be measured to
the nearest full second is to have the timer, stationed near

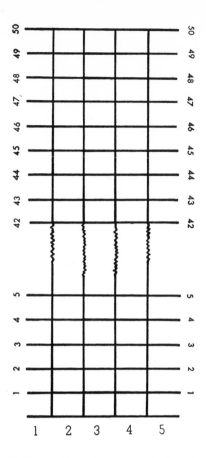

Figure 61. Field markings for mass timing of speed events.

1-5 = lanes for five runners
1-50 (sides) = one-yard zones for 50-yard course

the finish line, count the number of seconds aloud. The spotters watch the individual runners or swimmers and record the time called immediately before the individual reached the finish line.

When stop watches are not available, a metronome can be used. The sound can be supplemented by drum or by voice. The metronome can also be used in endurance tests where an exercise is repeated continuously for a considerable period of time at a set rate or speed of movement.

Lines can be marked on mat covers for convenience in scoring the standing broad jump. If only a few lines are drawn and measurement is desired to the nearest inch, a ruler may be used to measure from the nearest line to the imprint of the foot.

In conducting an event like the high jump, where the total number of trials is not predetermined, the group can be divided into squads according to ability. If ability is unknown, the group can be divided according to height, sending the taller students to one set of standards and the shorter to another. When only one set of standards or one jumping pit is available, small squads should· be used and they should be rotated to various events, in order to eliminate the time wasted while waiting for turns.

Several tests can be given at the same time by a central timer if all the tests require the same time interval. For example, the number of players who may simultaneously take the basketball Half-Minute Basket Shooting and the Passing test is limited only by the availability of baskets and wall areas. Each station then requires only a trained scorer, but no equipment other than the ball.

PRESENTATION OF TESTS

Before any testing is done, the students should be informed of the purpose of the test and how the results will be used. It is essential that the students be interested and desirous of putting forth their best efforts. The attitude toward tests is usually a reflection on the selection of tests, the administration of them, the use of test results, or the conditioning of the students. An unfavorable attitude will result when previous tests have been uninteresting or meaningless, or an undue amount of time has been taken away from the activity for testing. Tests will not be welcomed if the students think that too little use has been made of the test results, or if the tests have resulted in stiffness and soreness. Some groups will be motivated if an announcement is made in advance that the three best scores on each team or squad will be posted. If the tests are to be used as a partial basis for marking, this should be discussed in advance.

The same instructions should be given to all groups. Some tests include written directions to be read to the groups. When written directions are not available, the following principles* should be followed in preparing a set of directions:

1. The instructions should be as brief as possible, yet give an adequate understanding of what is to be done.

2. The instructions should include a demonstration.

3. The instructions should be adapted to the understanding of those persons being tested.

4. The order of instructions should be broken into units, and should be in the order of occurrence.

5. The instructions should stimulate interest and secure the maximum effort of all.

The instructions to pupils should be accompanied by instructions to examiners, mentioned earlier in the chapter under the heading Teaching the Assistants. Instructions should specify whether practice is permitted; if so, the number of trials should be indicated. An adequate and uniform amount of rest between trials should be provided so that fatigue will not affect the scores.

A demonstration of the test is usually advisable. The points to be emphasized should be thought of in advance and their order planned. An example of this is the softball field test, described in Chapter VI.

6. Demonstrate and explain as follows:

"Stand here as though on base. There is a supply of balls behind you. Take one of them, ready to throw."

Demonstrate a good throw to wall B, catch it as it returns, pivot and throw quickly to the target.

Take another ball and demonstrate a weak throw to wall B, retrieve it and return to base, throw quickly to the target.

"Note that a poor throw will cost you time to field it, that you must touch base while the ball is in your hand as though making a double play; throw immediately to the target. A wild throw will be ineffective at the target, but a slow deliberate throw will take time and earn a penalty for you by excess time.

---

*Adapted from McCall, William A.: How to Measure in Education, New York, The Macmillan Company, 1922, pp. 235-248.

"Note also that there is a supply of balls waiting for you and that you may take the successive trials as rapidly as you feel able to do so."

All the points that apply in presenting a good demonstration for instructional purposes apply here, such as having the group placed where it can see and hear, giving a picture of the "whole" first, and stressing the positive rather than the negative. An opportunity for questions should be given after the demonstration.

Careful planning of the administration of tests is essential if the tests are to have value and if time is to be conserved for other phases of the instructional program. The teacher who is inexperienced in administering tests should plan in advance and write out his plans with the same care and detail as he used in student teaching. Preparation and care in the collection of test data will amply repay the test administrator for the additional time expended.

REPORTS TO THE STUDENTS

If at all possible, the student should know what his score is at the time he finishes the test. He should also have some basis for knowing whether that score is good or poor. This information can be given to him by a squad leader if achievement scales have been constructed on scores made by previous classes of the same age and ability. Or older children may be taught to read scales posted on a bulletin board and to translate the raw scores into achievement scores.

If composite scores and achievement scores cannot be given to students on the day tests are given they should be ready for the next lesson. Again class time can be saved by having scores posted on the bulletin board or by giving the squad report to the squad leader so that he can inform his members. The most convenient way may depend upon which type of score sheet has been used.

Almost any type of scale can be explained very simply to even primary children. The average can be defined non-technically as the middle or typical score, with some better, some poorer, but a lot of them very close to the average. If quartiles are used there are two groups above and two below this average, in each direction one group similar to the average, one group differing from it.

479

On all achievement scales 50 is the average; the higher the score the better it is. Scores can be compared from one test to another on such scales. Each student should attempt to raise his score if the same test is given later.

When using T-scales, do not attempt to explain that the scale ends at approximately 20 or 80. To do so would destroy much of the motivational value gained by selecting the T-scale. The heavy concentration of scores in the 40's and 50's on the T-scale is in keeping with the definition of the average.

The percentile scales tend to put more of an emphasis on the comparison of one student with the others. Help the student to a general understanding of whether his performance is good or poor, and then attempt to improve his performance as much as possible. The scale is merely a device for telling how much he improves. The comparison between his own successive scores is far more important than a comparison with the performance of others. If students are concentrating on some particular skill such as a track event which can be measured very objectively, or time for swimming a certain distance, the raw score is apt to be meaningful, and one that is remembered from one practice session or competitive event. In that case no achievement scale is necessary, and daily improvements are easily measured and understood.

In some instances it is desirable for the student to keep a cumulative record of his performance. This would be an individual score card similar to the department's individual record card, or a syllabus or workbook. This procedure is frequently used with college students. It has proven to be good motivation and a means of helping the more mature student to appreciate his capacities, his needs, and his progress.

Written tests should be given some time prior to the last meeting of the class. The examination should be discussed during the following lesson and grades given to the student. It is usually best not to return an objective test to the students for the discussion. Having the papers often distracts from the discussion. Also passing out an examination may lead to loss of questions and therefore inability to use them in the future. In grading the written examination the teacher should note those questions which are most frequently missed, or should get a tally of responses done on the examination so she will know the relative difficulty

of the questions and content represented. The discussion
should cover the subject matter involved in the questions
most frequently missed, and should not involve a discussion
of the questions themselves. This discussion, like the
writing of the examination, should be an educational experience.

FILES AND RECORDS

The most fundamental rule in measurement is to make
only those measures which will serve the student either directly or indirectly. Even data for research should fit
this rule, as it is assumed research leads to improved
learning opportunities for these same students, or students
to follow. Similarly no permanent records should be maintained which are not serving the student in some way. Ob-
servance of these rules will do much to keep the records
brief and concise enough to be feasible.

To be of most help the record system should conform to
the following points:

1. Each student should have an individual record card
or composite record. Alphabetical file permits easy use of
the cards.

2. Cumulative records should be made over a period of
time, usually the 3, 4, 6 or 8 years the student is in a
particular school.

3. The record card should be as complete as possible.
It usually includes health, skill and guidance records. The
records for Health Service and physical education may be
combined if offices are adjacent.

4. Each record should be clearly dated so that in the
future it can be clearly understood with reference to the
others.

5. Tests should be clearly identified so that one knows
whether to compare subsequent scores.

6. The record card should be so planned that reports
can be legible. In an attempt to get a variety of material
on the card, don't crowd unduly. Choose a larger file card.

7. The record card should be on a standard filing card
size.

8. The records must be kept up-to-date.

9. The files should be confidential, used only by the teacher, the student, and counsellor if the school has one.

ADMINISTRATION OF KNOWLEDGE TESTS

Procedure

Administration of knowledge tests is relatively simple. However, there are certain details which need to be planned carefully in advance and carried out at the time of the examination. It is only through such planning that accurate information can be obtained of relative levels of knowledge of the students. Planning will also result in student recognition of fairness to all.

The room should be quiet, well-ventilated, and adequately lighted. The students should be comfortable and the situation conducive to concentration. For that reason it is desirable to give the examination in a classroom rather than in the gymnasium. Most schools will be able to provide a classroom if arrangements are made in advance. The seats should be well spaced or students seated in alternate seats. This becomes less important when answer sheets are used. (See Figure 62.) Books and wraps should not be brought into the room.

Answer sheets and mimeographed directions for their use can be handed the students as they enter the room. Pencils may also be given out at the door or a check made later to see that everyone is equipped. Special pencils must be used in institutions where equipment and/or service is provided for machine scoring of objective examinations. In this case, pencils are most efficiently given out at the door as students enter and collected as they leave.

Directions for the test should be in written form. If the directions are general and used for all tests, they can be placed on a separate sheet from the test. When the directions are specific to a particular test, they can be placed on the test itself, usually on the outside cover.

Be sure that each student receives but one copy of the test and that all copies are collected at the end of the examination period. If the copies are numbered consecutively, a check can be made quickly to see that all have been

482

Number of test form: _____

Please do not write in space below.

_____ W

_____ R

ANSWER SHEET

Name: _____ _____ Activity: _____
    (last name)   (first name)

Classification: _____ (Date: _____, 19___. Instructor: _____

Sample for multiple choice:

	1	2	(X)	4	5
0.	( )	( )	( )	( )	( )

	1	2	3	4	5
1.	( )	( )	( )	( )	( )
2.	( )	( )	( )	( )	( )
3.	( )	( )	( )	( )	( )
4.	( )	( )	( )	( )	( )
5.	( )	( )	( )	( )	( )
6.	( )	( )	( )	( )	( )
.					
.					
.					
25.	( )	( )	( )	( )	( )
	1	2	3	4	5

	1	2	3	4	5
26.	( )	( )	( )	( )	( )
27.	( )	( )	( )	( )	( )
28.	( )	( )	( )	( )	( )
29.	( )	( )	( )	( )	( )
30.	( )	( )	( )	( )	( )
31.	( )	( )	( )	( )	( )
.					
.					
.					
50.	( )	( )	( )	( )	( )
	1	2	3	4	5

Sample for true-false:

	(X)	2	3	4	5
0.	( )	( )	( )	( )	( )

	1	2	3	4	5
51.	( )	( )	( )	( )	( )
52.	( )	( )	( )	( )	( )
53.	( )	( )	( )	( )	( )
54.	( )	( )	( )	( )	( )
55.	( )	( )	( )	( )	( )
56.	( )	( )	( )	( )	( )
.					
.					
.					
75.	( )	( )	( )	( )	( )
	1	2	3	4	5

Figure 62. Sample answer sheet for knowledge tests.

483

returned   Students should be asked to record the number
of the test on the answer sheet. Since this enables the instructor to locate the student who has failed to hand in the
test, it discourages the practice of retaining them. As
further insurance against allowing questions to get into cir-
culation, each student should be required personally to hand
in the three forms: answer sheet, directions, and copy of
the test. Students should hand in papers when finished, to
avoid copying questions.

When all students are to have the same amount of time,
the test should be distributed face down, and the students
told to wait for a signal before starting. Instructions can
be read, questions answered about procedure, and any typographical errors mentioned before starting. After the starting signal no questions should be necessary. No help should
be given in the interpretation of questions, since this tends
to give an unfair advantage to the person asking the question and causes distracting interruptions.

Directions

The following sample of <u>Directions</u> may serve as a guide.

Use an answer sheet to mark your answers to each of the
questions in this test. Take the answer sheet now and print
your name, classification, name of activity in which you are
being tested, and other information indicated. Write the
number of your test copy in the blank space in the upper
left-hand corner of your answer sheet. Then finish reading
these directions.

Questions 1 to 50 in this test are of the multiple
choice type, consisting of a question followed by several
possible answers. Several may be good responses, but you
are to find the <u>best</u> answer.

On the answer sheet you will find as many sets or rows
of parentheses ( ) as there are questions in the test. The
number to the left of each row of parentheses corresponds
to the number of the question.

To answer a question, first decide which is the best
answer, then find the row of parentheses on the answer sheet
numbered the same as the question. Then place a cross (X)
in the parentheses corresponding to the choice you have made,
counting from the left. If the first response is correct or

best, place a cross in the first pair of parentheses in the set; if the second response is correct or best, place a cross in the second pair of parentheses, and so forth. All omissions in this section will be counted as errors; there will be no penalty for guessing.

Questions 51 to 75 are of the true-false type. If the statement is entirely true, place a cross (X) in the first pair of parentheses; if partially or entirely false, place the cross in the second set of parentheses. All omissions will be scored as errors. The sample questions have been marked correctly on the answer sheet.

Answer the questions in the order in which they are given, but do not linger too long over difficult items. Skip those and return later if time permits. If you do skip an item, be sure to skip the corresponding row of parentheses on the answer sheet. If you change your mind about a question, thoroughly erase your first answer. Never place more than one cross in any row!

Do not begin work until you are told to do so. If you have any questions, ask them now.

Answer Sheets

Answer sheets, commonly used in wide-scale testing in academic subject matter, have so many advantages that they should be in more common usage in physical education. A few advantages are listed below:

1. They save paper, stencils, and secretarial time as the test forms can be used repeatedly.

2. They can be scored more accurately and conveniently than is possible in turning through several pages of the test for each student's answers.

3. They save teacher time.

4. There is a saving of student time, because the student is familiar with the answer sheet and the procedure for answering.

A master answer sheet that can be used for either multiple choice or true-false questions in any test where the total number of questions does not exceed seventy-five, is shown in Figure 62. This sheet can be made to accommodate more questions by reducing the size of the type or having it printed rather than reproducing it on the typewriter.

Keys

Punched keys for use in scoring answer sheets can be made quickly and easily by following the directions listed below:

1. Attach a blank answer sheet to a piece of light-weight cardboard with paper clips, inserting a piece of carbon paper between the two. Manila filing folders are of suitable weight.

2. Label the key with the name of the examination.

3. Trace a few of the question numbers, to be cut out later and used as a guide when superimposing the key on the answer sheets.

4. Place crosses in all the appropriate parentheses, indicating correct answers.

5. Remove the dummy answer sheet and carbon paper and with a paper punch cut out all the crosses on the cardboard sheet. A paper punch with wide jaws is best for this purpose, since it will avoid the necessity of cutting the cardboard. A smaller punch can be used if the cardboard is cut lengthwise into thirds. After completing the punching, the cardboard can be put together with transparent tape. Use a punch that compares closely in size of hole with the amount of space within the parentheses on the answer sheet.

6. Trim the left-hand margin of the cardboard so that it will just cover the question numbers on the answer sheet. Cut out the marks which were made previously on selected question numbers. These indentations in the margin of the key will permit more accurate and quick placement of the key on the answer sheets.

7. Check to see that the holes have been properly punched by placing the key on the dummy of correct answers.

Scoring

In scoring, the cardboard key is superimposed on the answer sheet and carefully placed in its proper position. A red dot may be placed in each hole where no cross appears. The number of errors can then be counted and recorded on the answer sheet. Previous to the application of the key, the answer sheet should be scanned for any questions in which

486

two answers may have been placed. If any are found a red line should be drawn through the entire row of brackets. The red line will then appear as errors to be counted with the red dots placed in the empty holes. If the answer sheets are returned to the student it will identify the questions on which errors were made.

The score on multiple choice questions is usually the sum of correct responses. This may be obtained by subtracting the number of errors, counted as above, from the total number of questions. Or it may be counted as the number of crosses seen through the holes without a red line drawn through them. The true-false questions may be scored in the same way or they may be scored by subtracting the number of errors from the number answered correctly. In the latter method the answer sheet should be scanned for questions omitted and marked with a green line through the row of brackets so that these questions will not be counted as errors against the student. If correction is to be made for guessing, the test directions should indicate "Do not guess."

After all papers are scored a frequency distribution should be made of the scores. This will serve as the basis for a percentile or grade report to the students. In preparation for the discussion with the students, a check should be made on those questions missed most frequently. It may even be desirable to do a frequency distribution of errors. All answer sheets or other materials returned to the students for the discussion should be collected again after the discussion.

Before the answer sheets are destroyed an item analysis should be made of all questions which have not previously been so examined.

SELECTED REFERENCES

1. Brophy, Kathleen: Target for Testing Accuracy in Softball Throwing. Softball-Volley Ball Guide, American Association for Health, Physical Education and Recreation, Washington, D. C., p. 29, 1939.

2. Bovard, John F., Frederick W. Cozens and E. Patricia Hagman: Tests and Measurement in Physical Education. Philadelphia, W. B. Saunders Company, Chapter 19, 1949.

3. Hughes, William Leonard, and Esther French: The Administration of Physical Education. New York, Ronald Press, Chapter 13, 1954.

4. Larson, Leonard A., and Rachel D. Yocum: <u>Measurement and Evaluation in Physical, Health, and Recreation Education</u>. St. Louis, The C. V. Mosby Company, Chapter 19, 1951.

5. Lindquist, E. F., Editor: <u>Educational Measurement</u>. Washington, D. C., American Council on Education, Chapters 10, 11, 17, 18, 1951.

6. McCloy, C. H., and Norma D. Young: <u>Tests and Measurements in Physical Education</u>, Third Edition. New York, Appleton–Century–Crofts Company, Chapters 32 and 33, 1954.

7. McGraw, L. W.: A Comparison of Methods of Measuring Improvement. <u>Research Quarterly</u>, 22: p. 191, May 1951.

8. Nessler, Joan: Human Variations in Measurement Techniques. M. A. thesis, State University of Iowa, 1952.

9. Schmithals, Margaret, and Esther French: Achievement Tests in Field Hockey for College Women. <u>Research Quarterly</u>, 11: p. 840, October 1940.

INDEX

490